THE DIARY OF JOHN EVELYN

JOHN EVELYN (1620–1706), the second son of a substantial
landowner of Wotton in Surrey, and grandson of a gunpowder
monopolist, was always a man of independent means, though
not wealthy until 1699, when he inherited the estate at
Wotton. In 1637 he went to Balliol College, Oxford, as a
Fellow Commoner; from there he went on briefly to read law
at the Inner Temple, London. In his early years he travelled
extensively, visiting Holland and the Low Countries in 1641,
and between 1643 and 1645, avoiding the Civil War in
England, toured France, Italy, and Switzerland. In 1647 he
married Mary, daughter and heiress of Sir Richard Browne,
the Royalist Ambassador to France, whose confiscated estate,
Sayes Court near Deptford, Evelyn had by 1653 repurchased
and embellished.

He was a founding member of the Royal Society and an eye-
witness of many decisive events during his long life: the
Restoration of Charles II, the Second Dutch War, the Plague,
and the Great Fire of London. In 1664 he published his
famous and influential work *Sylva, or a Discourse on Forest
Trees*, and later became Councillor for Foreign Plantations,
mainly those in North America. He was made a Commissioner
of the Privy Seal by James II in 1685 and in 1693 retired to
Wotton, where he supervised his grandson and heir's education and marriage. Of his eight children only one survived
him when he died in 1706 at the age of eighty-five.

JOHN BOWLE is the author of many books, including *Western
Political Thought*, *Henry VIII*, *Charles I*, *The English Experience*, *Politics and Opinion in the Nineteenth Century*, *Hobbes
and his Critics*, and *John Evelyn and his World: A Biography*.
He became a history lecturer at Wadham College, Oxford, in
1947, and was made Leverhulme Research Fellow in 1950. He
has been Visiting Professor in the USA and Belgium, and now
lives in Oxford.

THE WORLD'S CLASSICS

The Diary of
John Evelyn

*Selected and Edited with
an Introduction by*
JOHN BOWLE

Oxford   New York

OXFORD UNIVERSITY PRESS

1985

Oxford University Press, Walton Street, Oxford OX2 6DP
London New York Toronto
Delhi Bombay Calcutta Madras Karachi
Kuala Lumpur Singapore Hong Kong Tokyo
Nairobi Dar es Salaam Cape Town
Melbourne Auckland

and associated companies in
Beirut Berlin Ibadan Mexico City Nicosia

Oxford is a trade mark of Oxford University Press

The Diary of John Evelyn was first published in six volumes
by the Clarendon Press in 1955
The one-volume abridged Oxford Standard Authors edition was
published by Oxford University Press in 1959
This selection first published 1983
First issued as a World's Classics paperback 1985

British Library Cataloguing in Publication Data

Evelyn, John, 1620–1706
The diary of John Evelyn.—(The World's Classics)
1. Great Britain—History—Stuarts, 1603–1714—Sources
I. Title II. Bowle, John, 1905–
942.06′092′4 DA370

ISBN 0–19–281529–6

Library of Congress Cataloging in Publication Data

Evelyn, John, 1620–1706.
The diary of John Evelyn.
(World's Classics)
Originally published: 1983.
Bibliography: p. Includes index.
1. Evelyn, John, 1620–1706. 2. Great Britain—History—Stuarts, 1603–1714. 3. Great
Britain—Court and courtiers—Biography. I. Bowle, John. II. Title.
DA447.E9A3325 1985 941.06′092′4 [B] 85–340

ISBN 0–19–281529–6 (pbk.)

Printed in Great Britain by
Hazell Watson & Viney Limited
Aylesbury, Bucks

Contents

Contents

Introduction

I

JOHN EVELYN is famous as a diarist, or, more accurately, as the author of memoirs; and in his own day he won celebrity as *Sylva* Evelyn, the writer of *Sylva, a Discourse of Forest Trees*, which, published in 1664, when landowners were restoring estates devastated during the Civil Wars and Interregnum, found a large and lasting public. He was also a pioneer of more open and attractive gardening, contrasting with the formal Tudor and early Stuart fashions, a connoisseur of architecture, painting, and coinage, and a versatile amateur of experimental science.

His immense *Diary* runs to six volumes in the definitive annotated edition by E. S. de Beer (Clarendon Press, 1955), and the one-volume slightly shortened version (Oxford University Press, 1959), also edited by de Beer, covers 1307 pages. The present selection covers about a third of the one-volume edition.

The Diaries were bound to be long for they extend from 1620 in the reign of James I to 1706 in the reign of Queen Anne, and cover the transformation of England from an enterprising but still minor country on the verge of empire to one of the great powers of Europe and the world, victorious in the Marlborough wars. Even more important, they also cover the momentous change in the climate of opinion from the 'Ancient' to the 'Modern', when the kind of baroque English of Burton's *Anatomy of Melancholy* was superseded by the clear prose of Dryden and Swift and by the neo-classical confidence of the age of Newton, prelude to the eighteenth century, while the old Conciliar Monarchy of Divine Right was adapted to a more constitutional form of government by the Revolution of 1688.

After avoiding the Civil Wars by travel abroad, Evelyn was an eager eye-witness of decisive events; and after the Restoration of 1660 he went everywhere and knew nearly everyone of importance. He also revised his *Diary* twice: the bound up manuscript *Kalendarium*, the main source, covers his life from 1620 to 1697 and continues on loose sheets until 1706; but most of it was written up from contemporary notes retrospectively. The first part, from the beginning up to the visit to Rome in 1644, was written in 1660; the second, from 1644 to 1684, written in 1680–84, and only from 1684 onwards does it become a contemporary Diary. The *Kalendarium* is thus at once an unconscious self portrait and – principally – a considered memoir.

It was not written for publication, and only quite by chance was the first selection ever published. In 1813 Lady Evelyn, widow of Sir Frederick Evelyn, the diarist's great-great-grandson, was conversing in the Evelyn house at Wotton, Surrey, with William Upcott, a minor librarian and bibliophile, who, when asked his hobbies, replied 'Collecting manuscripts and autographs'. 'Autographs!' she exclaimed, 'What do you mean by autographs? Surely you don't mean old letters such as these?' Then, opening a drawer, she showed him a heap of manuscripts lately used for cutting out patterns for a dress. Upcott pounced upon the find and at once discovered their importance; whereat Lady Evelyn declared with easy-going insouciance, 'Oh, if you like papers like that, you shall have plenty, for *Sylva* Evelyn and those who succeeded him kept all their correspondence, which has furnished the kitchen with abundance of waste paper.' She then instructed her housekeeper to 'take the key of the ebony cabinet, procure a basket' and 'bring down some bundles'. So Upcott discovered the original manuscript of the *Kalendarium*.

But Lady Evelyn was not much interested. She merely remarked, 'Bless me if here isn't old *Sylva*'s diary, why I haven't seen it for years!', and concluded that it would neither interest the public nor be worth the expense of printing. But, alerted by Upcott, a neighbouring antiquary with more social standing now became interested, and before she died Lady Evelyn had permitted the Revd William Bray, aged seventy-nine and assisted by Upcott, to make the first selection of *Memoirs Illustrative of the Life and Writings of John Evelyn*, published in 1818.* Such were the vicissitudes of the *Kalendarium*.

In spite of Lady Evelyn's doubts, the *Memoirs* sold well, and by an irony of fate led to the publication of Pepys's *Diary*, destined to overshadow Evelyn's own reputation with the general public. For where Pepys was an open-hearted character who revealed his intimate life, Evelyn was evasive and reserved, and Bray's selection left out anything shocking to a public fast becoming evangelical and prudish, and depicted Evelyn as an honorary early Victorian. And indeed, though himself the grandson of a business tycoon who had made a great fortune out of gunpowder, Evelyn was extremely fastidious and suffered from a Puritanical guilt from which Pepys was happily emancipated.

II

Evelyn was a good family man, and this selection opens with an affectionate and perceptive account of his parents. His father, Richard, had inherited a large and wealthy estate at Wotton from the original George, who in 1589, the year after the battle against the Armada had shown up the deficiency of gunpowder in the Navy, had been granted the patent to manufacture it throughout most of England. Having surpassed all competitors, grandfather George had made a vast fortune and, after investing the proceeds in land, launched twenty-four children and himself outlived all but six of them. His son John carried on the business, and the diarist's father, Richard, settled down as a rich country gentleman at Wotton.

On most of the Continent the Evelyns would not have been accepted into even the minor *noblesse*; but the flexible English establishment accepted them for their wealth and they became armigerous gentry. John Evelyn, in the third generation, had all the sentiments and the fine manners of his class, and, when the future Duke of Marlborough began to rise in the world, looked down on the Churchill family as originally minor office holders and provincial squires. Moreover, in 1625 Charles I nationalized the gunpowder business, the Evelyn patent ran out, and the family connection with 'black powder' lapsed, leaving the founder's estates a reputable source of wealth and status.

Evelyn's father was an affluent and independent country gentleman, who did his duty as High Sheriff of the County, entertained lavishly in traditional style and had no interest in the Court. He sent his eldest son and heir George to Oxford, and intended John for Eton; but John, abetted by his maternal grandmother, characteristically avoided this plan and lived mainly at Lewes, Sussex, until he was sixteen. For Richard had married

Eleanor Standsfield, heiress of a landowner in that neighbourhood, a lady who, worn out with births and miscarriages, had died in 1635 when John, who took after her in piety and method, was fourteen. With this prosperous and conventional background – his father disapproved of his artistic talent ('Painting and such things will do you no good hereafter') – in 1637 John went up as a Gentleman (or Fellow) Commoner to Balliol College, Oxford.

Unlike his near contemporary John Aubrey, for whom Oxford was a liberation and a joy after a restricted boyhood, Evelyn did not make much of it, and the entries in the pocket books he kept there (still in the library at Balliol College) are meagre. Soon, like many of the Caroline gentry, he took Chambers, along with his brother, at the Middle Temple to learn the rudiments of Law.

Evelyn appears to have been a vague and rather wayward undergraduate, with no particular purpose or ambition, and certainly little interest in the Law; but in 1640 his conventional upbringing was disrupted by the early death of his father. Wotton, the main property, went to his elder brother, but even as a younger son John Evelyn was left, not rich, but independent. The conflict of King and Parliament was now imminent, and in 1641 Evelyn decided to 'absent himself from this ill face of things at home'. That summer, 'a young Gent apt for all Impressions', he set out for his first tour abroad to the Dutch and Spanish Netherlands.

The Holland of Rembrandt and Vondel was still at war with Spain, but the long conflict had been the making of the Protestant United Provinces, already a great commercial sea and colonial power which had profited from the blockade of Antwerp, and where the Calvinist oligarchy had been unable to prevent religious toleration. Evelyn records his first expedition to the Continent in vivid detail – his first encounter with a culture that made England seem provincial. He then proceeded to the Spanish Netherlands, where Rubens had died the year before, saw his first fine Jesuit baroque church in Antwerp, and, in the autumn of 1641, returned by Brussels and Ostend. His first experience abroad had been a revelation.

Back in England, by October 1642 the Civil War had begun at the battle of Edgehill; but Evelyn, by temperament no warrior, only belatedly joined the King's army threatening London; he records 'I came in with my horse and Armes just at the retreate.' After a winter at Wotton, he again decided to 'evade the doing of very unhandsome things' by further travel abroad, and in November 1643 set out for France, not, as he wrote, 'Just to count Steeples' and tour 'like a goose swims down a river', but to practise an 'intelligent and taciturn observation'.

He spent Christmas in Paris, then the cultural capital of Europe and for the time being, since Louis XIV was only five, under the Regency of Anne of Austria, the Dowager Queen of Louis XIII. He carefully and fully records the sights, and in the spring of 1644 he moved down to Orléans, Blois, and Tours, where he improved his French; then, by boat down the Rhône to Valence, he arrived in September at Avignon and so to Marseilles and his first sight of the Mediterranean. His account of the Royal Galley slaves is particularly vivid; in spite of atrocious conditions, they appeared 'Cherefull and full of vile knavery'.

Evelyn's tour of Italy, extending to Genoa, Florence, Rome, Naples, Venice, and Padua, he afterwards wrote up in such detail from fashionable guide books that relatively little of the account can here be included: but the famous Italian cities and works of art made a profound impression on him and gave him standards for the rest of his life. A highlight of the tour was the *cavalcado* celebrating the enthronement of Pope Innocent X.

He returned by way of the then dangerous Simplon pass, where his companion, a belligerent Captain Wray, got into trouble with the Swiss because his dog had killed a goat, and descending the valley of the upper Rhône Evelyn fetched up in Geneva, where he developed and recovered from smallpox. Thence he proceeded to Paris, thankful that he had 'gotten so neare home', and there during the winter of 1646–7 he recuperated: 'the only time in my whole life I spent most idly'.

In June 1647, aged twenty-six, he married Mary Browne, ten years his junior, and daughter of Sir Richard Browne, the Royalist Ambassador to France. She proved a devoted wife and brought him the chance to buy her father's property at Sayes Court, Deptford, which became their cherished home until, in 1699, Evelyn inherited Wotton since George had died without a male heir.

The first Civil War, which Evelyn had prudently avoided, was now over; but, in spite of some cautious reconnaissance, Evelyn did not settle in England until after the execution of Charles I in 1649, and the defeat of Charles II at Worcester in 1651 had made it expedient to make the best of the Republic.

By January 1653 he had purchased his father-in-law's property at Sayes Court, settled there with his wife and their first son, and was 'setting out the overall Garden' which would become a show-piece. They detested what they considered the usurpations of Cromwell and the heavy taxation they imposed, but were most exasperated because the Anglican services were banned, including the keeping of Christmas. But the Republican Government was anxious to conciliate the crypto-Royalist gentry of substance, and the Evelyns were not persecuted; it is indeed remarkable how their social life went on. Evelyn complains; but, unlike the loyal Wiltshire gentry in the Penruddocke rising of 1655, he was not taking any risks. The *Diary* is particularly illuminating on such a characteristically English attitude; in 1654 Evelyn took his wife on a sight-seeing tour to Oxford, Stonehenge and the Cotswolds, and on to Cambridge and Ely, all attractively recorded.

Then, at last, with the death of Oliver Cromwell and the collapse of his regime, an entirely unexpected prospect opened, and with the Restoration of 1660 Evelyn, like Charles II, came into his own. Contacts made with the exiled royal court in Paris now bore fruit and he found himself in high favour. He witnessed the King's joyous entry into London: 'I stood in the strand, and beheld it, and blessed God.' The King now 'owned him particularly' as his 'old Aquaintance', and he recorded how the 'carkass of that arch-rebell Cromwell was dugg up' and hanged at Tyburn. All his versatile interests now had scope; he was nominated by the King to the Council of the reconstituted Royal Society, Prince Rupert confided his new method of engraving or 'Mezzo-Tinto', and – had Evelyn desired the honour – he might have been a Knight of the Bath.

In the spring of 1661 Evelyn was 'wonderfully astonish'd' at the Election ceremonies at Westminster School by the lively abilities of the boys, though – with his continental experience – shocked at their Anglicized pronunciation of Latin; and he wrote a brisk pamphlet on the 'inconveniencie of the aer and smoak of London', dedicated to Charles II. The monarch promised to act on it, but was defeated by the vested interests concerned. He went yachting with the King and the Duke of York, a new sport derived from the Dutch, and held the candle while Cooper, the miniaturist, was drawing the King's profile to make a stamp for the new money. He found Catherine of Braganza's 'olivaster' complexion 'sufficiently unagreeable' when in May 1662 she arrived at Portsmouth; at Sayes Court he entertained the Queen Mother, Henriette Marie, 'who recounted many observable stories of the sagacity of some Dogs that she had formerly had'; and he approved the new fashion of skating in St James's Park 'after the manner of the Hollanders'.

In February 1664 Evelyn published *Sylva*, his most famous book commissioned two years earlier by the Royal Society to promote the planting and preservation of timber for the Navy. It is practical, comprehensive, thorough, summing up the ideas then prevalent, and it was followed by the *Gard'ner's Almanack*, an '*Hortulan Calendar*' covering the entire year. His Diary records how he planted elms at Sayes Court and how the King planted elms at Greenwich, and how Charles with his own hands and Evelyn's crayon sketched the plan of a rebuilt Whitehall – 'which royal draft' Evelyn 'reserved as a rarity'. Still in his mid-thirties, he was at a peak of his career, as is reflected by the Diary; and *Sylva*, in the long run, contributed to the wooden walls of Nelson's Navy.

When by 1665 public affairs took a turn for the worse and the Second Dutch War broke out, Evelyn was nominated a Commissioner for Kent and Sussex to provide for the sick, wounded, and prisoners to be expected in such important districts. He was brought into contact with Clarendon, Buckingham, Albemarle and other great men, and travelled about the Kentish coast in a 'cold buisy but not unpleasant Journey'. But the Great Plague was now spreading in London, and by the summer Evelyn sent all his family down to Wotton, while, with singular courage, he himself resolved to stay at his post, though even St James's was a 'dismal passage', coffins exposed, shops shut and 'mournfull silence'. As more prisoners came in, Evelyn and Pepys did their best for them, 'with no money provided almost for the doing of it', and Evelyn was 'peremptory' to Albemarle that 'unless we had £10,000, the prisoners would sterve'. Some Dutch prizes were sold off for cash, and Evelyn, still in London and 'invironed with multitudes of poore pestiferous creatures', himself survived.

In March 1666 he tried, with the King's support, to promote a permanent Infirmary for those disabled by the war, then with Christopher Wren surveyed the 'General decays of Old St. Pauls, that ancient and venerable church . . . to set downe the particulars what was fit to be done'.

There was no time to act on them: on 2 September 1666, 'this fatal night, about ten, began that deplorable fire' – the Great Fire of London. Evelyn wrote a vivid and circumstantial account of it – here included; of how the Thames was covered with floating goods and the fields with carts and tents while the houses blazed and 'all the skie were of a fiery aspect . . . God grant mine eyes may never behold the like . . . the noise and crakling and thunder of the impetuous flames, the shreeking of Women and Children . . . the fall of Towers'. He describes how Charles II and the Duke of York fought the fire in person, the King 'showing his affection for his people and gaining theirs'. And, after the worst was over, Evelyn on foot explored the ruins, observed calcified stone and melted lead. War, Plague, and Fire had combined, he thought, to punish the nation for ingratitude to God for the Restoration. But in June 1667 the Dutch captured Sheerness, entered the Medway and blockaded the Thames, 'a Dreadfull Spectacle as ever any English men saw, and a dishonour never to be wiped off'. Evelyn had to remove his own best treasures from Sayes Court.

Public opinion blamed Lord Chancellor Clarendon, whom Charles commanded to surrender the Geat Seal. Evelyn, to whom he had long been 'a particular kind friend', 'found him in his bedchamber very sad'. He thought him the victim of the 'boufoones and Ladys of Pleasure' at Court, and last saw him in his garden 'sitting in his Gowt Wheele Chaire . . . he looked and spoke very disconsolately'. On 29 November 1667 Clarendon fled to France and banishment for life.

Charles II now had to manage parliament through shifty and factious politicians, who played upon the religious fear and fanaticism following the Civil War and Interregnum. The rudiments of political 'parties' now emerged – the Tories, High Anglican and Royalist; the Whigs, the remnant of the Republican Calvinist and Independent interest. Evelyn disliked this faction-fighting and turned to artistic and acadcmic interests. His wife had now borne six sons, but in the usual seventeenth-century way only one had survived infancy and was now, at fourteen, at Trinity College, Oxford. In June 1669 Evelyn attended the first Encaenia in the newly completed Sheldonian, an occasion he fully describes;

and having arranged for the presentation to the University of the Arundel Marbles from the collection of the late Earl of Arundel he was accorded an honorary Doctorate. By contrast to this grand occasion, the following year he was persuaded to visit a Bear-Garden – 'a rude and dirty passetime'. He also visited Newmarket Heath, 'sweete turf and down, like Salisbery plaine, the Jockeys breathing their fine barbs and racers'.

By January 1671 Evelyn had made a fortunate and famous discovery. Walking in the fields near Sayes Court, he chanced to look through the window of a 'poor thatched house' to see a young man carving in wood a 'large crucifix of Tintorets' – work of such 'studious exactness' that Evelyn had never in all his travels seen before. The youth turned out to be Grinling Gibbons; and Evelyn had him bring his carving to Court. Charles II, a monarch of taste, was interested; Wren took Gibbons up, and he became the most famous wood carver in England.

That year Evelyn also found his widest official scope as one of the King's Council for Foreign Plantations. It included the Duke of York, Prince Rupert, the Dukes of Buckingham and Ormond, and the Earl of Lauderdale. They were concerned mainly with the development of the West Indies and the English Colonies in North America. This important business (he fully records the cautious handling of the Puritan Massachusetts) appealed to Evelyn more than the King's own way of life, and he was shocked by the Monarch's 'very familiar discourse ... with Mrs. Nellie [Nell Gwyn] as they cal'd an impudent Comedian, she looking out of her Garden on a Tarrace at the top of the Wall, and – standing on the greene Walke under it: I was heartily sorry at this scene'. Evelyn, indeed, though a pious Anglican, had a strong streak of the prudish Puritan, and his diary is pervaded by laborious accounts of sermons, of which he was a formidable connoisseur. Few of them will be found in this selection; but they meant much to him, as did his habit of anxious propitiatory prayer and his regular thanks to God at the end of years of misfortune, for sparing him.

Even when, sedately married in middle age, in 1673 he began a romantic friendship with Margaret Blagge aged twenty-one, it was religiously high-minded; and when, after her marriage to Sidney Godolphin, she died in 1678 in childbirth, he wrote with rare emotion: 'this stroake did pierce me to the utmost depth ... never was a more virtuous and inviolable friendship'. He even composed an elaborate life of her, stressing her austere piety.

Politics, meanwhile, would not go away. Evelyn records fully the iniquities of Titus Oates and the crisis of 1678-9 over the alleged Popish Plot, an early example of whipped-up popular hysteria. He soon considered Oates a 'profligate wretch' whose evidence 'should not be taken against the life of a dog'; and found it more congenial to help found Chelsea Hospital for 'emerited soldiers', which, he insisted, should include a library in case a few of them might like to read. But the Rye House or 'Protestant' Plot to assassinate Charles II and York made even the King 'very melancholy': 'The Lord in Mercy', exclaimed Evelyn, now in his mid-sixties, 'avert the sad omen that we do not provoke him farther!' In spite of the King's political finesse in allowing the Whig extremists enough rope to hang themselves and so secure the legitimate succession of York, the Duke's Catholicism boded ill for a Protestant and insular country.

Since Evelyn had known Charles II fairly well, he is particularly illuminating on his character, when in February 1685, aged only fifty-four, he died, 'surpriz'd in his bed chamber by an Apopleck-tical fit' – 'A Prince of Many Virtues and many great Imperfections, Debonaire, easy of accesse . . . his countenance fierce, the voice greate . . . a lover of the sea . . . An excellent Prince doubtlesse had he been lesse addicted to Women.'

James II seemed at once set 'to bring in Poperie amain'; but Evelyn thought him able, and was relieved when, after his rebellion, Monmouth in the West 'gave it over and fled', to be executed with 'five chopps' by a clumsy headsman. He even predicted – for here the *Memoirs* become a contemporary diary – 'much happiness to this nation as to its political government', fervently though he wished that the King were 'of the National religion'. But as James II's Catholic policy developed, coincident with Louis XIV's persecution of the Protestants in France, Evelyn became more uneasy, torn between conscience and the fear of civil strife. The trial of the seven bishops and the birth of a Prince of Wales added to his alarm, and, like most Englishmen of property, by 1688 he feared civil war; for James still had an army larger than the expedition landed on 5 November by William of Orange at Torbay. But the King in fear 'forsook himself' and his subjects; and Evelyn describes William, very foreign, 'stately serious and reserved' with his Dutch guards in Whitehall. The *Diary* is particularly revealing on how the supposedly 'Glorious Revolution' was in fact only just muddled through, many conservatives 'aledging the danger of dethroning' as putting the whole social order at risk, and hoping for a Regency. Evelyn has to implore God so to compose the crisis 'that we may be at last a Nation and a Church under some fixt and sober establishment'; but for a long time all seemed in jeopardy with James in Ireland supported by the French and with William's Continental Coalition not yet in action; indeed, the hasty change of monarch still appeared but 'a sad Revolution in this sinful Nation'. Evelyn's view is probably representative.

In spite of James II's defeat at the Boyne, Evelyn long continued to fear a French invasion, until in May 1692 he could at last record the 'utter ruine of the French Fleet' off Cape La Hogue. But he seems unappreciative of William III's gruelling campaigns in the Low Countries and of his patient diplomacy in creating a Grand Alliance. He also distrusted Marlborough, 'the first who betrayed and forsooke his Master K: James'; and when in February 1702 William III was thrown from his horse hunting and died, Evelyn still thought the country in a very 'dangerous conjuncture', with all Europe poised to enter 'the most dangerous Warr that it ever suffered', and 'unprovided to resist the deluge of the French'. But the populace showed little grief; and Queen Anne – 'an English queen with an English heart', as Mary Evelyn put it – was immediately and peacefully proclaimed.

Evelyn's family life had long had a new setting. In 1691 George of Wotton's only son, aged thirty-five, had died of a stroke, having already three years before had a 'fit' through drinking healths to the Prince of Orange in riotous company, and John Evelyn and his surviving son 'Young John' had become the heirs of Wotton. There had been opposition from George's daughters and grand-daughters, but, after some wavering, George had determined to bequeath the estate to the male line. In May 1694 the Evelyns had left Sayes Court to live with George at Wotton, and when in 1699 George had died, in his eighty-third year, Evelyn had inherited an estate of about 7,500 acres. He had paid off the other claimants and settled down to a 'sedate and amicable composure'.

Sayes Court now had to take its chance. In 1696 it had been let to Admiral Benbow, not exactly a 'polite tenant', then early in 1698 requisitioned by the King for the young Tsar Peter of Muscovy, who 'had a mind to see the building of ships'. His household had proved 'right nasty', broken the furniture and 'damnified' the precious garden. Evelyn had avoided paying his respects to his alarming sub-tenant, and in April had thankfully recorded 'the Czar of Mosco went from my house towards Russia'.

Much had also gone wrong in Evelyn's family. 'Young John', overshadowed by his father, had never been a worldly success: he was intelligent and humorous, but too easy-going. Evelyn, of course, had arranged his marriage – to the step daughter of the proprietor of an estate at Radley, now the site of Radley College – and had allowed him £500 a year and sent his son, Jack, to Eton. But in 1692 'Young John' had been reduced to a Commission-ership in the Revenue in Dublin, whence after four years he had returned so ill that in 1699 Evelyn wrote 'To my exceeding grief and affliction after a languishing illness . . . died my remaining son, John . . . leaving me one grandson, now at Oxon: whom I beseech A. God to preserve.' Though he caught smallpox at Balliol, this boy, Jack, survived; he was charming, intelligent and even able to cope with his grandfather's overwhelming solicitude. As Evelyn's heir, he became the main interest of his old age.

This was as well, for only one of Evelyn's daughters had survived. In May 1685, soon after the death of Charles II, the talented and beloved Mary had died of smallpox, aged eighteen: 'Ô how desolate hast Thou left us, sweete, obliging, happy creature!' Then Elizabeth, aged seventeen, though 'bred up with the utmost circumspection', had eloped with a young man whom the Evelyns thought unsuitable, and by August had also died of smallpox. There remained Susanna, 'a good Child, religious, Ingenious, and qualified with all the ornaments of her sex', who in April 1693, the year before Evelyn became heir to Wotton, had married William Draper, the already affluent heir to a large estate. Surviving the perils of childbirth, she, and her husband, became a support of the Evelyns' declining years, which were increasingly clouded by his gloomy religious obsessions and political anticipations.

With old age, Evelyn, so inconsequent in youth, reverted to his family type, and became the possessive and ambitious man of property, determined to promote his descendants' fortunes. But where his father had been an independent country gentleman who had kept clear of the Court, now, with the growing power of central government and the need to keep up with growing wealth, Evelyn and his kind had become dependent on government patronage. And here he was lucky in his friendship with Sidney Godolphin, widower of his beloved Margaret, who, now Lord Godolphin and in 1702 Lord High Treasurer, disposed of great patronage. Moreover, his son, Francis, had made friends with young Jack at Eton; so, upon the inheritance of Wotton, Evelyn's plan for Jack's advancement took shape, and he was married in 1704 to Godolphin's niece, Ann Boscawen, daughter of Edward Boscawen (of substantial Cornish gentry) and his wife Joel, Lord Godolphin's sister. After long and tenacious negotiations, Jack, the heir to an unencumbered estate and through Godolphin's patronage now a Commissioner of the Prizes at £500 a year, was set up in life to continue the Evelyn line at Wotton. Evelyn's private victory coincided with the resounding public victory at Blenheim. He lapsed into decline with growing infirmities but undiminished faith, and died at the age of eighty-five on 27 February 1706, cared for by Mary, who survived him by six years.

III

Such, by way of introduction to the *Diary*, are the major landmarks of Evelyn's life. But while the Selection records them, it contains many other facets of Evelyn's versatile mind. He had a sharp eye for the exotic, and admirably describes the 'Entrance of the Russian Ambassador' to the Court of Charles II, clad 'after the Eastern manner, rich furrs, caps; some carrying Haukes, furrs, Teeth, Bows etc.', and how he delivered his speech in 'the Russe language alowd, but without the least motion of his body'. Again, he records how the 'Morocco Ambassador' was received with 'a string of pearls oddly woven in his Turbant'; 'I fancy the old Roman habite was little different as to the Mantle.'

Evelyn was always fascinated by strange animals, and often exactly describes them, while meticulous on the very peculiar experiments conducted by the Royal Society, and on the risky operations then performed by doctors ignorant of anaesthetics. For he was a man of the late Northern Renaissance, interested in everything, and living before the fragmentation of specialized knowledge; at once a humanist and a Christian. Indeed, in a wider view, Evelyn is singularly representative of his time. Francis Bacon, Viscount St Albans, had advocated 'renovating' knowledge for the deliberate 'betterment of man's estate', but had never brought himself to believe that the Earth went round the Sun: Evelyn, a much younger man who shared Bacon's interest in experiments, accepted that it did. But, though one of the founders of the Royal Society, he had little conception of the kind of ordered universe as depicted by Newton; he believed that Providence might at any moment intervene to punish mankind for sin, and thought nature unfathomably mysterious. Without the optimism that set in with the 'Moderns', he was haunted by an exacting and vengeful God; and although in France by the 1680s Fontenelle, President of the French Academy of Science, was adumbrating the novel idea of intellectual 'progress', Evelyn, though an admirer of Boyle, never really assimilated it. Though full of eager and versatile curiosity, he had, perhaps fortunately, little flair for abstractions, and so the better set down the lasting record of his experience of life.

To many readers he will perhaps be most attractive for his love of gardens: as when a brief entry in the *Diary* seems to transcend time when, at thirty-two, he 'plants the ortchard' at Sayes Court, 'new moone, wind west'; or when in old age he plants elms for his descendants at Wotton; or when he writes in a Plan of a Garden Book, 'The model, which I perceive you have seen will abundantly testify my abhorring of those painted and formal projections of our cockney gardens and plots, which appear like gardens of paste board and marchpane and smell more of paint than of gardens and verdure.'

JOHN BOWLE

Oxford 1982

A Chronology of John Evelyn

1620   31 October: John Evelyn born.

1625   27 March: James I and VI dies. Succeeded by Charles I.

1635   29 September: Evelyn's mother dies.

1637   9 May: Goes up to Balliol College, Oxford, as a Fellow Commoner.

1640   27 April: Sent to Middle Temple to study law.

        24 December: Father dies.

1641   12 May: Lord Strafford beheaded.

        21 July: First visit to Holland and the Spanish Netherlands.

1642   22 August: Outbreak of English Civil War.

        3 October: Battle of Edgehill.

        11 November· Sails for France, where he spends two years travelling.

1644   13 October: To Italy.

1646   May: Crosses Simplon into Switzerland.

        Contracts smallpox.

        October: Returns to Paris.

1647   27 June: Marries Mary Browne, daughter of Sir Richard Browne, Royalist Ambassador to France.

        12 October: Returns to England, leaving his wife with her parents in Paris.

1649   21 January: Evelyn's translation of de la Motte Le Vayer's *De La Liberté et Servitude*, defending monarchy, published.

        30 January: Charles I beheaded.

        12 July: Evelyn to France.

1650   November: Portrait engraved by Robert Nanteuil.

1651   *The State of France* – shrewd advice to 'young gents apt for all impressions' – published.

        22 September: Battle of Worcester.

1652   6 February: Returns to England.

        4 June: Mary Evelyn arrives in England.

        24 August: Son Richard born.

1653   22 February: Buys back Sayes Court.

        8 June: Tour round England.

1655   14 January: Son John born.

1657   7 June: Son George born.

1658   27 January: Death of son Richard.

15 February: Death of son George.

3 September: Death of Oliver Cromwell.

1659   *A Character of England*, attacking Republican bad manners, supposedly by a 'visiting Frenchman', published. Begins unpublished *Elysium Britannicum* on gardens.

1660   Publication of *Apologie for the Royal Party* by a 'Lover of Peace and of his country'; followed by *The Late News from Brussels Unmasked, and His Majesty Vindicated*.

29 May: Restoration of Charles II.

17 October: Regicides executed at Charing Cross.

1661   January: Evelyn made a Fellow of the 'Philosophic Society', later to become the Royal Society.

23 April: Coronation of Charles II.

May: Writes *Fumifugium: or the inconveniencie of the aer and smoak of London dissipated*.

Publication of *Tyrannus, or the Mode in a discourse of Sumptuary Lawes*, denouncing 'forreign Butterflies'.

1662   Publication of *Sculpture or History and Art of Chalcography and Engraving on Copper*.

20 August: Admitted to the Council of the Royal Society.

15 October: Delivers his 'Discourse concerning Forest-trees' to the Royal Society.

1663   Charles II visits Sayes Court.

1664   Publication of *Sylva, or a Discourse of Forest Trees in His Majestie's Dominions*: this treatise brought Evelyn fame, and was supplemented in the same year by *Kalendarium Hortense, or the Gard'ners Almanack*, an 'Horticulan Calendar'.

28 October: Nominated a Commissioner for the Wounded and Prisoners of War.

1665   Outbreak of Second Dutch War.

Evelyn translates Arnould's Jansenist *Nouvelle Hérésie des Jesuits* as the *Mystery of Jesuitism* and Fréart de Chambrey's *Parallel of Ancient Architecture* adding his own *Account of Architects and Architecture*.

July: The Plague begins to spread.

1 October: Daughter Mary born.

1666   2 September: The Great Fire of London.

13 September: Presents to the King *A Survey of the ruines, and a Plot for a new Citty, with a discourse on it.*

1667   February: Publication of *Tract on Public employment with an Active life ... preferred to Solitude.*

11 June: The Dutch reach Chatham.

14 September: Daughter Elizabeth born.

19 September: Persuades Henry Howard to bestow the Arundel Marbles on the University of Oxford.

1668   Translates Roland and Fréart de Chambray on painting as an *Idea of the Perfection of Painting* with his own *Preface.*

20 May: Daughter Susanna born.

1669   7 July: Attends the Encaenia of the Sheldonian Theatre in Oxford and is given an Honorary Doctorate.

1670   6 March: Death of Brother Richard.

At King's command writes *Preface on Navigation and Commerce,* against the Dutch, published four years later.

1671   Discovers Grinling Gibbons at work in a cottage near Sayes Court and introduces his work to Christopher Wren and the King. Gibbons became Master Carver in wood to all the monarchs.

May: Appointed Standing Councillor on Plantations for Foreign Plantations.

1672   Outbreak of Third Dutch War.

Evelyn on Council for Trade and Commerce, and Secretary of Royal Society.

1673   Friendship with Margaret Blagge.

1674   *Navigation and Commerce Their Original and Progress* suppressed.

1676   26 April: Learns of Margaret Blagge's marriage to Sir William Godolphin.

1678   3 September: Margaret Godolphin gives birth to a son, Francis.

9 September: Death of Margaret Godolphin.

1 October: The Popish Plot.

1679   4 June: Dines with Samuel Pepys in the Tower, where Pepys had been committed 'for misdemeanors in the Admiralty'.

1680   24 February: Son John marries Martha Spencer.

30 November: Robert Boyle elected President of the Royal Society.

29 December: Lord Stafford (second son of Lord Thomas Howard, Earl of Arundel) beheaded.

1682   Discusses plans for Chelsea Hospital with Stephen Fox and Christopher Wren.

1685   6 February: Death of Charles II. Succeeded by James II.

      14 March: Daughter Mary dies of smallpox.

      23 April: Coronation of James II.

      June–July: The Monmouth Rebellion.

      27 July: Daughter Elizabeth elopes.

      29 August: Daughter Elizabeth dies of smallpox.

      3 September: Nominated a Commissioner of the Privy Seal by the King.

1688   November: Invasion of William of Orange.

      24 December: James II flees to France.

1689   23 February: William III and Mary II declared joint rulers.

      11 April: Coronation of William and Mary.

1690   11 July: William III defeats James II at the Battle of the Boyne.

1691   May: Chelsea Hospital completed.

1692   January: Robert Boyle dies.

1693   27 April: Daughter Susanna marries William Draper.

      Translation of La Quintiniye's *Instructions pour les jardins Fruitiers et potagers* as the *Compleat Gard'ner*. He thus spread the principles of Andrew Le Notre who had revolutionized Continental gardening, and the pamphlet had wide and salutary influence.

1694   4 May: Evelyns move back to Wotton.

      28 December: Queen Mary dies of smallpox.

1697   Publication of *Numismata*, an elaborate and rambling treatise on coins.

1698   6 February–21 April: Peter I of Russia and his retinue stay at Sayes Court.

1699   24 March: Only remaining son, John, dies.

      4 October: Death of brother George. Evelyn inherits the estate at Wotton.

      Evelyn writes his last work, *Memoirs to my grandson*, advising caution and good sense.

1702   Outbreak of the War of the Spanish Succession.

      March: William III dies. Succeeded by Queen Anne.

1703   26 May: Samuel Pepys dies.

1705   18 September: Grandson Jack, Evelyn's heir, marries Ann Boscawen, niece of Lord Godolphin.

1706   27 February: Evelyn dies.

Note on the Text

Manuscripts

Apart from the *Kalendarium*, already described, which is the main source of the *Diary*, Evelyn in 1697 wrote the *De Vita Propria* which amplifies the *Kalendarium* up to 1644 and is valuable for his early life.

Earlier Editions

The full title of Bray's edition is *Memoirs Illustrative of the Life and writings of John Evelyn comprising his Diary for the years 1620–1705–6 and a selection of his familiar letters, to which being joined the private correspondence between King Charles I and Sir Edward Nicholas also between Sir Edward Hyde afterwards Earl of Clarendon and Sir Richard Browne.* 2 vols. London, 1818–19.

W. Upcott edited a revised edition of Bray in 1827. J. Forster also edited an edition of the *Diary*, based on Bray, in 1854, which was reprinted in Bohn's edition, 1859. Bray was also reprinted in four volumes in 1879 with an introduction by H. B. Wheatley, and reissued in 1906. In the same year Austin Dobson also produced an edition in three volumes. It was not, however, until 1955 that a complete and definitive edition of the *Kalendarium* and the *De Vita Propria* edited by E. S. de Beer from the original manuscript appeared.

Upcott also in 1825 edited a full selection of Evelyn's *Miscellaneous Works*, which still provides the most convenient access.

Note on this Edition

Omissions additional to those in the one-volume Oxford Standard Authors edition are indicated by an ellipsis (...). Where one or more complete entries have been omitted the three dots appear on a line by themselves, thus:

...

Square brackets have been used for editorial intervention – either to incorporate passages from *De Vita Propria* (in which case 'V' appears after the opening bracket), or to supply letters or words omitted by Evelyn and to replace some of his most unfamiliar spellings by more recognizable ones.

The italicization has been modernized and the ampersand (&) expanded, but otherwise the text remains unaltered.

KALENDARIUM

My Journal & c:

*

Parentage and Upbringing
1620–1642

Evelyn's Family

I was borne about 20 minuts past two in the morning, on Tuesday being the xxxi, and last of October Anno 1620, after my Father had been married about 7 yeares, and that my Mother had borne him 3 Children viz. Two Daughters and one sonn, about the 33d Yeare of his age, and the 23d of my Mothers.

. . .

My Father, named Richard, was of a sanguine complexion, mix'd with a dash of Choler; his haire inclining to light, which (though exceeding thick) became hoary by that time he had attain'd to 30 yeares of age; it was somewhat curled towards the extremes; his beard, (which he ware a little picked, as the mode was,) of a brownish colour and so continu'd to the last, save that it was somewhat mingled with grey haires about his cheekes; which with his countenance was cleare, and fresh colour'd, his eyes extraordinary quick and piercing, an ample fore head, in summ, a very well composed visage and manly aspect: For the rest, he was but low of stature, but very strong: He was for his life so exact and temperat, that I have heard he had never in all his life been surpriz'd by excesse, being ascetic and sparing: His Wisdome was greate, and judgment most acute; of solid discourse, affable, humble and in nothing affected; of a thriving, neate, silent and methodical genius; discreetely severe, yet liberall upon all just occasions both to his Children, strangers, and servants; a lover of hospitality; and in briefe, of a singular and Christian moderation in all his actions; not illiterate, nor obscure; as having continu'd Justice of Peace, and of the Quorum; and served his Country in the Charge of high-Sheriff; being (as I take it) the last dignified with that office for Sussex and Surrey together the same Yeare, before their separation: He was yet a studious decliner of Honors and Titles; being already in that esteeme with his Country, that they could have added little to him, besids their burthen: In fine, a person of that rare conversation, that upon frequent recollection, and calling to memory some Passages of his life, and discourse, I could never charge him with the least passion, or inadvertancy: His estate esteem'd to be about £4000 per an: well wodded and full of Timber:

My Mother's name was Elianor, sole daughter, and heyresse of John Standsfield Esquire of an antient, and honorable Family (though now extinct) in Shropshire; and Elianor Comber, of a good and well knowne house in Sussex. She was borne 17. Nov: 1598 in Cliff Sussex, neere Lewes. She was of proper personage, well timber'd, of a browne complexion; her eyes and haire of a lovely black; of constitution more inclyn'd to a religious Melancholy, or pious sadnesse; of a rare memory, and most exemplary life: for Oeconomiq prudence esteem'd one of the most conspicuous in her Country, which render'd her losse universaly deplor'd, both by those who knew, and such as onely heard of her. Thus much in briefe touching my Parents: nor was it reasonable I should speake lesse of them, to whom I owe so much.

The Place of my birth was Wotton, in the Parish of Wotton or Black-Heath in the County of Surrey, the then Mansion house of my Father, left him . . . by my Grandfather, and now . . . my Eldest Brothers. . . . It is situated in the most Sothern part of the Shire, and though in a Vally; yet realy upon a very greate rising, being on part of one of the most eminent hills in England for the prodigious prospect to be seen from its summit, though by few observed . . . The house is large and antient, suitable to those hospitable times, and so sweetely environ'd with those delicious streames and venerable Woods, as in the judgment of strangers, as well as Englishmen, it may be compared to one of the most tempting and pleasant seates in the Nation for a great person and a wanton purse to render it Conspicuous: for it has risings, meadows, Woods and Water in aboundance; not destitute of the most noble and advantagious accommodations; being but within little more than 20 miles from Lond: and yet so securely placed, as if it were an hundred: from Darking 3 miles, 6 from Gilford 12 from Kingston which serves it aboundantly with provisions as well of Land as Sea: I will say nothing of the ayre because the praeeminence is universaly given to Surrey; the soile being dry and sandy; but I should speake much of the Gardens, Fountaines and Groves that adorne it were they not as generaly knowne to be amongst the most natural and most magnificent that England afforded til this later and universal luxury of the whole nation since abounding in such expenses, and which indeede gave one of the first examples to that elegancy since so much in vogue and followd, for the managing of their Waters and other elegancies of that nature: Let me add the contiguity of 5 or 6 Mannors, the Patronage of the Livings about it; and (what Themistocles pronounc'd for none of the least advantages) the good Neighborhod, all which conspire here to render it an honorable and handsom royalty, fit for the present Possessor my worthy Brother, and noble Lady, whose constant Liberality give them title both to the place, and the affections of all that know them . . .

Evelyn's Childhood

I had given me the name of my Grandfather, my Mothers Father, who together with a sister of Sir Tho: Evelyns of Long Ditton, and Mr. Comber, a neere relation of my mothers, were my susceptors. I had given me two handsom pieces of very curiously wrought, and gilt plate. The sollemnity yet (upon what accident I know not, unlesse some indisposition in me) was perform'd in the Dining rome by Parson Higham the present incumbent of the Parish, according to the forme prescribed by the then glorious CHURCH of ENGLAND.

1621. I was now (in reguard of my Mothers weaknesse, or rather costome of persons of quality) put to Nurse to one Peter, a neighbours wife, and tennant; of a good comely, brown, and wholsome-complexion, and in a most sweete place towards the hills, flanked with wood, and refreshed with streames, the affection to which kind of solitude, I succked in with my very milke. It appeares by a note of my Fathers that I succked till 17: Jan: 1622, or at least I came not home before.

1623. The very first thing that I can call to memory, and from which time forward, I began to observe, was, this yeare my

Youngest Brother, being in his Nurses armes, who being then two
Yeares and 9 dayes younger then my selfe, was the last child of my
deare Parents: My Bro: Richard was borne at 10 at Night: 9: Nov:
Saturday: 1622.

1624. I was not initiated into any rudiments till neere 4 yeares of
age; and then one Frier taught us at the Church-porch of Wotton;
and I do perfectly remember the greate talke and stirr about il
Conde Gundamar, now Ambassador from Spaine; for neere about
this time was the match of our Prince with the Infanta propos'd,
and the Effects of that Comet 1618 still working in the prodigious
revolutions now beginning in Europ, especialy in Germany, whose
sad commotions sprung from the Bohemians defection from the
Emperor Mathias, upon which quarell the Sweds brake in, giving
umbrage to the rest of the Princes, and the whole Christian world,
cause to deplore it as never since Injoying any perfect tranquility.

1625. I was this yeare (being the first of the reigne of King
Charles) sent by my Father to Lewes in Sussex, to be with my
Grandfather, with whom I pass'd my Child-hood: This was that
yeare in which the Pestilence was so Epidemical, that there dy'd in
Lond. 5000 a Weeke; and I well remember the strict Watches, and
examinations upon the Ways as we pass'd: and I was shortly after so
dangerously sick of a Feavor, that (as I have heard), the Physitians
despair'd of me.

. . .

1627. My Grandfather Standsfield dyed this Yeare on the 5. of
Feb: and I remember perfectly the solemnity at his funerall; he was
buried in the Parish Church of All-Soules, where my Grandmother
(his second Wife) erected him a pious Monument.

. . .

It was not till the yeare 1628 that I was put to learne my Latine
Rudiments, and to Write, of one Citolin, a Frenchman in Lewes.

1629. I very well remember that generall Muster, praevious to
the Ile of Rès expedition; and that I was one day awaken'd in the
Morning with the newes of the Duke of Buckinghams being slaine
by that wretch Felton, after our disgrace before La Rochelle.

And I now tooke so extraordinary a fansy to drawing, and
designing, that I could never after weane my inclinations from it, to
the expense of much precious tyme which might have been more
advantagiously employd: 1630 For I was now put to schoole to one

Mr. Potts in the Cliff; from whom on the 7th of Jan: (being the day after Epiphany) I went to the Free-schole at Southover neere the Towne, of which one Agnes Morley had been the Foundresse, and now Edw: Snatt the Master, under whom I remain'd till I was sent to the University. This yeare my Grandmother (with whom I sojourn'd) being married to one Mr. Newton a learned and most religious Gent: We went from the Cliff, to dwell at his house in Southover. I do most perfectly remember the jubilie which was universaly express'd for the happy birth of the Prince of Wales 29: May: now CHARLES THE 2D, our most gracious Sovraigne.

1631. There happen'd now an extraordinary dirth in Engl: corne bearing an excessive price: and in imitation of what I had seene my Father do, I began to observe matters more punctualy, which I did use to set downe in a blanke Almanac.

The Lord of Castelhavens arraignement for many shamefull exorbitances was now all the talke; and the birth of the Princesse Mary, afterward Princess of Orange.

1632. October 21 my Eldest sister was married to Edw: Darcy Esquire: who little deserved so excellent a person, a woman of so rare vertue: I was not present at the Nuptials; but I was soone after sent for into Surrey, and my Father would very willingly have weaned me from my fondnesse of my too indulgent Grand-mother, intending to have sent me to Eaton; but being neither so provident for my owne benefit, unreasonably terrified with the report of the severe discipline there; I was sent back againe to Lewes, which perversenesse of mine, I have since a thousand times deplor'd.

This was the first time, that ever my Parents had seene all their Children together in prosperity.

Whiles I was now trifling at home I saw London, where I lay one night onely, the next day dined at Bedington much delighted with the Gardens and curiosities there, as they then appear'd to me: Thenc we return'd to the Lady Darcys at Sutton, thence to Wotton, and the 16 of Aug: following 1633 back to Lewes.

1633. Nov: 3: this yeare was my Father made sherif the last (as I thinke) who served in that honorable office for Surry and Sussex befor they were disjoyned: he had 116 Servants in Liverys, every one liveryd in greene sattin doublets; divers Gentlemen and persons of quality besides waited on him in the same garbe and habit, which at that time (when 30 or 40 was the usual retinue of the High-Sherif) was esteem'd a greate matter; nor was this out of the least vanity, that my Father exceeded (who was one of the greatest decliners of it in the World) but because he could not refuse the Civility of his friends and relations who voluntarily came themselves, or sent in their Servants: But my Father was afterwards most unjustly and spitefully molested by that jeering Judge Richardson, for repreeving the execution of a Woman, to gratifie my L: of Lindsey then Admiral; but out of this he emerged with as much honor as trouble.

1634. The King made this Yeare his progresse into Scotland, and Duke James was borne.

Decemb: 15. my deare Sister Darcy departed this life, being ariv'd to her 20th yeare of age, in vertue advanc'd beyond her yeares, or the merit of her Husband the worst of men. It was believed that the indisposition caused by her prety infant, which was borne the 2d of June before, contributed much to her destruction; as infallibly both their deaths did to my Mothers, who not long survived her.

The 24 of December I was therefore sent for home the second tyme to celebrate the obsequies of my Sister, who was interr'd in a very honorable manner, in our Dormitory, joyning to the Parish-Church, where now her Monument stands.

1635. On Jan: 7th following I returned to Lewes:

But my deare Mother, being now dangerously sick, I was the 3d of Sept: following sent for to Wotton; whom I found so far spent, that all human assistance failing, she in a most heavenly manner departed this Life upon the 29 of the same moneth, about 8 in the Evening of Michaelmas-day. It was a malignant feavor which tooke her away, about the 37th of her age, and 22d of her marriage, to our irreparable losse, and the universal regret of all that knew her. Certaine it is, that the visible cause of her indisposition proceeded from griefe, upon the losse of her daughter, and the Infants that follow'd it; and it is as certaine, that when she perceived the perill, whereto its excesse had engaged her, she strove to compose her selfe, and allay it; but it was too late, and she was forc'd to succumb; Therefore summoning all her Children then living (I shall never forget it) she express'd her selfe in a manner so heavenly, with instructions so pious, and Christian, as made us strangely sensible of the extraordinary losse then imminent; after which, embracing every one of us in particular, she gave to each a Ring with her Blessing, and dismiss'd us. Then taking my Father by the hand, she recommended us to his care; and because she was extreamely zealous for the education of my Younger Bro: she requested my Father, that he might be sent with me to Lewes; and so having importun'd him that what he design'd to bestow on her Funeral, he would rather dispose among the poore (for that she feared, God had not a little punish'd her, for the pomp, and expense of my Sisters) she labourd to compose herselfe for the blessed change which She now expected. There was not a Servant in the house, whom she did not expressly send for, advise, and infinitely affect with her counsell; and thus she continu'd to employ her intervalls, either instructing her relations, or preparing of her selfe: for though her Physitians (who were Dr. Meverell, Dr. Clement, and Dr. Rand) had given over all hopes of her recovery, and Sir Sanders Duncomb tried his celebrated and famous powder upon her [V: This knight is say'd to have first brought the use of Sedanns from Naples into England, but I remember few persons of Reputation would make use of them a good while after, it being held a conveyance for voluptuous persons and Women of pleasure to their leu'd Rendivozes incognito.]; yet she was many days impairing, and endur'd the sharpest conflicts of her sicknesse with admirable patience, and a most christian resignation; reteining both her intellectuals, and ardent affections for her dissolution to the very article of her departure; which hapned, as I sayd, on the 29 of September after she had fallen into a Crisis by a profound sweate (the onely change through all her sicknesse) after which lay[i]ng her hand upon every one of her Children, and [having] taken solemn leave of my Father; with elevated heart, and eyes, she quietly expired, and resign'd her Soule to God.

Thus ended that prudent, and pious Woman in the flowre almost of her age, to the unconsolable affliction of her husband, irreparable losse of her Children, and universal regret of all that knew her: She was interrd as neere as might be, to her Daughter Darcy, the 3d of October, at night; but with no meane Ceremony.

It was the 3d of the ensuing November after my Bro: Geo: was gon back to Oxford, 'ere I return'd to Lewes, where I made way (according to instructions received of my Father) for my Bro: Rich: who was sent the 12th after.

This Yeare 1636, being extreamely dry, the Pestilence much increased in Lond, and divers parts of England.

The 13th of Feb: I was especialy admitted (and as I remember my other Bro:) into the Middle-Temple Lond: though absent, and as yet at Schoole.

There were now large contributions to the distressed Palatinate.

The 31 of October came my Father himselfe to see us, and return'd the 5t of November following.

The 10th of December he sent a Servant to bring us necessaries etc. and the Plague beginning now to cease.

The 3d. of Apr: 1637 I was sent for from Schoole; where till about the last Yeare I had been extreamely remisse in my studies; so as I went to the Universitie, rather out of shame of abiding longer at Schoole, than for any fitnesse, as by sad experience I found, which put me to relearne all that I had neglected, or but perfunctorily gaind.

Evelyn at Oxford

It was Apr: 5. that I return'd to Wotton (upon what occasion I do not well remember) and the 9th of May after, that I ariv'd at Oxford, where I was admitted Fellow-Communer of Balliol Colledge upon the 10th in the Chapell there, taking an Oath to be conformable to the Statutes, and Orders of that Society.

. . .

It appeares by a letter of my Fathers, that he was upon treaty with one Mr. Bathurst of Trinity Coll: (afterwards Doctor and Praesident) [V: since, and at present the most antient Doctor in the University, a person of admirable Parts and Learning president of that Colledge; to which he has built a very fine Chapell, and a monument for himselfe:] who should have been my Tutor; but least my Brothers Tutor Dr. Hobbs, (more zelous in his life, then industrious with his Pupils,) should receive it as an affront; and especialy for that Fellow-Communers in Balliol were no more exemptd from Exercise than the meanest Scholars there; my Father sent me thither to one Mr. Geo: Bradshaw (*nomen invisum*) yet the sonn of an excellent Father, beneficed in our Country of Surrey. I ever thought my Tutor had parts enough; but as his ambition and I fear vices made him very much suspected of the Colledg; so his grudg to the Governor of it Dr. Lawrence (whom he afterwards

supplanted) tooke up so much of his tyme, that he seldom, or never
had any opportunity to discharge his duty to his Scholars; which, I
perceiving, associated my selfe with one Jam: Thicknesse (then a
Young man of the foundation, afterwards fellow of the house) by
whose learned and friendly Conversation I received a great
advantage.

At my first arival Dr. Parkhurst was Master, after his discease
Dr. Lawrence, a Chaplaine of his Majesties and Margaret
Professor succeeded, an accute and Learned Person; nor do I so
much reproch his severity, considering that the extraordinary
remissenesse of discipline had (til his coming) much detracted from
the reputation of that Colledg.*

There came in my tyme to the Coll: one Nathaniel Conopios out
of Greece, from Cyrill the Patriarch of Constantinople, who
returning many yeares after, was made (as I understood) Bishop of
Smyrna. He was the first I ever saw drink Coffè, which custome
came not into England til 30 years after . . .

[V: At my Admission into the Coll: every Gent: was used to give a
Piece of Plate or Tankard, with their Escuchion and Inscription of
the Donor: Mine was in Books to the value of the plate, which was
all Coin'd into mony to inable the King to maintaine his Forces,
and Court, which was quartered about Oxon: The P[l]ate was Gon
but my Books remaine in the Library, which is absolutly the best of
any Colledge perhaps in Europe:]

Upon the 2d of July, being the first of the Moneth, I first
received the B: Sacrament of the Lords Supper in the Colledg
Chapell, one Mr. Cooper, a fellow of the house preching; and at
this tyme was the Church of England in her greatest splendor, all
things decent, and becoming the peace, and the Persons that
govern'd.

The most of the following Weeke I spent in visiting the
Colledges, and several rarities of the University, which do very
much affect young comers; but I do not find any memoranda's of
what I saw.

18 July, I accompanyd my Eldest Bro (who then quitted Oxford)
into the Country; and the 9 of Aug: went to visite my friends at
Lewes, whenc I returned the 12th [to] Wotton. 17 Sept: I received
the B: Sacrament at Wotton-Churh, and Octob: 23 went back to
Oxon.

5: Nov: I received againe the holy Comm: in our Coll: Chapell: one Prouse, a Fellow (but a mad one) preaching.

December 9, I offerd at my first exercise in the Hall, and answerd myne Opponent: and upon the 11th following declaymed in the Chapell before the Master, Fellows and Scholars according to the Custome: The 15th after, I first of all Oppos'd in the Hall.

The Christmas ensuing, being at a Comedy, which the Gent: of Excester-Coll: presented to the University, and standing (for the better advantage of seeing) upon a table in the Hall, which was neere to another in the darke; being constrain'd by the extraordinary presse to quit my station, in leaping downe to save my selfe I dash'd my right leg with such violence against the sharp edge of the other board, as gave me an hurt which held me in cure till almost Easter, and confined me to my study.

1638. The 22d of Jan, I would needes be admitted into the daincing, and Vaulting Schole; of which late activity one Stokes (the Master) did afterwards set forth a pretty booke, which was publish'd with many witty Elogies before it.

. . .

Apr: 13th my Father order'd that I should begin to manage myne owne Expenses; which ('til then) my Tutor had don, at which I was much satisfied.

. . .

The 9th [July] following, I went home to visite my friends and the 26t, with my Bro: and Sister to Lewes, where we aboad till the 31, and thence, to one Mr. Michaels of Haughton neere Arundel (where we were very well treated) and the 2d of Aug: to Portsmouth; and thence having surveyd the fortifications (a greate rarity in that blessed Halcyon tyme in England) my bro: Rich. and I passed into the Ile of Wight, to the house of my Lady Richards, in a place call'd Yaverland; but we returned to our Company the next morning, whom we overtooke at Chichester, where having viewed the Citty, and faire Cathedrall, we lodg'd that night, and the day following return'd home.

. . .

About the beginning of September I was so afflicted with a quartan Ague, that I could by no meanes get rid of it untill the December following: This was that fatal Yeare, wherein the rebellious Scots oppos'd the King, upon pretence of the introduction of some new Ceremonies, and the Booke of Comm: Prayer; and madly began our Confusions, and their owne destruction too, as it proved in event.

[1639.] I came back to Oxon (after my tedious indisposition, and to the infinite losse of my tyme) on the 14 of Jan: 1639, and now I began to looke upon the rudiments of Musick, in which I afterwards ariv'd to some formal knowledge, though to small perfection of hand because I was so frequently diverted, with inclinations to newer trifles.

. . .

May 20, accompany'd with one Mr. Jo: Crafford (who afterwards, being my fellow-traveller in Italy, there chang'd his Religion) I tooke a journey of pleasure to see our Summerset-shire Bathes, Bristoll, Cirencester, Malmesbury, Abington, and divers other townes of lesser note; cursorily view'd, and return'd the 25t.

July 9, my Father sent for me home, and the 11th I receiv'd the B: Sa: at Wotton.

16. Sept: I went to Lewes, returning not till the 26t: so it was the 8th of Octob. e're I went back to Oxon.

December 14 according to injunctions from the heads of Colledges, I went (amongst the rest) to the Confirmation in St. Maryes; where after Sermon, the Bishop of Oxon: lay'd his hands upon us, with the usual forme of benediction prescrib'd: But this receiv'd (I feare) for the more part, out of curiosity, rather then with that due preparation and advise which had been requisite, could not be so effectual, as otherwise that admirable, and usefull institution might have been; and as I have since deplor'd it.

1640. Jan: 21, came my Bro: Richard from Schole, to be my Chamber-fellow at the University: he was admitted the next day, and Matriculated the 31th.

Feb: 16 was a Comm: againe in our Coll: and upon March the 25. my Father happning to be sick, sent both for me and my Bro: to come to him.

Apr: 11th, I went to Lond, to see the solemnity of his Majesties riding through the Citty in State to the Short Parliament, which began the 13 following; a very glorious and magnificent sight, the King circl'd with his royal diademe, and the affections of his People. But

The day after I return'd to Wotton againe, where I stay'd (my

Fathers indisposition suffering greate intervalls) till Apr: 27th when I was sent to London to be first resident at the Middle-Temple: so as my being at the University, in reguard of these avocations, was of very small benefit to me.

Upon May the 5t following, was the Parliament unhapily dissolved: and the 20th I return'd with my Bro: Geor: to Wotton, who was upon 28 of the same Moneth married at Albury, to Mrs. Caldwell (an heyresse of an antient Licestershire family) where part of the nuptials were celebrated.

Inns of Court

June 10th, I repaired with my Bro: to the Tearme, to goe into our new Lodgings (that were formerly in Essex-Court) being a very handsome appartiment just over against the Hall-Court; but 4 payre of stayres high; which gave us the advantage of the fairer prospect; but did not much contribute to the love of that impolish'd study; to which (I suppose) my Father had design'd me, when he payd £145 to purchasse our present lives, and assignements afterwards.

London, and especialy the Court, were at this period in frequent disorders, and greate insolencies committed by the abus'd and too happy Citty: in particular the Bish: of Canterburys Palace at Lambeth was assaulted by a rude rabble from Southwark; my Lord Chamberlayne imprison'd, and many Scandalous Libells, and invectives scatter'd about the streetes to the reproch of Government, and the fermentation of our since distractions; so that upon the 25. of June I was sent for to Wotton; and the 27th after, my Fathers indisposition augmenting, by advice of the Physitians, he repaired to the Bathe.

The 31. I went againe to Lond: to visite one Mr. Duncomb, a Relation of my Brothers Lady, who lay mortaly sick there, and the next day return'd: But on the 7th after, my Bro: Geo: and I, understanding the perill my Father was in upon a suddaine attaque of his infirmity; rod post from Guildford towards him, and found him indeede extraordinary weake. Yet, so, as that continuing his course, he held out till the 8th of September, when I returned [with] him home in his Litter; being, as we conceiv'd, something repair'd in his health.

Octob: 15. I went to the Temple, it being Michaelmas Tearme: and Oct: 30, I saw his Majestie (comming from his Northern expedition) ride in pomp, and a kind of Ovation, with all the markes of an happy Peace restor'd to the affections of his People; being conducted through Lond, with a most splendid Cavalcade; and on November following, the third (a day never to be mention'd without a curse) to that long, ungratefull, foolish and fatal Parliament, the beginning of all our sorrows for twenty yeares after, and the period of the most happy Monarch in the World — quis talia fando — .

Death of Evelyn's Father

But my Father being by this time enter'd into a Dropsy, which was an indisposition, the most unsuspected, being a person so exemplaryly temperate, and of admirable regiment; hastened me back to Wotton December 12. where the 24th following, being Thursday, between 12 and one at noone, departed this life, that excellent man, and indulgent parent; reteining his senses, and his piety to the last; which he most tenderly express'd in blessing us, whom he now left in the World, and the worst of tymes, whilst he was taken from the evill to come.

It was a sad, and lugubr[i]ous beginning of the Yeare, when on the 2d of Jan: 1640/1, we at night follow'd the mourning hearse to the Church at Wotton; where (after a Sermon, and funebral Oration, by the Minister) my Father was interr'd neere his formerly erected Monument, and mingled with the ashes of our Mother, he deare Wife.

But thus we were bereft of both our Parents in a period when we most of all stood in neede of their Counsell and assistance; especially my selfe of a raw, vaine, uncertaine and very unwary inclination; but so it pleased God, to make tryall of my Conduct, in a conjuncture of the greatest and most prodigious hazards, that ever the Youth of England saw; and if I did not amidst all this, impeach my Liberty, nor my Vertue, with the rest who made ship-wrack of both; it was more the infinite goodnesse, and mercy of God, then the least providence or discretion of myne owne, who now thought of nothing, but the pursute of Vanity, and the confus'd imaginations of Young men.

. . .

Strafford Executed

. . . upon the 15 [April] I repaired to Lond: to heare, and see the famous Tryall of the Earle of Strafford, Lord Deputy of Ireland; who on the 22d of March before had been summoned before both houses of Parliament, and now appear'd in Westminster-Hall, which was prepar'd with Scaffolds for the Lords and Commons, who together with the King, Queene, Prince, and flowre of the Noblesse were Spectators, and auditors of the greatest malice, and the greatest innocency that ever met before so illustrious an Assembly. It was Tho: Earle of Arundell and Surrey Earle Martial of England who was made high Stuard upon this occasion, and the Sequell is too well known.

. . .

May: 7th I went againe to Lond: with my Bro: and on the 12th following beheld on Tower-hill, the fatal Stroake, which sever'd the wisest head in England from the Shoulders of the Earle of Strafford, whose crime coming under the cognizance of no human-Law, a new one was made, not to be a precedent, but his destruction, to such exorbitancy were things arived.

First Visit to Holland

. . . so upon July the 15, having procur'd a passe at the Costome-house where I repeated my oath of Allegeance, I went the 16th from Lond: to Graves-end, accompany'd with one Mr. Caryll, and our Servants, where we arived by 6 that Evening, with a purpose to take the first opportunity of a passage for Holland; but the Wind as yet not favourable, we had tyme to view the Blockhouse of that Towne, which answer'd to another over against it at Tilberry (famous for the Rendezvous of Queene Eliz: in the yeare 88:) which we found stor'd with 20 piece of Cannon, and other ammunition proportionable: The 19th we rod to Rochester, and having seene the Cathedrall, we went to Chatham to see the Sovraigne, a mo[n]strous Vessel so call'd, being for burthen, defense and ornament the richest that ever spread cloth before the Wind; and especially for this remarkable, that her building cost his Majestie the affections of his Subjects, who quarreld with him for a trifle (as it was manag'd by some of his seacret Enemys, who made this an occasion) refusing to contribute either to their owne safty, or his glory. We return'd againe this evening and [on] the 21, nine in the morning, embarqued in a Dutch Fregat bound for Flushing, convoyd and accompanied by five other stoute Vessells, whereoff one was a Man of Warr, whose assistance we might have needed, if the two Saile which we discover'd to make towards us about midnight (and with whom we all prepar'd for an encounter) had proved to be the enemy which we apprehended; but finding them Norrway-Marchands onely, as we approch'd, we at 4 in the morning discry'd the coast of Flanders, and by noone, with a fresh Gale (which made it the most pleasant passage could be wished) we landed safely at Flushing in Zeland.

And now me thought the Seane was infinitely chang'd, to see so prety and neate a towne in the frontier: Here we first went to view the Pr: of Oranges house and garden, the Wales whereof are washed with Neptune continualy; after that the State-house, which are generaly in all the Low countries magnificently built; but being desirous to over-take the LeAgure which was then before Genep, 'ere the summer should be too far expir'd, we went this Evening to Midelbrogh, another sweete towne in this Iland of Walcheria; and by night to Der-Veere, from whence upon the 23d we embarqued for Dort: I may not forget that being insufferably tormented with the stitch in my side, caus'd through the impetuous motion of the Wagon, which running very swiftly upon the pav'd Cause-ways, give a wonderfull concussion to such as are unacquainted with that manner of travelling; the Fore-man perceiving me ready to drop from my seate, immediately cur'd and easd me of my payne, by unbouttoning my doublet, and applying an handfull of couch-grasse to my side.

We passe from Der-Veere over many Townes, houses and ruines of demolish'd suburbs etc. which have formerly ben swallow'd up by the sea; at what time no lesse then eight of those Ilands had ben irrecoverably lost . . .

By reason of an adverse wind, we were this night constrain'd to Lodg in our Vessel; but on the next day we landed at Dort, the onely virgin, and first towne of Holland.

This Citty is commodiously situated on the river of . . . . . . by which it is furnish'd [with] all German Commodities, and especialy Rhenish-Wines and Timber: It hath almost at the extreamity a very spacious, and venerable Church; a stately Senat-house wherein was holden that famous Synod against the Arminians 1618; and in that hall hangeth a Picture of the Passion, an exceeding rare, and much esteemed piece.

It was in this Towne that I first observed the Storkes building on their Chimnies, and frequently feeding in the Streetes, without that any dares to molest them.

Being desirous to hasten towards the Army, I tooke Wagon this afternoone to Roterdam, whither we were hurried in lesse than an houre, though it be ten-miles distant; so furiously do these Fore-men drive. I went first to visite the greate Church; the Doole, and the Burse, the publique statue of the learned Erasmus, which of brasse and a goodly piece; as we pass'd, they shew'd us his house; or rather the meane Cottage wherein he was borne . . .

The 26, I pass'd by a strait, and most commodious River through Delft, to the Hague; in which journey, I observ'd divers Leprous poore Creatures dwelling, and permitted to ask the charity of passengers, which is convey'd them in a floating box that they cast out; they live in solitary huts on the brink of the Water; and I was told, contract their dissease from their too much eating of fish.

Ariv'd at the Hague, I went first to the Queene of Bohemias Court, where I had the honor to kisse her Majesties hand; and severall of the Princesses, her daughters: Prince Mauris was also there, newly come out of Germany: and my Lord Finch not long before fled out of England from the fury of the Parliament. It was a fasting-day with the Queene, for the unfortunat death of her husband, and therefore the Presence had been hung with black-Velvet, ever since his disscease; after some discourse with her Majestie we went to our Lodging, and spent the next day in contemplating that most divertissant, and noble Village.

The 28, I went, by the like passage to Leyden, and by the 29th to Utricht, being 30 English miles distant (as they reckon by houres). It was now Kermas, or a Faire in this Towne; the streetes swarming with Boores and rudenesse; so that early the next morning (having visited the antient Bishops Court, and the two very famous Churches) I satisfied my curiosity till my returne, and better leasure: The 30th we came to Rynen, where the Queene of Bohemia hath a neate, and well built Palace, or Country house, built after the Italian manner, as I remember; and so crossing the Rhyne, upon which this Villa is situated, lodged that night in a Country-mans house.

The 31, I passed by Nimegen, built upon the rising brinke of the
same River, having a strong Castle at one end of the Towne, which
doth greately improve the prospect: I went to see the Church, and
the Fort of Naseburg, built by Pri: Maurice when he wonn this
Citty, which in the time of Charles the 5t was an Imperial seate:
The place is in Gelderland.

*A Glimpse of the Wars**

Two days after, being Aug: 2d, we ariv'd at the LeAgue, where
was then the whole Army encamped about Genep, a very strong
Castle situated on the river Wahale, and Commanding all
Cuke-Land; but being taken now foure [or] 5 days before, we had
onely a sight of the demolitions, and upon the next Sunday was the
thankesgiving-Sermonds, perform'd in Coll: Gorings Regiment
(eldest sonne of the since Earle of Norwich) by Mr. Goffe, his
Chaplaine (now turn'd Roman, and Fa: Confessor to the Q:
Mother) his text being taken out of 107: Psal: v. 9th, and the
evening spent in shooting of the Canon, and other expressions of
Military Triumphs.

Now (according to the complement) I was receiv'd a Voluntéere
in the Company of Cap: Apsley, of whose Cap: Lieutennant,
Honywood (Apsley being absent) I received many civilities.

Aug: 3 at night we rod about the lines of Circumvallation, the
Generall being then in the field: The next day I was accommodated
with a very spatious, and commodious Tent for my Lodging, as
before I was with an horse, which I had at command, and an Hutt,
which during the excessive heates, was a very greate conveniency;
for the sun peircing the Canvass of the Tent, it was during the day
unsufferable, and at night, not seldome infested by the mists and
foggs, which ascended from the river.

Upon the 6t as the turne came about, I watched on a
horneworke, neere our quarters; and traild a pike; being the next
morning reliev'd by a company of French: This was our continual
duty, till the Castle was refortified, and all danger of quitting that
station secur'd.

The 7th I went to see a Convent of Franciscan Friers, not far
from our Tents, where we found them at their devotions; and both
their Chapell, and Refectory full of the goods of such poore people
as at the approch of the Army, had fled with them thither for

Sanctuary. On the day following I went to view all the trenches, aproches, and Mines etc. of the besiegers; and in particular I tooke speciall notice of the Wheele-bridg, which Engine his Excellency, had made, to run over the moate, when they storm'd the Castle; as it is since described (with all the other particulars of his seige) by the Author of that incomparable Worke, Hollandia illustrata: the incredible thicknesse of the Walls, and ramparts of Earth, which a mine had broaken, and crumbl'd all to ashes, did much astonish me.

Upon the 8, I din'd in the horse quarters, with Sir Robert Stone, and his Lady; Sir William Stradling and divers Cavaliers; where there was very good cheere, but hot service for a young drinker as I then was: so that being pretty well satisfied with the confusion of Armies, and seiges (if such, that of the United-Provinces may be call'd, where their quarters, and encampments are so admirably regular, and orders so exactly observed, as few Cittys, the best disciplin'd, do in the World exceede it, for all Conveniences) I tooke my leave of the Leaugre, and Camerades; and on the 12 of Aug. embarked upon the Wahal (where the Prince had made a huge bridge of boates), in the company of three grave divines, who entertaynd us a greate part of our passage with a long dispute concerning the lawfulnesse of Church Musick: Here we saild by the Towne of Teile, where we landed some of our fraight, and about five a clock we touch'd at a pretty Towne nam'd Bommel, that had divers English in Garnison; it stands upon Contribution Land, which subjects the environs to the Spanish incursions: We saild also by an exceeding strong fort, call'd Lovestine (the appellative of a well knowne party in Holland) famous for the Escape of the learned Grotius by a Stratagem of his Lady convey[ing him] out instead of a Trunk of Books and soone after by another Towne Worcom, but we landed at the opposite Gorcom that night; a very strong and considerable frontiere.

Rotterdam and Amsterdam

13 We arived late at Roterdam, where was at that time their annual Mart or Faire, so furnish'd with pictures (especially Landscips, and Drolleries, as they call those clownish representations) as I was amaz'd: some of these I bought and sent into England. The reason of this store of pictures, and their

cheapenesse proceede from their want of Land, to employ their Stock; so as 'tis an ordinary thing to find, a common Farmor lay out two, or 3000 pounds in this Commodity, their houses are full of them, and they vend them at their Kermas'es to very greate gaines.

Here I first saw an Eliphant, who was so extreamely well disciplin'd and obedient, that I did never wonder at any thing more: It was a beast of a mo[n]strous size, yet as flexible and nimble in the joynts (contrary to the vulgar tradition) as could be imagin'd from so prodigious a bulke, and strange fabrick; but I most of all admired at the dexterity, and strength of his proboscis, on which he was able to support two, or three men, and by which he tooke, and reached what ever was offer'd him; his teeth were but short being a femal, and not old, as they told us. I was also shew'd a Pelican, or rather (as I conjectur'd) the Onocratulus of Pliny, having a large bill, tip'd with red, and pointing downewards a little reflected; but what is most prodigious, the under part, annex't to a gullet, so wide, and apt to extend; and would easily have swallowd, a little child: The plumage was white, wall-eyd, the legge red and flatt footed; but in nothing resembling the picture, and description of the fabulous Pelican; which when I told the testy old-man who shew'd it; he was very wroth. There was also a Cock with 4 leggs; but what was most strange, with two rumps or vents, one whereof was at his breast; by which he likewise voyded dongue, as they assur'd us: There was with this fowle an hen having two large Spurrs growing out at her sides, and penetrating through the feathers of her wings.

Upon Aug. 17 I passed againe through Delft, visited the Church, where was the monument of Prince William of Nassau, a peace of rare art; There lyeth likewise intombed with him, his sonn and successor Grave Maurice.

The Senat-house of this Citty, hath a very stately Portico, supported with very choyce Pillars of black-marble; being, as I remember of one entire stone: and within, there hangs up a certaine weight[y] vessell of Wood (not much unlike to a butter-Churne) which the adventurous Woman that hath two husbands at one time is to weare for a time about the Towne, her head comming out at the hole, and the rest hanging on her shoulders, as a pennance for incontinency:

From hence we went the next day to see Risewick, a stately country house of the Prince of Oranges; but for nothing more remarkable then the delicious walkes planted with Lime-trees, and the moderne paintings within. We return'd this evening to the Hague, and the next day went to visite the Hoff, or Princes-Court, with the adjoyning Gardens, which were full of ornament, close-Walkes, Statues, Marbles, Grotts, Fountaines, and artificiall Musique etc. There is to this Palas a very stately Hall, not much inferior to ours of Westminster, hung round with Colours, and other Trophys taken from the Spanyard; and the sides below are furnish'd with shopps. I return'd the next day to Delft, and thence to Rotterdam, whenc againe to the Hague Aug: 20: (as my buisinesse requird, which was to bring some Company on their way) and that Evening ariv'd at Leyden where immediatly I mounted a Wagon, which that night (as late as it was) brought us to Harlaem and almost to the end of my Last Journey; for I tooke such a Cold, as was like to kill me: About 7 in the Morning, I came to Amsterdam, where being provided of a Lodging, I procur'd to be brought to a Synagogue of the Jewes (it being then Saturday) whose Ceremonies, Ornaments, Lamps, Law, and Scholes afforded matter for my wonder and enquiry: The Women were secluded from the men, being seated above in certaine Galleries by themselves, and having their heads mabbl'd with linnen, after a fantasticall and somewhat extraordinary fashion:

A Jewish Cemetery

From hence I went to a place (without the Towne) calld Over-kirk, where they had a spacious field assign'd them for their dead, which was full of Sepulchers, and Hebrew Inscriptions, some of them very stately, of cost: In one of these Monuments, looking through a narrow crevise, wher the stones were disjoynted, I perceived divers bookes to lye, about a Corps (for it seems [they use] when any learned Rabby dies, to bury some of his Bookes with him, as I afterwards learn'd): of these, by the helpe of a stick that I had in my hand, I raked out divers leaves, which were all writen in Hebrew Characters but much impair'd with age, and lying. As we return'd we stepp'd in to see the Spin-house of Amsterdam, which is a kind of Bride-well, where incorrigible and Lewd Women are kept in Discipline and Labour; but in truth all is so sweete and neate, as there seemes nothing lesse agreable then the persons and the place. Here we were shew'd an Hospital erected for poore Travelors and

Pilgrimes (as they told us) by Queene Eliz: of England, and another maintaind by the Citty. The State, or Senat-house of this vast Towne is (if the designe be perfected) one of the most costly, and magnificent pieces of Architecture in Europ; especialy for the materialls, and the Carvings, which exceedes all description . . .

Upon Soneday, I went to heare an English Sermon, at the Presbyterian congregation; where they had chalked up the Psalmes upon a slate, which were that day to be sung; so placed, as all the congregation might see it, without the bidding of a Cleark: There was after sermon a Christning celebrated according to their fansy, which was homely enough. I was told, that after such an age no Minister was permitted to preach but had his maintenance continu'd during life.

I now expressly chang'd my Lodging, out of a desire to converse amongst the Sectaries that swarm'd in this Citty, to which gaine made every new-fangle acceptable. It was at a Brownists house, where we had an extraordinary good Table; There was in pension with us my L: Keeper Finch, and one Sir Jo: Fotherbee; here I also found an English Carmelite, that was travelling through Germanie towards Rome with another Irish Gentleman. I went to see the Weesehouse, which is a foundation like our Charter-house in designe, for the education of decay'd Persons, Orphans, and poore Children, where they are taught severall occupations; and, as I learn'd, the Wenches are so well brought up to housewifry, that men of good worth (who seeke that chiefely in a Woman) frequently take their Wifes from this Seminary. Hence we were carried to see the Rasp-house, where the lusty Knaves are compelld to labour; and it is a very hard labour, the rasping of Brasill, and Log-wood for the Diers, appointed them by their Task-masters. Thence to the Dull-house, a place for mad persons and fooles, like our Bethleem: But none did I so much admire as an Hospitall for their lame and decrepid souldiers, it being for state, order and accommodations one of the worthiest things that I thinke the world can shew of that nature: Indeede it is most remarkable, what provisions are here made and maintain'd for publique and charitable purposes, and to protect the poore from misery, and the Country from beggers.

The Bourse

It was on a Sunday morning about 11, that I purposely went to the Bourse (after the sermons were ended) to see their Dog-market; which lasts till two after-noone. I do not looke on the structure of this Exchange to be comparable to that of Sir Tho: Gresshams in our Citty of Lond: yet in one respect it exceeds, that ships of considerable burthen ride at the very key contiguous to it; and realy it is by extraordinary industry, that as well this Citty, as almost generaly the Townes of Holland, are so accommodated with Grafts, Cutts, Sluces, Moles and Rivers, that nothing is more frequent then to see a whole Navy of Marchands and others environ'd with streetes and houses, every particular mans Barke, or Vessell at anker before his very doore, and yet the Streetes so exactly straite, even, and uniforme that nothing can be more pleasing, especialy, being so frequently planted and shaded with the beautifull lime trees, which are set in rowes before every mans house, affording a very ravishing prospect.

The next day we were entertain'd at a kind of Tavern, calld the Briloft, appertaining to a rich Anabaptist, where in the upper romes of the house were divers pretty Water workes rising 108 foote from the ground, which seem'd very rare, till the Engine was discovered: here were many quaint devices, fountaines, artificiall musique, noyses of beasts and chirping of birds etc: but what I most admir'd then, was a lamp of brasse, projecting eight soccketts from the middle stemm, like to those we use in Churches, which having counterfeit lights or Tapers in them, had streames of Water issuing, as out of their Wieekes or Snuffs: the whole branch hanging all this while loose upon a [s]talk in the middst of a beame, and without any other perceptible commerce with any pipe; so that unlesse it were by compression of the ayre with a syringe, I could not comprehend how it should be don. There was likewise shew'd as a rarity, a Chime of Purselan dishes, which fitted to clock-worke, rung many changes, and tunes without breaking.

At another place of this Citty, we saw divers other Water-workes; but nothing more surpriz'd me than that stately, and indeede incomparable quarter of the Towne, calld the Keisers-Graft, or Emperors Streete, which appeares to be a Citty in a Wood, through the goodly ranges of the stately and umbragious Lime-trees, exactly planted before each-mans doore, and just at the margent of that goodly Aquae-duct, or river, so curiously wharfed with Clincar'd, (a kind of White sun-bak'd brick) and of which material the spacious streetes on either side are paved. This part of Amesterdam is built, and gained upon the maine Sea, supported by Piles at an immense Charge, but with everlasting foundations. Prodigious it is to consider those multitudes, and innumerable Assemblys of Shipps, and Vessels which continualy ride before this Citty, which is certainely the most busie concourse of mortall men, now upon the face of the whole Earth and the most addicted to commerce: Nor must I forget the Ports* and Issues of the Towne, which are very noble Pieces of Architecture, some of them modern; and so are their Churches (though more Gotick) where in their Turrets or Steeples, (which are adorn'd after a particular manner for cost, and invention) the Chimes of Bells are so rarely manag'd, and artificialy rung, that being curious to know whither the motion were from any extraordinary Engine, I went up into that of St. Nicholas (as I take it) where I found one who play'd all sorts of Compositions from the tablature before him, as if he had fingerd an Organ; for so were the hammers fastned with wyers, to severall keyes, put into a frame 20 foote below the Bells, upon which (by help of a Wooden instrument not much unlike a Weavers Shuttle that guarded his hand) he struck on the keys, and playd to admiration; all this while, through the clattering of the Wyers, dinn of the too neerely sounding bells, and noise that his wooden-gloves [made], the confusion was so greate, that it was impossible for the Musitian to heare any thing himselfe, or any that stoode neere him; Yet to those, who were at a distance, and especialy in the streetes, the harmony, and the time were most exact and agreable. The South-Church is richly paved with Blak, and White-marble: The West is a new fabric: Generaly, there are in all the Churches in Holland Organs, Lamps, Monuments etc: carefully preserved from the fury, and impiety of popular reformers, whose zeale has foolishly transported them in other places rather to act like madmen, then religious.

Upon St. Bartholomews-day I went to Hundius's shop to buy some Mapps, greately pleasd with the designes of that indefatigable Person: Mr. Bleaw, the setter-forth of the Atlas's and other Workes of that kind is worthy seeing: At another shop I furnish'd my selfe with some shells, and Indian Curiosities; and so towards the end of August quitted the Towne, returning back againe to Harlem by that straite River which runs betweene them; and in earnest it is a most stupendious prospect, to looke back upon Amsterdam at the end of this River cutt 10 miles in length as straite as a line without the least flexure, and of competent breadth to saile by one another: By the way it is not to be omitted, we were shew'd a Cottage where they told us dwelt a Woman, who had then been married to her 25th Husband; and being now a Widdow, was prohibited to marry for the future; yet it could not be proved, that she had ever made any of her husbands away, though the suspicion had brought her divers times to trouble.

Harlem is a very delicat Towne, and hath one of the fairest Churches of the Gotique designe, I had ever seene: There hang in the Steeple (which is very high) two Silver-bells, which they report were brought from Damiate in Egypt, by an Earle of Holland, in memory of whose successe, they are rung out every Evening. In the Nave or body of the Church, hang the goodliest branches of brasse for tapers that ever I had seene, esteemed of greate value for the curiosity of the Workmanship: also a very faire payre of Organs, which I could not find they made any use of in Divine-Service or so much as to assist them in their singing of Psalmes (as I suppos'd) but onely for shew, and to recreate the people before and after their Devotions, whilst the Burgomasters were walking and conferring about their affaires:

There likewise hangs up, neere the West-Window (as I remember) two modells of Shipps, compleately equipp'd, in memory of that invention of Saws under their keeles, with which they cutt the Chayne before the port of Damiate. Having visited this Church, the Fishmarket, and made some enquiry about the Printing-house, the Invention whereof is sayd to have been in this towne, I return'd to Leyden, that renowned University of Batavia . . .

The 28 [August] I went to see their Colledg, and Schooles, which are nothing extraordinary; and was Matriculated by the then Magnificus Proffessor who first in Latine demanded of me where my Lod[g]ing in the Towne was; my Name, Age, birth; and to what faculty I addicted my selfe; then recording my Answers in a Booke, he administred an Oath to me, that I should observe the Statutes, and Orders of the University, whiles I stay'd, and then deliver'd me a tickett, by virtue whereof I was made Excise-free; for all which worthy Priveleges, and the paines of Writing, he accepted of a Rix-dollar. Here was the famous Dan: Heinsius, whom I so long'd to see; as well as the E[l]zivirian Printing house and shop, renown'd for the politenesse of the Character, and Editions of what he has publish'd through Europ. I went also to visite their Garden of Simples, which was indeede well stor'd with exotic Plants, if the Catalogue presented to me by the Gardiner be a faithfull register. But amongst all the rarities of this place I was much pleasd with a sight of their Anatomy Schole, Theater and Repository adjoyning, which is very well furnish'd with Naturall curiosities; especially with all sorts of Skeletons, from the Whale and Eliphant, to the Fly, and the Spider, which last is a very delicat piece of Art, as well as Nature, how the bones (if so I may name them) of so tender an Insect, could possibly be separated from the mucilaginous parts of that minute animal. Here is the Sceletus of a Man on Horse-back, of a Tigar, and sundry other creatures: The Skinns of Men and Women tentur'd on frames and tann'd: Two faire and entire Mummies, Fishes, Serpents, Shells, divers Urnes; The figure of Isis cut in wood of a greate Proportion and Antiquity; a large Crocodile; The head of the Rynoceros; The Leomarinus, Torpedo, many Indian Weapons, Curiosities out of China, and of the Eastern Countries; so as it were altogether [impossible] to remember all, or take particular notice of them; though I could not forget that knife which they here shew'd us, newly taken out of a Drunken Dutch-mans gutts, by an incision in his side, after the sottish fellow had swallow'd it, when tempting to make himselfe vomit, by tickling his throat with the handle of it, he let it slip out of his fingers into his stomac, and had it taken out againe by the operation of that dextrous Chyrurgeon, whose Picture is together with his Patients preserv'd in this excellent Collection, and both the Persons living at my being in Holland.

. . .

I was the next day brought acquainted with a Burgundian-Jew who had married an Apostate Kentish-Woman: I asked him divers questions, and, amongst the rest, remember he told me that the World should never end: That our Soules transmigrated; and that even those of the most holy persons did Pennance in the bodys of bruits after death; and so he interpreted the banishment and salvage life of Nebucadnezar. That all the Jewes should rise againe and be lead to Jerusalem: That the Romans onely were the occasion of our Saviours death, whom he affirm'd (as the Turkes do) to be a greate Prophet but not the Messias: He shewed me severall bookes of their devotion, which he had translated into English for the instruction of his Wife; and told me that when their Messias came all the Ships, Barkes, and Vessells of Holland should by the powers of certaine strange Whirle-winds, be loosed from their Ankers and transported in a moment to all the desolat ports and havens throug[h]out the world, where ever the dispersion was, to convey their Breathren and Tribes to the Holy Citty; with other such like stuff, and so I tooke my leave of the lying-Jew, whom I found to be a merry dronken fellow; but would by no means handle any mony (for something which I purchas'd of him) it being Saturday; but bid me leave it in the Window of his house: meaning to receive it on Sonday following.

Sep: 1. I went hence to Delft, thence to Roterdam the next morning, and two days after back to the Hague againe to bespeake a Suite of Armor which I causd to be made to fit me, with the harnasse of an Horse man.

I now rod out of Towne to see the Monument of the Woman, reported to have borne as many Children as are dayes in the Yeare: The Basins wherein they were baptis'd, together with a large Inscription of the mat[t]er of fact is affixed to the Tomb, and inchased in a Compartiment of Carved Worke, in the Church of Lysdune, a desolate plase.

As I return'd we diverted to one of the Princes Palaces call'd the Hoff van Hounslers dyck, which is in truth a very magnificent Cloyster'd and quadrangular building: The Gallery is prettily paynted with severall huntings; and at one end thereof, a Gordian Knot, with severall rusticall Instruments so artificially represented, as would deceive an accurate Eye to discerne it from true Relievo. There is in this house a faire Staire-Case well contrived, having in the Domo, or Ceiling the rape of Ganymede painted, and other pendent figures, the Worke of F: Couenberg, of whose hand I bought an excellent drollery, which I afterwards parted with to my Bro: Geo: Evelyn of Wotton, where now it hangs: To this Palace joynes a faire Garden and Parke, curiously planted with Limes.

Being furnish'd at the Hague with some things which I wanted, I returned September 8th towards Roterdam through Delfts-haven,

and Seedam, where was at that time Coll: Gorings Winter-
quarters: This Towne has heretofore been very much talk'd of for
Witches.

An Unlucky Queen Mother

September 10th I tooke Wagon for Dort, to be present at the
Reception of Queene-Mother Maria de Medices Dowager of
France, Widdow of Henry the Greate, and Mother to the French
King Lewes xiiith, and Queene of England, whence she newly
ariv'd toss'd to and fro by the various fortune of her life; From this
Citty she design'd for Collin,* conducted by the Earle of Arundell,
and the Here van Brederod: I saw at this enterview the Princesse of
Orange, and the Lady her daughter, afterward married to the
house of Brandenbourg: There was little remarkable in this
reception befitting the greatenesse of her Person, but an universal
discontent, which accompany'd that unlucky Woman whereever
she went. The next day I return'd to Roterdam to dispatch a servant
of mine with some things into England.

Sep: 12th, I went towards the Busse passing by the Schone of the
Grave, a most invincible fort, neere to which is another calld Jack a
tra, not far from Ingle: We arrived at Bosleduc on Sep: 16. at the
time when the new Citadell was advancing with innumerable
hands, and incomparable inventions for the draining of the Waters
out of the Fenns and Moraces about it, being by Bucketts, Mills,
Cochleas, Pumps and the like. Here were now 16 companies, and 9
tropes of Horse: They were also cutting of a new River to passe
from the towne to a Castle not far from it, and here we split our
skiff terribly, falling fowle upon another through negligence of the
Master, who was faine to run on ground to our no little hazard: At
our arrival a Souldier conveyed us to the Governor, where our
names were taken, and our Persons examin'd very strictly.

17th I was permitted to walke the round, and view the Workes;
and obtained Licence to visite a prety Convent of Religious Women
of the Order of St. Clara, permitted (it seemes) to enjoy their
Monastery and maintenance undisturb'd by articles and capitula-
tions at the Surrender of the Towne, now 12 yeares since; Where
we had a Collation and very Civil entertaynement. They had a very
neate Chapell, in which the heart of the Duke of Cleve, their
Founder lies inhum'd under a plate of Brasse: Within the Cloyster

is a Garden, and in the middle of it an over-growne Lime-tree, out of whose stem, neere the roote, issue 5 upright and exceeding tall suckers or boles, the like whereof for evenesse and height I had not observd.

The Chiefe Church of this City is curiously carved within, and without; furnish'd with a paire of Organs, and a magnificent Font, or Baptistery all of Copper. The 18, I went to see that most impregnable Fort and Towne of Hysdune, where I was exceedingly oblig'd to one Coll: Crombe, the Lieutenant-Governor, who would needes make me accept the honor of being Cap: of the Watch, and to give the Word this night. The Fortification is very irregular; but esteem'd one of the most considerable for strength, and situation, not onely of the Neither-Lands, but of the World.

On the 18 we departed towards Gorcum, in which passage we discover'd a Party lurking on the shore neere Bomel; but they were to[o] weake to atacque us, being in a Mart-Ship, and well provided to receive them: Here, Sir Kenelme Digby travelling towards Colin met us. The next morning we ariv'd at Dort, passing by the Decoys where they catch innumerable quantities of Fowle.

The Spanish Netherlands*

On the 22d I went to Roterdam againe to receive a Passe, which I expected from the Cardinal Infanta, then Governor for the K: of Spaine his Bro: in Flanders, being desirous to see that Country in my returne for England whither I was now shaping my Course: And within two days after, having obtain'd another from his Highnesse the Pr: of Orange, upon the 24th of September I departed through Dort, attempting to sayle by the Keele, an obscure harbor so call'd, which the winds not permitting, we were constrayn'd to lye that night at Anker: 25th the next morning we made another Essay, but were againe repuls'd as far as Dort: The 26t, we put to sea afresh from the Keele; but a suddaine storme rising, with the Wind, and the Women (passengers) out-cries, we were forc'd to retyre into Harbor, where there lay threescore Vessells expecting fairer Weather. But we, impatient of the tyme, and inhospitablenesse of the Place set out againe the next morning early having the tyde propitious, though a most contrary and impetuous wind, passing so tirrible and overgrowne a Sea, as put us all in very greate jeopardy of our Lives; for we had much ado to keepe our selves above water, the billows breaking so desperately upon our Vessell, 'til it pleased God about noone to drive us in at a Towne calld William-Stat, a Place garnison'd by the English, where the Governor hath a faire house; the Workes, and especialy the Counterscarp is worthy of note, curiously hedg'd with a quick, and planted with a stately row of Limes on the Ramparts. The Church is of a round structure with a Cupola: Here I encounter'd two Polish noble-men, who were travelling out of Germany, and had beene in Italy, very accomplish'd persons.

It was now the 28 of Sept: when failing of an appointement, I was constrain'd to returne againe to Dort, for a Bill of Exchange; but it was the 1 of Octob: 'ere I could get back, when at the Keele I numberd 141 Vessells, who durst not yet adventure this fowle Passage: but we animated by the Master of a stout Barke, after a small encounter of Weather ariv'd by 4 that Evening at Stenebergen; In which passage we sailed over a Sea call'd the Plaet, which is an exceeding dangerous Water by reason of two contrary tydes which meete very impetuously: Here, because of the many Shelfes we were forc'd to tyde it along the Channell in sight of two prety Townes call'd Oude Towne, and Sommers Dyke: but 'ere we could gaine the Place the ebb was so far spent, that we were compell'd to foote it at least a league in a most pelting shower of raine. This is an exceeding impregnable fort..

Octob: 2. with a Gent: of the Rhyne-graves, I went in a Cart (for it was no better, nor other accommodation could we procure) of two Wheeles and one horse to Bergen-op-Zome; by the way meeting divers partys of his Highnesse Army, now retiring towards their Winter-Quarters; the Convoy-Skiffs riding by thousands, alongst the harbour. Having viewed the Workes (which are wonderfull strong) and the Fort, built heretofore by our Country-men the English, adjacent to the Towne; the Church and Market-place, we spent the night with severall Commanders and Souldiers [then] in the Towne. The next morning imbarked (for I had refus'd a Convoy of Horse which was offered me) and came early to Lillo, landing short of the Fort, by reason the tyde was against us, which constrain'd us to Land on the beach, where we marched halfe-leg-deepe in mudd, ere we could gaine the Dyke, which for being 5 or 6 miles distant from Lillo we were forced to walke on foote very wett, and discompos'd: Then entering a Boate

we pass'd the Ferry, and came into the Castle; being first examin'd
by the Sentinel, and conducted to the Governor, who demanded
my Passe, to which he set his hand, and asked 2 Rixdollars for a fee,
which me thought appeared very unhandsome in a Souldier of his
quality; I told him, that I had already purchas'd my Passe to the
Commissaries at Roterdam, at which, in a great fury snatching the
Paper out of my hand, he flung it scornefully under a table, and bad
me try whether I could get to Antwerp without his permission: But
when I drew out the mony, he return'd it as scurvily againe; bidding
me pay 14 dutch shill: to the Cantore or Searcher for my contempt,
which I was also glad to do with a greate deale of Caution and
danger, conceiling my Spanish-passe, it being a matter of
Imprisonment; for that the States were therein treated by the
names of Rebells; Besides all these exactions, I g[a]ve the
Commissary 6 shill: more, to the Souldiers something, and 'ere
perfectly cleare of this Severe Frontiere 31 stivers to the
Man-of-Warr who lay blocking up the River, twixt Lillo, and the
opposit Sconce call'd Lifkinshoeek; Two such Fortresses, as for
their circuit are hardly to be paralleld in all Europ besides. Thus on
4 of Octob: being (as I remember) Sonday, we passed the Forts of
Santa Cruce; St. Philippo, Callò, and St. Maria all appertaining to
the Spaynard: Out of St. Maria's came some Dons a'board us; and
now I made use onely of my other Passe, to which one of them put
his hand, receiving 6 guilders as a gratuity; These after they had
sufficiently searched our Vessel, left us very courteously: Then we
pass'd by another Man-of-Warr to which we Lower'd o[u]r
top-saile, and so after many importunate accidents of this nature
twixt these two jealous States, we at last ariv'd safe at Antwerp
about 11 in the morning.

Here so soone as I had provided me of a Lodging (which are in
this Citty very handsome and convenient) I lost little tyme; but with
the conduct of one Mr. Lewkner, spent the afternone (being a little
refresh'd) in seeing divers Churches, Coledges, Monasteries etc: I
exceedingly admir'd that sumptuous and most magnificent Church
of the Jesuites, being a very glorious fabrique without; and within
wholy incrusted with marble inlayd and polish'd into divers
representations of histories, Landskips, Flowers etc. Upon the high
Altar is plac'd the Statue of the B: Vergin and our Saviour in
White-marble, which has a bosse in the girdle consisting of a very

faire and rich Saphyre, with divers other stones of price. There hang up in this Church divers Votive tables and Reliques, containing the Pictures or Emblemes of severall dissasters, and recoveries. The Quire is a most glorious piece; and the Pulpet supported with fowre Angels, adorn'd with other carvings and rare Pictures wrought by the hand of Rubens now newly deceased: I went hence unto the Vrou-kirke or Notre Dame d'Anvers, which is the Cathedrall of this Citty: It is a very venerable fabrique, built after the Gotick manner, and especialy the Tower, which is in truth of an excessive height: This I ascended, that I might the better take a view of the Country about it, which happning on a day when the sunn shone exceedingly hot, and darted the rayes without any interruption, afforded so bright a reflection to us who were above, and had a full prospect of both the Land and Water about it, that I was much confirm'd in my opinion of the Moones being of some such substance as this earthly Globe consists of; perceiving all the subjacent Country (at so smale an horizontal distance) to repercusse such a light as I could hardly looke against; save where the River, and other large Water within our View appeard of a more darke and uniforme Colour, resembling those spotts in the Moone, attributed to the seas there etc. according to our new Philosophy and the Phaenomenas by optical Glasses: I number'd in this Church 30 priveleg'd Altars, whereof that of St. Sebastians was rarely paynted.

. . .

Octob: 5. I visited the Jesuites-Scholes (which for the fame of their method and institution, I had greately desir'd to see): they were divided into 4 Classes with a several Inscription over each of them; as, Ad majorem Dei gloriam the 1. Over the 2d was Princips diligentiae; the 3d Imperator Byzantiorum; over the 4th and Upmost Imperator Romanorum; under these, the Scholars and Pupils had their Places or formes, with titles and priority according to their proficiency: Their dormitorys and Lodgings above, were exceeding neate; Prisons they have for the offenders, and lesse diligent; a Court to recreate themselves in, wherein is an Aviary of Birds; besides Eagles, Foxes, Monke[y]s etc. to divert the Boys withall at their times of remission. To the house joyn'd a Music, and Mathematical Scholes where they were also initiated into those Studys; and lastly a pretty Chapell. I pass'd hence to the greate Streete which is built after a more Italian mode, in the middle whereof is erected a glorious Crucifix of White and black-marble greater then the life. This is a very faire and noble Streete; cleane, and sweete to admiration.

The Oesters-house, belonging to the East-India Company is a most beautifull Palace, adorn'd with more then 300 Windows: From hence walking into the Gun-garden I was suffer'd to see as much of the Citadell as is easily permitted to strangers: It is doubtlesse the most matchlesse piece of modern Fortification in the World; for all contrivances of force, and resistance; incomparably accommodated with Logiaments for the Souldiers, and magazines of Warr: The Graffs, ramparts, and Platformes are stupendious. Returning hence by the Shop of Plantine, I bought some bookes for the namesake onely of that famous Printer: But there was nothing about this Citty, which more ravished me then those delicious shades and walkes of stately Trees, which render the incomparably fortified Workes of the Towne one of the Sweetest places in Europ; nor did I ever observe a more quiet, cleane, elegantly built, and civil place then this magnificent and famous Citty of Antwerp, which caused me to spend the next day in farther contemplation of it, and reviewing what I had seene before; some few Palaces, Churches, Convents and Ports etc. 'til Evening, when I was invited to Signor Duerts, a Portuguese by nation, an exceeding rich Merchant, whose Palace I found to be furnish'd like a Princes; and here his three Daughters, entertain'd us with rare Musique, both Vocal, and Instrumental, which was finish'd with an handsome Collation: And so I tooke leave of the Ladys, and of sweete Antwerp as late as it was, embarquing my selfe for Bruxelles upon the Scheld, in a Vessel which deliver'd us to a second boate (in another River) drawn or taw'd by horses. In this passage we frequently chang'd our Barge by reason of the Bridges thwarting our Course so frequently: Here I observed many numerous Familys to inhabite their Vessells and floating dwellings, which were so built and divided by Cabines, as few houses on land enjoy'd better accommodation; stor'd with all sorts of Utensiles; neate, Chambers, a pretty Parlour, and kept so sweete and polite, as nothing could be more refreshing: The rivers on which they are drawne, being very cleare, and still waters and passe through a most pleasant Country on both the bankes: We had in our Boate a very good Ordnary, and excellent Company: The Cutt is as straite as a line can possibly lay it for the space of 20 English-miles; and what I much admir'd was, neere the mid-way, another artificial River, which intersects this at right-angles; but upon an eminence of Ground, which is therefore caryed in a Channel or Aqaeduct of stone so far abouve the other, as that the Waters neither mingle, nor hinder one anothers passage. We came to a Towne call'd Villefrow where is a very faire Castle, and here all the Passengers went on shore to Wash at a certaine fountaine issuing out of a Pillar, and so came abord againe. On the Margent of this long tract, are aboundance of Shrines, and Images defended from the injuries of the Weather, by the Niches of stone wherein they are placed. Thus at 9 in the Morning, being Octob: 7th we ariv'd at Bruxelles, where after I had a little dispatch'd some addresses; I went first to visite the State-house neere the Market-Place; being for the carving in free-stone a most laborious, and [strangely] finish'd Piece; well worth the observing.

. . .

Octob: 8: (being the Morning I came away) I went to see the Princes Court, which is an antient confus'd building, large and irregular, not much unlike the Hofft, at the Hague; for there is here likewise a very large Hall, where they vend all sorts of Wares: Through this we passed by the Chapell which is indeede rarely [arch'd] and in the middle of it (at present) the Hearse or Catapalco of the late Arch-dutchesse, the wise and pious Clara Eugenia: Out of this, we were by a Spanyard conducted to the Lodgings, tapissryd with incomparable Aras; and adorn'd with many excellent pieces of Rubens; old, and young Breugle, Titian, Steen-wick; with stories of most of the late actions in the Netherlands. The Library I would very faine have seene; but by an accident, we could not at this tyme; Yet peeping through the key-hole, I perceived that the Bookes were placed in Presses, which were onely cancell'd* with gilt-wyre. There is a faire Terrace which respects the Vine-yard, in which upon Pedestalls are fix'd the Statues of all the Spanish Kings of the house of Austria; the opposite Wales paynted by Rubens, being an history of the late tumults in Belgia; in the last piece, the Arch-Dutchesse shutts a greate payre of Gates upon Mars, who is made comming forth out of Hel, arm'd, and in a menacing posture; which, with that other of the Infantas taking leave of Don Phelip the IVth is a most incomparable table. From this we walked into the

Parke, which for being intirely within the Walles of the Citty is particularly remarkable; nor lesse divertissant, then if in the most solitary recesses; So naturally it is furnish'd with whatever may render it agreable, melancholy and Country-like: for here is a stately Heronry; divers springs of Water and artificial Cascads, Rocks, Grotts, one whereoff being compos'd of the Extravagant rootes of trees, and so cunningly built and hung together with Wyres, lookes very Extravagantly ... There is likewise a faire Aviary; and in the Court next it are kept divers sorts of Animals, rare and exotic fowle; as Eagles, Cranes, Storkes, Bustars, Pheasants of Severall kinds, and a Duck having 4 Wings etc: In another division of the same Close, Connys of an almost perfect yellow Colour: There was no Court now in the Palace, the Infanta Cardinal, who was the Governor of Flanders being dead but newly, and every body in deepe Mourning, which made us quitt the Towne sooner than happly we should else have don.

Lord Arundel*

It was now neere eleaven, when I repaird to his Majesties Agent Sir Henry De Vic, who very courteously receivd me and accommodated me with a Coach and six-horses, which carried me from Bruxelles to Gant, where it was to meete my Lord of Arundel, Earle Martial of England, who had requested me when I was at Antwerp to send it for him, if I went not thither my selfe.

Thus taking leave of Bruxelles, and a sad Court, yet full of Gallant Persons (for in this small Cittye the acquaintance being universal, Ladys and Gentlemen I perceiv'd had greate diversions and frequent meetings) I hasted towards Gant: Upon the Way, I met with divers little Wagons, pretily contriv'd and full of pedling Merchandises, which were drawne by Mastive-Dogs, harnass'd compleately like so many Coach-horses; in some 4, in others six, according to the Charge they drew; as in the Towne of Bruxelles it selfe I had observed: In Antwerp I saw (as I remember) 4 dogs draw 5 lusty Children in a Charriot to my greate astonishment; the Master commands them whither he pleases, crying his Wares about the streetes.

I baited by the Way to refresh our horses at a prety Towne call'd Ouse, and by 6 that Evening ariv'd at Ghendt.

Ghendt is an extravagant Citty of so vast a Circumference, that it is reported to be no lesse then 7 Leagues in compasse; but there is not an halfe part of it now built; much of it remaining in feilds and desolate pastures, even within the Wales, which has marvailous strong Gates towards the West, and two faire Churches, in one of which I heard a Sermon. Here I beheld the Palace wherein John of Gaunt, and Charles the Vt were borne, whose statue stands erected in the Market-place upon an high Pillar, with his sword drawn, to which (as I was told) the Magistrates and Burgers were wont to repaire upon a certaine day every yeare, with roaps about their necks, in toaken of submission and pennance for an old Rebellion of theirs: but now the Weede is changed into a blew ribbon. Here is planted the Basilisco, or monstrous gun so much talked of. [The] Ley and Scheld meeting in this vast Citty divide it into 26 Ilands which are united togethere by many bridges somewhat resembling Venice.

This night I supp'd with the Abbot of Andoyne, a pleasant and courteous Priest:

Octob: 8: I passed by Boate to Bruges, taking in a Convoy of 14 Musqueteeres by the way at a Redout, because the other side of the River being contribution land, was subject to the inrodes and depredations of the borduring States. This River was cut by the famous Marq: Spinola, and is, in my judgment, a wonderfull piece of Labour, and worthy publique worke, being in some places forced through the maine rock to an incredible depth for 30 miles: At the end of each mile is built a small Redout which communicats a line to the next; and so the whole way, from whence we received many volyes of shot in complement to my Lord Marshall who was in our Vessell a passenger with us: Thus about 5 that Evening we were met by the Magistrates of Bruges, who came out to convoy my Lord to his Lodging at whose cost he was entertayn'd that night. The morning after we went to see the State-house and adjoyning Aquaeduct; the Church and Market-place, where I remember we saw Cheezes, and Butter pild up like heapes of Mortar: Also the Fortifications and grafts, which are incredibly strong and large:

The 9th we ariv'd at Ostend, by a straite and artificial River: Here with leave of the Captaine of the Watch, I was caryed to survey the river and harbour which fortifies one side thereof: The East and South are mud and earth Wales, one of the strongest places in my life I had seene . . .

Octob: 10, I went by Wagon (accompany'd with a jovial Commissary) to Dynkirk, the journey was made all on the sea sands: On our arivall we first viewed the Court of Guards, The Workes, Towne-house and new Church (which is indeede very beautifull within) and another wherein they shew'd us an excellent piece of our B: Saviours bearing the Crosse. The Harbour in two Channells coming up to the Towne was choaked with a multitude of Prizes. From hence I the next day marched 3 English miles towards the Packet-boate being a pretty Fregat of 6 Gunns, which embarked us for England about 3 in the afternoone: At our going off the Schrnken fort (against which our Pinnac ankerd) saluted my L: Martial with 13 great gunns, which we answerd with 3. and so (not having the Wind favourable) after a little motion, ankerd that night before Calis: About midnight we weigh'd, and at 4 in the morning being not far from Dover, we could not yet make the Peere till 4 that afternoone, the wind proving contrary and driving us Westward; but at the last we got on shore, being the afternoone of Octob: 12th.

From Dover I that night rood Post to Canterbery, where I visited the Cathedrall, now in greatest splendor, those famous Windoes being intire, since demolish'd by the Phanatiques: The next morning by Sitinbourn, I came to Rochester; and thence to Graves-End, where a Light-horse-man (as they call it) taking us in, we spent our tide as far as Greene-Wich, whence after we had a little refresh'd at the Colledge (for by reason of the Contagion then in Lond: we baulked the Inns) we came to London, landing at Arundel Stayers, where I tooke leave of his Lordship, and retyr'd to my Lodgings in the Middle Temple, being about two in the morning the 14th of October.

Octob: 16 I went to see my Bro: at Wotton, being the 31 of this Moneth (unfortunate for the Irish rebellion which brake out the 23) one and twenty Yeares of age.

No: 7: I received the B: Sac, at the Church of Wotton; and in the afternoone went to give my L: Martial a Visite at Albury:

Nov: 8 I went to Lewes to see my friends in Sussex, accompany'd with my two Brothers. The 13th I return'd, and the 23d to Lond: where on the 25t following I saw his Majestie ride through the Citty, after his comming out of Scotland and a peace proclaym'd, with greate acclamations and joy of the giddy people.

Decemb: 15, I was elected one of the Comptrollers of the Middle-Temple-Revellers, as the fashion of the Young Students and Gentlemen was; the Christmas being kept this Yeare with greate Solemnity; but being desirous to passe it in the Country, I got leave to resigne my Staffe of Office, and went with my Bro: Richard to Wotton . . .

. . .

[1642. January] 29, I went againe to Lond, where I stayd till 5 March following, studying a little; but dauncing and fooling more:

. . .

The 23d Mar: I tooke a journey with my Brothers to Northampton faire to buy some saddle horses, and returnd the 28 by St. Albans, where we visited the Church, and the ruines of old Verulame, where the L: Chancelor Bacons contemplative monument is the sole ornament worth remembring.

Civil War and Travel: France
1642–1644

[July] 30th to Ditton: Sep: 2, to Wotton: Octob: 3d to Chichester, and thence the next day to see the Seige of Portsmouth; for now was that blody difference betweene the King and Parliament broaken out, which ended in the fatal Tragedy so many yeares after: It was on the day of its being render'd to Sir William Waler, which [gave] me opportunity of taking my leave of Coll: Goring the Governor now embarquing for France:

On the 6t I went from Portsmouth to [Southampton], lay at Winchester, where I visited the Castle, Schole, Church and K: Arthyrs round table; but especialy the Church and its Saxon Kings Monuments, which I esteemed a worthy antiquity: On the 7th I return'd to Wotton by Farne-ham and Guildford.

Octob: 3d was fought that signal Battaile at Edgehill:
31 I was 22 yeares of age.

A Discrete Participation

No: 12: was the Battaile of Braineford* surprisingly fought, and to the greate consternation of the Citty, had his Majestie (as 'twas beelieved he would) pursu'd his advantage: I came in with my horse and Armes just at the retreate; but was not permitted to stay longer then the 15th by reason of the Armys marching to Glocester, which had left both me and my Brothers expos'd to ruine, without any advantage to his Majestie. [V: I came with my Horse and Armes, and with some mony presented to his Majestie by my Bro: was assigned to ride Volunteere, amongst the Gent: in Pr: Ruperts Troop, who was general of the Horse: But the King marching to Glocester, by which the Gentlemen whose Estates were in Surry and Sussex lay in the immediate power of the Rebells, and would certainely have ben seized as delinquents; nothing of my appearing in Armes, being known, I was advis'd, to obtaine of his Majestie, leave to Travell; since my Estate in the County, would have maintained more against his Majestie, than I could, for him: So as having a Passe procur'd me by sir Ed: Nicholas, then Secretary of state, and a friend of our Family, (whence he had his rise in greate measure) under his Majesties hand, I began to resolve on my Returne and preparation to passe into France:]

. . .

[1643 March] the 11th I went to see my L: of Salisburys Palace at Hatfeild; where the most considerable rarity besides the house, (inferior to few for its Architecture then in England) was the Garden and Vineyard rarely well water'd and planted: They also shewd us the Picture of Secretary Cicil in Mosaique-worke very well don by some Italian hand.

I must not forget what amaz'd us exceedingly on the night before; viz, a shining clowd in the ayre, in shape resembling a sword, the poynt reaching to the North; it was as bright as the Moone, the rest of the skie being very serene; it began about 11 at night, and vanish'd not 'til about one, seene by all the South of England.

. . .

May 2d I went to Lond; where I saw the furious and zelous people demolish that stately Crosse in Cheapeside: The 4th I return'd with no little regrett for the Confusion that threaten'd us:

On the 15, to Lond: againe returning the 17th and resolving to possesse my selfe in some quiet if it might be, in a tyme of so greate jealosy, I built (by my Brothers permission,) a study, made a fish-pond, Iland and some other solitudes and retirements at Wotton, which gave the first occasion of improving them to those Water-Workes and Gardens, which afterwards succeded them, and became the most famous of England at that tyme. [V: It was now, that yet Balancing whether I should go immediatly abroad, or stay a while to see what Issue this difference between the K. and Parliament would produce, that I made (by my Bro: permission) the stews and receptacles for Fish, and built a little study over a Cascade, to passe my Malencholy houres shaded there with Trees, and silent Enough:]

. . .

The 12th [July] I return'd, and sent my Black-manage-horse and furniture with a friend to his Majestie then at Oxford.

23 July, The Covenant being pressed, I absented my selfe; but

finding it impossible to evade the doing of very unhandsome things; and which had been a greate Cause of my perpetuall motions hitherto betweene Lond: and Wotton: October the 2d, I obtayn'd a Lycense of his Majestie dated at Oxford, and sign'd by the King, to travell againe, so as on November 6, lying by the way at Sir Ralph Whitfeilds at Bletchinglee, (whither both my Brothers had conducted me) I arived at Lond: on the 7th and two dayes after tooke boate at the Tower-Wharfe, which carryd me as far as Sittinburne, though not without danger, I being onely in a payre of Oares expos'd to an hidious storme; but it pleas'd God, that we got in before the perill was considerable: From thence by Post I went to Dover accompany'd with one Mr. Thicknesse a very deare friend of mine:

First Landing in France

On the 11th having a reasonable good Passage, though the Weather were snowy and untoward enough, we came before Calais; where as we went on shore, mistaking the tyde, our shallop struck with no little danger on the sands; but at length we gott off.

Calais is an extraordinary well fortified Place consider'd in the old Castle, and new Citadell reguarding the Sea: The Haven consists of a long banke of Sand lying opposite to it: The Market-place and Church are very remarkeable things, besides those reliques of our once dominion there, so as I remember there was engraven in stone upon the front of an antient dwelling which was shew'd us, these words God save the King, in English, together with the name of the Architect and date: The Walls of the Towne are likewise very substantial, but the situation towards the Land not Pleasant in the least, by reason of the Marishes and low-grounds about it. The next day (being the 12th) after diner we tooke horse with the Messagere, hoping to have that night ariv'd at Bollogne; but there fell so greate a Snow, accompanied with hayle, raine and suddaine darknesse, as we had much a doe to retrive the next Village; and in this passage being to goe crosse a Vally where a Causeway and a Bridge was built over a small river, the raine that had fallen making it now an impetuous streame for neere a quarter of a mile, my horse slipping his [footing] had almost been the occasion of my perishing: This night we none of us went to bed, for the Souldiers in those parts leaving little in the Villages, we had enough to do to get ourselves dry by morning, between the fire and the fresh straw:

The next day early we ariv'd at Bollogne, where we were willing to recover some rest, though to the losse of a day:

Boullogne is a double towne, one part of it situate on an high rock or downes; the other call'd the Lower Towne is yet with a greate declivity towards the Sea; both of them defended by a strong Castle which stands on a notable Eminence: Under the Towne runs the River de Liane, which is yet but an inconsiderable brooke: This place is yet both a County, and a Bishoprick, but for nothing more remarkable to us, then the Seige of Hen: 8., when he made use of those letherne greate Gunns, which I have since beheld in the Tower of Lond: with this motto on them, Non Marte Opus est, cui non defficit Mercurius, if at least the history be true, which my L: Herbert doubts:

The next morning, through some danger of Partys surprizing us, we came to Monstreuil; It is built on the Summit of a most conspicuous hill, environd with faire and ample Meadows; but all the Suburbs had been from time to time ruin'd, and now lately burnt by the Spanish inroads. This Towne is exceedingly fortified with two very profound ditches, yet without Water; The walls about the Bastions, and Citadell are a noble piece of Masonry: The Church is more glorious without then within: The Market-place large, but the Inhabitans miserably poore.

From Montreuil we came the next day to Abbeville (having passd all this way in continual expectation of the Volunteeres as they call them) a Towne that affords a most gracious aspect towards the hill from whence we descended; nor indeede dos it deceive the Eye, for it is handsomly built, and has many pleasant and usefull streames passing through it, the maine river being the Somme which dos after wards discharge it selfe into the Sea at St. Valery almost in view of the Towne. The Principal Church is a very handsome piece of Gotique Architecture, and the Ports and Ramparts swee[t]ly built and planted for defence and ornament: In the morning they brought us choyce of Gunns and Pistolls to sell at reasonable rates, and neately made, being here a merchandize of greate account so as the Towne abounds in Gun-Smiths.

Henc we advanc'd to Beavais, another Towne of good noate, and the first Vineyards we came at: The next day to Beaumont, and the morrow to Paris, having taken our repast at St. Denys within t[w]o Leagues of that greate Citty.

St. Denys is a towne considerable onely for its stately Cathedrall, and Dormitory of the French Kings who lye there inhum'd, as ours at Westminster: Not omitting the Treasury esteemed one of the richest in Europ.

Treasures of St. Denys

The Church was built by K: Dagobert, but since much enlarged, being now no lesse then 390 foote long and 100 in bredth: 80 in height without comprehending the cover; it has also a very high shaft of stone, and the gates are of brasse:

Here whiles the Monke conducted us, we were shew'd the antient, and moderne Sepulchers of their Kings beginning from the founder to Lewes his son, with Charles Martel, Pepin [his] son, and father of Charlemagne, these lye in the Quire, and without more then as many more; amongst the rest Bertrand du Gues[c]lin Constable of France; in the Chapell of Charles V. all his posterity, and neere him that magnificent Sepulchre of Francis the first, with his Children, Warrs, Victories and Triumphs engraven in Marble: In the Nave of the Church lyes the Catap[h]alc or hearse of Lewes XII. Hen: 2d; a noble tomb of Fr: 2, and Charles IX.

. . . A greate head of pure Gold miter'd, and cover'd with very faire rubies, Saphyrs Topazes and a world of Pearles, it being the head of their greate St. Denys, supported by two Angels: There is likewise his Chalis, Crosse and Pastoral ring, with his booke, Inkern, Pilgrims Staffe, all coverd with gold: The Image of St. Hilary in a large Chrystal, a bone of his arme, the Collar and miter are full of precious stones and pearles almost numberlesse: Besides these divers other Saints. A Church of plate made after the Model of Noster Dame at Paris full of Reliques: Some of the Prophet Isaias bones in a silver Cofin. The Stole and Pallium of Pope Stephen the 3d. The body of St. Lewes: The Crowne of Charlemagne full of admirable stones, his 7 foote high Septer, and hand of Justice: The agraffe of his royal mantle beset with diamonds and rubies; his sword, belt, and spurrs of Gold: The Crowne of St. Lewes coverd with precious stones, amongst the rest one vast Ruby uncut, of inestimable value weighing 300 carrats,

under which is set one of the thornes of our B: S: Crowne: his
Sword, Seale and hand of Justice: The two Crownes of Hen: IVth,
his Scepter, hand of Justice and Spurrs: The 2 Crownes of His
sonn Lewes: In the Cloake-Royall of Anne de Bretagne is a very
greate and rare Rubie: divers bookes cover'd with solid Plates of
Gold, and studded with precious stones. Two Vasas of Berill; two
incomparable Vasas of Achate* whereof one is esteemed for
bignesse, Colour and carving imboss'd, the best now to be seene in
the World: By a special favour I was permitted to take the measure
and dimensions of it: The story on it is a Bacchanalia and sacrifice
to Priapus, a very holy thing, and fit for a Cloyster: It is realy
antique and indeede the Noblest jewell there. There is also a large
Gundola of Chrysolite, an huge Urne of Porphyrie; another of
Calcedone: A Vasa of Onyx, the largest I had ever seene of that
stone: Two of Chrystal: A morcel of one of the Water-potts our
Saviour did his first Miracle in. The Effigies of the Q: of Saba, of
Julius, Augustus, Marc Antony, Cleopatra and others upon
Saphyrs, Topazes, Agates, and Cornelians: That of the Q: of Saba
has a Morish face: That of Julius, and Nero Achats so rarely
colour'd and cut, as could not be nobler: He shew'd us a Cup in
which Solomon was us'd to drinke: An Idol of Apollo upon a greate
Amethist.

  There lay in the Window a miroir of a kind of stone sayd to have
been the Poet Virgils: Charlemaynes Chesse-men, full of Arabique
Characters, and as greate as bowles: In the Presse next the doore
the brasse Lanterne full of Chrystals, sayd to have conducted Judas
and his Company to apprehend our B: S: There was a faire
Unicornes-horne sent by a K: of Persia; it was about 7 foote long:
The onely tallon or claw of a Griffon that ever I saw: In another
Presse (over which stands the Picture in Oyle to the life, of their
Orleans Amazon with her Sword) the Effigies of the late French
Kings in Wax like ours at Westminster, coverd with their Robes,
and a world of other rarities I was forc'd to passe over: But thus
having rewarded our Courteous Fryer, we tooke horse for Paris,
where we ariv'd about five in the afternoone; in the Way observing
divers faire Crosses of stone erected, and carv'd with flowr de
Lyces, at every fu[r]long's end, where they affirme St. Denys
rested, and layd downe his head after Martyrdome, carying it from
the Place where this Monastery is builded.

Paris

We lay at Paris at the Ville de Venize, where after I had something refresh'd, and put my selfe in equipage, I went to visite Sir Rich: Browne, his Majesties Resident with the French King:

On the 5 of December, came the Earle of Norwich, Extraordinary Ambassador, whom in a Coach and six horses I went to meete, at the Palais of Monsieur de Bassompieres, at Chaliot, where I had the honor to see that gallant Person his Gardens, Tarraces and rare Prospect: My L: was waited on by the Master of the Ceremonies, and a very greate Cavalcade of men of Quality to the Palais Cardinal. Where on the 23d he had Audience of the Fr: King and the Q: Regent his Mother, in the Golden Chamber of Presence; from thenc I conducted him to his Lodging in the rüe St. Denys and so tooke my Leave.

December 24 I went with some company to see some remarkable places about the Citty; as the Isle, and how 'tis encompassed by the Seine and Oyse rivers: The City is divided into thre[e] Parts, whereof the Towne is greatest: The City lyes betwixt it and the University in forme of an Iland; Over the river Seine is built a stately bridg (call'd Pont Neuf,) by Hen 3d 1578, finished by Hen: 4th his Successor: It consists of 12 Arches, in the middst of which ends the poynt of an Iland handsomely built about with artificers houses. The Bridg above is very commodiously divided into one large Passage for Coaches, and two for footemen 3 or 4 foote higher, and of convenient breadth for 8, or 10 to goe on brest; all of hewn free-stone the best I thinke in Europ and growing in the very streetes, though more plentifully at Mont-Martyre within a mile of it. On the Middle of this stately bridge upon one side stands that famous statue of Henry le grand on horse-back exceeding the natural proportion by much, and on the 4 faces of a stately Pedestal (which is all compos'd of various sorts of Polish'd-Marble and rich mouldings) is engraven in brasse Inscriptions of his Victories, and most signal actions: The statue and horse is of Copper, being the Worke of the greate John di Bolognia, and sent from Florence by Ferdinando the first, and Cosimo the second, Unkle and Cousin to Mary di Medices wife of Henry, whose statue it represents: The Place where it is erected is enclos'd with a very strong and beautifull grate of Yron; about which there are allways Montebancs shewing their feates to the idle passengers. From hence is a rare

Prospect towards the Louver, and Suburbs of St. Germaines, the [Isle] du Palais and Notre Dame. At foote of this Bridge is a water-house, at the front whereof a greate height is the Story of our B: Saviour and the Woman of Samaria powring Water out of a bucket; above a very rare dyal of severall motions with a chime etc: The Water is conveyd with huge Wheeles, pumps and other Engines from the river beneath: But the confluence of the People, multitude of Coaches and severall accidents passing every moment over this Bridge is the greater miracle, and to a new Spectator, a most prodigious, yet agreable diversion: Other bridges there are as that of Notre dame, the Pont au Change etc. fairly built with houses of stone which are layd over this river; onely the Pont St. Anne landing the Suburbe of St. Germaines at the Thuilleries is built of Wood, having likewise a Water-house in the middst of it, and a statue of Neptune (as the other) casting Water out of a Whales mouth of lead; but much inferiour to the Samaritans.

The University lyes South-West on an higher grownd, contiguous to, but the lesser part of, Paris: The[y] reckon no lesse than 65 Colleges, but they in nothing approch ours at Oxford for state and order: Within the University dwell the Booksellers: Onely the Scholes (of which more hereafter) are very regular:

The Suburbs are those of St. Denys, Honoré, St. Marcel, Jacques, St. Michel, St. Victoire, and St. Germaines which last is the largest and where the nobility and Persons of best quality are seated: And truely Paris, comprehending the Suburbs is certainely for the material the houses are built with, and many noble and magnificent piles, one of the most gallant Cittys in the World, and best built: large in Circuit, of a round forme, infinitly populous; but situat in a botome environd with gentle declivities, which renders some places very durty, and makes it smell as if sulphure were mingled with the mudd: Yet is it pav'd with a kind of freestone of neere a foote square which renders it more easy to walke on then our pibbles of London:

On Christmas-Eve I went to see the Cathedrall Nostre Dame . . . This is the prime church of France for dignity, having Archdeacons, Vicaries, Cannons, Priests and Chaplaines good store, to the number of 127. It is also the Palace of the Archbishop: The young king being now there with a greate and martial Guard, who enter'd the Nave of the Church with their drumms and Fifes, at their ceasing was entertaind with the Church musique, and so I left him.

[1644.] Jan: 4 I passd with one Mr. Jo: Wall an Irish gent, who had been a Frier in Spaine, and after Reader in St. Isodor's Chayre at Rome; but now, I know not how, getting away, pretended himselfe a souldier of fortune, and absolute Cavaliere, having as he told us been Cap: of horse in Germany . . .

A Wit at the Sorbonne

The next day we went into the University, and enter'd into the College of Navarre, which is a well-built spacious Quadrangle, having a very noble Library; Thenc to the Sorbonne, an antient fabrique built by one Robert de Sorbonne whose name it retaynes; but the restauration which the late Cardinal de Richlieu has made to it of most excellent moderne building . . . We enter'd into some of the Scholes, and in that of Divinity we found a grave Doctor in his chaire with a multitude of Auditors, who all are Writers after his dictats, this they call a Course: After we had sate a little, up starts our Cavalier and ru[d]ely enough begins to dispute with the Doctor, at which (and especialy to see a fellow clad in the Spanish habit which is in Paris the greatest bugbare imaginable) both the Scholars and Doctor fell into such a fit of laughter, as no body could be heard speake for a while; but silence being obtaind, he began to speake Latine, and make his Apology in so good a style, that their derision was turn'd to admiration, and beginning to argue, he so baffled the Professor that with universal applause they all rose up and did him very greate honors, waiting on us to the very streete and Coach, and testif[y]ing a greate deale of satisfaction.

On the 6t, I alterd my Lod[g]ing to the rüe de Seine. The 18 I tooke a Master of the French Tongue.

Feb: 2d I heard the newes of my Nephew Georges birth; which was on Jan: 15: English style 1645.

Feb: 3d I put my selfe in mourning for the French Kings death Lewes xiii . . .

. . .

The Tuileries

. . . [February 9] I this day finish'd with a Walke in the greate Garden of the Thuilleres, which is rarely contriv'd for Privacy,

shade, company, by Groves, Plantations of tall trees, especialy that
in the middle being of Elmes, the other of Mulberys; and that
Labyrinth of Cypresse; not omitting the noble hedges of Pomegranads, the fountaines, Piscianas, Aviary, but above all the
artificial Echo, redoubling the words so distinctly, and as it is never
without some faire Nymph singing to its gratefull returns: standing
at one of the focus's, which is under a tree or little Cabinet of
hedges, the Voyce seemes to descend from the Clowds; and at
another, as if it were under grownd: This being at the botome of
the Garden, we were let into another, which being kept with all
imaginable accuratenesse, in reguard of the Orangery, precious
Shrubbs, and rare fruites, seem'd a Paradise: From a Tarrac in this
Place we might see so many Coaches (as late in the yeare as it was)
going towards the Course (which is a place neere adjoyning of
neere an English mile long, and planted with 4 rows of Trees,
making a large Circle in the middle) that one would Conceive were
impossible to be maintaind in the whole Citty: This Corso is wall'd
about neere breast-high with squar'd freestone, has a very stately
Arch at the Entry, with noble Sculpture and statues about it, built
by Mary di Medices; and here it is that the Gallants, and the Ladys
of the Court take the ayre and divert themselves, as with us in
Hide-Parke, the middle Circle being Capable to containe an
hundred Coaches to turne commodiously, and the larger of the
Plantations for 5 or 6 Coaches a breast:

. . .

Fontainebleau

The Next day, being Mar: 7th, I set forwards with some
Company, towards Fontaine Bleau, which is a sumptuous Palace of
the Kings (like ours of Hampton-Court) about 14 leagues from the
Citty: by the Way we passe through a Forest so prodigiously
encompassd with hidious rocks of a Certaine whiteish hard stone,
congested one upon another in Mountainous heights, that the like I
believe is no where to be found more horrid and solitary: It
abounds with Staggs, Wolves, Boares and sometimes more savage
bea[s]ts, there being not long after, a Lynx or Ownce killd amongst
them who had devowrd some passengers: Upon the Summite of
one of these gloomy Precipices, intermingled with Trees and
Shrubbs and monstrous protuberances of the huge stones which

hang over and menace ruine, is built an Hermitage: passing these
solitudes, not without howrly expectation of Rogues who frequently
lurke about these denns and do mischiefe (and for whom we were
all well appoynted with our Carabines) we arived that Evening at
the Village, where we lay at the Horne, going the next morning
early to the Palace: The Fabrique of this house is nothing so stately
and uniforme, as Hampton Court: but Fra: the 1st began much to
beautifie it; most of all Hen: 4th, and not a little the last King: It
abounds with very faire Halls, Chambers and Gallerys: In the
longest which is 360 foote long and 18 broad is paynted with the
Victoryes of that greate Prince Grand-father to the present: That of
Francis the i: cal'd the grand Galery, has all the Kings Palaces
paynted on it: Above these in 60 pieces of incomparable Worke the
history of Ulysses out of Homer don by Primaticcio in Fresca in the
tyme of Hen: 3d and esteemed amongst the most renown'd in
Europ for the designe: The Cabinet is full of incomparable
Pictures, especialy a Woman of Raphael: In the Hall of the Guards
is a piece of Tapissry painted on the wall very naturally,
representing the Victoryes of Charles the 7th against our Country-
men. In the Sale des Festines, is a rare Chimny-piece, and Hen:
4th on horse-back of White-marble esteemed worth 18000
Crownes: Clementia and Pax nobly don: Upon Columns of Jasper
2 Lyons of Brasse: The new stayres, and an halfe Circular Court is
of modern and good Architecture, and so is a Chapell built by
Lewes XIIIth all of Jasper and severall incrustations of Marble
through the inside: Having seene the romes we went to the Volary
which has a Cupola in the middle of it; also greate trees and
bushes, it being full of birds who dranke at two fountaines: There is
also a faire Tennis-Court, and noble stables; but the Beauty of all
are the Gardens: In the Court of the Fountaines stand divers
Antiquities, and statues, a Mercury especialy: In the Queenes
Garden is the figure of a Diana making a fountayne with a world of
other brasse statues: The Greate Garden being 180 thoises long
and 154 wide has in the Center the Fountayne of Tyber in a
Colossean figure of brasse, with the Wolfe over Romulus and
Rhemus: also at each corner of the Garden rises a fountaine. In the
Garden of the Piscina is an Hercules of White-marble; next is that
of Pines, and without that a Canale of an English mile in length, at
the end of which rises three jettos in the forme of a flowre de lys of

an exceeding height; at the margent are incomparable Walkes planted with trees: Here the Carps come familiarly to hand: Hence they brought us to a Spring which they report being first discover'd by a dog, gave occasion of beautif[y]ing this place both with the Palace and Gardens; The White and horrid rocks at some distance in the Forest yeald one of the most august and stupendious prospects imaginable. The Parke about it is very large, and the Towne full of noble-mens houses.

. . .

Norman Orchards

On the 18 with one Sir Jo: Cotton a Cambridg-shire Knight I went a journey into Normandy: The 1 day we passed by Gaillon which is the Archbishops of Roüens Palac, the Gardens are highly commended, but we went not in, intending to reach Pontoise by dinner: The Towne is built in a very gallant place, has a noble Bridge over the Oise, and is bravely refreshd with Fountaines. This is the first Towne in Normandy and the farthest terroire that the Vineyards extend on this side the Country, which is fuller of Playnes, Wood and Enclosures, with some downes towards the sea very like England. We lay this night at a small Vilage calld Magny; The next day descending an extraordinary steepe hill we din'd at Fleury; and after riding 5 leagues downe St. Catherine to Rouen, which affords a goodly Prospect to the ruines of that Chapell and mountaine. This Country dos so abound with Wolves, that a sheep-heard whom I met told us, one of his Companions was strangled by one but the day before, and that in the middst of his flock: The feilds are most of them planted with Peares, and Apples and other Cider fruites: It is also plentifully furnish'd with quarries of stone and slat, and hath Yron in aboundance.

I lay at the White Crosse in Rouen which is a very large Citty, situat on the Seine, having two smaller rivers besides calld the Aubelt and Lobes: There stand yet the ruines of a magnificent bridge of stone now supplyd by one of boates onely, to which there come up Vessells of considerable burthen: The other side of the Water consists of Meadow; and there have the reformed a Church: The Cathedrall of the Citty is Nost[r]e Dame, built as they acknowledge by the English, and inded some English words graven in Gotic Characters upon the Front seeme to confirm it. The

Towers and whole Church is full of Carving: It has 3 steeples with a Pyramid; in one of these I saw the famous bell so much talk'd off, being 13 foote in height, 32 large, the diameter 11, and we[igh]ing 40000 pounds: In the Chapel d'Amboise, built by a Cardinal of that name, lyes his body, with severall faire monuments: The Quire has behind it a greate Dragon paynted on the Wall, which they affirme to have don much harme to the Inhabitans till vanquish'd by St Romain their Archbishop, for which there is an annual Procession. It was now neere Easter, and many Images were exposd, with scenes and stories representing the Passion made up of little Puppets, to which there was great resort and devotion with offerings. There is before the Church a faire Palace. St. Owen is another goodly Church and Abby with very fine Gardens belonging to it: Here the King hath Lodgings when he makes his progresse through these parts.

The structure where the Court of Parliament is kep[t] is very magnificent, containing very faire halles and chambers, especialy La Chambre d'orée. The Towne house is also well built; and so are some gentlemens houses; but the most part of the rest are of Timber like our Merchants of London in the wodden part of the Citty.

Upon Easter moneday we went from Rouen, din'd at Totes, a solitary inn betweene that and Diepe where we ariv'd March 21: This Towne is situated betwene two Mountaines not unpleasantly; is washed on the north by our English Seas: The Port is commodious, but the entrance difficult: It has one very ample and faire streete, in which a pretty Church: In the afternoone I walked up the hill to view the Fort Pollet which consists of a strong Earth-Worke and commands the Haven, as on the other side dos the Castle which is also well fortified with the Citadel before it; nor is the towne it selfe a little strong: This place exceedingly abounds in workemen that make and sell curiosities of Ivory and Tortoise shells, in which they turne, and make many rare toyes; and indeed whatever the East Indys afford of Cabinets, Purcelan, natural and exotic rarities are here to be had with aboundant choyce:

The Coast

The 23d we passd all along by the Coast, a very rocky and rugged way, which forc'd [us] many times to alight till we came to Haver de

Grace, where we lay that night: The next morning we were admitted to see the Citadell which is both very strong and regular, and in reguard of its situation altogether impregnable: It is also excellently stor'd with Artillery and ammunition of all sorts, the works furnish'd with faire brasse Canon; the allogiaments of the Garnison very uniforme, a spacious place for drawing up the souldiers, a pretty Chapell, and faire house for the Governor. The Duke of Richlieu being now in the Fort we went to salute him who received us very civilly, and commanded that we should be shew'd what ever we desired to see: That which I tooke more especiall notice of was this motto upon the Canon, out of the Prince of Latine Poets – Ratio Ultima Regum: The Citadel was built by the late Card: de Richlieu, unkle of the present duke, and may be esteemed one of the strongest in France: The haven is very capacious: When we had don here we embarqued our selves and horses to passe over to the other side, being about 4 or 5 leagues to a Towne calld Homfleur, where dissembogues the Seine into the sea: The place seemes to be a poore fisher-towne, observable for nothing so much as the odd, yet usefull habites which the good-Women weare, of beares and others skinns, as of ruggs etc. at Diepe and all along those maritime Coasts: The 25, being the day after we ariv'd at Caen, a very noble and beautifull Towne situat on the river Orne which passes quite through it, joynd onely by a bridg consisting of one intire arch: We lay at the Angel, where we were very well usd, the place being aboundantly furnish'd with Provisions at a cheape rate. The most considerable object is the greate Abby and Church, large and rich; built after the Gotish manner, with two spires . . . at the West end, and all of stone . . .

. . .

From Caen we went on the 28th towards Paris . . .

. . .

Orléans

. . . On the 19 of Aprill I tooke leave of Paris, and by the way of the Messenger agreed for my Passage to Orleans:

The Way from Paris to this City (as indeede most of the roades of France) is paved with a small square free-stone; so that the Country dos not much molest the Travelor with dirt and ill way as ours in England dos; onely 'tis somewhat hard to the poore horses feete which causes them to ride more temperately, seldome going out of the trot, or *grand pas*, as they call it:

We passed by divers Wall'd Townes or Villages as the manner is frequently to secure them: Amongst others of note Chartres* and Estampes where we lay the first night: This has a faire Church: The next day we had excellent Way; but had like to come short home; for no sooner were we entred two or three leagues into the Forest of Orleans (which extends it selfe for many miles) after dinner; but the Company behind us, were set on by Rogues who shooting from the hedges and frequent Covert, slew fowre upon the spot, the rest flying: Amongst the slayne was a Captaine of Swisses of the Regiment of Picardy, a person much lamented: This disaster made such an Alarme in Orleans at our arival; that the Prevost-Martial with his assistants going in pursuite, brought in two whom they had shot, and exposed them in the greate Market-place, to see if any would take cognizance of them. I have greate Cause to give God thankes for this Escape . . .

. . . The 21 I went about to view the Citty, which is very well built of stone, upon the side of the Loyre; about the middle of the river is a very prety Iland full of Walkes, and faire Trees with some houses; this is contiguous to the Towne by a stately bridge of stone, reaching to the opposite suburbs, built likewise upon the edge of an hill from whenc is a beautifull prospect: At one of the extreames of the bridge are strong toures; and about the middle neere one side, the statue of the Virgin Mary or Pieta, with a Christo Morto in her lap, as big as the life:

'Jane d'Arc . . . Virago'

At one side of the Crosse kneels Charles the vith arm'd, and at the other Jane d'Arc the famous Pucele arm'd also like a Cavalier with boots and spurrs, her hayre dischevel'd as the Virago who deliver'd the Towne from our Countrymen, what time they beseig'd it: The valiant Creature being afterward burnt at Rouen for a Witch. The figures are all cast in Copper with a Pedistall full of Inscriptions, as well as a faire Columne joyning to it, which is all adornd with flowre de lyces and a Crucifix, with two saints, proceding as it were from two branches out of its Capital: The Inscriptions upon the Crosse are in Latine . . .

To this is made an annual procession, with a Masse sung before it on the 12 of May, with infinite Ceremony and Concourse of people:

The Wine of this Place is so grosse and strong that the Kings Cup-bearers are (as I was assurd) sworne never to give the King any of it: But it is else a very noble liquor, and much of it transported into other Countrys:

The Language for being here spoken in greate purity, as well for divers other Priveleges, and the University, makes the Towne to be much frequented by strangers, especialy Germans; which causes the English to make no long sojourne here; but such as can drinke and debauch:

The Citty stands in the County of Beaulse, was once styld a Kingdome, afterwards a Dutchy, as at present, and belongs to the 2d sonne of France: Many Councils have been celebrated here, and some Kings Crown'd. The University is very antient: divided now by the students into that of 4 Nations French, High-dutch, Normans and Picardins who have each their respective protectors, severall Officers, Treasurers, Consuls, Seal'es etc. There are in it two reasonable faire Libraries publique: whenc one may borrow a booke to on[e]s Chamber, giving but a note under hand, which is a costome extraordinary, and a confidence that has cost many Liberarys deare. The first Church I went to visite was that of St. Croix: It has been a stately fabric but now much ruind by the late Civil Warrs: They report the towre of it, to have beene the highest in France: There is the beginning of a faire reparation: about this Cathedrall is a very Spacious Cymeterie.

The Towne hous is also very nobly built, with an high towre to it: The Streetes, Market-place (some whereof are deliciously planted with Limes) are both ample and very straite; so exquisitely paved with a kind of pibble, that I have not seene a neater Towne in France: In fine, this Citty was by Francis the first esteemed the most agreable in his vast dominions:

On the 28, taking Boate on the Loir, I went towards Blois; the passage and River, being both very divertissant: Thus we went by Mehun, and Baugency where we din'd: Thence to a little Towne call'd St. Dieu where we repos'd that night. Thence quitting our Barke we hired horses to carry us to Blois by the Way of Chambourg, a famous house of the Kings built in the middle of a solitary Parke by Fran: I: the Enclosure is a Wall, and full of deere:

That which made me desirous of seeing this Palace was the extravagance of the designe, especialy the Stayre-Case mention'd by the Architect Palladio: The[y] report 1800 worke-men were employ'd in this fabrique together during the space of twelve yeares, which makes me wonder it was not finish'd, it being no greater than divers Gentlemens houses in England; both for rome and circuit. The Carvings are indeede very rich and full: The Stayre Case is devis'd with 4 Entries, or ascents, which thwart one another so, that though 4 severall persons meete, yet they never come in sight, but by the small loope holes, till they land: It consists of 274 stepps as I remember, and is indeede a worke very extraordinary; but of far greater expense, than use or beauty: The Chimnys of the house appeare like so many Towres: About the whole is a large deepe moate; The Country about it full of Corne and Wine, with many faire noblemens houses.

Blois

Being ariv'd at Blois this Evening, on the 30th of April which was the morrow I went to view the Towne, which is both very hilly, uneven and rag[g]ed.

The situation is on the side of the Loire, having suburbs joynd by a stately bridg of stone, upon which is a Pyramid with an Inscription I could not read as I passed:

The Castle has at the Entery Lewes the 12 on horseback in stone as big as the life, under a Gotic State . . . Under this a very wide payre of Gates nailed full of Wolves heads and Wild Boares: Behind the Castle the Present Duke Gastion had begun a faire building, through which we walked into a large Garden, esteemed for its furniture one of the rarest in Europ, especialy for simples and exotic plants, in which he takes extraordinary delight: On the right hand is a longe Gallery full of antient Statues and Inscriptions both of Marble and Brasse: The length of it being 300 paces, divides the Garden into higher and lower ground: having a very nob[l]e fountaine: There is likewise the Portraiteure of an Hart taken in the forest by Lewes the 12th which has 24 Antlers on its head. Henc we went to the Collegiat Church of St. Saviours, where we saw many Sepulchers of the Earles of Blois.

On Sunday, being May-day, we walked up into the Pall-mall, which is very long and so nobly shaded with tall trees (being in the middst of a greate Wood) as, unlesse that of Tours, I had not seene a statlier: from hence we proceeded, with a friend of mine through the adjoyning Forest to see if we could meete any Wolves, which are here in such numbers, that they often come and take the Children out of the very Streetes; for all which, will not the Duke (who is Sovraigne here) permitt them to be destroy'd: Thus we walked 5 or 6 miles out right, but met with none. Yet a Gentleman, who was resting himselfe under a tree, with his horse grazing by him; told us that halfe an houre before two Wolves had set upon his horse, and had in probability devour'd him but for a dog which lay by him that frighted them: At a little Village at the end of this Wood we eate excellent Creame; and visited a Castle which was there builded on a very steepe Cliff: so we return'd:

Bloys is a towne where the Language is exactly spoken, the Inhabitans very courteous, the ayre so good that it is for that cause the ordinary nursery of the Kings Children; and the People so ingenious, that for Goldsmiths Worke, and Watches no place in France affords the like: The Pastures about the river are very rich and pleasant.

. . . And now we come within sight of Tours whither we were designd for the rest of the tyme I resolv'd to spend in France, the sejourne being so absolutely agreeable:

Tours

Tours is situat on the easy side of an hill on the river of Loyre, having a faire bridg of stone cald St. Edme: the Streetes very long, straite, spacious, well built, and exceeding cleane: The Suburbs very greate and pleasant, joynd to the Citty by another bridg: On the 5, we were carry'd about the Towne to see severall places; especialy St. Martins both Church and Monastry, which is a vast piece of Gotic building, having 4 Square toures, faire Organs, a stately Altar, where they shew strangers the bones and ashes of St. Martine, with other reliques. From hence we walk'd to the Mall, which is without comparison the noblest for length, and shade the best in Europ, having 7 rowes of the talest and goodliest Elmes I had ever beheld, the innermost of which do so embrace each other, and at such a prodigious height, as nothing can be more solemn and majestical: Here we play'd a party or two, and then walked about the Towne Walles, which are built of square stone fill'd with

Earth, and having a moate; no Citty in France exceeding it in beauty or delight.

. . .

On the 8th, I went to see their Manifactures in silke (for in this Towne they drive a very considerable trade with Silk-Wormes) their pressing and wateri[n]g the Grograns and Chambletts: with weights of an extraordinary poyse put into a rolling Engine.

Here I tooke a Master of the Language, and studyed the tongue very dilligently; recreating my selfe sometimes at the Maill, and sometymes about the Towne.

. . .

A Recalcitrant Spaniard

Aug: 1: My Valet de Chambre, One Garro, a Spaynard, borne in Biscay, for some misdemeanors, I was forc'd to discharge; he demanded of me (besides his Wages) no lesse then 100 Crownes to cary him to his Country, which I refusing to pay, as no part of our agreement; he had the impudence to arest me, and serve me with a Processe: so the next day I was call'd on to appeare in full Court, where both our Advocats pleaded before the Lieutennant Civile: But it was so unreasonable a pretence, that the Judge had not patience to heare it out, but immediately acquitting me, was so civil, as after he had extreamely reproch'd the Advocate who tooke part with my servant, he rose from the Bench, and making a courteous excuse to me, that being a stranger I should be so barbarously usd, conducted me through the Court to the very streete dore: This Varlet afterwards threaten'd to Pistol me.

The next day I waited on the Lieutennant to returne him thankes for his greate humanity:

On the 18 came the Queene of England to Towers newly ariv'd in France, and taking this Citty in her way to Paris; she was very nobly receiv'd both by people and Cleargy, who went to meete her with all the Train'd bands: After the Harangue, the Archbish: entertaind her Majestie at his owne Palac, Where I did my duty to her: The 20th, she set forwards towards Paris.

Sep: 8: came two of my Kindsmen from Paris to Towers, where I settled them in their Pension and exercises.

On the 14 we tooke post for Richlieu, passing by l'Isle Bouchart, a Village in the way.

. . .

... On the 16th we returnd to Towers; from whence after 19 Weekes sejourne we went towards the more Southern parts of France minding now to shape my Course so as I might Winter in Italy:

September 16th with my friend Mr. Thicknesse, and our guide, we went the first day 7 leagues to a Castle cal'd Chenonceaux built by Cath: di Medices, and now belonging to the Duke of Vendosme; it stands on a bridg: In the Gallery amongst divers other excellent statues, is that of Scipio Africanus of Oriental Alabaster ...

... we tooke horse for Varenne, an obscure Village where we lay that night; The next day we deviated some what out of the way to see the towne of Bourbon l'Archambaut, from whose antient and ragged Castle is deriv'd the name of the present Royal Family of France. The Castle stands on a flinty rock, over looking the Towne: In the middst of whose streetes are some Bathes of medicinal Waters, some of them excessive hott, but nothing so neately wald, and adornd as ours in Sommersetshire ...

On the 26t we ariv'd at Rouanne, where we quitted our Guide, and tooke Post for Lions:

...

Lyons

The 27th we rod post by Pont-Charu to Lions which being but 6 leagues we soone accomplish'd, having made 85 leagues from Toures in 7 dayes:

Here at Lions at the Lion d'or, rüe de Flandre I encounter'd divers of mine acquaintance who comming from Paris, were design'd for Italy: We lost no time in se[e]ing the Citty, because of being ready to accompany these Gentlemen in their journey: Lions is incomparably situated upon a Confluence of Rivers Saone and Rhodanus, which washes the Walls of the Citty in a very rapid streame ...

Truffles: 'a certaine earth-nut, found out by an hogg'

Sept: 30 we bargain'd with a Waterman to transport us as far as Avignon upon the River; so we embarqued from Lions, and got the first night to Vienne in Dauphine: This is an Archbishoprick and the Province gives title to the Heyre aparent of France; here we lay, and supp'd; having (amongst other dainties) a dish of Truffles, which is a certaine earth-nut, found out by an hogg, train'd up to it, and for which those Creatures, are sold at a greate price: It is in truth an incomparable meate: We were shewd the ruines of an Amphi-theatre, reasonable entire, and many handsome Palaces: especialy that of Pontius Pilat, which we saw, not far from the Towne at the foote of a solitary Mountaine, neere the River, having 4 pinacles: Here 'tis reported he pass'd his exile, and precipitated himselfe into the Lake not far from it: The house is modernly built, and seemes to be the seate of some Gentleman; being in a very pleasent place though somewhat melancholy.

. . .

. . . we came to Valence, a Capital Citty, carr[y]ing the title of a Dutchy; But the Bishop is now sole Lord Temporal of it, and the Country about it: The Towne having an University famous for the Civil Law is much frequented: but the Churches are none of the fairest, having been greately defac'd in the time of the Warrs: Yet are the Streets full of pretty fountaines: The Citadell strong, and Garnisond: Here we pass'd that night, and the next morning by Pont St. Esprit, which is 2412 yards in length and consists of 22 Arches; in the Pillars or piles of the Arches are Windoes (as it were) to receive the Water when it is high and full; here we went on shore, it being very dangerous to passe the bridg with a boate:

Avignon

Hence leaving our barque, we tooke horse (se[e]ing but at some distance the Towne and Principality of Orange) and lodging one night on the Way ariv'd by noone at Avignon: This Citty has belong'd to the Popes ever since Clem: the 6ts tyme, being Anno 1352, alienated by Jeane Queene of Naples and Sicily. Entring the Gates of this towne the Souldiers at the Guard tooke our Pistols and Carbines from us, and examin'd us very strictly; after that having obtain'd the Governors leave, and Vice-Legat to tarry for 3 dayes, we were civily conducted to our lodging.

The City is plac'd on the Rhodanus, and divided from the newer part, or Towne (which is situate on the other side of the River) by a very faire bridge of stone, which has been broken, at one of whose extreames is a very high rock on which a strong Castle well furnish'd with Artillery. The Walls of the City (being all square huge free stone) are absolutely the most neate and best in repaire that in my life I ever saw: It is full of well built Palaces . . .

We were in the Arsenale, Popes Palace, and in the Synagogue of the Jewes, who are in this towne distinguish'd by their red hats:

Vaucluse so much renound for the solitude of the learned Petrarch, we beheld from the Castle; but could not goe to visite it, for want of time; being now taking Mules, and a guide for Marcelles:

Sep: 30 we lay at Loumas, the next morning came to Aix; having pass'd that most dangerous and extreamly rapid river of Durance: In this tract all the Heathes or Commons are cover'd with Rosemary, Lavander, Lentiscs and the like sweete shrubbs for many miles together, which to me was then a very pleasant sight:

Aix is the chiefe Citty of Province, being a Parliament and Presidial towne, with other royal Courts and Metropolitan jurisdiction: It is well built, the houses exceeding high, and Streetes ample: The Cathedrall St. Sauveurs is a noble pile, adornd with innumerable figures (especialy that of St. Michael). The Baptistarie, the Palace, the Court, built in a most specious Piazza are very faire: The Duke of Guizes house is worth the seeing, being furnish'd with many Antiquities in, and about it. The Jesuites have also here a royal Colledge, and the City is an University.

Marseilles

From hence Octob: 7 we had a most delicious journey to Marselles throug[h] a Country, sweetely declining to the South and Mediterranean Coasts, full of Vine-yards, and Olive-yards, Orange trees, Myrtils, Pomegranads and the like sweete Plantations, to which belong innumerable pleasantly situated Villas, to the number of above 15 hundred; built all of Free-stone, and most of them in prospect shewing as if they were so many heapes of snow dropp'd out of the clowds amongst those perennial greenes: It was almost at the shutting in of the Gates that we got in at

Marcelles: This Towne stands on the Sea-Coast upon a sweete rising; tis well wall'd, and has an excellent Port for Ships, and Gallys, securd by an huge Chayne of Yron which draw crosse the harbour at pleasure; and there is a well fortified tower: besides this, there are also three other Forts or small Castles, especialy that cald the If built on a rock: Ratonneau, and that of St. John strongly garnison'd. But the Castle commanding the Citty, is that of Nostre dame de la Guard: In the Chapel hang up divers Crocodiles Skinns:

Galleys and Galley Slaves

We went then to Visite the Gallys being about 25 in number. The Captaine of the Gally royal gave us most courteous entertainment in his Cabine, the Slaves in the interim playing both on loud and soft musique very rarely: Then he shew'd us how he commanded their motions with a nod, and his Wistle, making them row out; which was to me the newest spectacle I could imagine, beholding so many hundreds of miserab[l]y naked Persons, having their heads shaven cloose, and onely red high bonnets, a payre of Course canvas drawers, their whole backs and leggs starke naked, doubly chayned about their middle, and leggs, in Cupples, and made fast to their seates: and all Commanded in a trise, by an Imperious and cruell sea-man: One Turke amongst them he much favourd, who waited on him in his Cabine, but naked as he was, and in a Chayne lock'd about his leg; but not coupled.

Then this Gally, I never saw any thing more richly carv'd and Guilded (the Sovraigne excepted) and most of the rest were exceeding beautiful: Here, after we had bestow'd something amongst the Slaves, the Cap: sent a band of them to give us musique at dinner where we lodged. I was amaz'd to contemplate how these miserable Catyfs lye in their Gally, considering how they were crowded together; Yet was there hardly one but had some occupation or other: by which as leasure, in Calmes, and other times, permitts, they get some little monye; in so much as some have after many Yeares of cruel Servitude been able to purchase their liberty: Their rising forwards, and falling back at their Oare, is a miserable spactacle, and the noyse of their Chaines with the roaring of the beaten Waters has something of strange and fearfull in it, to one unaccostom'd. They are ruld, and chastiz'd with a bulls-pizle dry'd upon their backs, and soles of their feete upon the least dissorder, and without the least humanity: Yet for all this they are Cherefull, and full of vile knavery: We went after dinner to see the church of St. Victoire, where that Saints head is reserv'd in a shrine of silver which weighs 600 lbs: Thence to Nostre Dame, exceedingly well built: This is the Cathedrall: Then the Duke of

Guizes Palace; The Palais of Justice; the Maison du Roy. But there is nothing more strange than the infinite numbers of slaves, working in the Streets, and carying burthens with their confus'd noises, and gingling of their huge Chaynes: The Chiefe negoce of the Town is silkes and drougs out of Africa, Syria and Egypt: Also Barbara-horses which come hither in great numbers: The Towne is governd by 4 Captaines, and has 3 Consuls, and one Assessor: Three Judges royal; The Marchants have also a Judge for ordinary causes: Here we bought Umbrellos against the heate, and consulted of our jorney to Canes by Land, for feare of the Pickaron Turkes who make prize of many small Vessells about these parts, finding never a Gally bound for Genöa whither we were design'd . . .

Oct: 10, as we proceeded on our way we passd by the ruines of a stately Aquæ-duct; the soile about the Country being rocky; yet full of Pines, and rare simples:

Cannes

On the 11th we lay at Canes, which is a small port on the Mediterranean; here we agree'd with a Sea-man to transport us to Genöa, so having procurd a bill of Health (without which there is no admission at any Towne in Italy) we embarq'd on the 12 of Octob: touching at the Ilands of St. Margaret, and St. Honore, lately retaken from the Spanyards with so much bravery by Prince Harcourt: here, having payd some small duty, we bought divers trifles offerd us by the Souldiers but without going on Land: Thenc we Coasted within 2 leagues of Antibo which is the utmost towne of France: Thence by Nice a Citty in Savoy, built all of brick, which gives it a very pleasant aspect towards the sea, having a Castle built very high that commands it: Thus we also sail'd by Morgus now cald Monaco (having passd Villa Franca, heretofore Portus Herculis); where ariving after the Gates were Shut we were forc'd to abide in our Barque all night, which was put into the haven, the wind comming contrary; In the morning we were hastned away having no time permitted us (by our avaritious Master with whom we had made a bargaine) to goe up to see this strong and considerable Place: it now belongs to a Prince of the family of the Grimaldi of Genoa, who has put both it and himselfe under protection of the French: The situation (for that I could contemplat at pleasure) is on such a promontory of solid stone and rock, as I never beheld the like: The towne-Walls very fayre: Within it we were told was an ample Court, and a Palace furnish'd with the most princly and rich moveables imaginable, also collection of Statues, Pictures, and especially of Massie plate to an infinite value.

Italy and Switzerland
1644–1646

Next we saild by Menton, and Vintimiglia, being the first Citty of the Republique of Genöa; supp'd at Onela where we ankerd and lay on shore, The next morning we coasted in view of the Ile of Corsica, then passd St. Remes, all whose rivage is incomparably furnish'd with Ever-greens Orange, Citron, and even Date-trees: Port Mauritio, Where we also lay; The next morning by Drano, Araisso famous for the best Corrall fishing, which here growes in aboundance upon the rocks, deepe, and continualy coverd with the Sea: By Albenga, and Finale a very faire and strong Towne belonging to the K: of Spayne, for which reason a Monsieur in our Vessell was extreamely afraide, as likewise the Patron of our Barke (for that they frequently catch a French Prize, as they creepe by these shores, to go into Italy) who ply'd both sayles and Oares to get under protection of a Genoeze-Gally that passd not farr before us, and in whose company we sayld a Lee as far as the Cape of Savona: a Towne built at the rise of the Apennines; for all this Coast (except a little at St. Remes) is an high and steepe mountainous ground, consisting all of rock-marble, without any grasse, tree, or rivage, most terrible to looke on: A strange object it is to consider how some poore cotages stand fast on the declivities of these precipices, and what steps they ascend to them; but they consist of all sorts of most precious marbles:

A Risky Voyage

Here on the 15, forsaking our Gally we encounterd a little foule Weather, which made us creepe Terra, Terra as they call it; and so a Vessell that encounter'd us advis'd us to do: But our Patron, striving to double the point of Savona, making out into the Wind, put us all into an incredible hazard; for blowing very hard from Land 'twixt those horrid gapps of the Mountaines, it set so violently, as rais'd on the sudaine a[n] over growne Sea, so as we could not then by any meanes recover the Weather shore for many houres, inso much that what with the Water already enterd, and the confusion of fearfull Passengers (of which one was an Irish Bishop and his Bro: a Priest, confessing some as at the Article of Death) we were almost uterly abandon'd to despaire; Our Pilot himselfe giving us for gon: But so it pleas'd God on the suddaine (and as now we were almost sinking downe right, wearied with pumping, and laving out the Water) to appease the Wind, that with much adoe and greate perill we recover'd the Shore, which we now kept within lesse then halfe a league, in view and sent of those pleasant Villas, and fragrant Orchards which are situated on this Coast, full of Princly retirements for the Sumptuousnesse of their buildings and noblenesse of the plantations; especialy those at St. Pietro d'Arena, from whence (the wind spiring as now it did) might perfectly be smelt the peculiar joys of Italy, in the natural perfumes of Orange, Citron, and Jassmine flowres, for divers leagues to seaward.

Genoa

Octo: 16 we got to Anker under the Pharos or Watch-towre erected on an high rock, at the mouth of the Mole of Genoa; the weather being yet so fowle, that for two houres at least we dast not stand in to the haven: Towards the evening adventur'd and came on shore by the Prattique-house, where after strict examination of the Syndics, we were had to the Ducal Palace, and there our names beeing taken, we were conducted to our Inne, which was at one Zacharias an Englishmans, where we were almost amazd at the consideration of the danger we had escaped, never thinking to have seene that evening alive: I shall never forget a story of our host Zacharye, who upon the relation of our perill, quitted us with another of his owne, being ship-wrack'd as he affir[m]'d solemnly, in the middle of a greate sea some where in the West-Indies: That he swam no lesse then 22 leagues to another Iland, with a tinder-box wraped up in his hayre, which was not so much as wett all that way: That picking up the Carpenters tooles with other provisions in a Chest, he and the Carpenter, that accompany'd him (good swimmer[s] it seemes both) floated the Chest before them, and ariving at last in a place full of Wood, they built another Vessell, and so escaped; the rest being all cast away: After this story we no more talk'd of our danger, for Zachary put us quite downe, though we were all Travellors.

Octob: 17 accompany'd with a most courteous Marchand, who had long liv'd in the Towne, calld Mr. Tomson, we went to vieue the rarities: The Citty is built in the hollow, or boosome of a Mountaine, whose ascent is very steepe, high and rocky; so as from the Lanterne, and Mole, to the hill it represents the Shape of a Theater; the Streetes and buildings so ranged one above the other; as our seates are in Playhouses: but by reason of their incomparable materials, beauty and structure: never was any artificial sceane more beautifull to the eye of the beholder; nor is any place certainely in the World, so full for the bignesse of well designed and stately Palaces; as may easily be concluded by that rare booke in a large folio, which the greate Virtuoso and Painter Paule Rubens has publish'd, that containes but one onely Streete and 2 or 3 Churches.

The first Palace of note that we went to Visite was that of Hieronymo del Negros, to which we pass'd by boate crosse the harbour; here I could not but observe the suddaine and devlish passion of a sea-man who plying us, was intercepted by another fellow, that interposd his boate before him, and tooke us in; for the teares gushing out of his eyes, he put his finger in his mouth and almost bit it off by the joynt, shewing it to his antagonist, as an assurance to him of some bloudy revenge, if ever he came neere that part of the harbour any more: And indeede this beautifull Citty is more stayn'd with such horrid acts of revenge and murthers, than any one place in Europ, or haply the World besides where there is a political government; which renders it very unsafe to strangers: This makes it a gally matter to carry a knife about one whose poynt is not broken off.

. . .

There are in this Citty innumerable other Palaces of particular Curiositys . . . two Gardens are full of Orange-trees, Citrons and Pomegranads, Fountaines, Grotts and Statues; amongst which one of Jupiter of a Colossal magnitude, under which is the Sepulchre of a beloved dog, for which one of this family receivd of the King of Spaine 500 crownes a yeare during the life of that faithfull animal. The Conserve of Water here is a most admirable piece for art, and so is likewise that incomparable grotto over against it.

We went hence to the Palace of the Dukes, where is also the Court of Justice; Thence to the Marchants Walke rarely covered: Neere the Ducal Palace we saw the publique Armory, which was almost all new, and one of the neatest kept and order'd that I had ever seene, for the quantity, being sufficient for 30000 men: Here we were shew'd many rare inventions and engines of Warr peculiar to that Armory, as in whose state gunns were first put in use: The Guarnison of the Towne consists chiefly of Germans and Corsicans:

We went the next day to see the famous Strada Nova, which is the same I formerly mentioned to have ben designd by the famous Rubens: It is for statlinesse of the buildings, paving and evenesse of the Streete, certainly far superior to any in Europ for the number of houses: That of Don Carlo d'Orias is a most magnificent and prowd structure: Here in the Gardens of the house of the old Marquis Spinola I saw such huge Citrons hanging on the trees, applyd like our Abricotts to the Walles, that one would have believd incredible should have been supported by so weake branches: This whole Streete is built of polish'd Marbles etc:

Having thus spent the tyme in seeing the Palaces we went next to see the Churches which are nothing lesse splendid then the Palaces; That of St. Francis being totaly built of Parian marble: St. Laurenzo in the navil (as it were of the City) of white and black polish'd stone, the inside wholy incrusted with marble, and other precious materials; where, on the Altar of St. John stand those 4 sumptuous Columns of Porphyrie; here we were shew'd that prodigious Emrald so greately esteem'd by the Friers; being it may be one of the largest in the world.

. . .

They are much affected to the Spanish mode and stately garbe in this Citty, where (by reason of the narownesse of their Streetes) they passe onely in their Sedans and Litters, and not in Coaches.

Gulf of Spezia

Octob: 19, we agreed with a Filuca and embarqud towards Ligorne; but the sea being this day very high (but not very dangerous, in reguard the billows did not breake) we resolv'd for feare of a storme to put in at Porta Venere, which we made, betweene two such narrow and horrid rocks, as the waves dashing with extraordinary velocity against them, put us in no small perill; but we were soone deliverd into as greate a Calme, and a most ample harbor, being the Golpho di Specia; whence we could see Plinies Delphini Promontorium, now cald Cap fino . . .

Pisa

The next day by morning we ariv'd at Pisa, where I met with my old friend Mr. Tho: Henshaw, who was then newly come out of Spaine, and from whose Company I never parted till more then a yeare after:

Pisa, for the famous mention thereof in History, whiles it contended with Rome, Florence, Sardinia, Sicily, and even Carthage herself, is as much worthy the seeing as any city in Italy:

The Palace and Church of St. Stephano (where the order of Knighthod cald by that name was instituted) drew first our curiosity, the outside theroff being altogether of polish'd marble; It is within full of tables relating to their Order, over which hang divers banners and pendents, with severall other Trophes taken by them from the Turkes, against whom they are particularly oblig'd to fight; being, though a religious Order; yet permitted to marry: At the front of the Palace stands a fountaine, and the Statue of the greate duke Cosimo.

The Campanile or Settezonio, built by one John Oenipont a German, consists of severall orders of pillars; 30 in a row, designd to be much higher: It stands alone, on the right side of the Domo or Cathedrall, strangely remarkable for this, that the beholder would expect every moment when it should fall; being built exceedingly declining by a rare adresse of the imortal Architect: and realy I take it to be one of the most singular pieces of workmanship in the World; how it is supported from immediately falling would puzzle a good Geometrician.

The Domo standing neere it is a superbe structure beautified with 6 Colomns of great antiquity; and the gates are of brasse of admirable workmanship: Here is the Cemitere cald Campo Santo, made of divers Gally ladings of earth, brought formerly from Jerusalem, which being of a Carcofagus nature consumes dead bodys in the space of fourty houres. Tis clo[i]stred about with marble Arches, and here lyes buried the learned Philip Decius who taught in this University.

At one side of this Church stands an ample and well wrought Marble Vessell, that heretofore containd the Tribute of the City payd yearely to Cæsar: it is plac'd as I remember on a Pillar of Opite stone with divers other antique Urnes: Neere to this and in the same feild is the Baptisterie of San Giovanni built of pure white marble, and coverd with so artificial a Cupola, that the voice or word utter'd under it seemes to breake out of a Clowd: The Font and Pulpit supported with 4 lyons is of inestimable value for the preciousnesse of the materials: The Place where all these buildings stand they call the Area: Hence we went to see the Colledge to which joynes a Gallery so furnish'd with natural rarities, stones, minerals, shells, dryd Animals, Scelletos etc, as is hardly to be seene the like in Italy: to this the Physique-Garden lyes, where is a noble Palme tree from which I gatherd a long branch: It has also very fine Waterworkes in it. The River Arno it is which runs quite through the middle of this stately Citye, whenc that Streete is nam'd Longarno, so ample that even the Greate Dukes Gallys (built in the Arsenale here) are easily conveyd to Livorno; but what is most worth observeing is that incomparable sole Arch which stretches from banke to banke, the like of which (serving for a bridge) is no where in Europe; That which renders it so famous is the extreame flatnesse of it. The Duke has also in this Towne a Stately Palace, before which Ferdinando the 3ds statue is plac'd: over against it, is the Exchange all built of Marble. Since this Citty came to be under the Dukes of Tuscany [it] is extreamely depopulated and thinn of Inhabitants; though there be hardly in Italy, any which exceedes it for stately Edifices: Yet the situation is very low and flat; which accommodates it with Spacious Gardens and even feilds within the Wales of it.

Livorno: a Slave Market

Octob: 21 we tooke Coach to Livorno (where I furnish'd my selfe with a bill of Exchange) through the Greate Dukes new Parke, full of huge Corke-trees, the under wood all Myrtils: amongst which were many Buffolos feeding which is [a] monstrous kind of wild Ox, short-nosd, and with hornes revers'd; those who worke with them, command them as our Beare-Wards do the Beares, with a ring through the nose and a Coard: Much of this Parke, as well as a greate part of the Country about it, is very fenny and of very ill ayre.

Ligorne is the prime port belonging to all the Dukes Territories; heretofore a very obscure towne, but since Ferdinando at present has so strongly fortified it (after the moderne way) draind the marches, by cutting that Channell thence to Pisa, navigable for 16 miles, and raised a Mole, emulating that of Genoa to secure the shipping, it is becom a Port of incredible receipt; Strengthend with divers fanales and Skonces: It has also a Place for the Gallys where they lye very safe: [V: It is said that this Port with all its Accommodations, was design'd and caried [on], by Duke Dudly, who pretended to be Duke of Northumberland, but claiming Title by a Spurious branch, and not legitimate, was entertain'd at Florence, and made one of the Dukes Councill: His knowledge in Maritime Affaires etc appeares to be very greate, by the 3 greate Volumes publish[ed] in the Italian tonge, intitl'd *Arcano del Mare*:] Just before the sea is an ample Piazza for the Market, where are erected those incomparable Statues, with the fowre slaves of Copper much exceeding the life for proportion; and in the judgment of most Artists one of the best pieces of modern Worke that was ever don.

Here is in Ligorne, and especialy this Piazzo, such a concourse of Slaves, consisting of Turkes, Mores and other Nations, as the number and confusion is prodigious; some buying, others selling; some drinking, others playing, some working, others sleeping, fighting, singing, weeping and a thousand other postures and Passions; yet all of them naked, and miserably Chayn'd, with a Canvas onely to hide their shame: Here was now a Tent erected, where any idle fellow, weary of that trifle, might stake his liberty against a few Crownes; which if lost (at Dice or other hazard) he was immediately chaynd, and lead away to the Gallys, where he was to serve a tearme of Yeares, but whence they seldome returnd; and many sottish persons would in a drunken bravado trye their fortune. The houses of this neate Towne are very uniforme, and excellently paynted a fresca on the out wales, being the representation of many of their Victories against the Turkes: The houses though low (in reguard of the Earth-quakes which frequently happen here to their greate terror, as did one during my being in Italy) are very well built; and the Piazz[a], with the Church, whose 4 Columns at the Portico are of black marble Polish'd, is very fayre and commodious; and gave the first hint to the building both of the

Church and Piazza in Covent-Garden with us, though very imperfectly pursu'd.

From Livorno Octo:22 I tooke Coach againe to Empoly, where we lay, and the next day ariv'd at Florence, being recommended to the house of one Sig: Baritiere in the Piazza dal Spirito Santo, where I was exceedingly well treated:

Florence

Florenc is situated at the foote of the Apennines, the west part full of stately Groves, and pleasant Meadows, beautified with more then a thousand houses and country Palaces of note, appertaining to Gentlemen of the Towne:

The river Arno, which glids in a broad, but very shallow channell, runs through this Citty, dividing it as 'twere in the middle, and over this passe fowre most sumptuous bridges: of Stone: On that which was neerest our quarter stands in white marble the 4 seasons; on another, are the Goldsmits shops; at the head of the former stands a Columne of Opite upon which a Statue of Justice with her balances and Sword cut all out of Porphyrie, and for this the most remarkable, that 'twas the first which (after many yeares that art was utterly lost), had ben carv'd out of that hard material and brought to perfection; which they say was don by hardning the tooles in the juice of certayne herbs: This Statue was erected in that corner, for that there Cosimo was first saluted with the newes of Siennas being taken. Neere this is the famous Palazzo di Strozzi consisting of a rustique manner, a Princly piece of Architecture if any in the World be. Hence we went to the Palace of Pitie built by that family, but of late infinitely beautified by Cosimo, with huge Square stones, with a terrace at each side rustic uncut balustradoed, with a fountain that ends in a Cascade seene from the greate gate and so a vista to the Gardens of the Dorique, Ionic and Corinthian Order, in which nothing is more admirable than the vacant Stayre-case, Marbles, Statues, Urnes, Pictures, Court, Grotto and Water-workes: In the Quadrangle where is a huge jetto of Water in a Volto of 4 faces, and noble statues at each Square, especially the Diana of Porphyrie above the grotto: I remember we were shew'd a monstrous greate Load-stone: The Garden is full of all Variety, hills, dales, rocks, Groves, aviaries, Vivaries, fountaines, Especialy on[e] of 5 Jettos, the middle basin being one of the longest stones that ever I saw: and what ever may render such a Paradise deligh[t]full; and to this the Duke* has added an ample Laboratorie, over against which a fort standing on a hill, where they told us his highnesse Treasure is kept I saw in this Garden a rose grafted on an Orange Tree: much topiarie work and Columns in Architecture about the hedges: In this Palace it is the Duke ordinarily resides, living with his Swisse Guards after the frugal Italian way, and even Selling what he can spare of his Wines, at the Cellar under his very house: and which was odd, wicker bottles dangling over the very chiefe Entrance into the Palace; serving for a Vintners bush.

Next we went to see the Church of Santo Spirito where the Altar and Reliquary is most rich, and full of precious stones, especialy 4 pillars of a kind of Sepentine, and some of blew: Hence to another of the Dukes Palaces cal'd Palazzo Vecchio, before which is the statue of David, and Hercules killing of Cacus, the worke of Baccio Bandinelli, the other of Michael Angelo . . .

. . .

The Duke's Beasts

From this place we went to see the Dukes Cavalerizzo, where the Prince has a stable of incomparable Horses of all Countries, Arabs, Turks, Barbs, Gennets, English etc: which are continualy exercisd in the menage. Nere this is the Place where are kept several Wild-beasts, as Wolves, Catts, Bares, Tygers, and Lions: I tooke greate pleasure to see what an incredible height one of the Lyons would leape, for which I caused to be hung downe a joynt of mutton: They are loose in a deepe, Walld-Court, and therefore to be seene with much more delight than at the Tower of Lond, in their grates.

. . .

[V: On the [27th] I purchased the Pietra Comm[e]ssa Pieces for my Cabinet; bespoke 4. rare small statues of stucci made onely by that rare Artist Vincetio Brocchi: Collecting some Prints and drawings I went to see the renowned Church, Chapell and Library of St. Laurences in which the Medicean Family are buried, with Banners over them . . . Thus having run thro the most memorable buildings and Curiositys of this noble Citty: we went to see the Manufactors of Silke, Damask, Velvet etc, which they report brings a yearly Revenu of two Millions of Gold; the streetes are most of the[m] spacious, strait, and pav'd with flat broad Coarse Marble: which makes them very Cleane and faire; the Houses unive[r]saly well built of stone exceeding high, and of good Order; But the Inhabitans very thinn in them.

Siena

29 We tooke Horse for Sienna, alighting at Poggio Imperiale a house of Pleasure of the Duke, little distant from Florence, but having little time to Consider it, we refer'd it for our coming back from Rome:

We lay this night at st. Cassiano, and I think next day at Barbarini, a small Town, whence P. Urbans family: Then at Poggio Bunci famous for Snuff Tabacco, which the Italians of both sexes take excessivly, we dined, and that night arived at Sienna: (Note, that Snuff was not taken in England at this time nor some yeares after:) – this famous Citty stands on several rocky Hills, which makes it uneven, has an old ruin'd Wall about it, over-grown with Caper shrubs: but the Air is incomparable, whence divers passe the heates of Summer there; Provisions cheape, the Inhabitans Courteous, and the Italian purely spoken. The Citty at a little distance presents the Traveller with an incomparable Prospect, occasion'd by the] many playne brick Towers, which (whilst it was a Free state) were erected for defence; the tallest where off is call'd the Mangio, standing at the foote of the Piazza, which we went first to see the next day after our arival: At the entrance of this Tower is a Chapel (open towards the Piazza) of marble well adornd with Sculpture: On the other side is the Signioria or Court of Justice, this is very well built, a la Moderna, of brick; and indeede the Brick of Sienna is so rarely made, that it lookes almost as well as Porphyrie it selfe, having a kind of naturall politure. There is in this Senate-hous a very faire hall, where they sometimes recreate the People with publique Shews and Operas, as they call them . . .

The Piazza compasses the faciata of the Court and Chapel, and being made with descending steps, much resembles the figure of an Escalop-shell, with the white ranges of Paving intermix'd with the incomparable brick we described, and with which generally the towne is well paved, which renders it marvailously cleane . . .

. . . After this we walk'd to the Sapienza, which is the University or Coledge rather, where the high Germans enjoy many particular priveleges, who addict themselves to the Civil Law: And indeede this Place has produc'd divers excellent Scholars; besides those three Popes Alex:3, Pius the 2d and the 3d of that name, the learned Æneas Silvius, both of that antient house of the Piccolomini.

The Chiefe streete is calld Strada Romana. Pius the 2d has built a most stately Palace of Square stone, with that incomparable Portico joyning neere to it.

This Towne is commanded by a Castle, which hath to it 4 bastions, and a Garison of Souldiers, neere which a list to ride horses in, much frequented in summer by the Gallants.

Not far hence is the Church and Convent of the Dominicans, where in the Chapel of St. Catharine of Sienna, they shew her head, the rest of her body being translated to Rome: Then we went up to the Domo or Cathedral, which is both without and within of large square stones of black and white marble polish'd, of inexpressable beauty; as likewise is the front, being much adorn'd with Sculpture and rare statues . . .

. . .

An Encounter with a Cardinal

Nov:2d We went from Sienna, desirous to be present at the Cavalcad of the new Pope Innocentio decimo, who had not as yet made the grand Procession to st. Jo: de Laterano: We set out by Porto Romano, the Country all about the towne being rare for hunting and Game; so as Wild-Boare and Venison is frequently sold in the shops in many of the Townes about it: And first we pass'd neere Mont Oliveto, where the monastrie of that Order is pleasantly situated, and worth the seeing: Passing over a bridg (which by the Inscription shews it to have been built by Prince Matthias) we went through Buon-Convento famous for the Death of the Emperor Hen: 7th who was here poyson'd in the holy Eucharist: Thence we came to Torniero where we din'd. This Village lyes in a sweete Vally in view of Mount Alcini famous for the rare Muscatello; twas heretofore Mons Ilicinus. After 3 miles more we goe by St. Querico, and lay at a Privat Osteria neere it, where, after we were provided of Lodging, in came Cardinal Donghi a Genoeze by birth, now come from Rome; He was so civil as to entertaine us with greate respect, hearing we were English, for that he told us he had been once in our Country; amongst other discourse, he related how a Dove was seene to sit upon the Chayre in the Conclave, at the Election of Pope Innocent, which he magnified as a greate good Omen, with several other particulars which we enquir'd of him, till our Suppers parted us: I remember he came in great state, with his owne Bed-stead, and all the furniture; yet would by no meanes suffer us to resigne the room we had taken up in the Lodging before his arival.

An Airy Prospect

We rod next morning by Monte Pientio, or as vulgarly Monte Mantumiato, which is of an excessive height, ever and anon peeping above any Clowds with its snowy head; till we had climed to the Inn at Radicofany, built by Ferdinando the Greate Duke for the necessary refreshment of travellers in so inhospitable a place: as we ascended, we enter'd a very thick, soled and darke body of Clowds, which look'd like rocks at a little distance, which dured us for neere a mile going up; they were dry misty Vapours hanging undissolved for a vast thicknesse, and altogether both obscuring the Sunn and Earth, so as we seemed to be rather in the Sea than the Clowdes, till we having pierc'd quite through, came into a most serene heaven, as if we had been above all human Conversation, the Mountaine appearing more like a greate Iland, than joynd to any other hills; for we could perceive nothing but a Sea of thick Clowds rowling under our feete like huge Waves, ever now and then suffering the top of some other mountaine to peepe through, which we could discover many miles off, and betweene some breaches of the Clowds, Landskips and Villages of the subjacent Country: This was I must acknowledge one of the most pleasant, new and altogether surprizing objects that in my life I had ever beheld . . .

Sad Fate of a Bishop

On the 4th of November being next morning after a little riding we descend towards the Lake of Bolsena, which from hence (being above 20 miles in circuit) yeilds a most incomparable Prospect: neere the middle of it are 2. small Ilands, in one of which is a Convent of melancholy Capucines, and where those of the

Farnezian family are interr'd: Pliny, calls it Tarquiniensis Lacus, and talkes of divers floting Ilands about it, but they appeard not to us, The Lake is invironed with mountaines; at one of whose sides we pass'd towards the Towne Bolsena, antiently Vulsinium, very famous in antiquity, as testifie divers rare sculptures in the Court of st. Christianas Church, the Urne, and Altar and Jasper Columns. After 7 miles riding (passing through a certaine Wood heretofore sacred to Juno) we came to Mount Fiascone, the head of Falisci, a famous people in old tyme, and heretofore Falernum, as renown'd for the excellent Wine, as now for the story of the Dutch Bishop, who lyes buried in Favionos Church with this Epitaph:

Propter Est, Est dominus meus mortuus est:

because he had drunke too much of the Wine; for it seemes he had commanded his Servant, to ride before, and (enquiring where the best liquor was,) to write Est* upon the Vessells.

From Monte Fiascone we travell a plain and pleasant Champion to Viterbo, which presents it selfe with much state a farr off, in reguard of her many lofty pinacles and Towres; neither dos it deceive the expectation; for it is so exceedingly beautified with publique fountaines, especialy that at very entrance of the Port (being all of brasse, and adornd with many rare figures) as salutes the Passenger with a most agreable object and refreshing waters . . .

. . .

Arrival in Rome

I came to ROME on the 4th of November 1644 about 5 at night, and being greately perplex't for a convenient lodging, wandred up and downe on horse back, till one conducted us to one Monsieur Petits, a French mans, who entertaind strangers, being the very utmost house on the left hand as one ascends Monte Trinità, formerly Mons Pincius, neere the Piazza Spagnola. Here I alighted, delivered my horse to the Veturino, and having bargain'd with mine host for 20 crownes a moneth, I causd a good fire to be made in my Chamber, and so went to bed being very wet.

The very next morning (for resolv'd I was to spend no moment idly here) I got acquaintance with several persons that had long lived in Rome; being especialy recommended to Father John a Benedictine Monke, and Superior of his Order for the English

Colledg of Doway; a Person (to say truth) of singular learning, Religion and humanity; also to Mr. Patric Cary, an Abbot, and brother to our Learned Lord Falkland, a pretty witty young priest; but one that afterwards came over to our church: Dr. Bacon, and Gibbs, Physitians who had dependance of Cardinal Caponi, the latter an incomparable Poet; with Father Cortnèe the Chiefe of the Jesuites in the English Coledge, My Lord of Somerset: Bro: to the Marquis of Worcester, and some others: from whom I receiv'd instructions, how to behave our selves in Towne, what directions, Masters, and bookes to take in search and view of the Antiquities, Churches, Collections etc: and accordingly, the next day, being November 6t, I began to be very pragmatical.

And in the first place (as our Sights-man, for so they name certaine Persons in Rome, who get their living onely by leading strangers about to see the Citty) we first went to see the Palace of Farnezi, which is a most magnificent square structure, built by Michael Angelo of the 3 Orders of Columns, after the antient manner, and in a time when Architecture was but newly recovered from the Gotic barbarity: The Court, being square is tarrass'd, having two payre of staires which leade into the upper roomes; which conducted us to that famous Gallery painted by Caraccio, and then which nothing is certainely more rare of that Art in the whole world, so deepe, and well studied are all the figures, that it would require more judgment than, I confesse, I had, to determine whether they were flat, or emboss'd: Thence we pass'd into another painted in Chiaro e Scuro, representing the fabulous History of Hercules, then we went out on a Tarrace where was a pretty garden even on the leads, for it is built in a place of the Citty, that has no extent of grow[n]d backwards: The greate Sale is wrought by Salviati, and Zuccharo; furnish'd with statues, one of which being modern is the figure of a Farnese, in a triumphant posture of white marble, worthy of Admiration.

. . .

The Forum

On the 7th we went into Campo Vacino by the ruines of the Templum Pacis, built by Titus Vespatianus, and thought to be the biggest and most ample as well as richly furnish'd of all the Roman Dedicated places; It is now an heape, rather then a Temple; yet dos the roofe, and Volto, continue firme, shewing it to have formerly been of incomparable workmanship: This goodly structure was (none knows how) consumed with fire, the very night (by all computation) that our B: Saviour was borne.

. . .

The Capitol

The Capitol, to which we climed, by a very broad ascent of degrees, is built about a square Court, at right hand of which, going up from Campo Vacino gusshes a plentifull streame from the statue of Tybur in Porphyrie, very antique, and another representing Rome; but above all is admirable the figure of Marforius, casting [water] into a most ample Concha. The front of this Court is crown'd with an incomparable fabrique, containing the Courts of Justice, and where the Criminal Notary sitts, and others: In one of the Halls, they shew the statues of Greg: the 13th and Paule the 3d with several others: To this joynes an handsome Towre, the whole faciata adorn'd with noble Statues both on the out side, and battlements, ascended by a double payre of staires and a stately posario. In the center of the Court stands that incomparable Horse bearing the Emp: Marcus Aurelius of Corinthian mettal, as big as the life, placed on a Pedistal of marble, with an inscription, and esteemed one of the noblest pieces of worke now extant in the world, antique, and very rare . . .

. . .

St. Peter's

On the 19 I went to visite St. Pietro, that most stupendious and incomparable Basilicam, far surpassing any now extant in the World, and perhapps (Solomons Temple excepted) any that was ever built:

The largenesse of the Piazza before the Portico is worth observing, because it affords you a noble prospect of the Church; crowded up, for the most part in other places, where greate Churches are erected: In this is a fountaine out of which gushes a river, rather than a streame, which ascending a good height, breakes upon a round embosse of Marble into millions of pearles, which fall into the subjacent bason: making an horrible noise: I esteem this, one of the goodliest fountaines that ever I saw.

The next which surprizes your wonder is that stately Obelisque, transported out of Ægypt, and dedicated by Octavius Augustus Nepot: to Julius Cæsar, whose Ashes it formerly bore on the sumit; but being since overturn'd by the Barbarians, was re-erected with vast Cost, and a most stupendious invention by Dominico Fontana Architect to Sixtus V . . .

. . . I tooke notice of some Coaches which stood before the stepps of the Ascent, of which, one belonging to Card: Medicis had all the metall worke of Massie Silver, viz, the bow behind and other places; and indeede the Coaches at Rome, as well as Covered Wagons, which are also much in use, are generally the richest and largest that ever I saw . . .

. . .

The Lateran

November 20 I went to visite that antient See, and Cathedral of St. John de Laterana, and the holy places thereabout: This is a church of extraordinary devotion, though for outward forme not comparable to st. Peters, being of Gotique Ordonance: Before we went into the Cathedral the Baptisterie or Fonte of st. Jo: Baptist presented it selfe, it being formerly part of the Greate Constantines Palace, and as sayd his chamber, where by st. Silvester he was made a Christian; it is of an Octagonal shape, having before the entrance 8 faire Pillars of rich Porphyrie, the nobles[t] doub[t]lesse in the world, consisting of one intire piece, their Capitells of divers orders, underpropping divers lesser Columnes of white-marble that support a noble Cupola, the moulding whereof is incomparably wrought. In the Chapell which they affirme to have been the lod[g]ing chamber of this Emperor all Women are prohibited to enter, for the malice of Herodias who caus'd him to loose his head: Here are deposited divers sacred Reliques of st. James, Mary Magdalen, st. Mathew etc and two goodly pictures: Another Chapel or Oratory neere it, is cald st. Jo: the Evangelist well adorn'd with Marbles and Tables, especialy those of Cavalier Gioseppe, and of Tempesta in fresca.

. . .

Cavalcado of Innocent X*

The 23d of this Moneth of November was the sollemne, and

greatest ceremony of all the state Ecclesiastical, viz, the Cavalcado or Procession of his Sanctity Pope Inn[o]centius X to st. Jo: de Laterano which standing on the stepps of Ara Celi neere the Capitoll, I saw passe in this manner.

First went a guard of Swizzers to make way, and divers of the Avantguard of horse Car[ry]ing Lances: next follow'd those who caried the robes of the Cardinals, all two and two: then the Cardinals Mace-bearers, The Caudatari on Mules, The Masters of their horse: The Popes Barber, Taylor, Baker, Gardner and other domesticall officers all on horse back in rich liveries: The Squires belonging to the Guard. Then were lead by 5 men in very rich liverys 5 noble Neapolitan Horses white as Snow, coverd to the ground with trappings gloriously embrodered, which is a Service payd by the King of Spaine for the Kingdomes of Naples and Sicily pretended fœdatorys to the Pope: 3 Mules of exquisite beauty and price trapped in Crimson Velvet, next followd 3 rich Litters with Mules, the litters were empty: After these the Master of the horse alone, with his Squires: 5 Trumpeters: The [C]amerieri estra muros: The Fiscale and Consistorial Advocates: Cappellani, Camerieri di honore, Cubiculari and Chamberlaines cald Secreti, then followed 4 other Camerieri with 4 Capps of the dignity Pontifical, which were Cardinals hatts carried on staffs: 4 Trumpets, after them a number of Noble Romans and Gentlemen of quality very rich, and follow'd by innumerable Staffieri and Pages: The Secretaries of the Cancellaria, Abbreviatori-Acoliti in their long robes and on Mules: Auditori di Rota, The Deane of the Roti, and Master of the Sacred Palace, on Mules, with grave, but rich foote Clothes, and in flat Episcopal hatts: Then went more of the Roman and other nobility Courtiers with divers pages in most rich liveries on horseback; After them 14 drums belonging to the Capitol: Then the Marshals with their Staves, The 2 Sindics: The Conservators of the Citty in robs of Crimson damasc; next them the knight Confalonier and Prior of the P. R: in velvet tocqus: Six of his holynesse's Mace-bearers: Then the Captaine or Governor of the Castle of St. Angelo upon a brave prancer: Next the Governor of the Citty, on both sides of these 2 long rankes of Swizzers. The Masters of the Ceremonies, The Crosse bearer on horse, with two Priests on each hand a foote, Pages footemen and guards in aboundance. Then next the Pope himselfe carried in a

Litter, or rather open chaire of Crimson Velvet richly embrodred, and borne by two stately Mules; as he went holding up his two fingers, and blessing the people and multitudes upon their knees, looking out of their windoes and houses with lowd viva's and acclamations of felicity to their new Prince: This was follow'd by the Master of his chamber, Cuppbearer, Secretary, Physitian. Then came the Cardinal Bishops, next the Cardinal Priests, Card: Deacons, Patriarchs, Archbishops, and Bishops all in their several and distinct habits; some in red, others in greene flat hatts with tossles, all on gallant Mules richly trapp'd with Velvet, and lead by their servants in greate state and multitudes: After these the Apostolical Protonotari, Auditor and Tresurer, Referendaries. Lastly the Trumpets of the reareguard, 2 Pages of Armes in Helmets with might[y] feathers and Car[ry]ing Launces, 2 Captaines, Then the Pontifical [Standard] of the Church, The two Alfieri, or Cornets of the Popes light horse who all followed in Armor and car[ry]ing launces, which with innumerable rich Coaches, litters and people made up the Proceeding; but what they did at st. Jo: di Laterano I could not see by reason of the intollerable Crowd; so as I spent most of the day in admiring of the two Triumphal Arches, which had been purposely erected a few days before, and til now covered; the one by the Duke of Parma in the foro Romano; the other by the Jewes in the Capitol with flatering Inscriptions, but of rare and excellent Architecture, decor'd with statues, and aboundance of ornaments proper for the Occasion, since they were but temporary, and made up of boards, cloath etc painted and fram'd on the suddaine, but as to outward appearance solid and very stately. The night ended with fire-workes; that which I saw was that which was built before the Spa[n]ish Ambassadors house in the Piazza del Trinita, and another of the French: The first appeard to be a mighty rock, bearing the Popes Armes, a Dragon, and divers figures, which being set on fire by one who flung a Roquett at it, tooke fire immediately, yet preserving the figure both of the rock and statues a very long time, insomuch as 'twas deemed ten thousand reports of squibbs and crackers spent themselves in order: That before the French Ambass: Palace (which, I also saw) was a Diana drawne in a Chariot by her doggs, with aboundance of other figures as big as the life which plaied with fire in the same manner; in the meane time were all the windows or the whole Citty set with innumerable Tapers, which put into lanterns of sconces of severall colour'd oyl'd papers, that the win'd may not annoy them, render a most glorious shew, in my conceite, nothing prettier; and besides these, there were at least 20 other glorious fire workes of vast charge and rare art for their invention before divers Ambassadors, Princes and Cardinals Palaces, especialy that on the Castle of st. Angelo, being a Pyramid of lights of an excessive height fastned to the ropes and cables which support the standard-pole; Thus were the streetes this night as light as day, full of Bonfires, Canon roaring, Musique pla[y]ing, fountaines running Wine in all excesse of joy and Triumph.

. . .

[December] 12 I went againe to st. Peters to see the Chapells, Churches, and Grott, under ground, viz, under the whole Church (like our st. Faiths under Paules,) in which lye interr'd a world of Saints, Martyrs, and Popes; amongst the rest Hadrian the 4th, our Countryman, in a chest of Porphyrie: st. Jo: Chrysostom, Petronella; the heads of st. Jacobus minor, st. Lukes, st. Sebastians, and our Thomas of Beccket: A shoulder of st. Christopher, an Arme of Joseph of Arimathea: Longinus; besides 134 more Bishops, Souldiers, Princes, Scholars, Cardinals, Kings, Empp: and their wives to[o] long to particularize.

Hence we walked into the Cemitery [called] Campo Santo, the earth consisting of severall ship Loads of mould transported from Jerusalem, which has the vertue to consume a Carcasse in 24 houres: To this joynes that rare Hospital, where was once Neros Circus, and next to this the Inquisition house and Prison the inside whereoff, I thanke God, I was not curious to see. To this joynes his Holinesse's Horse-Guards.

Christmas in Rome

On Christmas-Eve at night I went not to bed, by reason that I was desirous to see the many extraordinary Ceremonyes perform'd then in their Churches, as mid-night Masses, and Sermons; so as I did nothing all this night but go from Church to Church in admiration at the multitude of sceanes, and pageantry which the Friers had with all industry and craft set out to catch the devout women and superstitious sort of people with, who never part from them without droping some mony in a vessell set on purpose: But especialy observable was the pupetry in the Church of the Minerva, representing the nativity etc: thenc I went and heard a Sermon at the Apollinare by which time it was morning.

On Christmas day his holynesse sa[y]ing Masse, the Artillery at st. Angelo went off: and all this day was exposd the Cradle of our Lord:

27. A great Supper is given the poore at the Hosp: of s: Jo: Laterano.

29 We were invited by the English Jesuites to dinner being their greate feast of Tho: of Canterbury: We din'd in their common Refectory, and afterward saw an Italian Comedy Acted by their Alumni before the Cardinals.

. . .

The Papal Palace

[1645.] Jan: 18. I went to see the Popes Palace the Vaticane where he for the most part continualy keeps his Court: It was first built by P: Simachus, and since augmented to a vast pile of building by the Successors: That part of it added by Sixtus Vtus is most magnificent; this lead us into divers tarraces arched sub dio, painted with the historys of the Bible by Raphel, which are so esteemed, that Workmen come from all parts of Europe to make their studys from these designes; and certainely the whole World dos not shew so much art; the foliage and Grotesque is admirable about some of the Compartments: In another ro[o]m are represented at large Mapps and plotts of most Countries in the World in very vast tables, with briefe descriptions: The Stayres which ascend out of s: Peters Portico into the first hall, are rarely contriv'd for ease, These leade into Sala di Gregorio XIII, the walls wherof are halfe to the [roof]incrusted with most precious marbles of various colours, and Workes; so is also the pavement opere vermiculato; but what exceeds description is the Volto or rooff itselfe, which is so exquisitely painted, that 'tis almost impossible for the skillfullest eye to discerne whither it be the worke of the Pensil upon a flatt, or of a toole, cutt in a deepe Levati of stone: The Rota dentata in this admirable perspective at the left hand as one goes out, the stella etc àre things of art incomparable: Certainely this is one of the most Superb and royall Appartments in the world, much too beautifull for a guard of gigantique Swizzers who do nothing but drinke, and play at Cards in it . . .

. . .

The Pope's Pantofles

Now we came into the Popes Chapell, so much celebrated for the Judgement painted by M: Angelo Buonaroti, the contemplation of which incomparable Worke tooke up much of our tyme and wonder: It is a painting in freṣca, upon a dead Wall at the upper end of the Chapell just over the high Altar of a vast designe and miraculous fantsy, considering the multitude of Nakeds, and variety of posture: The roofe is also full of rare worke: Hence we went into the Sacristia, where we were shew'd all the most precious Vestments, Copes etc, and furnitures of the Chapell, One Priestly Cope with the whole suite had been formerly sent from one of our English Henrys, and is shewn for a greate rarity, as indeede it is: We saw divers of the Popes Pantofles that are Kissed on his foote, having rich jewells embrodred on the instup: they are covered with crimson Velvet: Also his Tyara or Triple Crown, divers Miters, Crosiers, Crosses etc all bestudded with precious stones, gold and Pearle to an infinite value: A very large Crosse carved (as they affirme) out of the holy Wood it selfe: a world of Utensils, of Chrystal, Gold, Achat, Amber and other costly materials for the Altar: The Sala Clementinas Suffito is painted by Cherubin Alberti, with an ample Landskep of Paul Brills. Then we went into those Chambers painted with the historys of burning Rome quenched by the procession of a Crucifix: The victory of Constantine over Maxentius: St. Peters delivery out of Prison, all of them by the hand of the famous Julio Romano, and are therefore cal'd amongst the Virtuosi, the Paynters Academy, because you shall never come into them, but you find some young man or other designing from them, a civility which in Italy they do not refuse them where any rare pieces of the old and best Masters are extant; and which is occasion of breeding up many excellent men in that Profession: From hence we were conducted into a New Gallery, whose sides had painted on them most of the famous Places in Italy Townes and Territories, rarely don; and upon the Roofe the chiefe Acts of the Ro: Church since St. Peters pretended See there; It is doubtlesse one of the most magnificent Galleries this, in Europ:

Out of this we came into the Consistory, which is a very noble roome, the Volto painted in Grotesque as I remember: The Upper end of it has a Throne, elevated, and a baldachino or Canopy of state for his holynesse, over it: From hence through a very extraordinary long Gallery (longer I thinke, then the French Kings at the Louvre) but onely of bare wales, we were brought into the Vaticane Library . . .

This Library is doubtlesse the most nobly built, furnish'd, and beautified in the World, ample, stately, light and cherefull, looking into a most pleasant Garden: The Walls and roofe are painted; not with Antiqu[e]s, and Grotesc's (like our Bodlean at Oxford) but Emblemes, Figurs, Diagramms, and the like learned inventions found out by the Wit, and Industry of famous Men, of which there are now whole Volumes extant: There were likewise the Effigies of the most Illustrious men of Letters and Fathers of the Church, with divers noble statues in white marble at the entrance, viz. Hippolitus and Aristides: The Generall Councils, are likewise painted upon the side Walls: The largest roome was built by Sixtus Quintus 100 paces long, at the end is the Gallery of printed books: then the Gallery of the D: of Urbans Librarie amongst which are MSS: of incomparable Miniature, and divers China, Mexican, Samaritan, Abyssin and other Oriental books: As to the ranging of the bookes, they are all shut up in Presses of Wainscot, and not expos'd on shelves to the naked ayre; nor are the most precious mix'd amongst the more ordinary, which are shew'd to the curious onely; Such as are those two Virgils written in Parchment, of more then a thousand yeares old; the like a Terence: The Acts of the Apostles in Golden Capital Letters: Petrarchs Epigramms written with his owne hand: Also an Hebrew Parchment made up in the antient manner from whence they were first cal'd Volumina, with the Cornua, but what we English do much enquire after, the Booke which our Hen: 8, writ against Luther . . .

. . .

On the Road to Naples

January 27. Having agreed with the [Procachio] for Lusty Mules, [accompanied] wih Sir John Manwood (formerly Governor of Dover Castle, an old Souldier, that had Maried the famous Sir Jo: Ogles Daughter Mrs. Eutresia) Mr. Thomas Henshaw [and] Mr.

Borgh a Dutch Gentleman, that speaking perfect English pass'd
unsuspected in our Company (the [Spaniards] at that time having
Wars with Holland) two Cortizans in Mans Apparell, who rid
astride, booted, Sworded and Spurd, and whereof one was
marvelous pretty, and the Milaneze Squire Signor Jo: Baptist their
Gallant, our Servants and some others, we set out from the Latine
Port towards Naples: The firs[t] part of our way was well pav'd and
full of Antiquities especially antient Sepulchers, Inscriptions and
ruines; for it was [their] manner to bury much by famous
high-roads, where they also placed their Statues, thereby inciting
the minds of Men to gallant actions by the memory of their
examples: In the right hand we saw the [Aquæduct] of Ancq
Martius, and those of Claudius, and the new ones of Sixtus Vth,
being a stately peice of Arch work for near 20 Miles: Then we enter
the Via Appia 'till we came near Frascati which we left on the other
hand, riding by the Wood and Lake celebrated for the fiction of
Heleon and Diana, thence to Veletri, a Towne heretofore of the
Volsci where is a publique and faire statue of P: Urban the 8 in
brasse, and a stately Fountaine in the streete, here we lay, and
drank excellent Wine.

28 We dind at Sermoneta, descending all this morning downe a
stony mountaine, unpleasant, yet full of Olive-trees; and anon
passe a Towre built on a rock, kept by a small Watch or Guard
against the Banditi, who are very rife in these parts, daily robbing
and killing the Passengers, as my Lord Banbury and his Company
found to their cost, a little before: To this Guard we gave some
mony, and so were suffer'd to passe, which was still on the Appian
to the Tres Tabernæ (whither the Breathren came from Rome to
meete S. Paule Acts: 28:) The ruines wherof are yet very faire,
resembling the remainder of some considerable Edifice, as may be
judged by the vast stones, and fairenesse of the arched-worke. The
Country invironing this passage is hilly but rich; at the right hand
stretches an ample playne being the Pompt[i]ni Campi: We reposd
this night at Piperno in the Post-house without the Towne; and
here I was extreamely troubld with a sore hand which I brought
from Rome with me by a mischance, which now began to fester,
upon my base unlucky stiffne[c]ked trotting carrion Mule, and
which are in the world the most wretched beasts.

...

The day following we were faine to hire a strong [Convoy] of about 30 Firelocks to guard us through the Cork-Woods (much infested with the Banditi) as far as Nova fossa, where was the Appij Forum, and now stands a reveren'd Church with a greate Monastry, the Place where Tho: Aquinas both studied, and lyes buried: Here we therefore all alighted, and were most curteously received by the Monks, who shew'd us many Reliqus of their learned Saint; and at the high-Altar the print forsooth of the mules hoofe, which he caused to kneele before the host . . .

. . .

We ariv'd this night at Fundi, a most dangerous passage for robbing; and so we pass'd by Galbas Villa; and anon entred the Kingdome of Naples . . . The Via Appia is here a noble prospect, having before consider'd how it was carried through vast moun-taines of rocks for many miles, a most stupendious labour: here it is infinitely pleasant, beset with sepulchres and Antiquities, full of sweete shrubbs about the invironing hedges. At Fundi (here was Amiclas lost by silence) we had Oranges and Citrons for nothing, the trees growing in every corner infinitely charged with fruite, in all the poore peoples Orchyards:

29 We descried mount Cæcubus, famous for the generous Vine it heretofore produc'd, and so rid onward the Appian-Way beset with Myrtils, Lentiscus, bayes, Pomegranads, and whole Groves of orange-trees, and most delicious shrubbs, till we came to Formiana, where they shew'd us Ciceros Tomb standing in an Olive-grove, now a rudes of huge stones without any forme or beauty; for here that incomparable Orator was Murther'd: I shall never forget how exceedingly I was delighted with the Sweetnesse of this passage, the Sepulchers mixed amongst the verdures of all Sorts; besides being now come within sight of that noble Citty Cajeta which gives a surprizing Prospect along the Tyrhen Sea, in manner of a Theater; and here we beheld that strangly cleft Rock, an hideous and frightfull spectacle; which they have a tradition hapn'd upon the Passion of our B: Saviour: But the hast of our Procaccio suffer'd us not to dwell so long on these objects, and the many antiquities of this Towne as we desired:

At Formia we saw Ciceros Grott, dining at Mola, and passing Senuessa, Garigliano (where once the Citty Minterna) and beheld the ruines of that vast Amphitheatre and Aquæduct yet standing;

The River Liris which bounded the old Latium, Falernus, or Mons Massicus, celebrated for its wine, now nam'd Garo, and this night we lodg'd at a little Village call'd [S.] Agatha in the Falernian Feilds neere to Aurunca and Sessa. The next day, having passed Vulturnus, we come by the Torre di Francolesse where the valiant Hanibal in danger of Fabius Maximus escaped by debauching his Enemyes: And so we at last enter'd the most pleasant Plaines of Campania, now call'd Terra di Lavoro: In very truth I thinke the most fertile spot, that ever the Sunn shone upon: Here we saw the siender ruines of the once mighty Capüa contending at once both with Rome and Carthage for Splendor and Empire; now nothing but an heape of rubbish, with some goodly Vestigias of its pristine magnificence, discover'd in the remaining pieces of Temples, Arches, Theaters, Columns, Ports, Vaults, Collossas etc confounded together by the barbarous Goths and Longobards: There is yet a new Citty, neerer to the road by two miles, fairely raysd out of these heapes. The Passage from this Towne towards Naples (which is about 10, or 12 English post miles) is as straight as a line could lay it, and of a huge breadth, swarming with travellers more then ever I remember any of our greatest, and most frequented roads neere London: But what is extreamely divertissant, is the incomparable fertility of the feilds and grounds about it, which are planted about with fruit-trees, whose boles are serpented with excellent Vines, and they so exuberant, that 'tis commonly reported one Vine will loade 5 mules with its Grapes: but what much adds to the pleasure of these rusticities, is that the Vines climbing to the summit of the trees reach in festoons and fruitages from one tree to another, planted at exact distances, which shewing like a greene Chayne about a field, is pleasanter than any painting can describe it: Here likewise growes Rice, Canes for Suggar, Olives, Pomegranads, Mulberrys, Cittrons, Oranges, Figgs and infinite sorts of rare fruits: About the middle of the Way is the Towne Aversa, whither came 3 or 4 Coaches to meete our Lady travellers, of whom we now tooke leave, having ben very merry by the way with them, and the Capitano, who was their Gallant:

Naples

31 About noone We enterd the Citty of Naples, allighting at the 3 Kings, a Place of treatement to excesse, as we found by our very

plentifull fare all the tyme we were in Naples, where provisions are miraculously cheape, and we seldome sat downe to fewer than 18 or 20 dishes of the most exquisite meate and fruites, enjoying the Creature:

The morrow after our arival in the afternoone We hired a Coach to carry us about the Towne, and first we went to Visite the Castle of St. Elmo, built on an excessive high rock, whence we had an intire prospect of the whole Citty, which lyes in shape of a Theatre upon the Sea brinke, with all the circumjacent Ilands, as far as Capra, famous for the debauch'd recesses of Tiberius.

This fort is the bridle of the Whole Citty, and was well stor'd, and Garrisond with natural Spanyards: the strangenesse, of the precipice, and rarenesse of the Prospect in view of so many magnificent and stately Palaces, Churches and Monasteries, [with] the Arsenale, Mole, and distant Mount Vesuvius, all in full command of the Eye, is certainely one of the richest Landskips in the World: Hence we descended to another strong Castle, cald il Castello Nuovo, which protects the Shore, but they would by no intreaty permitt us to go in; the outward defence seemes to consist but in 4 tours very high, and an exceeding deepe graft, with thick Walls: Opposite to this is the Toure of St. Vincent, which is also very Strong: Then we went to the Vice-Roy's Palace, which is realy one of the noblest that I had seene in all Italy, partly old, and part of a newer Work, but we did not stay long here: Towards the Evening we tooke the ayre upon the Mole, which is a streete upon the rampart or banke raysed in the sea for security of their Gallys in Port, built as that of Genoä: here I observ'd an incomparable rich Fountaine built in the middst of the Piazza, and adornd with divers rare statues of Copper representing the Sirens and deities of [Parthenope], spouting large streames of Water into an ample Concha, all of cast mettall and infinite Cost: this stands at the entrance of the Mole, where wee mett many of the Nobility, both on horse-back, and in their Coaches to take the fresco from the sea, as the manner is, it being in the most advantagious quarter for good ayre, delight and prospect: Here we saw divers goodly horses who handsomly become their riders, the Neapolitan Gentlemen: This Mole is about 500 paces in length, and pav'd with a square hewn stone.

From the Mole we ascend to a Church, a very greate antiquity formerly sacred to Castor and Pollux, as the Greeke letters carv'd in the Architrave testify, and the busts of their two statues, converted now into a stately Oratory by the Theatines: Hence we went to the Cathedrall which is a most magnificent pile: and unlesse St. Peters in Rome certainly Naples exceeds all Cittys in the World for stately Churches and Monasteries: We were told that this day the Blood of St. Genuarius, and his head should be expos'd, and so we found it; but obtain'd not to see the miracle of the boiling of this blod, as was told us: The Next we went to see was St. Peters, richly adornd; the Chapel especialy, where the Apostle sayd Masse, as is testified on the Walle: After dinner we went to St. Dominic, where they shew'd us the Crucifix that is reported to have sayd these Words to St. Thomas: Bene de me scripsisti, Thoma. Hence to the Padri Olivetani famous for the monument of the learned Alexand: ab Alexandro.

. . .

. . . climbing a steepe hill we came to the Monastery of the Carthusians and Church, where (after we had turn'd about and considerd the goodly Prospect towards the Sea, and Citty; the one full of Gallys, and ships, the Other of stately Palaces, Churches, Monasteries, Castles, Gardens, delicious fields and meadows, Mount Vesuvius smoaking; the Promontory of Minerva, and Misenum; Capra, Prochyta, Ischia, Pausilipe, Puteoli and the rest, doubtlesse one of the most divertisant and considerable Vistas in the World) we went into the Church; which is most elegantly built; the very pavements of the common Cloyster being all layd with variously polish'd and rich marbles, richly figurd: here they shew'd a Massie Crosse of silver, much celebrated for the Workmanship and carving, and sayd to have ben 14 yeares in perfecting: The Quire also of this Church is of rare arte.

But above all to be admir'd is the yet unfinished Jesuites Church; a Piece, certainly if accomplish'd, not to be match'd in Europe: Hence we pass'd by the Palazza Caraffi full of antient and very noble statues; also the Palace of the Ursini.

The next day little, but visite some friends that were English merchants resident for their negotiation; Onely this morning at the Vice-roys Cavalerizzo, I saw the noblest horses that I had ever beheld, one of his sonns riding the Menage with that addresse and dexterity, as I had never seene any thing approch it.

Feb: 4th We were invited to the Collection of exotic rarities in the Museum of Ferdinando Imperati a Neapolitan Nobleman, and one of the most observable Palaces in the Citty: The repository full of incomparable rarities; amongst the Natural Herbals most remarkable was the Byssus Marina, and Pinna Marina: Male and femal Camelion; an Onacratulus and an extraordinary greate Crocodile: a Salamander; some of the Orcades Anates, held here for a strange rarity: The Male and female Manucodiata, the Male having an hollow on the back in which 'tis reported [the female] both layes, and hatches her Egg: The Mandragoras also of both Sexes: Papyrs made of severall reedes, and some of silke, tables of the rinds of Trees writen with Japonique characters; and another of the branches of Palme: many Indian fruites: a Chrystal that had a prety quantity of uncongeal'd Water within its cavity; a petrified fishers net: divers sorts of Tarantulas, being a kind of monstrous spiders, with lark-like clawes and somewhat bigger:

'Maddnesse of the Carnoval'

The next day we beheld the Vice-kings Procession which was very splendid for the Reliques, Banners and Musique which accompanied the B: Sacrament, which ceremony tooke up most of the morning.

The 6 We went by Coach to take the ayre, and see the diversions, or rather maddnesse of the Carnoval; the Courtisans (who swarme in this Citty to the number (as we are told,) of 30000 registred sinners, who pay a tax to the state for the Costome of their bodys) flinging eggs of sweete-water, into our Coach as we passed by the houses and windoes; and indeede this towne is so pester'd with these Cattel, that there needes no small mortification to preserve from their inchantments, whilst they display all their naturall and artificiall beauty, play, sing, feigne, compliment, and by a thousand studied devices seeke to inveagle foolish young persons: and some of our Company did purchase their repentance at a deare rate, after their returne.

The next day being Saturday we went 4 miles out of Towne on Mules to see that famous Vulcano or burning mountaine of Vesuvius; here we passe a faire Fountaine cal'd Labulla, which continualy boyles, supposed to proceede from Vesuvius . . .

The Bay of Naples

Being now approching the hill as we were able with our Mules, we alighted, crawling up the rest of the proclivity, with extraordinary difficulty, now with our feete and hands, not without many untoward slipps, which did much bruise us on the various colour'd Cinders with which the whole Mountaine is cover'd, some like pitch, others full of perfect brimstone, other metalique interspers'd with innumerable Pumices (of all which I made a collection) we at the last gain'd the summit, which I take to be one of the highest terraces in Europ (for 'tis of an excessive altitude) turning our faces towards Naples, it presents us one of the goodliest prospects in the World; and truely, I do not thinke there is a greater and more noble; all the Baiæ, Cuma, Elysian fields, Capra, Ischia, Prochita, Misenum, Puteoli, that goodly and gentile Citty, with a vast portion of the Tyrrhan Sea offering themselves to your view at once, and at so sweete and agreable a distance, as nothing can be more great and delightfull. The mountaine consists of a double top; the one pointed very sharp, and commonly appearing above any clowds; the other blunt; here as we approch'd we met many large and gaping clefts and c[h]asm's, out of which issu'd such sulphurous blasts and Smoake, that we durst not stand long neere them: having gaind the very brim of the top, I layd my selfe on my belly to looke over and into that most frightfull and terrible Vorago, a stupendious pit (if any there be in the whole Earth) of neere three miles in Circuit, and halfe a mile in depth, by a perpendicular hollow cliffe, like that from the highest part of Dover-Castle, with now and then a craggy prominency jetting out: The area at the bottom is plaine, like a curiously even'd floore, which seemes to be made by the winds circling the ashes by its eddy blasts: in the middle and center, is a [rising], or hill shaped like a greate browne loafe, appearing to consist of a sulphurous matter, continualy vomiting a foggy exhalation, and ejecting huge stones with an impetuous noise and roaring, like the report of many musquets discharging: This horrid Barathrum engaged our contemplation for some whole houres both for the strangnesse of the spectacle, and for the mention which the old histories make of it, as one of the most stupendious curiosities in nature, and which made the learned and inquisitive Pliny adventure his life, to detect the causes, and to loose it in too desperat an approch: It is likewise famous for the Stratagemm of the rebell Spartacus, who did so much mischiefe to the state, by his lurking and protection amongst these horid Caverns, when it was more accessible, and lesse dangerous than now it is: But, especialy, notorious it is, for the last conflagration, when in Ann: 1630 it burst out beyond what it had ever don since the memory of any history, spewing out huge stones, and fiery pumices in such quantity, as not onely invoron'd the whole mountaine, but totaly buried, and overwhelm'd divers Townes, people and inhabitants, scattering the ashes more then an hundred miles distance, and utterly devasting all those goodly Vineyards, where formerly grew the most incomparable Greco; when bursting through the bowels of the Earth it absorb'd the very Sea and with its whirling Waters drew in divers Gallys and other Vessells to their destruction; as is faithfully recorded: Some there are who maintaine it the very Mouth of hell it selfe, others of Purgatory, certainely it must be acknowledged one of the most horrid spectacles in the World: We descen'd with infinite more ease, than we climbd up; namely through a deepe Vallie of pure ashes (at the late erruption a flowing river of mealted, and burning brimestone) and so we came at last to our Mules, which with our Veturino, attended us neere the foote of the Mountaine.

On Sunday, we with our Guide goe to visite the so much celebrated Baiæ, and natural rarities of the Places adjacent: Here we enter the Mountaine Pausilipo, at the left hand of which they shewd us the Poet Virgils Sepulchre, erected on a very steepe rock, in forme of a Small rotunda, or cupulated Columne; but almost over growne with bushes, and wild bay-trees ... After we were advanc'd into this noble, and altogether wonderfull Crypta, consisting of a passage, spacious enough for 2 Coaches to go on breast, cut through a rocky mountaine (as reported, by the antient Cimmerii) for neere three quarters of a mile; others say by L: Cocceius, who employd no lesse then an hundred thousand men at worke on it for 15 dayes, we came to the mid-way, where there is an orifice, or Well, boar'd quite through the whole diameter of this vast Mountaine, which admitts the light into a pretty Chapel, hewn out of the natural rock, wherein hang divers lamps perpetualy burning: The Way is pav'd under foote; but it dus not hinder the dust, which rises so excessively in this much frequented passage, that we were forc'd at mid day, to make use of a Torch; and so at length, with no small astonishment we were deliverd from the

bowels of the earth into one of the most delicious, and incomparable Plaines in the World: the Orangs, the lemmons, Pomegranads,
and other fruites blushing yet upon the perpetualy greene trees, for
the Summer is here eternal; caus'd by the naturall and adventitious
heate of the earth, so warmed through the Subterranean fires, as
our guide alighting, and cutting up a turfe with his knife, and
delivering it to me, I was hardly able to hold it in my hands: This
Mountaine is exceedingly fruitfull in Vines, and there is nothing so
rare and exotic, which will not grow in these invirons: Now we
came to a lake of about two miles in circumference, inviron'd with
hills: The Water of it, is fresh and swete on the surface, and salt at
botome, some mineral-salt conjectur'd to be the cause; and 'tis
reported of that profunditude in the middle, as that it has no
botome soundable: The People call it Lago di Agnano, from the
multitude of Serpents, which involv'd together about the Spring fall
downe from the cliffy hills into it: and besides these it has no fish,
neither will any live in it: The first thing we did here, was, the old
experiment on a Dog, which we lead from that so mortal Cave
commonly nam'd Grotto del Cane or Charons Cave: It is not above
three, or four paces deepe, and about the height of a man, nor is it
very broad: In this Cave whatever has life presently expires; of this
we made tryal with two Doggs: which we bound with a Cord to a
short pole to guide him the more directly into the farther part of the
Den, where he was no soner enter'd, but without the least noyse or
so much as strugling, except that he panted for breath, lolling out
his tongue, his eyes being fixt, we drew him out dead, to all
appearance; but then immediately plunging him into the adjoyning
lake, within lesse space then halfe an houre, he recoverd againe,
and swimming to shore ran away from us: Another Dog, on whom
we try'd the former experiment of the Cave, without the application
of the Water, we left starke dead upon the shore: It seemes this has
also ben try'd on men, as well as beasts, as on that poore Creature
which Peter of Toledo caus'd to go in; likewise on some Turkish
Slaves, two Souldiers: and other foolehardy persons, who all
perished, and could never be recover'd againe by the Water of the
Lake, as are doggs, for which many learned reasons have ben
offer'd; as Simon Majolus in his booke of the Canicular dayes:
Colloq: 15 . . .

'The sweete retirements of the most opulent Romans'

Having well satisfied our curiosity among these Antiquities we retir'd to our Faluca, which row'd us back againe towards Puzzolo at the very place of St. Paules landing: Here keeping along the shore they shew'd us a place where the Sea-Water and Sands did exceedingly boyle: Thence to the Iland Nesis, once the fabulous Nymph: And thus we leave the Baiæ so renowned for the sweete retirements of the most opulent, and Voluptuous Romans, and certainely they were places of incomparable amœnitie, as their yet lasting and tempting site, and other circumstances of natural curiosities easily invite me to believe; since there is not certainely in the whole World so many stupendious rarities to be met with, as there are in the circle of a few miles which inviron these blissfull aboades:

Naples Again

Feb: 8. We went to see the Arsenal, which was well furnish'd with Gallies, and other Vessells: The Citty infinitely crowded with Inhabitans, Gentlemen and Merchants. The Government is held of the Pope by an annual tribute of 40000 ducats and a White-Genet; but the Spanyard trusts more to the power of those his natural Subjects there: Apulia and Calabria yeilding him neere 4 milions of crownes yearely to maintaine it: The Country is divided into 13 Provinces: 20 Archbishops: 107 Bish: The Estates of the Nobility in default of the masculine line reverting to the King: Besides the Vice-Roy, there is also (amongst the chiefe Magistrates) an high Conestable, Admiral, Chiefe-Justice, Great Chamb[e]rlaine, and Chancelor, with a Secretary who being prodigiously avaritious do wonderfully inrich themselves out of the miserable peoples labour, Silke, Manna, Sugar, Oyle, Wine, Rice, Sulphur, Alome; for with all these riches, is this delicious Country blest; the Manna falling at certaine seasons upon the adjoyning hills, in forme of a thick deuw: The very winter here is a summer, ever fruitefull, and continualy pregnant, so as in midst of February we had Melons, Cheries, Abricots and many other sorts of fruite: The building of the Citty is for the quantity the most magnificent of Europe, the streetes exceeding large, well paved, having many Vaults, and conveyances under them for the sullage which renders them very sweete and cleane even in the midst of winter: To it belongeth more then 3000

churches and monasteries, and those the best built and adornd in
Italy: they greately affect the Spanish gravity in their habite, delight
in good horses; the streetes are full of Gallants, in their Coaches,
on horseback, and sedans, from hence brought first into England
by Sir Sanders Duncomb: The Women are generally well featur'd,
but excessively libidinous; the Country people so jovial and
addicted to Musick, that the very husbandmen almost universaly
play on the guitarr, singing and composing songs in prayse of their
Sweete-hearts, and will go to the field commonly with their fiddle;
they are merry, Witty and genial; all which I much attribute to the
excellent quality of the ayre: The French they have a deadly hatred
to, so as some of our Company were flouted at for wearing red
Cloakes, as then the mode was:

'The Non ultra of my Travells'
Thus after two dayes respite, and feasting our senses with fine
sights and good cheere, I left this Ode, in our Hosts Albus (wherein
(as of many) it was his costome to desire his Guests to write their
Name and Impresse) as the Non ultra of my Travells; sufficiently
sated with rolling up and downe, and resolving with my selfe to be
no longer an Individuum vagum, if ever I got home againe; since
from the report of divers experienc'd and curious persons, I had
ben assur'd there was little more to be seene in the rest of the civil
World, after Italy, France, Flanders and the Low-Country, but
plaine and prodigious Barbarisme.

ODE.

Happy the man who lives content
With his owne Home, and Continent:
Those chiding streames his banks do curb
Esteemes the Ocean to his Orb;
Round which when he a Walke dos take,
Thinks t'have perform'd as much as Drake.
For other tongues he takes no thought
Then what his Nurse or Mother taught:

He's not disturb'd with the rùde Cries
Of the Procaccio's Up and Rise;
But being of his Faire possess'd
From Travelling sets up his rest:

In her soft armes no sooner hurl'd
But he enjoyes another World,*

Scornes Us who Travell Lands and Seas,
Thinkes there's no Countries like to his:
If then at Home, such Joyes be had,
Oh, how un-wise are We, how mad!

Neapoli 1644[5]*

Return to Rome

Thus about the 7th of Feb: we return'd to Rome by the same way we came, not daring to adventure by Sea (as some of our Company consulted) for feare of the Turkish Pyrates hovering upon that Coast; nor made we any stay, save at Albano to view the celebrated place and Sepulchre of the famous Duelists who decided the antient quarell betweene their imperious Neighbours with the losse of their lives; and to tast of the Wine no lesse famous: These two Brothers the Horacij and Cur[i]acij lye buried neere the high way, under two antient Pyramids of stone, some what decay'd and overgrowne with rubbish:

. . .

'The Academie of the Humorists'

The 17, I was invited (after dinner) to the Academie of the Humorists, kept in a spacious Hall, belonging to Signor Mancini, where the Witts of the Towne meete on certaine daies, to recite poems, and prevaricate on severall Subjects etc: The first that Speakes is cal'd the Lord, and stands in an eminent place, and then the rest of the virtuosi recite in order: by these ingenious Exercises the learn'd discourses, is the purity of the Italian Tongue daily improv'd: This roome is hung round, with enumerable devises or Emblemes all relating to something of *humidum* with Motos under them: Several other Academies there are of this nature, bearing the like fantastical titles: It is in this Accademie of the Humorists where they have the Picture of Guarini the famous Author of *Pastor fido*, once of this Society:

. . .

Contrasting Converts

The 25t invited by a Frier Dominican whom we usualy heard

preach to a number of Jewes, to be Godfather to a Converted Turk and a Jew, The Ceremonie was perform'd in the Church of S: Maria sopra la Minerva neere the Capitol, They were clad in White, then exorcis'd at their entering the church with aboundance of Ceremonies, when lead into the Quire, they were baptizd by a Bishop *in Pontificalibus*: The Turk lived afterwards in Rome, sold hot-waters, and would bring us presents when he met us, kneeling, and kissing the hemms of our Cloaks: But the Jew was believ'd to be a Counterfeit . . .

. . .

Easter in Rome

Good friday [April 14] we went againe to s. Peters, where the Volto, Launce, and Crosse were all three exposd and worship'd together: All the confession Seates fill'd with devout people, and the Night a procession of severall people that most lamentably whipped themselves till all the blood staind their clothes, for some had shirts, others upon the beare back, with vizors and masks on their faces, at every 3 or 4 stepps, dashing the knotted and ravelld whip-cord over their shoulders as hard as they could lay it on, whilst some of the religious Orders and fraternities sung in a dismal tone, the lights, and Crosses going before, which shewd very horrible, and indeede a heathnish pomp: The next day was much ceremonie at s. Jo: de Laterano, so as this whole weeke we spent in running from Church to Church, all the towne in buisy devotion, greate silence, and unimaginable Superstition: Easterday was awakn'd with the Guns againe from st. Angelo, we went to s. Peters, where the pope himselfe celebrated Masse, shew'd the Reliques formerly nam'd, and gave a publique benediction, and so we went to dinner:

Monday, we went to heare Music in the Chiesa Nova, and though there were aboundance of Ceremonies at the other greate Churches, and greate exposure of Reliques, yet being wearied with sights, of this nature, and the season of the Yeare (Summer at Rome being very dangerous, by reason of the heates,) minding us of returning Northwards, we spent the rest of the time in visiting such places as we had not yet sufficiently seene: onely I do not forget the Pops benediction of the *Confalone* or Standard, and giving the hallowed palmes; and on Mayday, the greate Procession of the Universitie, and the Mulatiers at st. Antonies, and their seting up a foolish May-pole in the Capitol, very ridiculous:

The Catacombs

We therefore now tooke Coach a little out of Towne, to visite the famous Roma Subterranea, being much like those of st. Sebastians: here in a Corn field, guided by two torches we crep't on our bellies into a little hole about 20 paces, which deliver'd us into a large entrie that lead us into severall streetes or allies, a good depth in the bowells of the Earth, a strange and fearefull passages for divers miles, as Bossius has describ'd and measur'd them in his book: we ever and anon came into pretty square roomes, that seem'd to be Chapells, with Altars, and some adorn'd with antient painting, very ordinary: That which renders the passages dreadfull is, the Skeletons and bodies, that are placd on the sides, in degrees one above the other like shelves, whereof some are shut up with a Course flat Stone, and Pro Christo or ☧ and Palmes ingraven on them, which are supposd to have ben Martyrs: Here in all liklyhood were the meetings of the Primitive Christians during the Persecutions, as Plinius Secundus describes them: As I was prying about, I found a glasse phiole as was conjecturd filld with dried blood, as also two lacrymatories: Many of the bodyes, or rather bones, (for there appeard nothing else) lay so intire, as if placed so by the art of the Chirugion, which being but touch'd fell all to dust: Thus after two or 3 miles wandring in this subterranean Meander we return'd to our Coach almost blind when we came into the day light againe, and even choked with smoake: A French bishop and his retinue adventuring it seemes too farr in these denns, their lights going out, were never heard of more.

A Tournament

We were entertain'd at Night with an English play, at the Jesuites where before we had dined, and the next at the Prince Galicanos, who himselfe compos'd the Musique to a magnificent Opera, where were Cardinal Pamphilio the Popes Nephew, the Governors of Rome, the Cardinals, Ambassadors, Ladies and a world of Nobilitie and strangers: after a Just and Turnament of severall young Gentlemen upon a formal Defy, which was perform'd in the Morning, to which we were invited, the prizes distributed by the

Ladies after the Knight Errantry way: The Launces and swords running at tilt at the Barrieres with a greate deele of clatter, but without any bloud shed, which gave much diversion to the Spectators, and was very new to us Travellers:

A Splendid Park

[May 3] The next day after dinner, Mr. Henshaw and I went againe to see the Villa Borghesi, having spent the Morning in attending the Enterance and Cavalcato of the Ambassador from the Gr: Duke of Florence, Card: Medices by the Via Flaminea: This Garden about a Mile without the Cittie, being rather a Park or Paradise contrivd and planted with Walkes and shades of Myrtils, Cypresse and other trees and groves, adornd with aboundance of Fountains, statues and Bass-relievos: Here they had hung large Netts to Catch Wood-Cocks: there were fine glades, and several pretty murmuring rivulets trickling downe the declining Walkes: There was also a Vivarie where among other exotic foules there was an Ostridge, besids a most capacious Aviarie and in another inclosd part, an heard of Deere: Before the Palace (which might become the Court of a greate Prince) stands a noble Fountaine of white Marble, inrich'd with statues: The walles of the house without are incrusted with excellent Basse relievos antique of the same marble, incornish'd with Festoones, and Niches set with statues from the very roofe to the foundation: A stately Portico joynes the Palace full of Statues, Columns, Urnes and other Curiosities of Sculpture . . .

. . .

Frascati

The 5 we tooke Coach and went 15 miles out of the Cittie to Frascati formerly Tusculanum, a villa of Card: Aldobrandini; built for a Country house but for its elegance, situation and accommodation of plentifull water, Groves, Ascents and prospect, surpassing in my opinion the most delicious places that my eyes ever beheld: Just behind the Palace (which is of excellent Architecture) and is in the center of the Inclosure, rises an high hill or mountaine all over clad with tall wood, and so form'd by nature, as if it had ben cut out by Art, from the summit whereof falls a horrid Cascade seeming rather a greate River than a streame, precipitating into a large Theater of Water representing a[n] exact and perfect Raine-bow when the sun shines out: Under this is made an artific[i]all Grott, where in are curious rocks, hydraulic Organs and all sorts of singing birds moving, and chirping by force of the water, with severall other pageants and surprizing inventions: In the center of one of these roomes rises a coper ball that continualy daunces about 3 foote above the pavement, by virtue of a Wind conveyed seacretly to a hole beneath it, with many other devices to wett the unwary spectators, so as one can hardly [step] without wetting to the skin: In one of these Theatres of Water, is an Atlas spouting up the streame to an incredible height, and another monster which makes a terrible roaring with an horn; but above all the representation of a storme is most naturall, with such fury of raine, wind and Thunder as one would imagine ones selfe in some extreame Tempest: To this is a Garden of incomparable walkes and shady groves, aboundance of rare Fruit, Orangs, Lemons, etc: and the goodly prospect of Rome above all description, so as I do not wonder that Cicero and others have celebrated this place with such encomiums. The Palace is indeede built more like a Cabinet, than any-thing compos'd of stone and morter, it has in the middle an Hall furnish[ed] with excellent Marbles, and rare Pictures, especialy those of Cavalier Gioseppe d' Arpino, and the movables are princely and rich, In a word this was the last piece of Architecture finishd by Giacoma de la Porta, who built it for Pietro Card: Aldobrandini in the time of Clement the 8th.

. . .

Tivoli

On the 6t. we rested ourselves, and next day in Coach tooke our last fare-well of visiting the Circumjacent places, and that was Tivoli, or the old Tyburtine: After about 6 miles from Rome we passe the Teverone, a bridge built [by] the Mother of Severus, Mammea, and so by divers antient Sepulchres, amongst others, that of Valerius Volusi, neere it the stinking sulphurous River over the Ponte Lucano where we found an heape or Turret full of Inscriptions, now call'd Plautius his Tomb. Ariv'd at Tivoli we went first to see the Palace d' Estè erected on a plaine, but where was formerly an hill: The Palace is very ample and stately: In the Garden at the right hand are plac'd 16 vast Conchas of marble jetting out Waters: in the midst of these stands a Janus quadrifrons that cast forth 4 girandolas, calld from the resemblance the Fontana di Speccho; neere this a Place for Tilting: before the Ascent of the Palace is that incomparable fountain of Leda, and not far from that 4 sweete and delicious Gardens; descending thence two pyramids of Water, and in a Grove of trees neere it, the Fountaines of Tethys, Esculapius, Arethusa, Pandora, Pomona and Flora, then the pransing Pegasus, Bacchus, The Grott of Venus, The two Colosses of Melicerta and Sybilla Tibertina, all of exquisite Marble, Coper and other suitable adornments, The Cupids especialy are most rare, pouring out Water, and the Urnes on which are plac'd the 10 Nymphs . . .

. . .

Difficulties of Exchange

The Bills of Exchange I tooke up from my first entering Italy 'til I went from Rome amounted but to 616 ducati di Banco, though I purchas'd many books, Pictures and severall Curiosities:

May: 18 But being now disappointed of Monies long expected, intending to see Lauretto, I was forc'd to returne by the same way I came, desiring if possible to be at Venice by the Ascention, and therefore diverted to take Legorne in the [way], as well to furnish me with Credit by a Merchant there, as to take order for the [transporting] such Collections as I had made at Rome; when on my Way, turning about to behold this once and yet glorious Citty, upon an Eminence of Ground I did not without some regret give it my last farewell –

. . .

We went . . . for Ligorne by Coach, where I tooke up 90 Crounes for the rest of my journey with letters of Credit for Venice, after I had sufficiently complaind of my defeate of Correspondence at Rome . . .

. . .

Bologna

This Towne belongs to the Pope, and is a famous University, situate in one of the fattest spots of Europe, for all sorts of Provisions: tis built like a ship, whereof the Torre d' Asinello may go for the Main-Mast: the Citty is of no great strength, a trifling Wall about it, and is in Circuit neere five miles, and 2 in length:

This Torre d'Asinello ascended by 447 stepps of a foote rise, seemes exceeding high, as being also but very narrow, and is the more conspicuous by another Tower cal'd Garisenda so artificialy built of brick (which increases the Wonder) as one would think it were allways ready to fall ... the whole Towne is so cloysterd, that one may passe from house to house through the Streetes without being exposd either to raine or Sun:

A Stately Persian

Before the stately Hall of this Palace [of the Legat] stands the Statue of Paule the 4th and divers others, also the Monument of the Coronation of Charles the 5t. The Piazza before it is absolutely the most stately in all Italy, St. Marks at Venice onely excepted; In the center of it is a Fountain of Neptune, a noble figure cast in Coper: I here saw a Persian walking about in a very rich vest of cloth of tissue, and severall other ornaments according to the fashion of their Country, which did exceedingly please me, he was a young handsom person of the most stately mîne I had ever observd: faine I would have seene the Library of St. Saviours famous for the quantity of rare Manuscripts, but could not, so we went to St. Francis's a glorious pile and exceedingly adorn'd within: After dinner I enquird out a Priest, and Dr. Montalbano, to whom I brought recommendations from Rome ...

Many of the Religious men here nourish those Lap-dogs had so in delicijs by the Ladies, which they sell, they are a pigmie sort of Spaniels, whose noses they breake whe[n] puppies, which in my opinion deformes them ...

...

From this pleasant Citty we went now towards Ferrara ... We parted from hence about 3 in the after noone, and went some of our way on the Chanell, and then Imbark'd upon the Po ... we Imbarkd in a stout Vessell (having made 30 on the Po) and thro[ugh] an artificial Chanell very strait, entred the Adice, which carried us by break of day into the Adriatic, and so sailing prosperously by Chioza (a Town upon an Iland in this sea) and Palestina, another; we came over against Malamocco (the chiefe port, and ankerage where our English Merchant men lie, that trade to Venice) where we arived about 7 at night, after we had stayed at the least two houres for our Permission to land, our Bill of Sanità being deliver'd according to costome: so soone as we came on shore we were conducted to the Dogana, where our Portmanteaus were visited, and so got to our lodging, which was at honest Signor Paulo Rhodomants at the Aquila Nera neere the Rialto, and one of the best quarters of the Towne. This journey from Rome to Venice, cost me 7: Pistoles and 13 Julios.

Venice

June. The next morning finding my-selfe extreamly weary, and beaten with my Journey, I went to one of their Bagnias, which are made, and treate after the Eastern manner, washing one with hot and cold water, with oyles, rubbing with a kind of Strigil, which a naked youth puts on his hand like a glove of seales Skin, or what ever it be, fetching off a world of dirt, and stretching out on[e]s limbs, then claps [on] a depilatorie made of a drug or earth they call Resina, that comes out of Turky, which takes off all the haire of the body, as resin dos a piggs. I think there is orpiment and lime in it, for if it lie on to long it burns the flesh: The curiosity of this Bath, did so open my pores that it cost me one of the greatest Colds and rheumes that ever I had in my whole life, by reason of my comming out without that caution necessary of keeping my selfe Warme for some time after: For I immediately began to visite the famous Places of the Citty And Travellers, do nothing else but run up and downe to see sights, that come into Italy: And this Citty, for being one of the most miraculously plac'd of any in the whole World, built on so many hundred Ilands, in the very sea, and at good distance from the Continent, deser[v]'d our admiration: It has neither fresh, nor any other but salt Water, save what is reserved in Cistrens, of the raine, and such as is daily brought them from Terra firma in boates: Yet it wa[nt]s nor fresh water, nor aboundance of all sorts of excellent Provisions, very cheape. 'Tis reported that when the Hunns overran all Italy, some meane fishermen and others left the Maine land, and fled to these despicable and muddy Ilands for Shelter, where in processe of time, and by Industry, it is growne to the greatnesse of one of the most considerable states in the World, consider'd as a Republique and having now subsisted longer, than any of the foure antient Monarchies, and flourishing in greate State, welth and glory by their Conquests of greate Territories in Italy, Dacia, Greece, Candy, Rhodes, Slavonia, and at present challenging the Empire of all the Adriatique Sea, which they yearly espouse, by casting a gold ring into it, with greate pomp and ceremony upon Ascension day: the desire of seing this, being one of the reasons, that hastned us from Rome: First the Dodge or Duke (having heard Masse) in his robes of State (which are very particular and after the Eastern) together with the Senat in their gownes, Imbarkd in their gloriously painted, carved and gilded Bucentoro, invirond and follow'd by innumerable Gallys, Gundolas, and boates filled with Spectators, some dressed in Masqu[e]rade, Trumpets, musique, and Canons, filling the whole aire with din: Thus having rowed out about a league into the Gulph, the Duke at the prow casts into the Sea a Gold ring, and Cup, at which a loud acclamation is Echod by the greate Guns of the Arsenale, and at the Liddo: and so we returned:

'Gundolas'

Two days after taking a Gundola which are their Water Coaches, (for land ones many old men in this Citty never saw any, or rarely a horse) we rowed up and downe the Channells, which are as our Streetes; These Vessells are built very long and narrow, having necks and tailes of steele, somewhat spreading at the beake like a fishes taile, and kept so exceedingly polish'd as giues a wonderfull lustre: some are adornd with carving, others lined with Velvet, commonly black, with Curtains and tassals, and the seates like Couches to lie stretch'd on, while he who rowes, stands on the very edge of the boate, upright, and with one Oare (bending forward as if they would precipitate into the Sea) rows, and turnes, with incredible dexterity, thus passing from Channell to Channell, and landing his fare or patron, at what house he pleases: The beakes of these vessells are not unlike the Roman antient Rostrums: The first thing I went to see of publique building was the Rialto, celebrated for passing over the grand Canale with one onely Arch, so large as to admitt a Gally to row thro[ugh] it, built of good Marble, and having on it, besides many pretty shops, three stately and ample passages for people, without any incumbrance, the 2 outmost nobly balustr'd with the same stone, a piece of Architecture to be admir'd. It was Evening and the Canale (which is their Hide-park, where the Noblesse go to take the aire) was full of Ladys and Gent; and there are many times very da[n]gerous stops by reason of the multitude of Gu[n]dalos, ready to sink one another, and indeede they affect to leane them so [on] one side, that one who is not accostom'd to it, would be afraid of over setting: Here they were singing, playing on harpsicords, and other musick and serenading their Mistriss's: In another place, racing, and other *passe tempi* on the Water, it being now exceeding hot: I went next day to their Exchange, a place like ours, frequented by Merchants, but nothing so magnificent; from thence my Guide had me to the Fondigo di Todeschi which is their magazine, and here the Merchants (as in a Coledge) having their lodging and diet many of them, especially Germons . . .

. . .

St Mark's Church

This famous Church is . . . Gotic, yet for the preciousnesse of the Materials . . . far exceeding any of Rome, St. Peters hardly excepted; and first I much admired the splendid historie of our B: Saviour, composd all of Mosaic over the faciata . . . and over the chiefe Gate, are 4 horses cast in Coper, as big as the life, the same that formerly were transported from Rome by Constantine to Byzantium, and thence by the Venetians hither . . . But when all is said, as to this Church, tis in my opinion much too dark, and dismal, and of heavy work: The fabric, as is much of Venice, both for bu[i]ldings and other fashions and circumstances much after the Greekes, their next neighbours:

. . .

Ascension Week

Twas now Ascension Weeke, and the greate Mart or faire of the whole yeare now kept, every body at liberty, and jollie; the Noblemen stalking with their Ladys on Choppines about 10 foote high from the ground. These are high heeld shoos particularly affected by these proude dames, or as some say, invented to keepe them at home, it being so difficult to walke with them, whence one being asked how he liked the Venetian Dames, replyd, they were *Mezzo Carne, Mezzo Legno*;* and he would have none of them: The truth is their Garb is very odd, as seeming allwayes in Masquerade, their other habite also totaly different from all Nations: The[y] weare very long crisped haire of severall strakes and Colours, which they artificially make so, by washing their heads in pisse, and dischevelling them on the brims of a broade hat that has no head, but an hole to put out their head by, drie them in the Sunn, as one may see them above, out of their windos: In their tire they set silk flowers and sparkling stones, their peticoates comming from their very armepetts, so high as that their very breasts flub over the tying place; so as they are neare three quarters and an halfe Aporn: Their Sleeves are made exceeding wide, under which their smock sleeves as wide and commo[n]ly tucked up to the shoulder, and shewing their naked arme, through false Sleeves of Tiffany girt with a bracelet or two: besides this they go very bare of their breasts and back, with knots of poynts richly tagg'd, about their shoulders and other places, of their body, which the[y] usualy cover with a kind of yellow Vaile of Lawn very transparant. Thus attir'd they set their hands on the heads of two Matron-like servants or old women to support them, who are mumbling their beades: Tis very ridiculous to see how these Ladys crawle in and out of their Gundolas by reason of their Choppines, and what dwarfes they appeare when taken down from their Wooden scafolds: Of these I saw neere 30 together stalking, halfe as high more, as the rest of the World; for Curtezans or the Citizens may not weare Chopines, but cover their bodies and faces with a vaile of a certaine glistring Taffata or Lustrèe, out of which they now and then dart a glaunce of their Eye . . .

An Opportunity Missed

There being at the time a ship bound for the Holy Land, I had now resolved to imbarke myselfe, intending to see Jerusalem, and others parts of Syria, Egypt, and Turky: but after I was provided of all necessaries, laied in Snow to coole our drink, bought some Sheepe, Poultry, Bisquit, Spirits and a little Cabinet of Drouggs etc. in case of sicknesse; our Vessell (whereof Cap: Powell was Master) happnd to be press'd for the service of the State, to Carry Provisions to Candia, which was now nuly attacqu'd by the Turkes; which altogether frustrated my designe, to my greate sorrow, it being but two or 3 daies before we hoped to set saile.

Padua

On the   of June we went to Padöa to the faire of their St. Anthony, in company of divers Passengers, the first Terra firma we landed at was Fusina, being onley an Inn, where we changed our Barge, and were then drawne up with horses through the River Brenta, a strait Chanell, as even as a line for 20 miles, the Country on both sides deliciously planted with Country Villas and gentlemens retirements, Gardens planted with Oranges, Figs, and other fruit, belonging to the Venetians. At one of these Villas we went on shore to see a pretty contrivd Palace: Observable in this passage was their buying their Water of those who farme the sluces, for this artificial river is in some places so shallow, that reserves of water are kept with sluces, which they open and shut with a most ingenious invention or Engine, so as to be governd even by a child: Thus they keep up the water, or dismisse it, till the next channell be either filled by the stop, or abated to the levell of the other; for which every boate pays a certaine dutie: Thus we stayd neere halfe an houre, and more at 3 severall interruptions, so as it was evening ere we got to Padoa: Which is a very antient Cittie, if the tradition of Antenors being the founder be not a fiction . . .

Venetian Arsenal

Thus having spent the day in rambling, I returnd the next to Venice: Our next sally was the Arsenal thought to be one of the best furnish'd in the World . . . The forge is 450 paces long, and one of them has 13 furnaces: There is one Canon weighing 16573 pounds cast whilst Henry the 3d dined, and put into a Gally, built, rigg'd and fitted for launching within that time: They have also armes for 12 Galeasses, which are Vessells to row of almost 150 foote long, and 30 large: not counting prow or poup, and contain 28 banks each 7. men, and so carry 1300 Men: with 3 masts: In another a Magazin for 50 Gallys, and place for some hundreds more: Here stands the Bucentaur, with a most ample deck, and so contriv'd, that the Slaves are not seene, having on the Poup a Thron for the Dodge to sit, when he gos in tryumph to espouse the Adriatic: here is also a gallery of 200 yards long for Cables, and over that a Magazine of hemp: Over against these their Saltpeter houses and a large row of Cells or houses to thrust their Gallys in, out of all Weather: Over the Gate, as we go out, is a roome full of greate and small Guns, some of which discharge 6 times at once: Then there is a Court full of Cannon bullets, Chaines, Grapples, Granados, etc: and over that Armes for 800000 men, and by themselves, armes for 400, taken from some that were in a plot against the State; together with weapons of offence and defence for 62 ships, 32 piece of Ordinance on Carriages taken from the Turks, and one prodigious Mortar-piece: In a word, tis not to be reckon'd up, what this large place containes of this sort: There were now 23 Gallys, and 4 Gally Grossi here of 100 Oares of a side: The whole Arsenal is walld about, and may be in Compasse about 3 miles, with 12 Toures for the Watch, besides that the sea invirons it: The Workmen who are ordinarily 500 march out of it in militarie order, and every evening receive their pay thro[ugh] a small hole in the gate, where the Governor lives.

A Proto-Guillotine

The next day I saw a wretch executed who had murther'd his Master, for which he had his head chop'd off by an Axe that slid down a frame of timber, betweene the two tall Columns in St. Marcs Piazzo at the sea brink; the Executioner striking on the Axe with a bettle, and so the head fell of the block:

. . .

English Hospitality

[August 7?] The next morning Cap: Powell (Master of the Vessell which had ben stop'd by the State, to go to Candy, and in which I was to Embark towards Turky) invited me on board, lying about 10 miles from Venice, where we had a good dinner, of English pouderd beefe, and other good meate, with store of Wine, and greate Gunns, as the manner is: After dinner the Captaine presented me with a stone he lately brought from Gran[d] Cairo, which he tooke from the Mumy-pitts, full of Hieroglypics, which I designd on paper, with the true dimensions and sent in a letter to Mr. [Henshaw], to communicate to Father Kircher, who was then setting forth his greate work *Obeliscus Pamphilius*, where it is described, though without mentioning my Name at all: The stone was afterward brought for me into England, landed at Wapping, where before I could heare of it, it was broken into severall fragments, and utterly defaced to my no small affliction: The Boate-swaine of the ship also gave me an hand and foote of rare [Mummy], the nailes wheroff had ben overlaid with thin plates of

Gold, and the whole body perfect, when he brought it out of Egypt, but the avarice of the Sailers and Ships Crue, brake it in pieces and divided the body among them, which was greate pitty: he presente[d] me also with 2 Egyptian Idols, and some loaves of the Bread which the Coptics use in the H: Sacrament, with other curiosities:

August: 8 I had newes from Padoä of my Election to be Syndicus Artistarum, which caused me (after two days idling in a Country Villa, with the Consul of Venice) to hasten thither, that I might dissingage my selfe of that honour, because it was not onely Chargeable, but would have hindred my progresse . . .

. . .

Evelyn leaves Venice

[1646. March] Having pack'd up my purchases, of Books, Pictures, G[l]asses, Treacle, etc (the making and extraordinary ceremonie whereof, I had ben curious to observe, for tis extremely pompous and worth seeing) I departed from Venice, accompanied with Mr. Waller (the celebrated Poet) now newly gotten out of England, after the Parliament had extreamely worried him, for attempting to put in execution the Commission of Aray, and for which the rest of his Collegues were hanged by the Rebells:

The next day, I tooke leave of my Comrades at Padoa, and receiving some directions from Cavallero Salvatico how to govern my selfe, being of late incommoded with a salt defluction from my head (for which I had a little before ben let blood) I prepard for my Journey towards Milan: It was Easter Monday, that I was invited to Breakfast at the Earle of Arundels; I tooke my leave of him in his bed, where I left that greate and excellent Man in teares upon some private discourse of the crosses had befaln his Illustrious family: particularly the undutifullnesse of his Grandson Philips turning Dominican Frier Since Cardinal of Norfolke, the unkindnesse of his Countesse, now in Holland; The miserie of his Countrie, now embroild in a Civil War etc: after which he causd his Gentleman to give me directions all written with his owne hand, what curiosities I should enquire after in my Journey, and so injoyning me to write sometimes to him, I departed: There staying for me below Mr. Henry Howard now duke of Norfolk, Mr. J: Digby son of Sir Kenh[e]lme Digby and other Gent:

Who conducted me to the Coach that stood ready at the doore.

. . .

In company then with Mr. Waller, one Cap: Wray (son to Sir Christopher, whose Father had ben in armes against his Majestie and therefore by no meanes wellcome to us) with another gent: one Mr. Abdy, a modest and learned man, we got that night to Vincenza, passing by the Euganian hills, celebrated for the Prospects, and furniture of rare simples, which are found growing about them: The Wayes were something deepe, but the whole Country flat and even as a bowling greene; the common fields lying square, and orderly planted with fruite-trees, which the Vines run upon and embrace for [many] miles, with delicious streames creeping along the ranges.

. . .

Milan

[May] Here, at approch of the Citty, some of our Company (in dread of the Inquisition, severer here than in any place of all Spaine) thought of throwing away some Protestant (by them call'd Heretical) books and papers: It was about 3 in the Afternoone that we came thither, where the Officers search'd us th[o]roughly for prohibited goods, but finding we were onely Gentlemen Travellers dismissd us for a small reward: so we went quietly to our Inn the 3 Kings, where for that day we refreshed ourselves, as we had neede.

. . .

A Scots Colonel

. . . Walking a turne in the Portico before the Dome a Cavaliero who pass'd by, hearing some of our Companie speaking English, looked a good while earnestly on us, and by and by sending his servant towards us, desird that we would honour him the next day at Dinner; This we looked on as an odd kind of Invitation, he not speaking at all to us himselfe: We returnd his Civilitie, with thanks, not fully resolv'd what to do, or what might be the meaning of it, in this jealous place: But on inquirie, 'twas told us he was a Scots Colonel, that had an honorable Command in the Citty, so we agreed to go: This Afternoone we were wholy taken up in seeing an Opera, represented by some Neapolitans, and performed all in excellent Musick, and rare Sceanes: in which there acted a celebrated Beauty:

Next morning we went to the Colonels, who had sent his servant againe to conduct us to his house; which in truth we found a noble Palace, richly furnish'd. There were also other Guest[s], all Souldiers, and one of them a Scotch man, but not one of all their names could we learn: At dinner he excusd his rudenesse, that he had not himselfe spoken to us, telling us it was his costome, when he heard of any English Travlors (who but rarely would be knowne to passe through that Citty, for feare of the Inquisition) to invite them to his house, where they might be free: And indeede we had a most sumptuous dinner, with plenty of Excellent provision, and the wine so tempting, that after some healths had gon about, and we rissen from Table, the Colonel leade us into his hall, where there hung up divers Colours, Saddle, bridles, pistols and other Armes, being Trophies which he had with his owne hands taken from the Enemy; and amongst them would needes bestow a paire of Pistols on Cap: Wray, one of our fellow Travelors, and a good drinking Gent: and on me, a Turkish bridle woven with silk and very Curiously embossd, with other silk Trappings, to which hung an halfe moone finely wrought, which he had taken from a Basshaw that he had slaine: With this glorious spoile, I rid the rest of my Journey as far as Paris and brought it afterwards into England.

His Tragic End

Then he shew'd us a stable of brave horses, with his Menage and Cavalerizzo. Some of the horses he causd to be brought forth, which he mounted, and perform'd all the motions of an Excellent horse-man: When this was don, and he alighted, contrary to the advice of his Groome and Pages, (who it seemes knew the nature of the beast, and that their Master was a little spirited with Wine) needes he would have out a fiery horse, that had not yet ben Menag'd, and was very ungovernable; but was else a very beautifull Creature: This he mounting, the horse getting the raines, in a full carriere, [rose] so de[s]perately, as he fell quite back, crushing the Colonell so forceably against the Wall of the Manege, that though he sat on him like a Centaure, yet recovering the Jade on all foure againe, he desir'd to be taken down, and so led in, where he cast himselfe upon a Pallet, where with infinite lamentation, after some time, we tooke our leaves of him, being now speechlesse; and the next morning coming to visite him, we found before the doore, the

Canopie, which they usualy carry over the Host, and some with lighted tapers, which made us suspect he was in very sad condition, and so indeede we found him, an Irish frier standing by his bed side, as Confessing him, or at least disguising a Confession and other Ceremonies, usd *in extremis*; for we afterwards learn'd, that the Gent: was a Protestant, and had this Frier his confident; which doubtlesse was a dangerous thing at Milan, had it ben but suspected: At our enterance he sighed grievously and held up his hands, but was not able to speake: After vomiting some bloud, he kindly tooke us all by the hand, and made signes, that he should see us no more, which made us take our leave of him with extreame reluctancy, and affliction for the Accident: This sad disaster made us Consult that very Evening about our departure from this Towne as soone as we could, not knowing how we might be enquird after, or engag'd, The Inquisition heare being so cruelly formidable, and inevitable on the least suspicion: The very next morning therefore discharging our Lodgings we agreed for a coach to Carry us to the foote of the/ Alpes, not a little concernd for the death of the Colonell, which we now heard of, and that had so courteously entertain'd us:

Lago Maggiore

The first day then we got as far as Castellanza, by which runs a spacious river into Lago Maggiore: Here at dinner were two or three Jesuites who were very pragmatical and inquisitive, whom we declind conversation with as decently as we could: so we pursu'd our journey through a most fruitfull plaine, but the weather wet and uncomfortable: At night we lay at Sesto and next morning (leaving our Coach) Imbarked in a boate to waft us over the Lago (being one of the largest in Europe) and whence we could perfectly see the touring Alps, and amongst them Il gran San Bernardo esteemed the highest mountaine in Europe, appearing some miles above the Clouds: Through this vast Water passes the River Ticinus which discharges itselfe into the Pó, by which meanes Helvetia transports her Merchandizes into Italy, which we now begin to leave behind us: Having now sail'd about 2 leagues we were hal'd on shore at Arona, a strong Towne belonging to the Dutchy of Milan, where being examind by the Governor, and paying a small duty, we were dismiss'd: Opposite to this Fort is Angiera, another small Towne;

the passage very pleasant, with the horrid prospect of the Alps, coverd with Pine trees, and Firrs and above them Snow: The next we pass'd was the pretty Iland, Isabella, that [lies] about the middle of the Lake, and has a faire house built on a Mount, indeede the whole Iland is a Mount, ascended by severall Terraces and walks all set about with Oranges and Citron trees, the reflection from the Water rendring the place very warme, at least during the Summer and Autumn: The next we saw was Isola, and left on our right hand the Ile of St Jovanni, and so sailing by another small Towne (built also upon an Iland) we ariv'd at night to Marguzzo an obscure village at the end of the Lake, and very foote of the Alpes, which now rise as it were suddainly, after some hundred of miles of the most even Country in the World, and where there is hardly a stone to be found, as if nature had here swept up the rubbish of the Earth in the Alpes, to forme and cleare the Plaines of Lumbardy, which hitherto we had pass'd since our coming from Venice:

In this wretched place, I lay on a bed stuff'd with leaves, which made such a Crackling, and did so prick my skin through the tick, that I could not sleepe: The next morning I was furnish'd with an Asse (for we could not get horses) but without stirrops, but we had ropes tied with a loope to put our feete in, that supplied other trappings, and thus with my gallant steede, bridld with my Turkish present, we pass'd thro a reasonable pleasant, but very narrow Vally, 'til we came to Duomo, where we rested, and having shew'd the Spanish passe, we brought from the Ambassador; The Governor would presse another on us: though onely that his Secretary might get a Croune: Here we exchang'd our Asses for Mules sure footed on the hills and precipices, as accustom'd to passe them, and with a Guide, which now we hired, we were brought that night, through very steepe, craggy, and dangerous passages, to a Village cal'd Vedra, being the last of the King of Spaines Dominion in the Dutchy of Milan a very infamous wretched lodging:

Crossing the Simplon in May

Next morning we mount againe through strange, horrid and firefull Craggs and tracts abounding in Pine trees, and onely inhabited with Beares, Wolves, and Wild Goates, nor could we any where see above a pistol shoote before us, the horizon being terminated with rocks, and mountaines, whose tops cover'd with Snow seem'd to touch the Skies, and in many places pierced the Clowdes. Some of these vast mountaines were but one intire stone, 'twixt whose clefts now and then precipitated greate Cataracts of Mealted Snow, and other Waters, which made a tirrible roaring, Echoing from the rocks and Cavities, and these Waters in some places, breaking in the fall, wett us as if we had pas'd through a mist, so as we could neither see, nor heare one another, but trusting to our honest Mules, jog on our Way: The narrow bridges in some places, made onely by felling huge Fir-trees and laying them athwart from mountaine to mountaine, over Cataracts of stupendious depth, are very dangerous, and so are the passages and edges made by cutting away the maine rock: others in steps, and in some places we passe betweene mountaines that have ben broken and falln upon one another, which is very tirrible, and one had neede of a sure foote, and steady head to climb some of these precipices, harbours for the Beares, and Woulv[e]s, who sometimes have assaulted Travellers: In these straits we frequently alighted, freezing in the Snow, and anon frying by the reverberation of the Sun against the Cliffs as we descend lower, where we meete now and then a few miserable Cottages, built so upon the declining of the rocks, as one would expect their sliding down: Amongst these inhabite a goodly sort of People having monstrous Gullets or Wenns of flesse growing to their throats, some of which I have seene as big as an hundred pound bag of silver hanking under their Chinns; among the Women especialy, and that so ponderous, as that to Ease them, they many of them were [a] linnen cloth, bound about their head and coming under the chin to support it, but *quis tumidum guttur miratur in Alpibus*? Their drinking so much snow water is thought to be the Cause of it, the men using more wine, are not so strumous as the Women: but the very truth is, they are a race of people, and many greate Water-drinkers here have not those prodigious tumors: It runs as we say in the bloud, and is a vice in the race, and renders them so ougly, shrivel'd and deform'd, by its drawing the skin of the face downe, that nothing can be more fritefull; to which add a strange puffing habit, furrs, and barbarous Language, being a mixture of corrupt high German, French, and Italian: The people are of gigantic Stature, extreamely fierce and rude, yet very honest and trustie: This night, through unaccessible heights, we came in prospect of Mons Sempronius, now Mount Sampion, which has on its summit a few hutts, and a Chapell: Approching this, Captaine Wrays Water Spaniel, (a huge filthy Curr, that had follow'd him out of England), hunted an heard of Goates downe the rocks, into a river made by the dissolutions of the Snow: Ariv'd at our cold harbour (though the house had in every roome a Stove), supping with Cheeze and Milke and wretched wine to bed we go in Cupbords, and so high from the floore, that we climb'd them by a Ladder, and as we lay on feathers, so are Coverd with them, that is, betweene two tickes stuff'd with feathers, and all little enough to keepe one warme: The Ceilings of the roomes are strangely low for those tall people.

Captain Wray's Adventure

The house was now . . . halfe cover'd with Snow, nor is there ever a tree or bush growing in many miles: from this unhospitable place then we hasted away early next morning, but as we were getting on our Mules, comes a huge young fellow, demanding mony for a Goate, Cap: Wrays Dog (he affirm'd) had kild the other day: expostulating the matter, and impatient of staying in the Cold, we set spurrs and endeavor'd to ride away, when a multitude of People, being by this time gotten together about us (it being Sonday morning and attending for the Priest to say Masse) stop our Mules, beate us off our saddles and imediately disarming us of our Carbines, drew us into one of the roomes of our Lodging, and set a guard upon us. Thus we continu'd Prisoners til Masse was ended, and then came there halfe a Score grimm Swisse, and taking upon them to be Magistrates, sate downe on the Table, and condemn'd us to pay the fellow a pistol for his Goate, and ten more for attempting to ride away: Threatning that if we did not do it speedily they would send us to another Prison, and keep us to a day of publique Justice, where, as they perhaps would have exaggerated the Crime, for they pretended we span'd our Carbines and would have shot some of them (as indeede the Captaine, was about to do) we might have had our heads cut off, for amongst these barbarous people, a very small misdemeanor dos often meete that animadversion: This we were afterwards told; and though the proceeding appeerd highly unjust, upon Consultation among ourselves, we thought it safer to rid our selves out of their hands, and the trouble we were brought in, than to expostulate it among such brutes, and therefore we patiently lay'd downe the mony, and with fierce Countenances had our Mules, and armes deliverd us, and glad to scape as we did: This was cold entertainement, but our journey after was colder, the rest of the Way having (tis sai'd) ben cover'd with Snow since the Creation; for that never man remember'd it to be without; and because by the frequent Snowing, the tracks are continualy fill'd up, we passe by severall tall Masts, set up, to guide Those who travell, so as for many miles they stand in ken of one another, like to our Beacons: In some places of divided Mountaines, the Snow quite fills up the Cleft, whilst the bottome being thaw'd, leaves it as it were a frozen Arch of Snow, and that so hard, as to beare the greatest weight, for as it snows often so it perpetualy freezes, and of this I was so sensible, as it flaw'd the very skin of my face: Beginning now to descend a little, Cap: Wrays horse, that was our Sumpter, (and carried all our bagage) plunging thro a bank of loose Snow, slid downe a firefull precipice, more than thrice the height of St Paules, which so incens'd the Cholerique Cavalier his Master, that he was sending a brace of bullets into the poore beast, least the Swisse, that was our Guide, should recover him and run away with his burden: but just as his hand was lifting up his Carbine, We gave such a Shout, and pelted the horse so with Snow balls, as with all his might plunging thro the Snow, he fell from another steepe place into another bottome neere a path we were to passe: It was yet a good while 'ere we got to him, but at last we recovered the place, and easing him of his Charge, hal'd him out of the Snow, where he had ben certainely frozen in, if we had not prevented it before night: It was (as we judg'd) almost two miles that he had slid and fall'n, and yet without any other harme, than the benumming of his limbs for the present, which with lusty rubbing and chafing he began to move, and after a little walking perform'd his journey well enough: All this Way (affrited with the dissaster of the Captaines horse) we trudg'd on foote, driving our Mules before us: and sometimes we fell, and sometimes slid thro this ocean of featherd raine, which after October is impassible: Towards night we came into a larger way, thro vast woods of Pines which cloth the middle parts of these rocks: here they were burning some to make Pitch and Rosin, piling the knotty branches, as we do to make Char-Coale, and reserving that which mealts from them, which harden into Pitch etc: and here we passd severall Cascads of dissolv'd Snow, that had made Channels of formidable depth in the Crevices of the Mountaines, and with such a firfull roaring, as for 7 long miles we could plainely heare it: It is from these Sourses, that the swift and famous Rhodanus, and the Rhyne which passe thro all France, and Germanie, derive their originals.

Late at night then we got to a Towne call'd Briga which is build at the foote of the Alpes in the Valtoline: Every doore almost had nailed on the outside, and next the Streete, a Beares, Wolfes or foxes-head and divers of them all Three, which was a Salvage kind of sight: but as the Alps are full of these beasts, the People often kill them:

The Upper Rhône Valley

The next morning we return'd our Guide, and tooke fresh Mules and another to conduct us to the Lake of Geneva, passing through as pleasant a Country, as that which before we had traveld, was melancholy and troublesome, and a strange and suddaine change it seem'd, for the reverberation of the Sunbeames darting from the Mountaines and rocks, that like a Wall range it on both sides, not above 2 flight shots in bredth for some hundreds of miles; renders the passage excessively hot: through such extreames we continud our Journey, whilst that goodly river the Rhone glided by us in a narrow and quiet chanell, almost in the middle of this Canton, and fertilizing the Country for Grasse and Corne which growes here in aboundance, for the Snow which waters it from the hills, brings downe with it a fertil liquor that dos wonderfully impregnat.

Sion

We ariv'd this night at a very pretty Towne, and Citty, for Sion (that is its name) is a Bishops seate, and the head of Valesia, and has a Castle: The Bishop who resides in it, has both Civile and Ecclesiastical Jurisdiction, and here our Host, (as the costome of these Cantons is) was one of the chiefest of the Towne, and having heretofore ben a Colonell in France us'd us exstreame Civily; being so displeas'd at the barbarous usage we received at Mount Sampion, as he would needes give us a letter, to the Governour of the Country, who resided at St. Maurice (which was in our Way to Geneva) to revenge the affront: This was a true old blade, and had

ben a very curious Virtuoso, as we found by an handsome collection
of Books, Medails, Pictures, Shells and other Antiquities; amongst
other things he shew'd us two heads and hornes of the true
Capricorne, which he told us, were frequently kill'd among the
Mountaines: One branch of them was as much as I could well lift,
and neere as high as my head, not much unlike the greater sort of
Goates, save that they bent forewards, by help whereof they climb
up, and hang on inaccessible rocks, from whence they now and
then shoote them, and spake prodigious things of their leaping
from crag to crag, and of their sure footing, notwithstanding their
being cloven footed, unapt on[e] would think to take hold, and
walke so steadily on those tirrible ridges as they do: On[e] of these
beames, the Coll: would have bestowed on me, but the want of a
Convenience to carry it along with me, caus'd me to refuse his
courtesie: He told me that in the Castle there were some Roman
and Christian Antiquities; and some Inscriptions he had in his
owne Garden; but our time being short I could not perswad my
Companions to stay and visite the places he would have had us
seene, nor the offer he made to shew us the hunting of the Beare,
Wolfe, and other wild beasts; inviting us to his Country house,
where he told us he had better Pictures, and other rarities: A more
debonaire brave Gentleman I never saw, nor could possibly expect
to find in this rude Country and among the blunt Swisse:
Wherefore the next morning, having presented his daughter (a
pretty Virgin, and well fashion'd) a small rubie ring, we parted
somewhat late from our generous Host: Passing through the same
pleasant valy, continue'd betweene the horrid mountaines on either
hand, and lying like a Gallery for many miles in length, and so got
to Martigni where we were also well entertain'd: The Houses in
this Country are all built of firr boards plain'd within, low and
seldom of above one storie: The People very Clownish, and
rustickly clad, after a very odd fashion, for the most part in blew
cloth, very whole and warme, nor with almost any variety or
distinction, twixt the gentlemen and common sort, by a law of their
Country, being exceedingly frugal: so as I saw not one begger
among them; add to this their greate honestie and fidelitie, though
exacting enough for what they part with: We paied the value of 20
shill: English for a days hire of one horse: Every man gos with a
sword by his side, and the whole Country well disciplind, and

indeede impregnable, which made the Romans have so ill successe against them; one lusty Swisse, at their narrow passages sufficient to repell a Legion: 'Tis a frequent thing here for a Young Trades man, or fermor to leave his Wife and Children for 12 or 15 Yeares, and seeke his fortune in the Warrs abroad in Spaine, France, Italy or Germanie and then returne againe to Work: I looke upon this Country, to be the safest spot of all Europ, neither Envyed, nor Envying, nor are any of them rich, nor poore; but live in greate Simplicity and tranquilitie, and though of the 14 Cantons halfe be Roman Catholics, the rest Reformed; yet they mutualy agree, and are confederate with Geneva and its onely security against its potent Neighbours: as their owne is, from being atack'd by the greater Potentates, by the Jealosie of their neighbours, who would be over balanc'd, should the Swisse (who now are wholy mercenarie, and Auxilliaries) be subj[e]cted to France or Spaine:

We were now ariv'd at St. Maurize, a large and handsome Towne, and residence of the President, where Justice is don: To him we presented our letter from Sion, and made known the ill usage we receiv'd for the killing of a wretched Goate; and which so incens'd him, as he sware, if we would stay, not onely to helpe us to our mony againe, but most severely to punish the whole rabble: but we were by this time past our revenge, and glad we were gotten so neere France, which we reckon'd as good as home: He courteously invited us to dine with him, but we excus'd ourselves, and returning to our Inn, whilst we were eating something before we tooke horse, the Governor had causd two pages to bring us a present of two huge Vessels of Cover'd Plate full of Excellent Wine, which we drank his health in, and rewarded the Youthes; The Plate were two vast boules, supported by 2 Swisses handsomly wrought after the German manner:

Evelyn Ill with Smallpox

This Civilitie, and that of our hosts at Sion, perfectly reconcild us to the hig[h]landers, and so proceeding on our journy, we passd this afternoone through the Gate which divides the Valois from the Dutchy of Savoy, into which we now were entering, and so thro Montei ariv'd that evening to Beveretta, where being extreamely weary, and complaining of my head, and little accommodation in the house, I caus'd one of our Hostesses daughters to be removed out of her bed, and went immediately into it, whilst it was yet warme, being so heavy with paine and drowsinesse, that I would not stay to have the sheetes chang'd; but I shortly after pay'd dearely for my impatience, falling sick of the Small Pox so soone as I came to Geneva; for by the smell of franc Incense, and the tale the good-woman told me, of her daughters having had an Ague, I afterwards concluded she had ben newly recoverd of the Small Pox: The paine of my head and wearinesse making me not consider of any thing, but how to get to bed so soone as ever I alighted, as not able any longer to sit on horseback: Notwithstanding this, I went with my Company the next day, hiring a bark to carry us over the Lake Lacus Lemanus, and indeede, sick as I was, the Weather was so serene and bright, the Water so Calme, and aire temperate, that, never had Travelers a sweeter passage: Thus we saild the whole length of the Lake, for about 30 miles, The Countries bordering on it, Savoy and Bearne, affording one of the most delightfull prospects in the World, the Alps, cover'd with Snow, though at greate distance, yet shewing their aspiring tops: They speake of Monsters and Tritons often seene in this Lake. Through this Lake, the River Rhodanus passes with that velocity as not to mingle with its exceeding deepe waters, which are very cleare, and breedes the most celebrated Troute, for largenesse and goodnesse of any in all Europ: I have ordinarily seene one of 3 foote in length, sold in the Merket for a small Price: and such we had in the Lodging where we abode, which was at the White Crosse: All this while I held up tollerably, and the next morning (having a letter for Signor John Diodati the famous Italian Minister, and Translator of the Holy Bible into that Language) I went to his house, and had a greate deale of discourse with that learned person: He told me he had ben in England, droven by Tempest into Deale, sailing for Holland, had seene London, and was exceedingly taken with the Civilities he receivd: He so much approv'd of our Church Government by Bishops; that he told me, The French Protestants would make no Scruple to submitt to it, and all its pomp, had they a King of the reform'd Religion, as we had: he exceedingly deplord, the difference now betweene his Majestie and his Parliament: After dinner came one Monsieur Saladine (with his little Pupil the Earle of Carnarvon) to visite us, offering to carry us to the Principal places of the Towne: But being now no more able to hold up my head, I was constrain'd to keepe my Chamber, imagining that my very eyes would have droped out, and this night felt such a stinging all about me that I could not sleepe: In the morning I was very ill: yet for all that, the Doctor (whom I had now consulted, and was a very learned old man, and as he sayd had ben Physition to Gustavus the greate King of Sweden, when he pass'd this way into Italy, under the name of Monsieur Garse, the Initial letters of Gustavus Adolphus Rex Sueciæ, and of our famous Duke of Boukingham returning out of Italy) perswaded me to be let bloud, which he accknowledg'd to me he should not have don, had he suspected the Small-Pox, which brake out a [day] after; for he also purg'd me, and likewise applied Hirudines ad anum, and God knows what this had produc'd if the spots had not appeard: for he was thinking of blouding me againe: Wherefore now they kept me warme in bed for 16 daies, tended by a vigilant Swisse Matron whose monstrous Throat, when I sometimes awake'd out [of] unquiet slumbers would affright me: After the pimples were come forth, which were not many, I had much ease, as to paine, but infinitly afflicted with the heate and noysomenesse; But by Gods mercy, after five weekes keping my Chamber, being purg'd, and visited by severall of the Towne: espec[i]aly Monsieur Saladine and his Lady, who sent me many refreshments, during my sicknesse: Monsieur Le Chat (my Physitian) to excuse his letting me bloud, told me it was so burnt and vitious, as it would have prov'd the Plague or spoted feavor, had he proceeded by any other method:

Geneva

The next day after my going abroad, I din'd at Mr. Saladines, and in the afternoone, went crosse the Water on the side of the Lake, to take a Lodging that stood exceeding pleasantly, about halfe a mile off the Citty, for better ayring; but I onely stayd one night, having no Company there save my Pipe; so as the next day, I causd them to row me about the Lake, as far as the greate Stone, which they call Neptunes rock, on which they say, Sacrifice was antiently offer'd to him: Thence I landed at certaine Chery-Gardens, and pretty Villas situate on the rivage, and exceedingly pleasant: Returning I visited their Conservatories of Fish, in which were Trouts of 6 and 7 foote long as they affirm'd: The River Rhone, which parts the Citty in the midest, dips into a Cavern under ground, about 6 miles from it, and afterwards rises againe, and runns its open Course, like our Mole or Swallow by Darking in Surrey. Next morning (being Thursday) I heard Dr. Diodati preach in Italian, many of that Country, especialy of his native Lucca being Inhabitants at Geneva, and of the Reformd religion: And now I was intent about seeing the Towne, which lies betweene Germanie, France, and Italy, so as those three Tongues are familiarly spoken by the Inhabitans: 'Tis a strong, well fortified Citty, part of it built on a rising ground; The houses are not despicable, but the high pent-houses (for I can hardly call them Cloysters) being all of wood; thro which the people passe drie, and in the shade winter and summer, exceedingly deforme the fronts of the buildings: Here are aboundance of Booke-Sellers, but Ill Impressions: These with Watches (of which store are made here), Chrystal, and excellent Screw'd Gunns, are the staple commodities: and all Provisions are good and cheape: One of the first things I went to see after I was gotten abroad, was the Towne-house, fairely built of stone . . .

The Territories about the Towne are not so large as many ordinary gentlemen have about their Country farmes; for which cause they are in continual watch, especialy on the Savoy side; but in case [of] any seige the Swisse are at hand . . . They shew'd us in this Senat house 14 antient Urnes, dug up as they were removing Earth in the fortifications:

Hence we walked a little out of Towne, to a spacious field, which they call Campus Martius, and well it may so be term'd, with better reason, than that of Rome at present, (which is no more a field, but all built into streetes) for here on every Sonday after the Evening devotions, this precise people, permitt their Youth to exercise Armes, and shoote in Gunns, and in the long and Crosse bowes, in which they are exceedingly expert, as reputed to be as dextrous as any people in the world; To encourage which, they yearely elect he that has won most prizes at the mark, to be their King: as the King of the Long bow, Gun, or Crosse-bow who weares that weapon in his hat in gold, with a crowne over it, made fast to the hatt like a broach: There is in this fild a long house wherein in severall presses, are kept their Armes, and furniture very neately; to which joynes a Hall, where on certaine times they meete and feast, and in the glasse windos, are the Armes and names of their Kings: At the side of the fild is a very noble Pall-Mall, but it turnes with an elbow; Also a bowling Place, a Tavern, and a True-table, and here they likewise ride their menag'd Horses; and it is the usual place of publique Execution, who suffer here, for any capital crime, tho committed in another Country, by which Law, divers fugitives have ben put to death, who have repaird hither for protection: amongst other severe punishments, Adultery is death: Having seene this field, and playd a game at Mall, I supp'd at Mr. Saladines. On Sonday, I heard Dr. Diodati preach in French and after the French mode in a Gowne with a Cape, and his hat on: The Church Government is severely Presbyterian; after the discipline of Calvine and Beza, who set it up; but nothing so rigid, as either our Scots, or English Sectaries of that denomination: In the afternoone Mon-sieur Morise a Young most learned person, and excellent Poet, chiefe Professor of the University: This was in St. Peters, heretofore a Cathedral, and a reverend pile: I[t] has 4 Turrets, on which stands a continual Sentinel, on another Cannons mounted: The Church within is very decent, nor have they at all defac'd the painted windows, which are full of Saints pictures, nor the Stalls, which are all carved with the Historie of our B: Saviour: a Spacious Church, of Gotic fabric:

In the afternoone I went to see the young townes men exercise in Mars field, where the Prizes were pewter plates, and dishes: 'Tis said that some have gain'd competent Estates, by what they have thus won: Here I first saw huge Balistæ or Crosse bows (such as they formerly us'd in wars, before Greate guns were known) shot in: They were placed in frames, and had might[y] screws to bend them, doing execution an incredible distance. They are most accurate at the long-bow, and Musquet, very rarely missing the smalest mark; and I was as buisy with the Carbine I brought with me from Bressia as any of them: After every shot, I found them go into the long house and clense their guns before they charg'd againe.

On Moneday I was invited to a little Garden without the Workes, where were many rare Tulips, Anemonies and other choice flowers: The [Rhodanus] running 'thwart the Towne out of the Lake, makes halfe the Citty Suburbs, [which] (in imitation of Paris) they call St. Germans fauxbourg, and it has a church of the same name: On Two Wooden bridges that go Crosse the river, are severall water Mills, and shops of Trades, especialy Smiths and Cuttlers, and betweene the bridges an Iland, in the midst of which a very antient Tower, said to be built by Julius Cæsar, at the end of the other bridge is the Mint, and a faire sun-dial.

. . .

Captain Wray in Love

[July] Whilst we thus linger'd in this famous Towne, not very much celebrated for beauties, (for even at this distance from the Alps, the gentlewomen have something full Throates,) our Captaine Wray, (afterwards Sir Will: Wray, eldest son to that Sir Christopher, who had ben both in armes against his Majesty for the Parliament) fell so mightily in love with one of Monsieur Saladines daughters, that with much perswasion, could he be gotten to think of his journey, into France, the season now coming on extreamly hot: My sicknesse and abode here cost me 45 pistols of gold to my Host, and 5 to my honest Doctor, who for 6 Weekes attendance and the Apothecarie, thought it so generous a reward, that at my taking leave, he presented me with his advice for the regiment of my health, written with his own hand in Latine.

. . .

Return to Paris

But I blesse God, I pass'd this Journey without any of these inconveniences, yet much observing the regiment prescribed me: It was an extraordinary hot, unpleasant season, and journey by reason of the Craggie Waies: The morning after we tooke, or rather purchased a boate, for it could not be brought back againe, because of the streame of the Rhodanus running here about. Thus were we two days going to Lions, passing by many admirable Prospects of Rocks and Cliffs, and neare the towne, down a very steepe declivitie of Water, for a full mile: From Lions, we proceeded the next morning, taking horse to Rohan, and lay that night at Tarrara: At Rohan it was we indulged ourselves, with the best that all France affords; for here the provisions are choice and plentifull: so as the supper we had, might have satisfied a Prince: We lay that night in Damask bedds (at Monsieur de Loups) and were treated like Emperours:

This Town is one of the neatest built in all France, on the brink of Loire and here we agreede with an old fisher, to row us as farr [as] Orleans:

The first night came we to Nevers, early enough to see the Towne, the Cathedral St. Cyre; the Jesuits Colledge, the Castle, or Palac of the Dukes, with the bridge to it is nobly built. Next day we past by La Charite, a pretty towne somewhat distant from the River, and here it was I lost my faithfull Spaniel (Piccoli) who had follow'd me from Rome; it seemes he had ben taken up by some of the Governors pages or foote-men, without recovery, which was a greate dis-pleasure to me, because the curr, had many usefull qualities: The next day we ariv'd at Orleans, taking our turn to row through all the former passages, and reckoning that my share amounted to little lesse than 20 legues; sometimes footing it through pleasant fields and medows, sometimes we shot at fouls and other birds, nothing came amisse, sometimes we play'd at Cards, whilst other sung, or were composing Verses; for we had the greate Poet Mr. Waller in our Companie, and some other ingenious Persons: At Orleans we abode but one day, the next (leaving our mad Captaine behind us) I arived at Paris, strangely rejoyc'd, after so many dissasters, and accidents, of a tedious Peregrination, that I was gotten so neere home, and therefore resolved to rest myselfe before I set on any farther Motion.

It was now October, and the onely time that in my whole life I spent most idly, tempted from my more profitable recesses; but I soone recovered my better resolutions, and fell to my study, and learning of the high-dutch and Spanish tongues, and now and then refreshing my Dauncing, and such exercises as I had long omitted, and which are not in such reputation among the sober Italians.

1647. January 28, I chang'd my Lodging in the Place de Monsieur de Metz neere the Abby of St. Germains, and thençe on the 12 feb: to another in Rüe Collumbiers, where I had a very faire Appartment, which cost me 4 pistols per Moneth: The 18 I frequented a Course of Chymistrie, the famous Monsieur Le Febure operating upon most of the Nobler processes: 3 March, Monsieur Mercure began to teach me on the Lute, though to small perfection.

In May I fell sick and had very sore Eyes, for which I was 4 times let blood. The 22d: My Valet de Chambre Hebert robbed me of the value of threescore pounds in Clothes and plate; but through the dilligence of Sir Richard Browne his Majesties Resident at the Court of France and with whose Lady and family I had contracted a greate Friendship (and particularly set my affections on a Daughter) I recoverd most of them againe; obtaining of the Judge (with no small difficulty) that the processe against my Theife, should not concerne his life, being his first fault.

Marriage: Paris and London
1647–1652

June 10th: We concluded about my Marriage, in order to which on 26: I went to St. Germans, where his Majestie (then Prince of Wales) had his Court, to desire of Dr. Earles, then one of his Chaplaines, and since, Deane of Westminster, Clearke of the Closset and Bishop of Salisburie, to come with me to Paris.

So on Thursday 27 June 1647 the Doctor Married us in Sir Richard Browne Knight and Baronet My Wifes fathers Chapell, twixt the houres of 11 and 12 some few select friends being present: And this being Corpus Christ feast, solemn[l]y observ'd in these Countries, the stretes were sumptuously hung with Tapissry, and strew'd with flowers.

July 13, I went with my Wife, and her Mother, to St. Cloud, where we collation'd, and were serv'd in Plate:

September 10th, being call'd into England to settle my affaires, after about 4 yeares absence (my Wife being yet very Young, and therefore dispensing with a temporarie and kind separation, whilst left under the care of an excellent Lady, and prudent Mother) I tooke leave of the Prince, and Queene:

Return to England

Octob: 4: I seald and declard my Will: and that morning went from Paris taking my journey thro Rouen, Dieppe, Ville-Dieu, St. Vallerie, where I staied one day, with Mr. Waller, with whom I had some affaires, and for which cause I tooke this Circle to Calice, where I ariv'd on the 11th and that night Imbarking in the Paquet-boate, was by one aclock gott safe to Dover; for which I heartily put up my Thankes to God, who had conducted me safe to my owne Country, and ben mercifull to me through so many aberrations: Hence taking Post, I ariv'd at London the next day at Evening, being the 2d of October New-style.*

On the 4th my Bro: George hearing where I was sent me horses and a kind Invitation, so on the 5t I came to Wotton the place of my Birth, where I found his Lady, my Sister, and severall of my friends and relations, amongst whom I refresh'd my selfe and rejoyc'd 'til the 10th, when I went to Hampton Court, wher I had the honour to kisse his Majesties Hand, and give him an Account of severall things I had in charge, he being now in the power of those execrable Villains who not long after mu[r]der'd him: Here I lay at my Co: Searjeant Hattons at Thames Ditton whence on the 13 I went to London, the next day to Sayes-Court (now my house) at Deptford in Kent, where I found Mr. Pretyman my Wifes Unkle, who had charge of it, and the Estate about it during my F in Laws Residence in France: on the 15th I went to lodge in my owne Chambers at the Middle Temple about the dispatch of my particular concernes. November the 7th I return'd againe to Wotton to visite my brother, and on the 9th my Sister, opened to me her Marriage with Mr. Glanvill: December 3: I went back to Deptford, and the next day to London, where I staied till 1648 January 14th when I went to Wotton to see my young Nephew, and thence to Baynards to visite my Bro: Richard, who came back with me on the 18th and stayd 'til 29, before my returne to London.

. . .

Aprill 3. I went to Wotton, thence to a place neere Henly cald Boyne, belonging to one Mr. Elmes, which I thought to have purchas'd and settled in; but we did not accord: So on the 5t I return'd, and the 10th to Lond:

26. There was a greate up-rore in Lond, that the Rebell Armie quartering at Whitehall would plunder the Cittie, who publish'd a proclamation for all to stand on their guard:

May: 4 Came-up the Essex petitioners for an agreement 'twixt his Majestie and the Rebells. 16 The Surry men addressd to the Parliament for the same, of which some were slayne and murder'd by Cromwells guards in the new Palace yard.

I now sold, the Impropriation of South Malling neere Lewes in Sussex to Mr. Kemp and Alcock for 3000 pounds:

23 I went to Deptford, and 30: to Lond: 29: to Dept: 30: Lond: about buisinesse:

There was a rising now in Kent, my Lord of Norwich being in the head of them and their first rendezvous in Broome-fild, next my house at Says-Court whence they went to Maidstone, and so to Colchester where there was that memorable siege:

June 27: I purchas'd the Manor of Hurcott in Worcestershire of my Bro: Geo: for 3300 pounds: on the 29 I return'd to Deptford.

. . .

Aug: 10th To Lond, return'd: 16 To Woodcoat to the Wedding of my Bro: Richard who married the Daughter and Coheire, of Esquire Minn lately deceased: by which he had a greate Estate both in Land and monie, upon the death of a Brother etc: Memorandum that the Coach in which the Bride and Bridegroome were, was over-turn'd in coming home, but no harme: 19 I return'd to Sayes-Court and: 22: to Lond: 25 return'd: 28 To Lond, and went to see the celebrated follies of Bartholomew faire.

September 8. I returnd to Deptford: 16 Came my lately married Bro: Richard and his Wife to visite me: 17 I shewed them Greenewich and her Majesties Palace, now possessd by the Rebells: 18 Went my Unkle Pretyman into France, and my Bro: return'd home. 25 I went to Lond: and next day to Wotton: 28 to Alburie to visite the Countesse of Arundel, return'd to Wotton. 30th To Woodcot and the 3d of Octob: to Lond: 7 to Says Court: 13 To Lond: 20 Return'd, next day came my Bro: Richd: with whom I went to Woodcot and on 26: To Lewes, in which journey I escaped a strange fall from my horse in the dark, from an high bank and deepe way about Chaylie: 31 I went to see my Mannor of Preston Beckhelvyn, and the Cliff house:

. . .

Decemb: 2: I lent 1000 pounds to Esquire Hyldiard on a statute: and this day sold my Mannor of [Hurcott] for 3400 pounds to one Mr. Bridges and on the 4th acknowlegd the fine.

4th I lent 1000 pounds to my Lord Vicount Montague, on a [Mortgage] of Horslay, in Surry: 10 I went to Deptford: 13 to Lond: The Parliament now sat up the whole night, and endeavord to have concluded the Ile of Wight Treaty, but were surprizd by the rebell Army, the Members disperssd, and greate confusion every where in expectation what would be next: I now also gave Mr. Christmas a Receipt for 5000 pounds which being deposited in his hands, had ben repay'd me at severall times.

. . .

'Horrid villanies' at Whitehall

18. I gott privately into the Council of the rebell Army at Whitehall, where I heard horrid villanies: 20: I return'd to Sayes-Court: 28 my Bro: George came and dined with me: Memorand This was a most exceeding wett yeare, neither frost or snow all the winter for above 6 days in all, and Cattell died of a Murrain every where:

... [1649. January] 13 I returned to S. Court: 17: To Lond: I heard the rebell Peters incite the Rebell powers met in the Painted Chamber, to destroy his Majestie and saw that Arch Traytor Bradshaw, who not long after condemn'd him. On the 19 I return'd home, passing an extraordinary danger of being drown'd, by our Whirries falling fowle in the night, on another vessell there at Anker, shooting the Bridge at 3 quarter Ebb, for which his mercy, God Almighty be prais'd.

21. was published my Translation of Liberty and Servitude, for the Preface of which I was severely threatn'd: 22d I went through a Course of Chymistrie at S. Court and now was the Thames frozen over, and horrid Tempest of Winds, so different was this part of the Winter from the former:

The King Murdered

The Villanie of the Rebells proceeding now so far as to Trie, Condemne, and Murder our excellent King, the 30 of this Moneth, struck me with such horror that I kept the day of his Martyrdom a fast, and would not be present, at that execerable wickednesse; receiving that sad [account] of it from my Bro: Geo: and also by Mr. Owen, who came to Visite this afternoone, recounting to me all Circumstances.

...

Art Collecting

[February 15] Web, at the Exchange has some rare things in miniature of Breugls, also Puti in 12 Squares, that were plunderd from Sir James Palmer: At Du Bois we saw 2 Tables of Puti, that were gotten I know not how, out of the Castle of St. Angelo by old Petit, thought to be Titians, he has some good heads of Palma, and one of Stenewick:

Bellcan shewd us an excellent Copy of his Majesties Venus

Sleeping, and the Satyre, with other figures; for now they had plunderd sold and dissipat[e]d a world of rare Paintings of the Kings and his Loyall Subjects: After all Sir William Ducy shewd me some excellent things in Miniature, and in Oyle of Holbeins Sir Tho: Mores head, and an whole figure of Ed: the Sixt: which were certainely his Majesties; also a Picture of Q: Elizabeth, the Lady Isabella Thynn, a rare painting of Rotenhamer being a Susanna, and a Magdalena of Quintine the black-smith. Also an Hen: 8th of Holben, and Francis the first rare indeede, but of whose hand I know not:

Paris Besieged

16: Paris being now streitly besieged by the Pr: of Condy, my wife being with her Father and Mother shut up, I writ to comfort her: next day went back to Says-Court . . .

27 Came out of France my Wifes Unkle, (Paris still besieg'd): being rob'd by sea of the Dynkirk Pyrats, I lost among other goods my Wifes Picture painted by Monsieur Bourdon: 28: Lond:

• • •

[March] 21 I receiv'd letters from Paris from my Wife and Sir Richard, with whom I kept a political Correspondence, with no small danger of being discover'd:

• • •

Aprill 2. To Lond, and Inventoried my Moveables, that had hitherto ben dispers'd for feare of Plundering: and writ into France touching my suddaine resolutions of coming over to them . . .

• • •

France Again

[July] 12 accompanied by my Co: Stephens, and my Sister Glanvill, who there supp'd with me, and return'd: Whence I tooke post immediately to Dover, where I arived by 9 in the morning, and about 11 that night went on board in a bark, Guarded by a Pinnace of 8 gunns, this being the first time the Pacquett boate had obtain'd a Convoy, having severall times before ben pillag'd: I carried over with me my Servant Ri: Hoare an incomparable writer of severall hands, whom I afterwards preferrd in the Prerogative Office, at returne of his Majestie. We had a good passage, though chased by a Pyrate for some houres, but he Durst not attaque our fregat and so left us: But we then chased them, til they got under the protection of the Castle at Calais: The vessell was a small Privateere belonging to the Prince of Wales: I was very sick at Sea, till about 5 in the morning that we landed, before the Gates were open: and so [did] my Lady Catherine Scot daughter to the Earle of Norwich, that follow'd us in a Shallop, with one Mr. Arth: Slingsby, who came out of England Incognito. At entrance of the Towne, the Lieutennant Governor being on his horse with the Guards let us passe Courteously: I went to visite Sir Richard Lloyd an English Gent: in the Towne, and walked in the Church, where the Ornament about the high Altar of black-marble is very fine, and there is a good picture of the Assumption: The Citadell seemes to be impregnable, and the whole Country about it, to be laied under Water by sluces for many miles.

16 We departed for Paris, in company with that pleasant Lady, Scott, one Slingsby, and a Spanish don call'd Sanchez whom I found to be a very good Schollar, and one that had seen the World: The 2d days Journey passing through Marquise there being a Faire that day, I lost a Spaniel which I brought with me out of England, taken up I suppose by the Souldiers: We were in all this Journey greately apprehensive of Parties, which caused us to alight often out of our Coach, and walke separately on foote with our Guns ready, in all suspected places.

1. August 3 afternoone we came to St. Denis, saw the rarities of the Church and Tresury and so to Paris in the Evening: The next day, came to Wellcome me at dinner my Lord High Treasure[r] Cottington, Sir Edw: Hide Chancellor, Sir Ed: Nicholas Secretary of State, Sir Geo: Cartret Governor of Jersey, Dr. Earles, having now ben absent from my Wife above a Yeare and halfe, and were very cherefull.

The rest of the Weeke was taken up with visites from, and to my friends: On the 18 I went to St. Germains to kisse his Majesties hands; In this Coach (which was my Lord Willmots), went Mrs. Barlow, the Kings Mistris and mother to the Duke of Monemoth, a browne, beautifull, bold, but insipid creature . . .

. . .

Cutting for the Stone

[1650.] 3 of May, at the Hospital of the Charitie, I saw the whole operation of Lithotomie namely 5 cut of the stone: There was one person of 40 years old had a stone taken out of him, bigger than a turkys Egg: The manner thus: The sick creature was strip'd to his shirt, and bound armes and thighs to an high Chaire, 2 men holding his shoulders fast down: then the Chirurgion with a crooked Instrument prob'd til he hit on the stone, then without stirring the probe which had a small chanell in it, for the Edge of the Lancet to run in, without wounding any other part, he made Incision thro the Scrotum about an Inch in length, then he put in his forefingers to get the stone as neere the orifice of the wound as he could, then with another Instrument like a Cranes neck he pull'd it out with incredible torture to the Patient, especially at his after raking so unmercifully up and downe the bladder with a 3d Instrument, to find any other Stones that may possibly be left behind: The effusion of blood is greate. Then was the patient carried to bed, and dress'd with a silver pipe accomodated to the orifice for the urine to passe, when the wound is sowed up: The danger is feavor, and gangreene, some Wounds never closing: and of this they can give shrewd conjecture by the smothnesse or ruggednesse of the stone: The stone pull'd forth is washed in a bason of water, and wiped by an attendant Frier, then put into a paper and writen on, which is also entred in a booke, with the name of the person, shape, weight etc of the stone, Day of the moneth, and Operator: After this person came a little Child of not above 8 or 9 yeares age, with much cherefullnesse, going through the operation with extraordinary patience, and expressing greate joy, when he saw the stone was drawn: The use I made of it, was to give Almighty God hearty thankes, that I had not ben subject to this Infirmitie, which is indeede deplorable:

An Adventure en Cavaliere

7. I went with my Lady Browne, and my Wife, together with the Earle of Chesterfield, Lord Ossorie and his Bro: to Vamber, a place neere the Citty, famous for the butter, when comming homewards (for we were on foote) my Lord Ossorie stepping into a Garden, the doore open; There step'd a rude fellow to it, and thrust my Lord, with uncivil language from entering in: upon this our young Gallants struck the fellow over the pate, and bid him aske pardon; which to our thinking he did with much submission, and so we

parted: but we were not gon far, but we heare a noise behind us, and saw people coming with gunns, swords, staves and forks, following, and flinging stones; upon which we turn'd and were forc'd to engage, and with our Swords, stones and the help of our servants, (one of which had a pistol), make our retreate for neere a quarter of a mile, when an house receiv'd us: by this time numbers of the baser people increasing, we got up into a turret, from whence we could discover their attempts, and had some advantage: however my L: Chesterfield was hurt in the face and back with a stone, his servant in the Eye and forehead, and Sir R: Bro: protecting his Lady with his Cloake, on the shoulder, and his Lady with such a blow on the head and side of her neck as had neere fell'd her: I myselfe was hurt on the shoulder: my servant La Roch (a stoute Youth) much hurt on the reines: 'Twas a greate mercy that though they were so many, they durst not come neere us with their hookes, and that their gunns did no Execution amongst us, tho fir'd: In the Scuffle one of them was thrust through the arme, another wounded, in his elbow, with his owne Gun, with which one of our Company struck him; We discharged one among them with our Pistol, what hurt it did [I] know not, and we had no more amunition: Being got up into the Turret and battail below over, they beset the house, but durst not attempt to come up, where they knew we had a trap-doore betweene us, whence we could easily repell them: At last, with much adoe, and making them understand the occasion of the quarell, we came to parlie, and the conclusion was, that we should all be that angry fellows prisoners: This we absolutely refuse'd: upon which they fell to attacque the house; but coming at last to consider that we might be persons of qualitie (for at first they tooke us for Burgers of Paris) the company began to slink away, and our Enemie to grow so mild, upon intercession of the Master of the house, and that we might come downe into the next chamber: I obtain'd leave also to Visite my Lord Hatton (comptroller of his Majesties Household) who with some others of our Companie, were taken prisoners in the flight, whom I found under 3 locks and as many doores one within another, in this rude fellows Masters house, who pretended to be steward to one Monsieur St. Germains one of the first Presidents of the grand Chamber de Parliament and a Canon of Notre Damme: In this Interim one of our Laquais escaping to Paris during the Scuffle;

went and caused the Bailife of St. Germains to come with his Guard and rescue us, which he did, accompanied with Sir Rob: Welch, Mr. Percy Church, and others, with Weapons, and immediately after Monsieur St. Germains himselfe, newes being brought him to Paris that his housekeeper was assaulted, upon which he expressd mighty revenge: But when he saw the Kings Officers, the Gentlemen and noblemen, with his Majesties Resident, and better understood the occasion, he was asham'd of the Accident, begging the fellows pardon, and desiring the Ladys to accept of their Submission, and a Supper at his house, whilst we found for all that, it grieved him to the heart, we had not ben some inferior persons, against whom he might have taken some more profitable advantage: The Bailife in the meanetime exaggerated the affront, (and indeede it was a greate one upon no manner of occasion offer'd on our part:) and would have fallen on the little towne, striking downe as many as he mett about the streetes and way. It was 10 a clock at night ere we got to Paris, guarded by Prince Griffith (a certaine Welch Hero, going under that name, and well knowne in England, for his extravagances) together with the Scholars of two Academies who came forth to assist and meete us on horseback; and would faine have alarm'd the Towne we received the affront from, which with much ado we prevented.

8: Deane Cousin preached on 5: Matt. 34. against using unlawfull meanes to escape persecution, applied to the calamity of our Nation

12 Complaint being come to the Queene and Court of France of the affront we had receiv'd at Vamber, The President was ordred to aske Sir R: Bro: his Majesties Resident, Pardon, and the fellow to make submission and be dismissd: There came along with him President Thou, the greate Thuanus's sonn and so all was composd: But I have often heard, that gallant Gent: my Lord Ossorie, affirme solemnly, that in all the Conflicts he was ever in at sea, or land (in the most desperate of both which he had often ben) he believed he was never in so much danger, as when these people rose against us: He was usd to call it the *Bataill de Vambre*, and remember it with a greate deale of Mirth, as an Adventure *en Cavaliere*.

...

A Visit to England

[June] 27 I seald my Will in presence of my Lord Stanhop and Mr. Radcliff etc and taking leave of my Wife and other friends, tooke horse for England, paying the Messager 8 pistols for me and my servant to Calais, seting out with 17 in Company well arm'd, some Portugezes, Swisse and French, whereof 6 were Captaines and Officers: We came the first night to Beaumont, next day to Baovais and lay at Poiz, and the next, without dining reach'd Abbeville, next din'd at Montrell, and proceeding met a Company of foote (being now within the inroades of the Parties, which dangerously infest this days Journey, from St. Omers and the Frontiers) which we drew very neere to, ready, and resolute to Charge through, and accordingly were ordered and led by a Captaine of our traine; but as we were on the speede, they cald out, and prov'd to be Scotch-men, newly landed and raisd men and few arm'd among them. This night we were well treated at Bollogne: Jun: 21 we march'd in good order, the passage being now exceeding dangerous, and got to Calais by a little after two: The sun did so scorch my face in this journey, as made all the Skin peele off: The 22d I din'd with Mr. Booth his Majesties Agent, and about 3 in the afternoone imbark'd in the Packet-boat (hearing there was a Pirate then also setting saile, we had security from molestation), and so with a faire S.W. Wind, in 7 houres we lande'd safe at Dover: The buisy Watch-man would have us to the Major to be searched, but the gent being in bed, we were dismiss'd: Next day being Sonday, they would not permit us to ride post, so that afternoone our Trunkes were visited, after which one Mr. De la Vall collation'd us: Next morning by 4 we set out for Canterbury, where I met with my La: Cathrine Scot whom that very day twelve moneth before, I met at Sea, going for France; she had ben visiting Sir Tho: Peyton, not far off, and would needes carry me in her Coach as far as Gravesend, with one Mr. Kingstone, that had long served the Venetian, and Duke of Parma: so dining at Sittinburne, we came late to Gravesend and so to Deptford, taking leave of my Lady about 4 the next morning extreamly weary. 27th I went to Lond: and was visited by severall friends: 1 July I paied 45 pounds to my Lady Hatton, so much taken up by me at Paris of my Lord her husband: 5. I supped in the Citty with my Lady K. Scot, at one Monsieur du bois's, where was a [Gentlewoman] cald Everard, that was a great Chymist: on the 7. I heard a Sermon at the Rolles Chapell on 1. Pet: 2. 7., relating to the Excellences of Christ. In the afternoone having a mind to see what doings was among the Rebells now in full possession at White-hall, I went thither, and found one at Exercise in the Chapell, after their Way, and thence to St. James's, where another was preaching in the Court abroad: having finish'd my businesse at London I return'd home where I found severall of my Wifes relations.

A Bathe at Wotton

... The Country was now much molested by Souldiers, who tooke away Gentlemens horses for the Service of the State as then call'd: 28 The Minister of Wotton preach'd on 6 Matt 13. on part of the Lords Prayer: 30 I din'd at Mr. Duncombs where I met many Gent: and Ladys, especialy one of them, viz. the Lady Ford, who was observ'd to Eate most prodigiously: After dinner I went to visite my Lord Vicount Montague, and returning to Wotton bath'd this Evening in the pond, after I had not for many years ben in cold Water ...

Channel Crossing: 'sufficiently discompos'd'

[August 12] I set out towards Paris, taking post at Gravesend, and so that night to Canterbury, where being Surpriz'd by the Souldiers, and having onely an antiquated passe, with some fortunate dexterity I got clear of them; though not without extraordinary hazard, having before counterfaited one, with successe, it being so difficult to procure one of the Rebells without entering into oathes, which I never would do, and at Dover Mony to the Searcher and officers was as authentique as the hand and Seale of Bradshaw himselfe. 13 I came to Dover, where I had not so much as my Trunk open'd: so at 6 in the Evening we set saile, the wind not favorable I was very sea-sick, coming to anker about one a Clock: about 5 in the morning we had a long-boate to carry us to land, though at good distance; this we willingly enter'd, because two Vessels were chasing us: but being now almost at the harbours mouth, through inadvertancy, there brake in upon us two such huge seas, as had almost sunk the boate, I being neere the middle up in Water: our steeres man, it seemes, apprehensive of the danger was preparing to leape into the sea, and trust his swimming: but seeing the vessell emerge, put her into the peere, and so God be thanked we got wet to Calais, where I went immediately to bed, sufficiently discompos'd: here I was visited by Sir Richard Lloyd. Next day (15: old. 25 New style) attending Company, (the passages towards Paris, being so infested with Volunteeres from the Spanish frontieres) I visited Collonel Fitz Williams and his Lady, who had ben the day before to see me: Then my Lord Strafford: I was also visited by Monsieur Zanches d Avila an acquaintance of mine. Next morning, the regiment of Picardy consisting of about 1400 horse and foote, and among them a Cap: whom I knew, being come to Towne; I tooke horses for myselfe and servant, and march'd under their Protection to Boulogne: 'Twas a miserable spectacle, to see how these tatter'd souldiers, pillag'd the poore people of their Sheepe, poultry, Corne, Catell, and whatever came in their Way: but they had such ill pay, that they were ready themselves to sterve: 27: I din'd at Montreull, and lay at Abb-Ville now past danger, and warning the poore people (infinitely inquisitive and thankfull) how the Souldiers treated their neighbours, and were marching towards them: The 28 we got to Pois, a Village belonging to the Mareshall de Crequey, it stands in a bottome, here we lay, dind next day at Bovais, lay at Beaumont, and so the 30, to Paris. As we pass'd St. Denis the people were in up-rore, the Guards doubl'd, and every body running with their goods and moveables to Paris; upon an Alarm'e that the Enemy was within 5 leagues of them; so miserably expos'd was even this part of France at this time: I lay this night at my old Hosts, in Rue Dauphine, and next morning went to see my Wife at her Fathers after 2 monethes absence onely.

. . .

'Batts as big as catts'

[October] 4 I went againe to see Monsieur Lincleres collection, to which was added, a new Grotto, and Bathing-place, hewe'd thro the buttments of the Arches of Pontnoeuf, into a wide vault, at the intercolumniation; so as the Coaches and horses thunder over on[e]s head: He assur'd me he found Batts as big as catts, and Ratts of a strange size:

I went this Evening to the Thuylleries, thence to the Palace of Orleans, in which I now tooke notice of that rich gilded and carved roofe in the Dukes Presence, with the Parquette'd floore: I had seldom seene a looking glasse of so large a size; The frame had a tree of Ivy twisted about it, in silver curiously wrought, and severall Tablets of historie enamell'd: Two fine Clocks on the table, and so returned home:

. . .

[November] 8 Monsieur Nanteuils presented me with my owne Picture, don all with a pen, an extraordinary curiosity . . .

. . .

Arab Customs

. . . [1651. January 8] After Evening Prayer came Mr. Wainsford to visite me, he had long ben Consul at Aleppo and told me many strange things of those Countries, the Arabs especialy: he affirm'd, that though they allowd common places of sinn; yet if any man of reputation had his daughter corrupted, he cutt her throat with his owne hands: That though the Arabs were poorely arm'd, they were capable of destroying the greatest powers of the Earth; by knowing how to cover, and conceale their Springs in those Sandy Deserts: That when their [Chief] will shew himselfe in State, all his greate men sit on their armour cover'd with a red Cloth: Their safty is their Excellent horses, [they] ride without Stirrops: dwell in long black Tents, made of a wooll like felt, that resists all weather: Their riches in Catell and Camels: Sometimes [they] threaten the Citties about them: Damascus itselfe pays them Contribution:

. . .

A Dromedary

. . . [February] 24 I went to se a Dromedarie, a very monstrous beast, much like the Camel, but larger, and with tufts of haire on the neck, knees, and thighs; and two bunches on its back about 3 foote one from the other . . .

. . .

Torture Observed

[March] 11 This morning I went to the Chastlett or prison, where a Malefactor was to have the Question or Torture given to him, which was thus: They first bound his wrists with a strong roope or smalle Cable, and one end of it to an iron ring made fast to the wall about 4 foote from the floore, and then his feete, with another cable, fastned about 6 foote farther than his uttmost length, to another ring on the floore of the roome, thus suspended, and yet lying but a slant; they slid an horse of wood under the rope which bound his feete, which so exceedingly stiffned it, as severd the fellows joynts in miserable sort, drawing him out at length in an extraordinary manner, he having onely a paire of linnen drawers on his naked body: Then they question'd him of a robery, (the Lieutennant Criminal being present, and a clearke that wrot) which not Confessing, they put an higher horse under the rope, to increase the torture and extension: In this Agonie, confessing nothing, the Executioner with a horne (such as they drench horses with) struck the end of it into his mouth, and pour'd the quantity of 2 boaketts of Water downe his throat, which so prodigiously swell'd him, face, Eyes ready to start, brest and all his limbs, as would have pittied and almost affrited one to see it; for all this he denied all was charged to him: Then they let him downe, and carried him before a warme fire to bring him to himselfe, being now to all appearance dead with paine. What became of him I know not, but the Gent: whom he robbd, constantly averrd him to be the man; and the fellows suspicious, pale lookes, before he knew he shold be rack'd, betraid some guilt: The Lieutennant was also of that opinion, and told us at first sight (for he was a leane dry black young man) he would conquer the Torture and so it seemes they could not hang him; but did use in such cases, where the evidence is very presumptuous, to send them to the Gallies, which is as bad as death. There was another fat Malefactor to succeede, wh[o] he said, he was confident would never endure the Question; This his often being at these Trials, had it seemes given him experience of, but the spectacle was so uncomfortable, that I was not able to stay the sight of another: It represented yet to me, the intollerable suffering which our B: S: must needes undergo, when his blessed body was hanging with all its weight upon the nailes on the Crosse.

. . .

Crabs of the Red Sea

[May] 21: The Deane on 1. Acts 9. 10. 11. describing the Ascension. That since our B: Saviour was to be received into the Heavens til his 2d Comming; how vaine it was to fancy a corporal

presence in the B: Sacrament, as the Romanists would impose: 23.
I went to take leave of the Ambassadors for Spaine, which were my
L. Treasurer Cottington and Hide Sir Edw: and as I return'd
visited Monsieur Morines Garden, and other rarities, especialy
Coralls, Minerals, Stones, and other natural Curiosities: particularly Crabs of the red-sea, the body no bigger than a small birds
egg, but flatter, and the 2 leggs or claws a foote in length: he had
aboundance of incomparable shells, at least 1000 sorts which
furnish'd a Cabinet of greate price, and a very curious collection of
Scarabies and Insects, of which he was compiling a natural historie;
also the pictures of his Choice flowers and plants in miniature: he
told me there were 10000 sorts of Tulips onely: he had also *Tallie
douces** sans nombre*: he had also the head of the Rynoceros bird,
which was indeede very extravagant; and one butterflie resembling
a perfect bird:

. . .

[August 20] I this day received safe, divers books and other
things I had sent for out of England, which were reported to have
ben taken by the Pyrates: but God be thanked it was otherwise:

. . .

29 Was kept a solemn fast, for the Calamities of our poore
Church, now trampl'd on by the Rebells:

. . .

A Narrow Escape
[September] 6 I went with my Wife to St. Germaines, to
Condoule Mr. Wallers losse: I carried with me, and treated at
dinner, that excellent and pious person, The Deane of Pauls Dr.
Steward, and Sir Lowes Dives, halfe brother to the Earle of Bristol,
who entertain'd us with his wonderfull Escape out of Prison in
White-hall, the very evening before he was to have ben put to
death, leaping down out of a jakes 2 stories high into the Thames at
high-Water, in the coldest of Winter, and at night: so as by swiming
he got to a boate that attended for him: tho' he was guarded with six
musqueteeres: That after this he went about in Womens habits,
and then in a Small-Coalemans; Then travell'd 200 miles on foote,
Embarked for Scotland, with some men he had raised, who coming
on shore were all surpriz'd and imprison'd on the Marq: of
Montrosses score, he not knowing any thing of their barbarous

murder of that Hero: This he told us was his 5· Escape, and none lesse miraculous, with this note, That the charging through 1000 men arm'd, or whatever danger could possible befall a man in his whole life, he believed could not more confound, and distract a mans thoughts, than the execution of a premeditated Escape, The passions of hope and feare being so strong: This Knight was indeede a valiant Gent: but not a little given to romance, when he spake of himselfe. I return'd to Paris the same Evening:

Mr. T. Hobbes Observes Louis XIV

The 7th of September I went to Visite Mr. Hobbs the famous Philosopher of Malmesbury, with whom I had long acquaintance: from whose Window, we [saw] the whole equipage and glorious Cavalcade of the Young French Monarch Lewis the XIVth passing to Parliament, when first he tooke the Kingly Government on him, as now out of Minority and the Queene regents pupilage: First came the [Captain] of the King's Aydes, at the head of 50 richly liveried: Next the Queene Mothers light horse an hundred: The Lieutennant being all over cover'd with Embroiderie and ribbans, having before him 4 Trumpets habited in black velvet, full of Lace, and Casques of the same:

Then the Kings light horse 200: richly habited, with 4 Trumpets in blew velvet embrodred with Gold, before whom rid the Count d'Olonne Coronet, whose belt [was all] set with Pearle: next went the grand Prevosts Company on foot, with the Prevost on horseback, after them, the Swisse in black Velvet toques led by 2 gallant Cavalieres habited in scarlet colour'd Sattin after their Country fashion, which is very fantastick: he had in his cap a pennach of heron, with a band of Diamonds, and about him 12 little Swisse boyes with halebards, which was very pretty: Then came the Ayde des Ceremonies; next the grandees of Court, and Governors of Places, Lieutenants Gen: of Provinces magnificently habited and mounted, among [them] one, I must not forget, the Chevalier Paul famous for many Sea-fights and signal exploits there, because 'tis said, he never had ben an Academist, and yet govern'd a very un-rully horse, and beside his rich suite, and Malta Crosse esteem'd at 10 thousand Crownes: These were headed with 2 Trumpets, and indeede the whole Troup cover'd with Gold and Jewells, and rich Caparisons were follow'd by 6 Trumpets in blew

Velvet also, præceeding as many Heraulds in blew Velvet Semé'd with floeur de lys, and Caduces in their hands, velvet caps: Behind them came one of the Masters of the Ceremonies, then divers Marishalls, and of the Nobility exceeding splendid, behind them Count d'Harcourt Grand Escuyr alone carrying the Kings Sword in a Scarf, which he held-up in a blew sheath studded with flor de lyss; his horse, had for reines two Scarfs of black Taffata: Then came The foote-men and Pages of the King aboundance of them, new liveried, and with white and red feathers: Next the Guard de Corps and other officers, and lastly appear[d] the King himselfe upon an Isabella Barb, on which a housse seméd with Crosses of the Order of the H.G. and floure de lyces: The King himselfe like a young Apollo was in a sute so coverd with rich embrodry, that one could perceive nothing of the stuff under it, going almost the whole way with his hat in hand saluting the Ladys and Acclamators who had fill'd the Windos with their beauty, and the aire with 'Vive Le Roy'. Indeede he seem'd a Prince of a grave, yet sweete Countenance, now but in the 14th yeare of his Age . . .

. . .

Battle of Worcester

22 Arived the newes of the fatal Battail at Worcester, which exceedingly mortified our expectations.

. . .

[October 29] This morning came newes and Letters to the Queene, and Sir Richard Bro: (who was the first had intelligence of it) of his Majesties miraculous Escape after the fight at Worcester, which exceedingly rejoic'd us.

. . .

1 December I receiv'd a Bill of Exchange being now resolv'ed to returne into England.

. . .

21 Came to Visite my Wife Mrs. Lane, the Lady who conveied the King at his Escape from Worcester to the sea-side.

. . .

1652. 1 Jan: After publique prayers in the Chapell, making up all Accompts, I prepard for my last Journey, being now resolvd to leave France [for] alltogether.

. . .

Journey to the Coast

29 Came aboundance of my French and English Acquaintance, and some Germans to take leave of me, and conducted me to the Coach and Horses; So about 12 a Clock (in an extraordinary hard Frost, that had continud a good while before,) we set forth and got that night to B[e]aumont. 30, at Beau[v]ais, 31 we found the wayes very deepe with Snow, and exceeding cold; din'd at Pois, lay at Berneè, a miserable Cottage, of miserable people in a Wood, and wholy unfurnish'd, but in a little time, we had sorry beds and some provision, which they told me they hid in the wood, for feare of the frontier Enemy, the Garisons neere them continualy plundering what they had: They told us they were often infested with Wolves: I cannot remember that I ever saw more miserable Creatures:

1 Feb: I din'd at Abbe Ville – afterward we met 2 Capuchin friers marching towards Paris. 2 din'd at Montreuill, lay at Bollogne 3 and came next day to Calis by 11 in the Morning; so I thought to have embarq'd in the Evening, but feare of Pyrates plying neere the Coast, I durst not trust our small Vessel, 'til Moneday following, when 2 or 3 lusty vessels were to depart:

. . .

Sayes Court and London
1652–1660

6 I Embark'd early in the Packet-boat, but put my goods in a Stouter Vessell: 'twas dark, but exceeding Calme weather, so as we got not to Dover till 8 at night; The other vessell out sailing us an houre and more:

Next morning came the Cleark of the Passage and Monsieur De la Vall to visite me, we supped together: 29: English style (having desir'd Mr. De la Valle to convey a letter to Monsieur Le Compt de Strade, to put him in mind of his promise, and that he would consigne the Picture to him) I tooke horse for Canterbury, thence to Sittenburne, thence, lying at Rochester, 30th to Gravesend, thence, in a pair of Oares, and so landed at Says-Court about 2 in the Afternoone, where I stayed Friday, Sat: and Sonday, to refresh, and looke after my packetts, and goods I brought:

Ireton's Funeral
[February] 1 I went to Lond: visited my Bro: his Lady and severall friends: 2: Came Mr. Davie Walker (one of his Majesties Bed-chamber) to visite me: 3 My Bro: Richard, La: Cath: Scott, Mr. Waller; at whose house I din'd. 4: I went to Visite my Co: Rich: Fanshaw, and received divers visites from friends: 5: My Bro: Glanvill came to see me, with whom I condold the death of my deare sister, a most ingenious and virtuous woman, and whom I exceedingly loved: Next day he sent me Mourning: and this day I saw the Magnificent Funeral of that arch-Rebell Ireton, carried in pomp from Somerset house to Westminster, accompanied with divers regiments of Souldiers horse and foote; then marched the Mourners, Generall Cromewell (his father in Law) his Mock-Parliament men: Officers, and 40 poore-men in gownes, 3 led horses in housses of black-Cloth: 2 horses led in black-Velvet, and his Charging horse all coverd over with embrodery and gold on crimson Velvet: Then the Guidons, Ensignes, 4 Heraulds, carrying

the armes of the State (as they cald it) namely the red Crosse, and Ireland, with the Casque, Wreath, Sword, Spurrs etc: next a [Charriot] Canopied, all of black Velvet, and 6 horses, in this the Corps, the Pall held up by the Mourners on foote: The Mace and Sword with other marks of his Charge in Ireland (where he died of the Plague) carried before in black Scarfs; Thus in a grave pace, drums coverd with cloth, souldiers reversing their armes, they proceeded thro the streetes in a very solemn manner. This Ireton was a stout rebell, and had ben very bloudy to the Kings party, witnesse his severity at Colchester; when in cold blood he put those gallant gent: Sir Charles Lucas and G. Lisle to death:

. . .

Evelyn Resolves to Settle

10 I went to Deptford; where having prety well settld my buisinesse in Lond: I made preparation for my settlement, no more intending to go out of England, but endeavor a settled life, either in this place, or some other, there being now so little appearance of any change for the better, all being intirely in the rebells hands, and this particular habitation, and the Estate contiguous to it (belonging to my F in Law, actualy in his Majesties service) very much suffering, for want of some friend, to rescue it out of the power of the Usurpers; so as to preserve our Interest, and to take some care of my other Concernes, by the advise, and favour of my Friends, I was advis'd to reside in it, and compound with the Souldiers; being besides, authoriz'd by his Majestie so to do, and encourag'd with a promise, that what was in Lease from the Crowne (if ever it pleas'd God to restore him), he would secure to us in Fee-ferme: I had also addresses, and Cyfers, to Correspond with his Majestie and Ministers abroad; upon all which inducements, I was persuaded to settle hence forth in England, having now run about the World, most part out of my owne Country neere 10 yeares: I therefore now likewise meditated of sending over for my Wife, whom as yet I had left at Paris:

. . .

22 I went with my Bro: Evelyn to Wotton, to give him what directions I was able about his Garden, which he was now desirous to put into some forme: but for which he was to remove a mountaine, that [was] over-growne with huge trees, and thickett,

with a moate, within 10 yards of the very house: This my Brother immediately attempted, and that without greate Cost for more than an hundred yards South, by digging downe the Mountaine, and flinging it into a rapid streame, which not onely carried the Land etc away, but filled up the moate, and leveld that noble arëa where now the Garden and fountaine is: The first occasion of my Bro: making this alteration, was my building of a litle retiring place betweene the greate wood East ward, next the Meadow, where some time after my Fathers death I made a triangular Pond or little stew, with an artificial rock, after my coming out of Flanders: 26: I went to visite Mr. Hylyard, to whose sonns I had ben serviceable in France: 28 I returned, visiting my Bro: Richard and Wife at Woodcot.

· · ·

[March] 1 I return'd to Says-Court: 5. Came my Bro: G. to visite me, brought Cromwells Act of Oblivion, to all that would submit to the Government: returnd that Evening . . .

· · ·

15 This night was an Ecclipse of the Moone, I writ Letters to my Wife etc: concerning my resolution of settling; also to the Deane touching my buying his Library, which was one of the choicest collection[s] of any private persons whatsover in England:

· · ·

16 I let bloud 9 ounces. 17 Sweate, and bathed, and went to Lond, to take order about my goods ariv'd out of France: I had ben exceedingly troubld with a swelling in my throat and neck, which fore-ran the Piles, and had now for 2 Springs indisposd me, but now prevented, by the Course I tooke and greate evacuations:

· · ·

29 Was that celebrated Eclipse of the Sun, so much threatned by the Astrologers, and had so exceedingly alarm'd the whole Nation, so as hardly any would worke, none stir out of their houses; so ridiculously were they abused by knavish and ignorant star-gazers.

30 Came my Bro. Geo: and Bro: Rich: with his wife to dine with me, and my little Nephew Geo: Evelyn brought to abide some time with me, if possible to reclaime him of his fondnesse to home, where he miserably lost his time: We went this afternoon to see the Queenes house at Greenewich, now given by the Rebells to

Bolstrood Whittlock one of their unhappy Counselors, keeper of pretended Liberties.
   ...

Mary Evelyn Returns

[May] 7 I had Letters from Paris, dated 11th May of my Wifes being with Child of her first, and returnd to Saies Court: 14 I went to Lond, and returnd: 17 came my Bro: to see me: 19 my Wife confirm'd to me her being quick: 20 To Lond, about my parting with my house in the Cliffe neere Lewes in Sussex: The next day I went to see the manner of chambletting silk and Grograns at one Monsieur La Dorees in Morefields; and thence to Coll: Morley (one of their Council of State, as then calld) who had ben my Schole-fellow, to request a Passe for my Wifes safe landing and the goods she was to bring with her out of France, which [he] courteously granted, and did me many other kindnesses, which was a greate matter in those daies: 22 return'd home ...

3 June I went to Lond, received Letter[s] from Coll: Morley to the Magistrates and Searchers at Rie to assist my Wife at her Landing, and shew her all civility: returned:

4 I set out for Rie to meete my Wife, now upon her journey from Paris, after she had obtain'd leave to come out that Citty, which had now ben besieged some time, by the Pr: of Condys armie, in the Time of the Rebellion: and after she had now ben neere 12 Yeares from her owne Country, that is since 5 yeares of age, at which time she went over: 5 I lay this night at Sennock, ariv'd the next at Rie, where was an Embargo, upon occasion of the late Conflict with the Holland Fleete, the two Nations being now in Warr; and which made sailing very unsafe: 6: Whitsonday, I went to Church (which is a very faire one) [heard] one of their Canters, who dismiss'd the Assembly rudely, and without any blessing: I was displeased when I came home, that I was present at it, having hitherto kept my Eares incontaminate from their new fangled service: Here I stayed til the 10th with no small impatience, when I walked over to survey the ruines of Winchelsea, that antient Cinq-port, which by the remaines and ruines of ample Streetes, and publique structures, discovers it to have formerly ben a considerable and large Citty, There are to be seene vast Caves and Vaults, Walls, and Towers, ruines of Monasteries, and of a sumptuous Church in which some

handsom monuments, especialy of the Templars buried just in the manner of those in the Temp: at Lond: This place being now all in rubbish, and a few despicable hovells and cottages onely standing, hath yet a Major: The sea which formerly renderd it a rich and commodious port, having now forsaken it: so we walked back to Rie:

11 About 4 in the after-noone, being at bowles on the Greene, we discoverd a Vessel, which proved [to] be that in which my Wife was, and got into harbour about 8 a clock that Eveni[n]g to my no small joy: They had ben 3 days at Sea, and hardly Escaped the whole Dut[c]h Fleete, through which the[y] pass'd taken for Fishers; which was a greate good fortune; there being 17 bailes of furniture, and other rich plunder, which I blesse God came all safe to land, together with my Wife, and my Lady Browne her mother, accompanying her Daughter: But my Wife discompos'd with being so long at sea, we set not forth towards home 'til the 14th, when hearing the Small-pox was very rife in and about Lond: and that my Lady had a greate desire to drink Tunbridge Waters; I carried them thither, where I staied in a very sweete place, private and refreshing, and also tooke the Waters my selfe a few daies, 'til the 23d when buisinesse calling me homewards, and to prepare for the reception of my little family (leaving them for the present in their Cottage by the Wells)

Evelyn Robbed

The morning growing excessivly hot, I sent my footman some hours before, and so rod negligently, under favour of the shade, 'til being now come to within three miles of Bromely, at a place calld the procession Oake, started out two Cutt-throates, and striking with their long staves at the horse, taking hold of the reignes, threw me downe, and immediately tooke my sword, and haled me into a deepe Thickett, some quarter of a mile from the high-way, where they might securely rob me, as they soone did; what they got of mony was not considerable, but they tooke two rings, the one an Emrald with diamonds, an [Onyx], and a pair of boucles set with rubies and diamonds which were of value, and after all, barbarously bound my hands behind me, and my feete, having before pull'd off my bootes: and then set me up against an Oake, with most bloudy threatnings to cutt my throat, if I offerd to crie out, or make any noise, for that they should be within hearing, I not being the person they looked for: I told them, if they had not basely surpriz'd me, they should not have made so easy a prize, and that it should teach me hereafter never to ride neere an hedge; since had I ben in the mid way, they durst not have adventur'd on me, at which they cock'd their pistols, and told me they had long guns too, and were 14 companions, which all were lies: I begg'd for my Onyx and told them it being engraven with my armes, would betray them, but nothing prevaild: My horses bridle they slipt, and search'd the saddle which they likewise pull'd off, but let the horse alone to grace, and then turning againe bridld him, and tied him to a Tree, yet so as he might graze, and so left me bound: The reason they tooke not my horse, was I suppose, because he was mark'd, and cropt on both Eares, and well known on that roade, and these rogues were lusty foote padders, as they are cald: Well, being left in this manner, grievously was I tormented with the flies, the ants, and the sunn, so as I sweate intollerably, nor little was my anxiety how I should get loose in that solitary place, where I could neither heare or see any creature but my poore horse and a few sheepe stragling in the Coppse; til after neere two houres attempting I got my hands to turne paulme to paulme, whereas before they were tied back to back, and then I stuck a greate while ere' I could slip the cord over my wrist to my thumb, which at last I did, and then being quite loose soone unbound my feete, and so sadling my horse, and roaming a while about, I at last perceiv'd a dust to rise, and soone after heard the rattling of a Cart, towards which I made, and by the help of two Country fellows that were driving it, got downe a steepe bank, into the highway againe; but could heare nothing of the Villains: So I rod to Colonel Blounts a greate justiciarie of the times, who sent out hugh and Crie immediately: and 25, The next morning weary and sore as I was at my wrists and armes, I went from Deptford to Lond, got 500 ticketts printed and dispers'd, by an officer of Gould Smiths-hall, describing what I had lost, and within two daies after had tidings of all I lost, except my Sword which was a silver hilt, and some other trifles: These rogues had paund my Rings etc for a trifle to a Goldsmiths Servant, before the tickets came to the shop, by which meanes they scap'd, the other ring was bought by a Victualer, who brought it to a Goldsmith, that having seene the ticket, seiz'd upon him; but whom I afterwards discharg'd upon the mediation of friends, and protestation of his innocency: Thus did God deliv[e]r me from these villains, and not onely so, but restor'd to me what they tooke, as twise before he had graciously don, both at sea and land, I meane, when I had ben rob'd by Pyrates and was in danger of a considerable losse at Amsterdam, for which and many, many signal preservations I am eternaly obligd to give thanks to God my Saviour.

. . .

[July] 10 I had newes of the taking of one of the knaves who robbd me, and was summon'd to appeare against him: so as on the 12, I was in Westminster Hall but not being bound over (nor willing to hang the fellow) I did not appeare, comming onely to save a friends baile who appeard for me; however the man being found [guilty], was turn'd over to the old bailey:

13 My Wife and her Mother came first to Deptford: next day her Bro: John Pretyman and severall friends to congratulate. 15 We all went to Lond: to returne Visites: In the meane time, I received a letter from Sir Tho: Peyton, and a petition from the Prisoner (whose father I understood was an honest old fermor in Kent) to be favourable which I was; not withstanding, others comming in, about a Rape, and that he had ben in Goaile before, he was condemn'd, but repriv'd by Sir Tho: I was told he was a bloudy rascal, and had murderd severall of his Majesties Subjects being a souldier in Ireland, and that had it not ben for his companion, a younger fellow, 'twas ten to one, but he had knock'd me on the head: This I came to know afterwards and that in the End, upon some other Crime, he being obstinate and not pleading, was press'd to death: one thing I remember, that he was one of the worst look'd fellows I ever saw.

. . .

[December] 25 Christmas day no sermon anywhere, so observd it at home, the next day we went to Lewsham, where was an honest divine preach'd on 21. Matt:9. celebrating the Incarnation, for on the day before, no Churches were permitted to meete etc: to that horrid passe were they come: 31 I adjusted all accompts, and renderd thanks to God for his mercys to me the yeare past.

. . .

The Garden at Sayes Court

[1653. January] 17 I began to set out the Ovall Garden at Says Court, which was before a rude Ortchard, and all the rest one intire fild of 100 Ackers, without any hedge: excepting the hither holly-hedge joyning to the bank of the mount walk: and this was the beginning of all the succeeding Gardens, Walkes, Groves, Enclosures and Plantations there:

21 I went to Lond: and sealed some of the Writings of my Purchase of Sayes-Court, returnd next day:

. . .

[February] 19 I planted the Ortchard at Says-Court, new Moone, wind West.

22 Was perfected the sealing, livery and sesin of my Purchase of Says Court My Bro: Geo: Glanvill, Mr. Scudamor, Offley, Co: William Glanvill, sonn to Serjeant Glanvil (sometime Speaker of the H: of Commons) Co: Steephens, and severall of my friends dining with me, it being also Shrove Tuesday; I paid for it 3500, my bargaine being 3200 pounds: cost 3500 pounds 300 pounds more than I bargain'd for:

. . .

[August] 13 I first began a Course of yearely washing my head with Warme Water, mingld with a decoction of Sweete herbs, and immediately, with cold Spring water, which much refreshd me, and succeeded very well with me divers yeares:

. . .

A 'Phanatical' Preacher

4 December: 'Til now I had met with no Phanatical Preachers, but going this day to our Church, I was surprizd to see a Tradesman, a Mechanic step up, I was resolv'd yet to stay, and see what he would make of it, his Text was 2. Sam. 23. 20 'and Benaiah sonn of Jehoiada – went downe also and slew a lion in the midst of a pit, in the time of Snow'.

That no danger was to be thought difficult, when God call'd for sheading of blood, inferring that now, the Saints were calld to destroy, temporal Governments, with such truculent, [anabaptisticall] stuff: so dangerous a Crisis were things growne to:

. . .

25 Christmas-day, no Churches [or] publique Assembly, I was

faine to passe the devotions of that blessed day with my family at home: 29. Came my Bro: E: and divers friends to dine with me:

· · ·

[1654] 5 May. I bound my [Laquay] Tho: Heath Apprentise to a Carpenter, giving with him 5 pounds, and new Cloathing: he thriv'd very well and became rich . . .

· · ·

Painted Ladies

10 My Lady Gerrard treated us at Mulbery-Garden, now the onely place of refreshment about the Towne for persons of the best quality, to be exceedingly cheated at: Cromwell and his partisans having shut up, and seiz'd on Spring Garden, which 'til now had ben the usual rendezvous for the Ladys and Gallants at this season: 11: My Bro: Evelyn treated us in the same manner:

11 I now observed how the Women began to paint themselves, formerly a most ignominious thing, and used onely by prostitutes. I return'd this evening home:

· · ·

26 My second new-Coach was brought home:

2 June I went to Lond [to] take leave of severall Relations and friends, resolving to spend some monethes amongst my Wifes friends etc in Wiltshire and other parts, to whom we had ben so uncessantly invited. 4: our Minister proceeded, to shew the difference 'twixt the animal and spiritual life.

A Tour in England

8 My Wife and I set out on our Journey, in Coach and 4 horses etc: din'd at Windsore, and saw the Castle, the Chapell of St. George: where they have laied our blessed Martyr K. Charles in the Vault, just before the Altar: The Church and Workmanship in stone (though Gotic) is admirable: The Castle it selfe, large in Circumference, but the roomes Melancholy and of antient magnificence: The keepe (or mount) hath besides its incomparable Prospect, a very profound Well, and the Terrace towards Eaton, with the Park, meandring Thames, swete Meadows yeilds one of the most delightfull prospects in the World; So that night we lay at Reading, saw my Lord Cravons house at Causam now in ruines, his goodly Woods felling by the Rebells: 9 Din'd at Marlborow, which

having lately ben fired, was now new built: At one end of this Towne we saw my Lord Seamors house, but nothing observable save the Mount, to which we ascend winding for neere halfe a mile: It seemes to have ben cast up by hand: Then we passd by Coll: Pophams, a noble Seate, Park and River; Thence by Newbery, a Considerable Towne, and Dennington Castle, famous for the Battail, seige, and that this last had ben the possession of old Geofrie Chaucer: Then Aldermaston, a house of Sir Humphry Forster built a la moderne: Also that exceedingly beautiful seate of my L: Pembrocks on the ascent of an hill, flank'd with woods and reguarding the river, and so at night 11 to Cadenham the Mansion of Ed: Hungerford Esquire, Unkle to my Wife where we made some stay:

. . .

Bath and Bristol

27 We all went to see Bathe, where I bathed in the Crosse bathe; amongst the rest of the idle diversions of the Towne, one Musitian was famous for acting a Changling; which indeede he personated strangely: The Faciate of this Cathedrall is remarkable for the Historical Carving: The Kings Bath is esteemed the fairest in Europe; The Towne is intirely built of stone, but the streetes narrow, uneven and unpleasant: Here we trifled and bath'd, and intervisited with the company who frequent the place, for health etc: till 30th and then went to Bristoll a Citty emulating London, not for its large extent, but manner of building, shops, bridge: Traffique: Exchange, Market-place etc. The Governor shew'd us the Castle, of no greate concernment: The City wholy Mercantile, as standing neere the famous Severne, commodiously for Ireland and the Western world: Here I first saw the manner of refining Suggar, and casting it into loaves, where we had collation of Eggs fried in the suggar furnace, together with excellent Spanish Wine; but what was most stupendious to me, was the rock of St. Vincent, a little distance from the Towne, the precipice whereoff is equal to any thing of that nature I have seene in the most confragose cataracts of the Alpes: The river gliding betwene them after an extraordinary depth: Here we went searching for Diamonds, and to the hot Well of Water at its foote: There is also on the side of this horrid Alp, a very romantic seate: and so we returned that Evening

to Bathe, and on the 1 of July to Cadenam, where on the Sonday, preachd Dr. Hayward Chaplaine to the late A: Bish: Lawde, on 15: Luke 7 describing the Joyes of Heaven at the conversion of a sinner:

4 Upon a Letter of my Wifes Unkle Mr. Pretyman, I waited back on her to London, passing by Hungerford towne (famous for its Troutes) I ariv'd at Deptford the next day, which was 60 miles, in the extreamity of heate:

Oxford

6 I saw [my] prety boy, return'd early to Lond, and the next day, met my Wife and company at Oxford, which being on the 7th was the Eve of the Act: 8 Next day was spent in hearing severall exercises in the Scholes, and after dinner the Procter opened the Act at St. Maries (according to custome) and the Prævaricators their drolery, then the Doctors disputed, and so we supp'd at Waddum Coll: The 9th Dr. French preechd at St. Maries on 12: Matt: 42, advising the Students the Search after true Wisdome, not to be had in the books of Philosophers, but Scriptures: in the afternoone the famous Independent Dr. Owen, perstringing Episcopacy: he was now Cromwells Vice-Chancellor: We din'd with Dr. Ward, Mathematical Professor since Bish: of Salisbury, and at night Supp'd in Balliol Coll: Hall, where I had once ben student and fellow Commoner, where they made me extraordinarily wellcome, but I might have spent the Evening as well.

10 On Monday I went againe to the Scholes to heare the severall faculties, and in the Afternoone tarried out the whole Act in St. Maries. The long speeches of the Proctors: The V: Chancelors, the severall Professars, Creation of Doctors, by the Cap, ring, Kisse etc: those Ceremonies not as yet wholy abolish'd, but retaining the antient Ceremonies and Institution: Dr. Kendal (now Inceptor amongst others) performing his Act incomparably well, concluded it with an excellent Oration, abating his Presbyterian animositie, which he withheld not even against that Learned and pious divine Dr. Hammond: The Act was closd, with the Spech of the V: Chancellor. There being but 4 In Theologie, 3 in Medicine, which was thought a considerable matter, the times consider'd: I din'd at on[e] Monsieur Fiats, a student at Excester Coll: and supped at a magnificent Entertainement in Waddum Hall, invited by my

excellent and deare Friend Dr. Wilkins, then Warden now Bishop of Chester: on the Eleventh was the Latine Sermon which I could not be at, invited, being taken-up at All-Soules, where we had Music, voices and Theorbes perform'd by some ingenious Scholars, where after dinner I visited that miracle of a Youth, Mr. Christopher Wren, nephew to the Bishop of Elie: then Mr. Barlow [since Bishop of Lincoln] Bibliothe[c]arius of the Bodlean Library, my most learned friend, who shewd me, together with my Wife, The rarities of that famous place, Manuscrip[t]s, Medails and other Curiosities. Amongst the MSS an old English Bible wherein the Eunuch mention'd to be baptizd by Philip, is cald the Gelding, and Philip and the Gelding went down into the Water etc, also the Original Acta of the Council of Basil, 900 years since, with the Bulla or leaden Affix, which has a silken Chord, passing thro every parchment: likewise a MS: of Ven: Beades of 800 years antiquity: together with the old *Ritual secundum Usum Sarum*, exceeding voluminous: Then amongst the nicer curiosities: The Proverbs of Solaman written in French, by a Lady every Chapter of a severall Character, or hand, the most exquisitely imaginable: An Hieroglypical Table, or Carta folded up like a Map, I suppose it painted on Asses hide, extreamely rare: but what is most illustrious, were the no lesse than 1000 MSS: in 19 Languages, espe[c]ialy Oriental, furnishing that new part of the Library, built by A: Bishop Lawd: some of Sir Kenhelme Digby, and the Earle of Pembroch: In the Closset of the Tower, they shew Josephs parti colourd Coate, A Muscovian Ladys Whip, some Indian Weapons, Urnes, Lamps: etc: but the rarest, is the Whole *Alcoran* written in one large sheete of Calico, which is made up in a Priests Vesture or Cape after the Turkish, and the Arabic Character so exquisitely written, as no printed letter comes neere it: Also a rolle of Magical Charmes or Periapta, divers Talismans, some Medails: Then I led my Wife into the Convocation house finely Wainscoted: The Divinity Schole and gotic Carv'd roofe; The Physick Or Anatomie Schole, adorn'd with some rarities of natural things; but nothing extraordinary, save the Skin of a Jaccal, a rarely Colour'd Jacatroo, or prodigious large Parot, two humming birds, not much bigger than our humble bee: which indeede I had not seene before that I remember. etc.

12 We went to St. Johns, saw the Library, and the 2 Skeletons, which are finely clense'd, and put together: observable are also the

store of Mathematical Instruments, all of them chiefly given by the late A: Bishop Lawd, who built here an handsome Quadrangle: Thence we went to New Coll: where the Chapell was in its antient garb, not withstanding the Scrupulositie of the Times: Thence to Christ-Church, in whose Library was shew'd us an Office of Hen: 8, the writing, Miniature and gilding whereof is equal if not surpassing any curiosity I had ever seene of that kind: It was given, by their founder, the Cardinal Wolsy: The Glasse Windos of the Cathedral (famous in my time) I found much abused: The ample Hall, and Columne that spreads its Capitel to sustaine the roofe as one gos up the Stayres is very remarkable: Next we walked to Magdalen Coll: where we saw the Library and Chapell, which was likewise in pontifical order, the Altar onely I think turn'd Table-wise: and there was still the double Organ, which abominations (as now esteem'd) were almost universaly demolish'd: Mr. Gibbon that famous Musitian, giving us a tast of his skill and Talent on that Instrument: Hence we went to the Physick Garden, where the Sensitive and humble plant was shew'd us for a greate wonder. There Grew Canes, Olive Tres, Rhubarb, but no extraordinary curiosities, besides very good fruit, which when the Ladys had tasted, we return'd in Coach to our Lodging.

Transparent Apiaries

13 We all din'd, at that most obliging and universaly Curious Dr. Wilkin's, at Waddum, who was the first who shew'd me the Transparant Apiaries, which he had built like Castle and Palaces and so ordered them one upon another, as to take the Hony without destroying the Bees; These were adorn'd with variety of Dials, little Statues, Vanes etc: very ornamental, and he was so aboundantly civill, as finding me pleasd with them, to present me one of these Hives, which he had empty, and which I afterwards had in my Garden at Says-Court, many Yeares after; and which his Majestie came on purpose to see and contemplate with much satisfaction: He had also contrivd an hollow Statue which gave a Voice, and utterd words, by a long and conceald pipe which went to its mouth, whilst one spake thro it, at a good distance, and which at first was very Surprizing: He had above in his Gallery and Lodgings variety of Shadows, Dyals, Perspe[c]tives, places to introduce the Species, and many other artif[i]cial, mathematical, Magical curiosities: A

Way-Wiser, a Thermometer; a monstrous Magnes, Conic and other Sections, a Balance on a demie Circle, most of them of his owne and that prodigious young Scholar, Mr. Chr: Wren, who presented me with a piece of White Marble he had stained with a lively red very deepe, as beautifull as if it had been naturall. Thus satisfied with the Civilities of Oxford: Dining at Farington a Towne which had newly ben fir'd, during the Warrs, and passing neere the seate of Sir Walter Pies, we came on the 13th to Cadenam, where on the 16 The Curate preach'd on his former Subject, like a Country parson, that tooke no greate paines: 16 We went to another Uncle and relation of my Wifes, Sir John Glanvill, a famous Lawyer formerly Speaker of the House of Commons; His Seate is at Broad-hinton, Where he now lived but in the Gate-house, his very faire dwelling house, having ben burnt by his owne hands, to prevent the Rebells making a Garison of it: Here my Co: Will: Glanvill (his eldest sonn) shewed me such a lock for a doore, that for its filing, and rare [contrivances], was a masterpiece, yet made by a Country Black-Smith: But we have seene Watches made by another, with as much curiositie, as the best of that Profession can brag off; and not many yeares after, there was nothing more frequent, than all sorts of Iron-Work, more exquisitely wrought and polish'd, than in any part of Europ; so as a dore lock, of a tollerable price, was esteem'd a Curiositie even among forraine Princes: We went back this Evening to Cadenham, and on the 19 to Sir Ed: Bayntons at Spie-Park, a place capable of being made a noble seate; but the humorous old knight, has built a long single house of 2 low stories, upon the precipice of an incomparable prospect, and landing on a bowling-greene in the Park; The house is just like a long barne, and has not a Windo, on the prospect side: After dinner they went to bowles, and in the meane time, our Coachmen made so exceedingly drunk; that returning home we escaped incredible dangers: Tis it seemes by order of the Knight, that all Gentlemens servants be so treated: but the Custome is barbarous, and much unbecoming a Knight, much lesse a Christian:

Salisbury and Wilton House

On the 20th We proceede to Salisbury; We went to see the Cathedral, which I take to be the compleatest piece of Gotic-

Worke in Europe, taken in all its uniformitie; a neate fabric, but the pillars (reputed to be cast) are of stone manifestly cut out of the cuarry: Most observable are those in the Chapter-house: There are some remarkable Monuments, particularly the antient Bishops founders of the church; Knights Templars, the Marques of Hartfords: Also the Cloysters of the Palace and Garden to it, and greate Mural dial.

In the afternoone we went to Wilton, a fine house of the E. of Penbrochs, in which the most observable are the Dining-roome in the modern built part towards the Garden, richly gilded, and painted with story by De Creete, also some other apartments, as that of Hunting Landskips by Pierce: some magnificent chimny-pieces, after the French best manner: Also a paire of artificial winding-stayres of stone, and divers rare Pictures: The Garden (heretofore esteem'd the noblest in all England) is a large handsome plaine, with a Grotto and Waterworks, which might be made much more pleasant were the River that passes through, clensed and rais'd, for all is effected by a meere force: It has a flower Garden not inelegant: But after all, that which to me renders the Seate delightfull, is its being so neere the downes and noble plaines about the Country and contiguous to it. The stables are well order'd, and yeild a gracefull front, by reason of the Walks of limetrees, with the Court and fountaine of the stable adorn'd with the Cæsars heads:

We return'd this evening by the Plaine, and 14 mile-race, where out of my Lords Hare-Waren we were entertain'd with a long course of an hare for neere 2 miles in sight: Neere this a Pergola or stand, built to view the Sports; so we came to Salisbury, and view'd the most considerable parts of that Citty, the Merket place, which together with most of the streetes are Watred by a quick current and pure streame, running through the middle of them, but are negligently kept, when with small charge they might be purged, and rendred infinitely agreable, and that one of the sweetest Townes in Europe; but as 'tis now, the common buildings are despicable, and the streetes dirty.

Stonehenge

22 We departed and dined at a ferme of my U. Hungerfords cald Darneford magna, situate in a Vally under the Plaine, most sweetly

water'd, abounding in Trowts and all things else requisite, provisions exceeding cheape: They catch the Trouts by Speare in the night, whilst they come wondring at a light set in the sterne: There were Pigeons, Conys, and foule in aboundance, and so we had an excellent dinner at an houres warning: After dinner continuing our returne we passd over that goodly plaine or rather Sea of Carpet, which I think for evennesse, extent, Verdure, innumerable flocks, to be one of the most delightfull prospects in nature and put me in mind of the pleasant lives of the Shepherds we reade of in Romances and truer stories: Now we were ariv'd at Stone-henge, Indeede a stupendious Monument, how so many, and huge pillars of stone should have ben brought together, erected some, other Transverse on the tops of them, in a Circular arëa as rudly representing a Cloyster, or heathen and more natural Temple: and so exceeding hard, that all my strength with an hammer, could not breake a fragment: which duritie I impute to their so long exposure: To number them exactly, is very difficult, in such variety of postures they lie and confusion, though they seem'd not to exceede 100, we counted onely 95: As to their bringing thither, there being no navigable river neere, is by some admir'd; but for the stone, there seemes to be of the same kind about 20 miles distant, some of which appeare[s] above ground: About the same hills are divers mounts raisd, conceiv'd to be antient intrenchments, or places of burial after bloudy fights: We now went by the Devizes a reasonable large Towne, so passing over Tan-hill (esteemed one of the highest in England) we came late to Cadenam: We had in this journey some disasters by a stonehorses getting loose: Stonehenge app[e]ares like a Castle at a distance.

23 Mr. Flea preachd on his former Text, still describing what ornaments a Christian should put on, to meete our B: Lord in.

27 I went to Hunting of a Sorel deare, and had excellent chase for 4 or 5 houres: The venison little worth, we expecting it should have ben a male:

. . .

Worcester

August 1 We set out towards Worcester, by the way (thick planted with Cider-fruit) we deviate to the holy Wells trickling out of a Vally, thro a steepe declivity toward the foote of greate-

Maubern hills: They are said to heale many Infirmities, As Kings-evil, Leaprosie etc: sore Eyes: Ascending a greate height above them, to the Trench dividing England from South Wales we had the Prospect of all Hereford shire, Radnor, Brecknock, Monmouth, Worcester, Glocester, Shropshire, Warwick, Derby-shire, and many more: We could discern Tewxbery, Kings-rode towards Bristol etc so as I esteeme it one of the goodliest Vista's in England.

2 This evening we ariv'd at Worcester, The Judges of Assise, and Sherifs just entering as we did: Viewing the Towne the next day, we found the Cathedral extreamely ruin'd by the late Warrs, otherwise a noble structure: The Towne is neately pav'd and very cleane, The goodly river Severne runing by it: It stands in most fertil Country:

. . .

York

17 To YORK the 2d Citty of England, fairely Waled, of a Circular forme, Waterd by the brave river Ouse, bearing Vessels of Considerable burdens, over which a stone bridge, emulating that of London, and built on: The Middle Arch larger than any I have seene in all England, with a rivage or Wharfe all of hewn stone which makes the river appeare very neate: but most remarkeable and worthy seeing, is St. Peters Cathedrall, which alone of all the greate Churches in England, had best ben preserv'd from the furie of the sacrilegious, by Composition with the Rebells, when they tooke the Citty, during the many incursions of Scotch and others: It is a most intire, magnificent piece of Gotic Architecture: The Skreene before the Quire is of stone, carv'd with flowers, running work and statues of the old Kings: The Monuments (many of them) very antient: Here as a greate rarity in these dayes, and at this time, they shew'd me a Bible and Common-prayer book cover'd with Crimson Velvet, and richly emboss'd with silver gilt: Also a Service for the Altar of Guilt wrought Plate, flagons, Basin, Eure, Chalices, Patins etc: with a gorgeous covering for the Altar, Pulpet etc: carefully preserv'd in the Vestrie: in the holow Wall whereof rises a plentifull Spring of excellent Water: I got up to the Toure, where we had Prospect towards Duresme, and could see Rippon, part of Lancashire, and the famous and fatal Marston Moore, the

Spaus of Knarsbrough, and all the invirons of that admirable Country.

Sir Ingoldsby has here a large house, Gardens and Tennis-Court; Also the Kings house; and church neere the Castle which was modernly fortified with a Palizad and bastions: The Streetes narrow, ill pav'd, the shops like London. 18 We went next day to Beverly, a large Towne, Two stately Churches, St. Johns and St. Maries not much inferior to the best of our Cathedrals. Here a very old Woman shew'd us the Monuments, and being above 100 yeares of age, spake the language of Q: Maries daies in whose time she was born, being the Widdow of a Sexton that had belonged to the Church, an hundred yeares. Hence we passe through a fenny-Country (but rich) to Hull, situate like Calais, modernly and strongly fortified with three Block-houses, of Brick and Earth: It has a good harbour for ships, and Mercat Place: The Water-house is worth seeing: famous also is this Town, (or rather infamous) for Hothams refusing enterance to his Majestie: and here ends the South of Yorkshire, so now we passe the Humber, which is an arme of the Sea, of about 2 leages breadth; 19 the weather was bad, but we cross'd it in a good barque over to Barton the first Towne in that part of Lincoln-shire, all Marsh ground 'til we came to Briggs famous for the plantations of Licoris, and then brave pleasant riding to Lincoln, much resembling Salisbury Plaine.

Lincoln

LINCOLN an old confusd towne, very long, uneven and confragose, steepe and raged, but has formerly ben full of good houses, especialy Churches and Abbies, especialy the Minster, comparable to that of York it selfe, abounding with marble pillars, a faire front: Here in was interrd Q. Elianor, loyal and loving Wife to her Husband out of whose wound she succked the poisond arrow: The Abbot founder, with rare carving in the stone: The Greate Bell or Tom as they call it: I went up the steeple to view the Countrie: The Cloyster and Bish: Palace: but the Souldiers had lately knocked off all or most of the Brasses which were on the Gravestones, so as few Inscriptions were left: They told us they went in with axes and hammers, and shut themselves in, till they had rent and torne of some barges full of Mettal; not sparing the monuments of the dead, so helish an avarice possess'd them.

. . .

Cambridge

1 September Cambridg, and went first to see St. Johns Colledge
and Librarie, which I think is the fairest of that Universitie: one
Mr. Benlous has given it all the ornaments of Pietra Commessa,
whereof a Table, and one piece of Perspective is very fine, other
trifles there also be of no greate value, besides a vast old song book
or Service, and some faire Manuscripts: This Coll: is well built of
brick: There hangs in the Library the Picture of Williams ABishop
of York, and sometime Ld: Keeper, my Kindsman, and their greate
benefactor. Next we saw Trinity Coll, esteemed the fairest
Quadrangle of any University in Europ, but in truth far inferior to
that of Christ-Church Oxford: the Hall is ample, and of stone, the
fountaine in the Quadrangle is gracefull, The Chapell and Library
faire, there they shew'd us the prophetic MS. of the famous
Grebner; but the passage and Emblem which they would apply to
our late King, is manifestly relating to the Swedish; in truth it
seemes to be a meere fantastic rhapsody, however the Title
bespeake strange revelations: There is an Office finely miniatur'd
MS, with some other antiquities given by the Countesse of
Richmond mother of Hen: 7: and the formention[ed] Bishop
Williams when Bishop of Lincoln: The Library is pretty well stor'd:
Here the Greeke Professor had me into another halfe Quadrangle,
cloistred and well built, and gave us an handsome Collation in his
owne Chamber: Then we went to Caius, then to Kings Coll, where
I found the Chapel altogether answerable to expectation, especialy
the roofe all of stone, which for the flatnesse of its laying and
carving may I conceive vie with any in Christendome; The
contignation of the roofe (which I went upon), weight, and artificial
joyning of the stones is admirable: The lights are also very faire:
The library is too narrow: here in one Ile, lies the famous Dr.
Collins so celebrated for his fluency in the Latine Tongue: from
this roofe we could discry Elie, and the Incampment of Sturbridge
faire now beginning to set up their Tents and boothes: also
Royston, New-Market etc: houses belonging to the King. Thence
we walked to Clare-hall of a new and noble designe, but not
finish'd: hence to Peterhouse formerly under the charge and
gover[n]ment of my worthy friend Dr. Jo: Cosin; deane of
Peterborow, a pretty neate Coll: and delicate Chapell: next to
Sidny, a fine College, Kathrine-hall, though meane structure, yet

famous for the learned B: Andrews once Master: then to Emanuel Coll: that zealous house, where to the Hall, they have a Parler for the fellows: The Chapell is reform'd *ab origine*, built N. and South, meanely built, as is the Librarie: Thence to Jesus Coll: one of the best built, but in a Melancholy situation: next to Christ Coll. very [nobly] built, especialy the modern part, built without the Quadrangle towards the Gardens, of exact Architecture: The Schooles are very despicable, and publique Librarie but meane though somewhat improved by the Wainscoting and Books lately added by the Bishop Bancrofts Library and M.SS: They shew'd us little of antiquity: onely K: Jamess Works, being his owne gift, and kept very reverently and was the onely rarity shewd us. The Mercat place of Chambridg is very ample and remarkable for old Hobsons the pleasant Carriers beneficence of a fountaine: But the whole Towne situated in a low dirty unpleasant place, the streetes ill paved, the aire thick, as infested by the fenns; nor are its Churches (of which St. Maries is the best) anything considerable in compare to Oxford which is doubtlesse the noblest Universitie now in the whole World. From Chambridge we went to Audley End and spent some time in seeing that goodly Palace built by Howard E. of Suffolck, and once Lord Treasurer of England: It is a mixt fabric, 'twixt antique and modern, but observable for its being compleately finish'd, and without comparison one of the statliest Palaces of the Kingdome, consisting of two Courts, the first very large, Wingd with Cloisters: The front hath a double Entrance: The Hall is faire, but somewhat too smale for so august a pile: The Kitchin leaded and Cellars very large and arched with stone, Celars I never saw any so neate and well dispos'd: These Offices are joynd by a Wing out of the way very handsomely: The Gallery is the most cherefull, and I thinke one of the best in England: a faire dining-roome, and the rest of the Lodgings answerable with a pretty Chapell: The Gardens are not in order, though well inclosed: It has also a Bowling ally, a nobly well walled, wooded and watred Park, full of fine collines and ponds, the river glides before the Palace, to which an avenue of lime-trees; but all this much diminishd by its being placed in an obscure bottome; for the rest a perfectly uniforme structure, and sh[e]wes without like a diademe, by the decorations of the Cupolas and other ornaments on the Pavilions: I observ'd that instead of railes and balusters, there is a bordure of Capital letters, as was lately also on Suffolck house neere Charing Crosse, built by the same L: Tress: This house stands in the Parish of Saffron Walden famous for the aboundance of Saffron there Cultivated and esteem'd the best of any forraine Country.

Having dined here, we passe thro Bishop Stratford a pretty waterd Towne, and so by London late home 3 to Sayes-Court after a parerration of 700 miles, but for the variety an agreable refreshment after my Turmoile and building etc.

. . .

Young Richard's Escape

[December] 31 By Gods special Providence we went not to Church, my wife being now so very neere her time: for my little sonne Richard now about 2 yeares old as he was fed with broth in the morning, a square but broad and pointed bone of some part of a ract of Mutton, stuck so fast in the Childs Throate and crosse his Weason, that had certainly choaked him, had not my Wife and I ben at home; for his mayd being alone with him above in the Nurserie, was fallen downe in a swone, when we below (going to Prayers) heard an unusual groaning over our head, upon which we went up, and saw them both gasping on the floore, nor had the Wench any power to say what the Child ail'd, or call for any help: At last she sayd, she believed a Crust of bread had choak'd her little Master, and so it almost had, for the eyes and face were s[w]ollen, and clos'd, the Mouth full of froath, and gore, the face black – no Chirurgeon neere: what should we doo?, we cald for drink, power it downe, it returnes againe, the poore babe now neere expiring. I hold its head down, incite it to Vomite, it had no strength, In this dispaire, and my Wife almost as dead as the Child, and neere despaire, that so unknown and sad an accident should take from us so pretty a Child: It pleased God, that on the suddaine effort and as it were struling his last for life, he cast forth a bone . . . I gave the child some Lucotellus Balsome for his Throat was much excoriated. Ô my Gracious God out of what a tender feare, and sad heart, into what Joy did thy goodnesse now revive us! Blessed be God for this mercy: Wherefore beging pardon for my sinns, and returning Thanks for this grace, I implord his providential care for the following yeare.

. . .

Birth of Young John

[1655. January] 14 About ½ after 10 in the Morning, was my Wife delivered of another Sonn, being my Third, but 2d living: *Benedictus sit deus in donis suis*: 16th I went to Lond: returnd the 18th and the same on foote, returning by Water 20th: I saw a live Camelion.

21 Mr. Malorie still pursued his 55 Esay 8. describing the incomprehensibility of Gods free Grace, to exceede both faith and reason, nay our very sinns, in a very pious discourse:

26 Was Christned my Sonne John by Sir Jo: Evelyn, Lady Gerrard, and his Unkle Will: Pretyman susceptors, Mr. Owen officiating at Says-Court, according to the rite of the Church of England:

. . .

A Cromwellian Warship

. . . [April 9] we went to see the greate Ship newly built, by the Usurper Oliver, carrying 96 brasse Guns, and of 1000 tunn: In the Prow was Oliver on horseback trampling 6 nations under foote, a Scott, Irishman, Dutch, French, Spaniard and English as was easily made out by their several habits: A Fame held a laurell over his insulting head, and the word 'God with us':

. . .

[August] 13 I went to Woodcot to condole with my Bro: R: upon the death of his Sonn.

. . .

[September] 17 Received 2600 pounds for the Mannor of Warley Magna in Essex, purchased by me some time since: The Taxes were so intollerable, that they eate up the Rents etc: surcharged as that County had ben above all others during our unnatural War . . .

. . .

The Ingenious Hartlib

[October] 27 To Lond about Sir N: Crisps designs: I went to see York-house and Gardens belonging to the former greate Buckingham: but now much ruin'd thro neglect. Thence to visite honest and learned Mr. Hartlib, a Publique Spirited, and ingeni[o]us person, who had propagated many Usefull things and Arts: Told

me of the Castles which they set for ornament on their stoves in
Germanie (he himselfe being a Lithuanian as I remember) which
are furnishd with small ordinance of silver on the battlements, out
of which they discharge excellent Perfumes about the roomes,
charging them with a little Powder to set them on fire and disperse
the smoke: and intruth no more than neede; for their stoves are
sufficiently nasty: He told me of an Inke that would give a dozen
Copies, moist Sheetes of Paper being pressed on it, and remaine
perfect; and a receit how to take off any Print, without injury to the
original in the least: This Gent: was Master of innumerable
Curiosities, and very communicative. I returnd home that evening
by water, and was afflicted for it with a Cold, that had almost kil'd
me. This day came there also forth the Protectors Edict or
Proclamation, prohibiting all ministers of the Church of England
from Preaching, or Teach any Scholes, in which he imitated The
Apostate Julian: with the Decimation of all the Royal parties
revenues thro-out England.

December 9 Mr. Mal: on 106 Psal: 4. 5. how Christ redeemed
his Elect: etc: 13 to Lond: 14: I visited Mr. Hobbs the famous
Philosopher of Malmesbury, with whom I had ben long acquainted
in France. – return'd that Evening – Now were the Jewes admit
ted –

. . .

25 There was no more notice taken of Christmas day in Churches;
wherefore

30 I went to Lond: where Dr. Wild (at St. Greg) preached the
funeral Sermon of Preaching, this being the last day, after which
Cromwells Proclamation was to take place, that none of the Ch: of
England should dare either to Preach, administer Sacraments, Teach
Schoole etc. on paine of Imprisonment or Exile . . .

. . .

Whitehall Still Intact

[1656. January] 11 I adventurd to go to White-Hall, where of
many yeares I had not ben, and found it very glorious and well
furnish'd, as far as I could safely go, and was glad to find, they had
not much defac'd that rare piece of Hen 7th and 8 etc. don on the
Walles of the Kings Privy Chamber. 14th I dined with Mr. Barckley

Son to my Lord Berckley of Ber: Castle, where I renewed my Acquaintance with my Lord Bruce, my fellow Tra: in Italy:

. . .

A Musical Prodigy

Mar: 4: This night I was invited by Mr. Rog: L'Estrange to heare the incomperable Lubicer on the Violin, his variety upon a few notes and plaine ground with that wonderfull dexterity, as was admirable, and though a very young man, yet so perfect and skillfull as there was nothing so crosse and perplext, which being by our Artists, brough[t] to him, which he did not at first sight, with ravishing sweetenesse, and improvements, play off, to the astonishment of our best Masters: In Summ, he plaid on that single Instrument a full Consort, so as the rest, flung-downe their Instruments, as acknowl[e]dging a victory: As to my owne particular, I stand to this hour amaz'd that God should give so greate perfection to so young a person: There were at that time as excellent in that profession as any were thought in Europ: Paule Wheeler, Mr. Mell and others, 'til this prodigie appeared and then they vanish'd, nor can I any longer question, the effects we read of in Davids harp, to charme maligne spirits, and what is said some particular notes produc'd in the Passions of Alexander and that King cf Denmark – 5. I return'd home:

. . .

[April] 11 To Lond: returned 12. Mr. Barkley, and Mr. Rob: Boyle that excellent person, a greate Virtuoso, Dr. Taylor and Dr. Wilkins dined with me at Sayes Court, when I presented Dr. Wilkins with my rare Burning-glasse; Afternoone we all went to Coll: Blount to see his new invented Plows: and so went with them to Lond:

. . .

28 I made up my grand Accompt with my U: Pretyman being 10376 pounds: 16s. 04d, which this day after long calling on him, was finish'd and mutualy discharged: 30: Came to dine with me my Bro: and their Wives, with severall other Relations.

. . .

[June] 14 Came to visi[t]e me the old Marquis of Argyle, since executed; the Lord Lothain and some other Scotch noblemen all strangers to me. Note, the Marqu[i]s, tooke the Turtle-Doves in the Aviary for Owles.

. . .

Colchester

[July] 7 I began my journey to see some parts of the North East of England; but the weather so excessive hot and dusty, I shortned my progresse – I lay this night at Ingulstone, 8 the next day to Colchester, a faire Towne but now wretchedly demolished by the late Siege; espe[c]ialy the suburbs all burnt and then repairing: The Towne is built on a rising, having faire meadows on one side, and a river, with a strong antient Castle, said to have ben built by K. Coilus father of Helena mother of Constantine the Greate of whom I find no memory, save at the pinacle of one of their Woolstaple houses, where Coilus has a statue of wood wretchedly carvd: The walles are exceeding strong, deeply trenched and fill'd with Earth. It has 6 gates and some Watch toures; and some handsome Churches; but what was shew'd us as a kind of miracle, at the outside of the Castle, the Wall where (Sir Charles Lucas and Sir Geo: Lisle those valiant persons who so bravely behav'd themselves in the late siege, and were barbarously shot to death and murderd by Ireton in cold blood and after rendission upon articles) the place was bare of grasse for a large space, all the rest of it abounding with herbage: For the rest, this is a raged, factious Towne, and now Swarming in Sectaries. Their Trading Cloth with the Dutch, and Baies and saies with Spaine; and is the only place in England where these stuffs are made unsophisticated. Famous likewise will this Place ever be for the strenuous resistance of those most Loyal Gent: etc: against the Rebells, when neere all the strong places and Townes in England had given up to the Conquerors, what time, they expected reliefe from the Scotch Army, defeated with his Majesty at Worcester: It is also famous for Oysters, and Erringo of rootes here about growing and Candied: Henc we went to Dedham a pretty Country Towne, and very faire Church, finely situated, the vally well watred: Here I met with Dr. Stokes a young Gent: but an excellent Mathematician: This is (as most are in Essex) a Clothing Towne, and lies in the unwholsome hundreds. 9 Hence to Ipswich in Suffolck, which is doubtlesse one of Sweetest, most pleasant, well built [Towns] in England. It has 12 faire Churches, many noble houses, especialy the Lord D'evorixe's etc – a brave Kay and commodious harbor, being about 7 miles from the maine: an ample Mercat-place, and here was born the greate Cardinal Woolsey, who began a palace here, which was not finish'd etc: I returnd to Dedham: At Ipswich I had the curiosity to visite some Quakers there in Prison, a new phanatic sect of dangerous Principles, the[y] shew no respect to any man, magistrate or other and seeme a Melancholy proud sort of people, and exceedingly ignorant: one of these was said to have fasted 20 daies, but another endeavoring to do the like perish'd the 10th, when he would have eaten, but could not . . .

. . .

[August] 11 Came to visite me my Co: R: Fanshaw, when I propos'd Mr. Woodhead to him, for Governor to my Lord of Corkes Sonns, requesting me to recommend some learned person etc: This Mr. Woodhead was a monkish solitary person (as afterwards I learned) and by some suspected for popish, but doubtlesse a most heavenly man:

. . .

A Compromise

[November] 23 A very wet day, had the Church office and sermon read to my Family, my Wife not well.

30 An accident keept me at home from Church also: Now indeede that I went at all to Church whilst these usurpers possess'd the Pulpet, was that I might not be suspected for a Papist, and that though the Minister were Presbyterianly affected, he yet was as I understood duly ordaind, and preachd sound doctrine after their way, and besides was an humble harmelesse and peaceable man.

December 1 I went to Lond, returnd next day: 7: our Minister proceeds, shewing that the first thing God gives is himselfe. 12 Came Doctor Clark to visite me, now recoverd of his long sicknesse. 13 To Lond: returnd: 14: our Preacher proceedes. 20: The deepe and greate Snow kept us from Church, but not from the publique Office at home;

. . .

A Valiant Spanish Gent

[1657. January] 10 I went to visite the Governor of Havana, a brave sober, valiant Spanish Gent: taken by Capt: Young of Deptford, when after 20 yeares being in the Indias and amassing greate Wealth, his lady, and whole family (excepting two [Sonns]) were burnt, destroyed, and taken within sight of Spaine: His Eldest Son, daughter and Wife perishing with immense treasure: One Sonn, with his brother of one yeares old were the onely saved: The young Gent: about 17: was a well complexion'd Youth, not olive colourd; he spake latine handsomly, was extreamely well bred, and borne in the [Charcas] 1000 miles south of the Equinoxial neere the mountaines of Potisi: had never ben in Europe before: The Governor was an antient Gent: of greate Courage, of the order of S: Jago: sore wounded, his arme and rib broken and lost for his owne share 100000 pounds sterling, which he seem'd to beare with exceeding indifference, and nothing dejected; after some discourse I went with them to Arundel house where they dined: They were now going back into Spaine, having obtaind their liberty from Cromewell. An example of human Vicissitude:

. . .

Protector Oliver Refuses the Crown

[March] The Protector Oliver, now affecting King-ship, is petition'd to take the Title on him, by all his new-made sycophant Lords etc: but dares not for feare of the Phanatics, not thoroughly purged out of his rebell army:

. . . [April] 21 I went to Lond: to consult Dr. Bate about taking preventing Physick: Thence to Visite my Lord Hatton, with whom I dined; at my returne I step'd into Bedlame, where I saw nothing extraordinarie, besides some miserable poore Creatures in chaines, one was mad with making Verses: and also visited the Charter-house, formerly belonging to the Carthusians; now an old neate, fresh solitarie Colledge for decaied Gent: It has a grove, bowling-greene, Garden: Chapell, hall etc where they eate in common: I likewise saw Christ-Church and Hospital, a very goodly building, Gotic: also the Hall, Schoole, Lodgings, in greate order, for the bring[ing] up many hundreds of poore Children of both sexes, and is a[n] exemplary Charity: There is a large picture at one end of the Hall, representing the Governors, founders, and

Institution: so on the 23d I returned home: 25. To Lond, return'd
that Evening. I had a dangerous fall out of the Coach in Covent
Garden, going to my Bro: but without harme, The Lord be praised:
26: our Viccar on his former subject: shewing how the old man,
dwelt even in the regenerate;

27 I tooke preventing Physick.

May: 1 Divers Souldiers quarter'd at my house, but I thank God,
went away the next day towards Flanders: 2: I tooke Physick. The
next-day (lying at Greenewich on the 4th) I went into Surrey with
my Co: G: Tuke, to see Baynards, an house of my Bro: Richards,
which he would have hired: We going in a Charriot drawne with
unruly young horses, one of which (they said) had already killed two
keepers, were often in very greate danger; so as after 20 [miles]
riding, we were forced to change our horses. This is a very faire and
noble house of my Bro: built in a park, and having one of the
goodliest avenue[s] of Oakes up to it, that ever I saw: There is also
a pond of 60 Ackers neere it: The Windos of the chiefe roomes are
of very fine painted glasse: but the situation excessively dirty and
melancholy . . . [13] There had ben at my house this afternoone
Laurence president of Olivers Council, and some other of his
Court Lords to see my Garden and plantations: 14. Came my Aunt
Hungerford to dinner:

                              . . .

7 June My Wife fell in Labour from 2 in the morning till 8½ at
night, when my fourth Sonne was borne, it being Sonday: he was
Christned on Wednesday on the 10th and named George (after my
Grandfathers name) my Bro: Rich: Evelyn: Co: George Tuke and
Lady Cotton susceptors etc: Dr. Jer: Taylor officiating in the
withdrawing-roome at Says-Court:

                              . . .

A Curious Cat

16 To Lond, returned: 18 I saw at Greenewich a sort of Catt
brought from the East Indies, shaped and snouted much like the
Egyptian Ratoone, in the body like a Monkey, and so footed: the
eares and taile like a Catt, onely the taile much longer, and the Skin
curiously ringed, with black and white: With this taile, it wound up
its body like a Serpent, and so got up into trees, and with it, would
also wrap its whole body round: It was of a wolly haire as a lamb,

exceedingly nimble, and yet gentle, and purr'd as dos the Cat.

. . .

July: 3 A ship blown-up at Wapping, shooke my whole house, and the chaire I was sitting and reading in [in] my study . . .

. . .

A 'Way-Wiser'

August 2: Our Minister on the same Text: 6: I went to see Coll: Blount who shewed me the application of the Way-Wiser to a Coach, exactly measuring the miles, and shewing it by an Index as one rid along: It had 3 Circles, one point[e]d to the number of rods: The other to the miles by 10, to 1000: with all the subdivisions of quarters etc: very pretty, and very usefull . . .

. . .

The East India Company

[November] 20 I went to Lond: to a Court of the E. India Comp; upon its new Union: where was much dissorder by reason of the Anabaptists, who would have the Adventurers obliged onely by an Engagement, without Swearing, that they might still pursue their private trade; but it was carried against them: and that Wednesday should be a Generall Court for Election of Officers; after Sermon, and prayers for good successe: The stock resolv'd on was 800000 pounds: (27) I tooke the Oath, at the E. India house, subscribing 500 pounds: and so returnd . . .

. . .

A Brush with the Soldiers

[December] 20 Viccar: proceeded: 25, I went with my Wife etc: to Lond: to celebrate Christmas day. Mr. Gunning preaching in Excester Chapell on 7: Micha 2. Sermon Ended, as he was giving us the holy Sacrament, The Chapell was surrounded with Souldiers: All the Communicants and Assembly surpriz'd and kept Prisoners by them, some in the house, others carried away: It fell to my share to be confined to a roome in the house, where yet were permitted to Dine with the master of it, the Countesse of Dorset, Lady Hatton and some others of quality who invited me: In the afternoone came Collonel Whaly, Goffe and others from Whitehall to examine us one by one, and some they committed to the Martial, some to Prison, some Committed: When I came before them they tooke my name and aboad, examind me, why contrarie to an Ordinance made that none should any longer observe the superstitious time of the Nativity (so esteem'd by them) I durst offend, and particularly be at Common prayers, which they told me was but the Masse in English, and particularly pray for Charles stuard, for which we had no Scripture: I told them we did not pray for Cha: Steward but for all Christian Kings, Princes and Governors: The[y] replied, in so doing we praied for the K. of Spaine too, who was their Enemie, and a Papist, with other frivolous and insnaring questions, with much threatning, and finding no colour to detaine me longer, with much pitty of my Ignorance, they dismiss'd me: These were men of high flight, and above Ordinances: and spake spitefull things of our B: Lords nativity: so I got home late the next day blessed be God: These wretched miscreants, held their muskets against us as we came up to receive the Sacred Elements, as if they would have shot us at the Altar, but yet suffering us to finish the Office of Communion, as perhaps not in their Instructions what they should do in case they found us in that Action . . .

. . .

Death of Young Richard

[1658. January] 27 After six fitts of a Quartan Ague it pleased God to visite my deare Child Dick with fitts so extreame, especiale one of his sides, that after the rigor was over and he in his hot fitt, he fell into so greate and intollerable a sweate, that being surpriz'd with the aboundance of vapours ascending to his head, he fell into such fatal Symptoms, as all the help at hand was not able to recover his spirits, so as after a long and painefull Conflict, falling to sleepe as we thought, and coverd too warme, (though in midst of a severe frosty season) and by a greate fire in the roome; he plainely expird, to our unexpressable griefe and affliction. We sent for Physitians to Lond, whilst there was yet life in him; but the river was frozen up, and the Coach brake by the way ere it got a mile from the house; so as all artificial help failing, and his natural strength exhausted, we lost the prettiest, and dearest Child, that ever parents had, being but 5 yeares and 3 days old in years but even at that tender age, a prodigie for Witt, and understanding; for beauty of body a very

Angel, and for endowments of mind, of incredible and rare hopes. To give onely a little tast of some of them, and thereby glory to God, (who out of the mouths of Babes and Infants dos sometimes perfect his praises) At 2 yeare and halfe old he could perfectly reade any of the English, Latine, french or Gottic letters; pronouncing the three first languages exactly: He had before the 5t yeare or in that yeare not onely skill to reade most written hands, but to decline all the Nounes, Conjugate the verbs, regular, and most of the irregular; learned out *Puerilis*, got by heart almost the intire Vocabularie of Latine and french primitives and words, could make congruous Syntax, turne English into Lat: and vice versa, construe and prove what he read and did, the government and use of Relatives, Verbs Transitive, Substantives etc: Elipses and many figure and tropes, and made a considerable progresse in Commenius's *Janua*; began himselfe [to] write legibly, and had a strange passion for Greeke: the number of Verses he could recite was prodigious, and what he remembred of the parts of playes, which he would also act: and when seeing a Plautus in ones hand, he asked what booke it was, and being told it was Comedy etc, and too difficult for him, he wept for sorrow: strange was his apt and ingenious application of Fables and Morals, for he had read Æsop, and had a wonderfull disposition to Mathematics, having by heart, divers propositions of Euclid that were read to him in play, and he would make lines, and demonstrate them: As to his Piety, astonishing were his applications of Scripture upon occasion, and his sense of God, he had learn'd all his Catechisme early, and understood the historical part of the Bible and N. Test: to a wonder, and how Christ came to redeeme Mankind etc: and how comprehending these necessarys, himselfe, his Godfathers etc were discharged of their promise: These and the like illuminations, far exceeding his age and experience considering the prettinesse of his addresse and behaviour, cannot but leave impressions in me at the memory of him: When one told him how many dayes a certaine Quaker had fasted in Colchester, he replied, that was no wonder; for Christ had sayd, That Man should not live by bread alone, but by the word of God: He would of himselfe select the most pathetical Psalmes, and Chapters out of Jobe, to reade to his Mayde, during his sicknesse, telling her (when she pittied him) that all Gods Children must suffer affliction: He declaim'd against the

Vanities of the World, before he had seene any: often he would desire those who came to see him, to pray by him, and before he fell sick a yeare, to kneele and pray with him alone in some Corner: How thankfully would he receive admonition, how soone be reconciled! how indifferent, continualy cherefull: Grave advise would he be giving his brother John, beare with his impertinences, and say he was but a Child: If he heard of, or saw any new thing, he was unquiet till he was told how it was made, and brought us all difficulties that he found in booke, to be expounded: He had learn'd by heart divers Sentences in Lat: and Greeke which on occasion he would produce even to wonder: In a word he was all life, all prettinesse, far from morose, sullen, or childish in any thing he said or did: The last time he had ben at Church, (which was at Greenewich) according to costome, I asked him what he remem-bred of the Sermon: Two good-things Father, replys he: *Bonum Gratiæ*, and *bonum Gloriæ* with a just account of what the preacher said: The day before he died, he cald to me, and in a more serious manner than usualy, Told me, That for all I loved him so dearely, I would give my house, land and all my fine things to his Bro: Jack, he should have none of them, and next morning when first he found himselfe ill, and that I perswaded him to keepe his hands in bed, he demanded, whither he might pray to God with his hands un-joyn'd, and a little after, whilst in greate agonie, whither he should not offend God, by using his holy name so oft, calling for Ease: What shall I say of his frequent pathetical ejaculations utter'd of himselfe, Sweete Jesus save me, deliver me, pardon my sinns, Let thine Angels receive me etc: so early knowledge, so much piety and perfection; but thus God having dressed up a Saint fit for himselfe, would not permit him longer with us, unworthy of the future fruites of this incomparable hopefull blossome: such a Child I never saw; for such a child I blesse God, in whose boosome he is: May I and mine become as this little child, which now follows the Child Jesus, that Lamb of God, in a white robe whithersoever he gos. Even so Lord Jesus, *fiat Voluntas tua*, Thou gavest him to us, thou has taken him from us, blessed be the name of the Lord, That I had any thing acceptable to thee, was from thy Grace alone, since from me he had nothing but sinn; But that thou has pardon'd, blessed be my God for ever Amen:

30 On the Saturday following, I sufferd the Physitians to have

him opened: Dr. Needham and Dr. Welles, who were come three days before, and a little time ere he expired, but was past all help, and in my opinion he was suffocated by the woman and maide that tended him, and covered him too hott with blankets as he lay in a Cradle, neere an excessive hot fire in a close roome; for my Wife and I being then below and not long come from him, being come up, and I lifting up the blanket, which had quite cove[re]d the Cradle, taking first notice of his wonderfull fresh colour, and hardly hearing him breath or heave, soone perceived that he was neere overcome with heate and sweate, and so doubtlesse it was, and the Child so farr gon, as we could not make him to heare, or once open his eyes, though life was apparantly in him: we gave him some thing to make him neeze but ineffectivly: Being open'd . . . they confidently affirm'd the Child was (as tis vulgarly cald) liver-growne, and thence that sicknesse and so frequent complaint of his side: and indeede both Liver and Splen were exceedingly large etc: After this I caused the body to be Cofin'd in Lead, and reposited him that night, about 8 a clock in the Church of Deptford, accompanied with divers of my relations and neighbours, among whom I distributed rings with this – *Dominus abstulit*: intending (God willing) to have him transported with my owne body, to be interrd at our Dormitorie in Wotton chur[c]h in my deare native County Surry, and to lay my bones and mingle my dust with my Fathers, etc: If God be so gracious to me; and make me as fit for him, as this blessed child was: Here ends the joy of my life, and for which I go even mourning to the grave: The L. Jesus sanctifie this and all other my Afflictions: Amen:

. . .

[February] 15 The afflicting hand of God being still upon us, it pleased him also to take away from us this morning my other youngest sonn George now 7 weekes languishing at Nurse, breeding Teeth, and ending in a Dropsie: Gods holy will be don: he was buried in Deptford Church the 17th following . . .

. . . [March] This had ben the severest Winter, that man alive had knowne in England: The Crowes feete were frozen to their prey: Ilands of Ice inclosd both fish and foule frozen, and some persons in their boates:

. . .

'Let bloud in the foote'

[April] 21 Being greately afflicted with the Hemerhoids [bleed-ing] very much, by reason of the purges which I tooke, stoping this day on a suddain taking cold, I was so ill, that I was not far from death, and so continud to the 23. when being let bloud in the foote, it pleas'd God to restore me after some time; Blessed [be] God.

. . .

June 2. An extraordinary storme of haile and raine, cold season as winter, wind northerly neere 6 moneths.

A Stranded Whale

3 A large Whale taken, twixt my Land butting on the Thames and Greenewich, which drew an infinite Concourse to see it, by water, horse, coach, on foote from Lond, and all parts: It appeared first below Greenewich at low-water, for at high water, it would have destroyed all the boates: but lying now in shallow water, incompassd with boates, after a long Conflict it was killed with the harping yrons, and struck in the head, out of which spouted blood and water, by two tunnells like Smoake from a chimny: and after an horrid grone it ran quite on shore and died: The length was 58 foote: 16 in height, black skin'd like Coach-leather, very small eyes, greate taile, small finns and but 2: a piked snout, and a mouth so wide and divers men might have stood upright in it: No teeth at all, but sucked the slime onely as thro a grate made of that bone which we call Whale bone: The throate [yet] so narrow, as would not have admitted the least of fishes . . .

. . .

. . . [August] The 10th to Sir Ambros Brown at Betchworth Castle in that tempestious Wind, which threw-downe my greatest trees at Says Court, and did so much mischiefe all England over: It continued all night, till 3 afternoone next day, and was S.West, destroying all our winter fruit . . .

September 3 Died that archrebell Oliver Cromewell, cal'd Protector . . .

. . .

'The joyfullest funerall that ever I saw'

. . . [November] 22 To Lond, to visite my Bro: and the next day saw the superb Funerall of the Protectors: 23 He was carried from

Somerset-house in a velvet bed of state drawn by six horses houss'd with the same: The Pall held-up by his new Lords: Oliver lying in Effigie in royal robes, and Crown'd with a Crown, scepter, and Mund, like a King: The Pendants, and Guidons were carried by the Officers of the Army, The Imperial banners, Atchivements etc by the Heraulds in their Coates, a rich caparizon'd Horse all embroidred over with gold: a Knight of honour arm'd *Cap a pè* and after all his Guards, Souldiers and innumerable Mourners: In this equipage they proceeded to Westminster μετ᾽ [πολλῆς] φαντασιας* etc: but it was the joyfullest funerall that ever I saw, for there was none that Cried, but dogs, which the souldiers hooted away with a barbarous noise; drinking, and taking Tabacco in the streetes as they went: I went not home til the 17th.

. . .

[1659. May] 5 I went to visite my Bro, and next day to see a new Opera after the Italian way in Recitative Music and Sceanes, much inferior to the Italian composure and magnificence: but what was prodigious, that in a time of such a publique Consternation, such a Vanity should be kept up or permitted; I being ingag'd with company, could not decently resist the going to see it, though my heart smote me for it: I returnd home:

7 Came the Ambassador of Holland and Lady to visite me, and staid the whole afternoone:

. . .

'No Government in the Nation'

. . . [October] We had now no Government in the Nation, all in Confusion; no Magistrate either own'd or pretended, but the souldiers and they not agreed: God Almight[y] have mercy on, and settle us . . .

. . .

Colonel Morley Tempted

[December] 10 I treated privately with Coll: Morley (then Lieutenant of the Tower, and in greate trust and power) concerning delivering it to the King, and the bringing of him in, to the greate hazard of my life; but the Colonel had ben my Schole-fellow and I knew would not betray me . . .

. . .

   . . . [1660. January 22] I went this afternoone to visite Colonel Morley, then Lieutennant of the Tower: of Lond. In the Chapell, a young man preach'd, on 7 Eccles: 9: against the passion of Anger very well: After dinner, I discoursd the Colonel, but he was very jealous, and would not believe Monk came in to do the King any service. I told him he might do it without him, and have all the honour; he was still doubtfull, and would resolve on nothing yet: so I tooke leave, and 23 went home, to see a sick person at my house at S. Court, and returnd the 26:

   . . .

General Monck Acts*

   [February] Generall Monke came now to Lond: out of Scotland, but no man knew what he would do, or declare, yet was he mett on all his way by the Gent: of all the Counties which he pass'd, with petitions that he would recall the old long interrupted Parliament, and settle the Nation in some order, being at this time in a most prodigious Confusion, and under no government, every body expecting what would be next, and what he would do. 5. A stranger made an excellent discourse on 1. Joh. 3. 1. concerning the greate Love of God, to Man. In the afternoone M: Chamberleyne on 1. Cor: 9. 26. of the active, and contending life of a Christian. 10: Mr. Gunn: on the fast. 31. Jer: as before: Now were the Gates of the Citty broken-downe by Gen: Monke, which exceedingly exasperated the Citty; the Souldiers marching up and downe as triumphing over it, and all the old Army of the phanatics put out of their posts, and sent out of Towne. 11 I visited Mr. Boyle, where I met the Earle of Corke. A signal day: Monk perceiving how infamous and wretched a pack of knaves would have still usurped the Supreame power, and having intelligence that they intended to take away his commission, repenting of what he had don to the Citty, and where he and his forces quarterd; Marches to White hall, dissipates that nest of robbers, and convenes the old Parliament, the rump-parliament (so cal'd as retaining some few rotten members of the other) being dissolved; and for joy wheroff, were many thousands of rumps, roasted publiquely in the Streetes at the Bonfires this night, with ringing of bells, and universal jubilee: this was the first good omen.

   . . .

... 17: I fell sick, and that very dangerously of a malignant feavor: From Feb: 17th to the 5 of Aprill I was detained in Bed, with a kind of double Tertian, the cruell effects of the Spleene and other distempers, in that extremity, that my Physitians Dr. Wetherborn, Needham, Claud, were in greate doubt of my recovery, and in truth I was brought very low, but it pleased God to deliver me also out of this affliction, for which I render him hearty thanks ...

During this Sicknesse came innumerable of my Relations and friends to visite me, and it retarded my going into the Country longer than I intended: however I writ, and printed a letter in defence of his Majestie against a wicked forged paper, pretended to be sent from Bruxells, to defame his Majesties person, Virtues, and render him odious, now when every body were in hopes and expectation of the Gen: and Parliaments recalling him, and stablishing the Government on its antient and right basis: In doing which towards the decline of my sicknesse, and setting-up long in my bed, had caused a small relapse, out of which it yet pleased God also to free mee, so as by the 14th I was able to go into the Country, which the Physitians advisd me to, which I accordingly did to my Sweete and native aire at Wotton ...

May. 3 Came the most happy tidings of his Majesties gracious Declaration, and applications to the Parliament, Generall, and People etc and their dutifull acceptance and acknowledgement, after a most bloudy and unreasonable Rebellion of neere 20 yeares. Praised be forever the Lord of heaven, who onely dost wondrous things, because thy mercys indure forever.

...

9 I was desired and designed to accompany my Lord Berkeley with the publique Addresse of the Parliament Gen: etc: and invite him to come over, and assume his Kingly government, he being now at Breda; but being yet so weake and convalescent, I could not make that journey by sea, which was not a little to my detriment etc: so I went to Lond to excuse my selfe, returning the 10th, having yet received a gracious message from his Majestie, by Major Scot and Colonel Tuke. 13 our Viccar Mr. Litler preached on 4: Matt: 10. Shewing the necessity of giving God bodily worship:

...

The Reign of Charles II
1660–1685

The Restoration

[May] 29 This day came in his Majestie Charles the 2d to
London after a sad, and long Exile, and Calamitous Suffering both
of the King and Church: being 17 yeares: This was also his
Birthday, and with a Triumph of above 20000 horse and foote,
brandishing their swords and shouting with unexpressable joy: The
wayes straw'd with flowers, the bells ringing, the streetes hung with
Tapissry, fountaines running with wine: The Major, Aldermen, all
the Companies in their liver[ie]s, Chaines of Gold, banners; Lords
and nobles, Cloth of Silver, gold and vellvet every body clad in, the
windos and balconies all set with Ladys, Trumpets, Musick, and
[myriads] of people flocking the streetes and was as far as
Rochester, so as they were 7 houres in passing the Citty, even from
2 in the afternoone 'til nine at night: I stood in the strand, and
beheld it, and blessed God: And all this without one drop of bloud,
and by that very army, which rebell'd against him: but it was the
Lords doing, *et mirabile in oculis nostris*: for such a Restauration was
never seene in the mention of any history, antient or modern, since
the returne of the Babylonian Captivity, nor so joyfull a day, and so
bright, ever seene in this nation: this hapning when to expect or
effect it, was past all humane policy.

. . .

[June] 4 I received letters of Sir R: Brownes landing at Dov[e]r,
and also Letters from the Queene, which I was to deliver at
White-hall, not as yet presenting my selfe to his Majestie by reason
of the infinite concourse of people: It was indeed intollerable, as
well as unexpressable, the greedinesse of all sorts, men, women and
children to see his Majesty and kisse his hands, inso much as he
had scarce leasure to Eate for some dayes, coming as they did from
all parts of the Nation: And the King on the other side as willing to
give them that satisfaction, would have none kept out, but gave free
accesse to all sorts of people: Wherefore addressing my selfe to the

Duke, I was carried to his Majestie when he was alone, and very few noblemen with him, and kissed his hands, being very gratiously receivd: which don I return'd home to meet 5 Sir R: Browne, who came not 'til the Eight, after a 19 yeares Exile, during which yet, he kept up in his Chapell, the Liturgie and offices of the Church of England, to his no small honour, and in a time, when it was so low and as many thought utterly lost, that in many Controversies both with Papists and Sectaries, our divines used to argue for the visibility of the Church from his Chapell and Congregation: I went to Lond: this Evening, the 9., when on Whitsonday Mr. Gunning preached on 59. Esay 20. 21. Mr. Chamberlaine in Afternoone on 20 Joh: 22: I was all this Weeke too and froo at Court, about buisinesse.

15 Mr. Gunning, on 16 Joh: 7. 11. 16 The French, Italian and Dutch Ministers came to make their addresse to his Majestie, one Monsieur Stoope pronouncing the harange with greate Eloquence . . .

18 I proposed the Ambassy of Constantinople for Mr. Henshaw, but my Lord Winchelsea struck in: Goods that had ben pillag'd from White-hall during the Rebellion, now daily brought in and restor'd upon proclamation: as plate, Hangings, Pictures etc:

20 I saw the Audience of the Duke of Brandenburg: 21 The Warwick-shire Gentlemen (as also did all the shires and chiefe Townes in all the three Nations) present their Congratulatory Addresse to his Majestie. This was carried by my L. of Northampton. I went home this Evening:

29 St. Peters day to Lond: 30 The Sussex Gent presented their Addresse to which was my hand; I went with it, and kiss'd his Majesties hand; when his Majestie was pleasd to owne me more particularly, by calling me his old Acquaintance, and speaking very graciously to me:

. . .

[July] 3 I went to Hide-park where was his Majestie and aboundance of Gallantrie:

4 I heard Sir Sam: Tuke harangue to the house of Lords, in behalfe of the Ro: Catholicks: and his account of the transaction at Colchester about the Murdering of my Lo: Capel, and the rest of those brave men, that sufferd in cold bloud, after Articles of reddition etc:

5 I saw his Majestie go with as much pompe and splendor as any Earthly prince could do to the greate Citty feast: (The first they invited him to since his returne) but the exceeding raine which fell all that day, much eclips'd its luster: This was at Guild-hall, and there was also all the Parliament men, both Lords and Comm: the streetes adorn'd with Pageants etc: at immense cost:

The Royal Touch

6 His Majestie began first to Touch for the Evil according to costome: Thus, his Majestie sitting under his State in the Banqueting house: The Chirurgeons cause the sick to be brought or led up to the throne, who kneeling, the King strokes their faces or cheekes with both his hands at once: at which instant a Chaplaine in his formalities, says, 'He put his hands upon them, and he healed them', this is sayd, to every one in particular: when they have ben all touch'd, they come up againe in the same order, and the other Chaplaine kneeling and having Angel gold, strung on white ribbon on his arme, delivers them one by one to his Majestie: Who puts them about the neck of the Touched as they passe: whilst the first Chaplaine repeates: 'That is the true light who came into the World': Then followes an Epistle (as at first a Gospell) with the Liturgy prayers for the sick with some alteration: Lastly the blessing, And then the Lo: Chamberlaine and Comptroller of the household, bring basin, Ewer and Towell for his Majestie to wash:

The King received a Congratulatory Letter from the City of Collogne in Germany, where he had ben sometime in his Exile: his Majestie saying they were the best people in the world: the most kind and worthy to him that ever he met: His two Bro: D. of York and Gloucester din'd With his Majestie . . .

. . .

28 I heard his Majesties Speech in the Lords house, passing the bills of Tunnage and poundage, Restauration of my L. Ormond to his Estate in Ireland, concerning the Commission of the Sewers, and Continuance of the Excise. In the afternoone I saluted the Æbish: of Armagh my old friend, formerly of London Derry: he presented severall Irish Divines etc: to his Majestie (This was Dr. Bramall): to be promoted Bishops in that Kingdome, most of the Bishops in all the 3 Kingdome, being now almost worne out, and Sees vacant . . .

. . .

A Commission Declined

... [August] 23. Came Duke Hamilton, Lord Lothein and severall Scotish Lords, to see my Garden: 25. Coll: Specer, Coll: of a Regiment of horse in our County of Kent, sent to me, and intreated that I would take Commission for a Troope of Horse, and that I would nominate my Lieutennant and Ensigns: but I thanked him for the honour intended me, and would by no meanes embrace the trouble. ...

[September] 13 In the middst of all the joy and jubilie, dies the Duke of Gloucester of the Small-pox, which put all the Court in Mourning: died the 13th in prime of youthe, a Prince of extraordinary hopes etc ... ...

Disbanding the Army

Octob: 6. I paied the greate Tax of Pole-mony, levied for the disbanding of the Army, 'til now kept up; I paid as Esquire 10 pounds and 1s: for every Servant in my house etc:

7 Our Viccar on 2. Cor: 11. 26: There dind with me this day a french Count with Sir S: Tuke, who came to take leave of me, being now sent over to the Queene-Mother to breake* the Marriage of the Duke with the Daughter of Chancellor Hide; which the Queene would faine have undon; but it seemes matters were reconcild, upon greate offers of the Chancellor to befriend the Queene, who was much indebted, and was now to have the settlement of her affaire go thro his hands:

11 I went to Lond: to be sworn a Commissioner of the Sewers; and this day were those barbarous Regicides, who sat on the life of our late King, brought to their Tryal in the old baily, by a Commission of *Oyer & terminer*: I return'd at night. ...

Regicides Executed

17 This day were executed those murderous Traytors at Charing-Crosse, in sight of the place where they put to death their natural Prince, and in the Presence of the King his sonn, whom they also sought to kill: take[n] in the trap they laied for others: The Traytors executed were Scot, Scroope, Cook, Jones. I saw not their

execution, but met their quarters mangld and cutt and reaking as they were brought from the Gallows in baskets on the hurdle: ô miraculous providence of God; Three days before suffered Axtel, Carew, Clements, Hacker, Hewson and Peeters for reward of their Iniquity: I returnd:

. . .

28 His Majestie went to meete the Queene Mother:

29 Going to Lond: about my affaires, My Lord Majors shew stop'd me in cheape-side: one of the Pageants represented a greate Wood, with the royal Oake, and historie of his Majesties miraculous escape at Bosco-bell etc:

31 Arived now to my 40th yeare, I rendred to Almighty God my due and hearty thanks:

. . .

[November] 3 Arived her Majestie Queene Mother in to England, whence she had ben now banished almost 20 years; together with her illustrious daughter the Princesse Henrietta, divers other Prin[c]es and noblemen accompanying them. I return'd home.

. . .

23 Being this day in the Bed-Chamber of the Princesse Henrietta (where were many great beauties, and noble-men) I saluted divers of my old friends and acquaintance abroad; his Majestie carying my Wife to salute the Queene and Prin[c]esse, and then led her into his Closet, and with his owne hands shew'd her divers Curiosities.

. . .

The Royal Society

[1661. January] I was now chosen (and nominated by his Majestie for one of that Council) by Suffrage of the rest of the Members, a Fellow of the Philosophic Society, now meeting at Gressham Coll: where was an assembly of divers learned Gent: It being the first meeting since the returne of his Majestie in Lond: but begun some years before at Oxford, and interruptedly here in Lond: during the Rebellion: This morning was another rising of the Phanatics in which some were slaine: his Majestie being absent; til the 10th. 12 I returnd home:

16 I went to the Philosophic Club: where was examin'd the Torricellian experiment . . .

. . .

A Posthumous Revenge

30 Was the first Solemn Fast and day of humiliation to deplore the sinns which so long had provoked God against this Afflicted Church and people: orderd by Parliament to be annualy celebrated, to expiate the Gilt of the Execrable Murder of the late King Char: I, our Viccar preaching on 21. Deut: 7. 8. on which he made a very pious, and proper discourse: This day (ô the stupendious, and inscrutable Judgements of God) were the Carkasses of that arch-rebell Cromewell, Bradshaw the Judge who condemn'd his Majestie and Ireton, sonn in law to the Usurper, draged out of their superbe Tombs (in Westminster among the Kings), to Tyburne, and hanged on the Gallows there from 9 in the morning til 6 at night, and then buried under that fatal and ignominious Monument, in a deepe pitt: Thousands of people (who had seene them in all their pride and pompous insults) being spectators: looke back at November 22: 1658, and be astonish'd – 'And [fear] God, and honor the King, but meddle not with them who are given to change'.

. . .

A Missed Appointment

[March] 13 I went to Lambeth with Sir R: Brownes pretence to the Wardenship of Merton Coll: in Oxford, to which (as having about 40 years before ben student of that house) he was unanimously elected, one fellow onely excepted: now the statutes of that house being so, that unlesse every fellow agree, the election devolves to the Visitor, who is the A: Bish: of Canterbury, his Grace gave his vote to Sir T. Clayton resident there, and the Physick Professor; for which I was not at all displeas'd; because though Sir Rich: miss'd it, by much ingratitude and wrong of the Arch-Bishop (Clayton being no fellow) yet it would have hindred Sir Richard from attending at Court, to settle his greater Concernes, and prejudicd me: he being so much inclined to have pass'd his time in a Collegiate life, very unfit for him at that time for many reasons. So

I tooke leave of his Grace, who was Dr. Juxon, formerly L: Treasurer in the reigne of Charles I.

Mezzotinto Revealed

This after noone his hig[h]nesse Prince Rupert shewed me with his owne hands the new way of Graving call'd Mezzo Tinto, which afterwards I by his permission publish'd in my Historie of Chalcographie, which set so many artists on Worke, that they soone arived to that perfection it is since come, emulating the tenderest miniature.

. . .

April: 1 I din'd with that greate Mathematicia[n] and virtuoso Monsieur Zulecum, Inventor of the Pendule Clock and Phæ-nomenon of Saturns anulus; he was also elected into our Society: 4. I return'd home:

8. To Lond: 11 returnd: 12 Our Viccar on 2. Phil. 8. 13 I went to Parsons Greene to visite Mr. Rowland Chap: to my L. Mordaunt, now sick to death: 14 our Viccar on 4. Rom: 24, I received the H. Communion: 19 To Lond: about Says-Court buisinesse: Saw the bathing and rest of the Ceremonies of the Knights of the Bath preparatory to the Coronation, it was in the Painted Chamber in Westminster: I might have received this honour, but declined it: The rest of the ceremony was in the chapell at White-hall where their Swords being laid on the Altar, the Bishop deliverd them etc: 21. I heard part onely of a Sermon at St. Martines:

. . .

Coronation of Charles II

23 Was the Coronation of his Majesty Charles the Second in the Abby-Church of Westminster at all which Ceremonie I was present: The King and all his Nobility went to the Tower, I accompanying my L: Vicount Mordaunt part of the Way: This was on Sunday: 22: but indeede his Majestie went not 'til Early this morning, and proceeded from thence to Westminster . . . This magnificent Traine on horseback, as rich as Embroidery, velvet, Cloth of Gold and Sil: and Jewells could make them and their pransing horses, proceeded thro the streetes, strew'd with flowers, houses hung with rich Tapissry, Windos and Balconies full of Ladies, The Lond: Militia lining the ways, and the sevrrall

Companies with their Banners and Loud musique ranked in their orders: The Fountaines runing wine, bells ringing, with Speeches made at the severall Triumphal Arches: At that of the Temple Barre (neere which I stood) The Lord Major was received by the Baylife of Westminster who in a Scarlet robe made a Speech: Thence with joyfull acclamations his Majestie passed to White-hall: Bonfires at night and the next day being st. Georges he went by Water to Westminster Abby: when his Majestie was entered, the Deane and Prebends brought all the Regalia, and deliverd them to severall Noble-men, to beare before the King, who met them at the West dore of the church, singing an Antheme, to the Quire: Then came the Peres in their Robes and Coronets etc in their hands, til his Majestie was placed in a Throne elevated before the Altar: Then the Bish: of Lond (the A Bishop of Canterbury being sick) went to every side of the Throne to present the King to the People, asking if they would have him for their King, and do him homage, at which they shouted 4 Times 'God Save K. Ch: the 2d': Then an Anthem sung: Then his Majesty attended by 3 Bishops went up to the Altar, and he offerd a pall, and a pound of Gold: Then sate he downe in another chaire during the sermon, which was preached by Dr. Morley then B: of Worcester on   after Sermon the K: tooke his Oath before the Altar, to [mainetaine] the Religion, Mag: Charta and Laws of the Land: Then the Hymn 'Veni S. Sp.', then the Leitany by 2 Bish. Then the L: AB: of Cant (present but [much] indisposd and weake) said, Lift-up your hearts: Then rose up the King, and put off his robes and upper garments; and was in a Wastcoate so opened in divers places as the A: Bishop might commodiously anoint him, first in the palmes of his hands, then was sung an Anthem and prayer, Then his breast, and twixt the shoulders, bending of both armes, and lastly on the crowne of the head: with apposite hymns and prayers at each anoynting: Then closed and buttned up the Wastcoate, which was don by the Deane: Then was a Coyfe put on and the Colobium, Syndon or Dalmatic, and over this a Supertunic of Cloth of Gold, with buskins and sandals of the same, Spurrs, The Sword, a prayer being first saied over it by the A.Bish. on the Altar before 'twas girt on: by the L: Chamberlain: Then the Armill, Manteles etc: Then the A:B: placed the Crowne Imperial on the Altar, prayed over it, and set it on his Majesties Head, at which all the Peres put on their Coronets etc. Anthems and rare musique playing with Lutes, Viols, Trumpets, Organs, Voices etc. Then the A B: put a ring on his Majesties finger: Then the K. offered his Sword on the Altar: which being redeemed, was drawn and borne before him: Then the AB: deliverd him the Scepters with the Dove in one hand, and the other in the other with the Mond: Then the K. kneeling the A: Bish: pronounc'd the blessing: Then ascending againe his Regal Throne and 'Te Deum' singing all the Peeres did their Homage by every one touching his Crowne: The ArchBish and rest of the Bish: first kissing the King: Then he received the H: Sacrament, and so disrobed, yet with the Crowne Imperial on his head, accompanied with all the nobility in the former order, he went on foote upon blew cloth, which was spread and reachd from the West dore of the Abby, to Westminster Stayres where he tooke Water in a Triumphal barge to White-hall. where was extraordinary feasting:

24 I presented his Majestie with his Panegyric in the Privy Chamber, which he was pleasd most graciously to accept: etc. also to the L. Chancelor and most of the noble men who came to me for it, and dined at the Marq: of Ormonds now made Duke, where was a magnificent feast, and many greate persons:

A Redoubtable Snake

25 I went to the Society where were divers Experiments in Mr. Boyls Pneumatique Engine. We put in a Snake but could not kill it, by exhausting the aire, onely made it extreamly sick, but the chick died of Convulsions out right, in a short space:

. . .

May 1 I went to Hide Park to take the aire, where was his Majestie and an inumerable appearance of Gallantry and rich Coaches etc: it being now a time of universal festivity and joy: etc:

. . .

A Westminster School Election*

13 I heard, and saw such Exercises at the Election of Scholars at Westminster Schoole, to be sent to the Universitie, both in Lat: Gr: and Heb: Arabic etc in Theames and extemporary Verses, as wonderfully astonish'd me, in such young striplings, with that readinesse, and witt, some of them not above 12 or 13 years of age: and pitty it is, that what they attaine here so ripely, they either not

retaine, or improve more considerably, when they come to be men: though many of them do: and no lesse is to be blamed their odd pronouncing of Latine, so that out of England no nation were able to understand or endure it: The Examinants or Posers were Dr. Duport Greek professor at Cambridge: Dr. Fell: Deane of Christchu[rc]h, Oxon: Dr. Pierson, Dr. Alestree, Deane of Westminster and any that would:

14 His Majestie was pleased to discourse with me concerning severall particulars relating to our Society, and the Planet Saturne etc: as he sat at Supper in the withdrawing roome to his Bed-Chamber.

Experiments with Poisons

15 We made sevverall experiments on Vipers, and their biting of Dogs and Catts, to make tryall of a stone presented us from the E: Indias a pretended cure: 16. I dined at Mr. Garmus the Resident of Hamburg, who continud his feast neere 9 whole hours, according to the Custome of his Country; though no greate excesse of drinking, no man being obligd:

. . .

22 Was the Scotch-Covenant burnt by the common hangman in divers places of Lond: ô prodigious change! This after [noone] at our Society were severall discourses concerning poisons. Sir Jo Finch told us of an exquisite poyson of the D: of Florences that kill'd with a drop: That drawing a threit and needle dipt in it thro a hens thigh it perish'd immediatly, but if an hot needle were thrust after it, it cured the wound. This was tried also on a dog, successfully: That any thing thus killed, the limb affected being suddainly cut off the rest eate moste delicately and tender, without any detriment to the Eater: Hereupon Dr. Charleton affirm'd that having killed a Linnet with Nux Vomica suddainly: a Sea-Gull eating that bird died also immediately, and some other animal that prey'd on that Gull the Venume in force after the third Concoction . . .

. . .

[June] 19 Discourses at our Society about poysons againe. We gave Nux Vom: to birds that killed them out-right, afterwa[r]ds, because some writers affirmed Sublimate was its conterpoyson, we tried it on other birds, but it succeded not:

. . .

. . . [July:] 17 I went to Lond. at our Assembly: we put a Viper and slow-worme [or] Aspic to bite a Mouse, but could not irritate them to fasten at all . . .

. . .

[September] 13 To Lond: 14. I presented my *Fumifugium** dedicated to his Majestie who was pleased I should publish it by his special Command; being much pleasd with it:

. . .

22 Our Viccar on 26. Matt: 39: An exceeding sickly wet Autumne after a very wet summer:

Yachting with the King

October 1 I sailed this morning with his Majestie [on] one of his Yaachts (or Pleasure boates) Vessells newly known amongst us, til the Dut[c]h E. India Comp. presented that curious piece to the King, and very excellent sailing Vessels. It was on a Wager betweene his other new Pleasure boate, built fregate-like, and one of the Duke of Yorks, the wager 100 pounds. The race from Greenewich to Gravesend and back: The King lost it going, wind Contrary, but sav'd stakes returning: There were divers noble Person[s] and Lords on board: his Majestie sometimes steering himselfe: There attended his Barge and Kitchin boate: I brake fast this morning with the king, at returne in his smaller Vessell, he being pleasd to take me and onely foure more who were Noble-men with him: but dined in his Yacht, where we all Eate together with his Majestie. In this passage his Majestie was pleasd to discourse to me about my Book inveing against the nuisance of the Smoke of Lond: and proposing expedients how by removing those particulars I mention'd, it might be reformd; Commanding me to prepare a Bill, against the next session of Parliament; being (as he said) resolved to have something don in it . . .

. . .

. . . [November] 15 I dind with the Duke of Ormond: his Grace told me there were no Moules in Ireland, nor any Ratts 'til of late, and that but in one County; but a mistake that Spiders would not live there; onely not poyson: Also that they frequently took Salmon with dogs . . .

. . . [24] This night his Majestie fell into discourse with me Concerning Bees etc: 26: I saw Hamlet Pr: of Denmark played: but

now the old playe began to disgust this refined age; since his
Majestie being so long abroad . . .
. . .

Deep Play at Court

. . . [1662. January] This evening (according to costome) his
Majestie opned the Revells of that night, by throwing the Dice
himselfe, in the Privy Chamber, where was a table set on purpose,
and lost his 100 pounds: the yeare before he won 150 pounds: The
Ladys also plaied very deepe: I came away when the Duke of
Ormond had won about 1000 pounds and left them still at passage,
Cards etc: at other Tables, both there and at the Groome-porters,
observing the wiccked folly vanity and monstrous excesse of
Passion amongst some loosers, and sorry I am that such a wretched
Custome as play to that excesse should be countenanc'd in a Court,
which ought to be an example of Virtue to the rest of the kingdome.
. . .

A 'rare limmer'

10 Being call'd into his Majesties Closet, when Mr. Cooper (the
rare limmer) was crayoning of his face and head, to make the
stamps by, for the new mill'd mony, now contriving, I had the
honour to hold the Candle whilst it was doing; choosing to do this
at night and by candle light, for the better finding out the shadows;
during which his Majestie was pleasd to discourse with me about
severall things relating to Painting and Graving etc:
. . .

A Royal Visit

16 Having notice of his R: Highnesse the Duke of Yorks
intention to visite my poore habitation and Garden this day, I
returned; where he was pleasd to do me that honour of his owne
accord: and to stay some time viewing such things as I had to
entertaine his curiosity; after which he caused me to dine with him
at the Treasurer of the Navys house, and to sit with him coverd at
the same table: There were with his Highnesse The Duke of
Ormond and severall Lords: Then they viewed some of my
Ground, about a project of a Sasse or receptacle for ships to be
moored in; which was laied aside, as a fancy of Sir Nic: Crisp etc:

After this I accompanied the Duke to an East India vessel that lay at Black-Wall, where we had Entertain[me]nt of several curiosities: among other spiritous drinks, as Punch etc, they gave us Canarie that had ben carried to, and brought back from the Indies, which was indeede incomparably good: So I returned to Lond, with his highnesse. This night was acted before his Majestie the Widow, a lewd play:

. . .

Death of Elizabeth of Bohemia

[February] 17 This night was buried in Westminster the Queene of Bohemia (after all her sorrows and afflictions being come to die in her Nephews armes the King) and this night, and the next day fell such a storme of Haile, Thunder and lightning, as never was seene the like in any mans memorie; especialy the tempest of Wind, being South-west, which subverted besids huge trees, many houses, innumerable Chimnies, among other that of my parlor at Says Court, and made such havoc at land and sea, as severall perish'd on both: Divers lamentable fires were also kindled at this time: so exceedingly was Gods hand against this ungratefull, vicious Nation, and Court. 19. at our Assembly, discourses of Vegetation without Earth, for which I was ordered to prepare some experiments . . .

. . .

The Portuguese Queen*

[May] 30 The Queene arived, with a traine of Portugueze Ladys in their mo[n]strous fardingals or Guard-Infantas: Their complexions olivaster, and sufficiently unagreable: Her majestie in the same habit, her foretop long and turned aside very strangely: She was yet of the handsomest Countenance of all the rest, and tho low of stature pretily shaped, languishing and excellent Eyes, her teeth wronging her mouth by stiking a little too far out: for the rest sweete and lovely enough: This day was solemnly kept the Anniversary of his Majesties Birth, and restauration . . .

. . .

[2 June] I had newes sent me from home, that a Swarme of my Bees tooke flight, and hived them selves betweene a Cabine in his Majesties ship, the Oxford fregat; which telling the King of he tooke for a good omen; desiring me that none should disturb them.

I saw the rich Gudola sent his Majestie from the state of Venice, but it was not comparable for swiftnesse to our common wherries, though managed by Venetians . . .

Hampton Court

Hampton Court is as noble and uniforme a Pile and as Capacious as any Gotique Architecture can have made it . . . The Queene brought over with her from Portugal, such Indian Cabinets and large trunks of Laccar, as had never before ben seene here: The Greate hall is a most magnificent roome: The Chapell roofe incomparably fretted and gilt: I was also curious to visite the Wardrobe, and Tents, and other furniture of State: The Park formerly a flat, naked piece of Ground, now planted with sweete rows of lime-trees, and the Canale for water now neere perfected: also the hare park: In the Garden is a rich and noble fountaine, of Syrens and statues etc: cast in Copper by Fanelli, but no plenty of Water: The Cradle Walk of horne-beame in the Garden, is for the perplexed twining of the Trees, very observable etc: Another Parterr there is which they call Paradise in which a pretty banqueting house, set over a Cave or Cellar; all these Gardens might be exceedingly improved, as being too narrow for such a Palace . . .

. . . [July] 31. I sate with the Commissioners about reforming the buildings and streetes of London, and we ordered the Paving of the Way from st. James's north, which was a quagmire, and also of the Hay-market about Piqudillo, and agreed upon Instructions to be printed and published for the better-keeping the Streetes cleane: so returnd home:

. . .

The Queen Mother at Sayes Court

[August 14] This After-noone her Majestie Queene-Mother (with the Earle of St. Albans, and many greate Ladys and persons) was pleased to honour my poore Villa with her presence, and to accept of a Collation, being exceedingly pleased, and staying 'till very late in the Evening: The day following Came also my Lord Chancellor Earle of Clarendon (and Lady) his purse, and Mace borne before him, to Visite me, who likewise Collation'd with us, and was very merry: They had all ben our old acquaintances in Exile, during the Rebellion; and indeede this greate person was ever my friend etc: his sonn, my L: Corneberry was here too:

. . .

[August 17] I din'd at Mr. V. Chamberlaines, and then went to see the Q: Mother, who was pleased to give me many thanks for the Entertainement she receiv'd at my house, after which she recounted to me many observable stories of the Sagacity of some Dogs that she had formerly had.

The Royal Society's Arms

20: To Lond: I was this day admitted, and then Sworne one of the present Council of the Royal Society, being nominated in his Majesties Original Graunt, to be of this first Council, for the regulation of [the] Society, and making of such Laws and statutes as were conducible to its establishment and progresse: for which we now set a part every Wednesday morning, 'till they were all finished: My Lord Vicount Brounchar (that excellent Mathematitian etc) being also, by his Majestie, our Founders, nomination, our first [President]: The King being likewise pleas'd to give us the armes of England, to beare in a Canton, in our Armes, and send us a Mace of Silver guilt of the same fashion and bignesse with those carried before his Majestie to be borne before our President on Meeting-daies etc: which was brought us by Sir Gilbert Talbot, Master of his Majesties Jewelhouse.

. . .

A Water-Triumph

23 I this day was spectator of the most magnificent Triumph that certainely ever floted on the Thames, considering the innumerable number of boates and Vessels, dressd and adornd with all imaginab[l]e Pomp: but above all, the Thrones, Arches, Pageants and other representations, stately barges of the Lord Major, and Companies, with vari[o]us Inventions, musique, and Peales of Ordnance both from the vessels and shore, going to meete and Conduct the new Queene from Hampton Court to White-hall, at the first time of her Coming to Towne, [far] exceeding in my opinion, all the Venetian Bucentoro's etc on the Ascension when they go to Espouse the Adriatic: his Majestie and the Queene,

came in an antique-shaped open Vessell, covered with a State or Canopy of Cloth of Gold, made in forme of a Cupola, supported with high Corinthian Pillars, wreathd with flowers, festoones and Gyrlands: I was in our new-built Vessell, sailing amongst them.

. . .

'Discourse concerning Forest-trees' delivered

[October] 15 I this day delivered my Discourse concerning Forest-trees to our Society upon occasion of certaine Queries sent us by the Commissioners of his Majesties Navy: being the first Booke that was Printed by Order of the Society, and their Printer, since it was a Corporation:

. . .

A Muscovite Ambassador

[November] 27 I went to Lond: to see the Enterance of the Russian Ambassador whom his Majestie ordered should be received with much state, the Emperor his Master having not onely ben kind to his Majestie in his distresse, but banishing all Commerce with our Nation during the Rebellion: and first then the Citty Companies and Traind bands were all in their stations, his Majesties Army and Guards in greate order: his Excellency came in a very rich Coach, with some of his chiefe attendants; many of the rest on horse back, which being clad in their Vests, after the Eastern manner, rich furrs, Caps, and carrying the present, rendred a very exotic and magnificent shew: Some carrying Haukes, furrs, Teeth, Bows, etc:

. . .

[December] 29 To Lond: Saw the Audience of the Moscovy Ambassador, which was with extraordinary State: for his retinue being numerous, all clad in vests of several Colours, and with buskins after the Eastern manner: Their Caps of furr, and Tunicks richly embrodr[e]d with gold and pearle, made a glorious shew: The King being sate under the Canopie in the banqueting house, before the Ambassador went in a grave march the Secretary of the Embassy, holding up his Masters letters of Credence in a crimson-taffaty scarfe before his forehead: The Ambassador then deliverd it, with a profound reverence to the King, the King to our Secretary of State; it was written in a long and lofty style: Then came in the present borne by 165 of his retinue, consisting [of] Mantles and other large pieces lined with Sable, Black fox, Ermine, Persian Carpets, the ground cloth of Gold and Velvet, Sea-morce teeth aboundance, Haukes, such as they sayd never came the like; Horses, said to be Persian, Bowes and Arrows etc: which borne by so long a traine rendred it very extraordinary: Wind musick playing all the while in the Galleries above: This finish'd and the Ambassador conveyed by the Master of Ceremonies to York house, he was treated with a banquet, that cost 200 pounds, as I was assured: etc: I returned home.

. . .

. . . [1663. February 15] This night some villans brake into my house and study below and robb'd me to the Value of 60 pounds in plate, mony and goods.

. . .

Charles II at Sayes Court

[April] 30 Came his Majestie to honor my poore Villa with his presence, viewing the Gardens and even every roome of the house; and was then pleased to take a small refreshment: There was with him the Duke of Richmont, E: of St. Albans, L: Lauderdail and severall Persons of quality:

. . .

The King's Guards

. . . [July] 4: I saw his Majesties Guards being of horse and foote 4000 led by the Generall, The Duke of Albemarle, in extrordinary Equipage and gallantrie, consisting of Gent: of quality, and Veterane Souldiers, excellently clad, mounted and ordered, drawn up in batallia before their Majesties in Hide-parke, where the old Earle of Cleavela[n]d trailed a Pike, and led the right-hand file in a foote Company commanded by the Lord Wentworth his sonn, a worthy spactacle and example, being both of them old and valiant Souldiers: This was to shew the French Ambassador Monsieur Cominges: There being a greate Assembly of Coaches etc in the Park . . .

. . .

Planting Elms

[1664. April] This Spring I planted the home field and West field about Says-Court, with Elmes; being the same Yeare that the Elmes were also planted by his Majestie in Greenewich park.

. . .

A Tour to Cornbury

. . . [October] 17. I went with my L: V. Count Cornbury to Cornebury in Oxfordshire, to assist the Planting of the Park and beare him company, with Mr. Belin, both virtuous and friendly Gent: also with Mr. May, in Coach and six horses, din'd at Uxbridge, lay at Wicckam: 18 at Oxford, went through Woodstock where we beheld the destruction of that Royal Seate and Park by the late Rebels: and ariv'd that Evening at Cornbury, an house built by the Earle of Denby, in the midle of a Sweete dry Park walled with a Dry-wall: The house of excellent free stone, abounding in that park, a stone that is fine, but never swets or casts any damp: tis of ample receite, has goodly Cellars, the paving of the hall admirable, for the close laying of the Pavement: We design'd an handsome Chapell that was yet wanting, as Mr. May had the stables which indeede are very faire, having set out the Walkes in the Park, and Gardens: The Lodge is a prety solitude, and the Ponds very convenient; The Parke well stored. Hence on the 20: we went to see the famous Wells natural, and artificial Grotts and fountains calld Bushells Wells at Ensham: this Bushell had ben Secretary to my L. Verulam: It is an extraordinary solitude: There he had two Mummies, a Grott where he lay in an hamac like an Indian: Hence we went to Dichley an antient seate of the Lees, now Sir Hen: Lees, a low antient timber house, with a pretty bowling greene: My Lady gave us an extraordinary dinner: This Gent: Mother was Countesse of Rochester, who was also there, and Sir Walt: Saint Johns: There were some Pictures of their ancesters not ill Painted; the Gr: Grandfather had ben Knight of the Gartyr, also the Picture of a Pope and our Saviours head: so we returned to Cornbury:

23 Mr. Nash (formerly Præceptor to my Lord) preachd at Charlbery the Parish-Church, on 18 Luke 18: 24: We dined at Sir Tim: Tyrills at Shotover: this Gent: married the daughter and heyre of Bishop Usher A:B: of Armagh that learned Prælate: th[e]y

made a greate entertainement: There is here in the Grove, a fountain of the coldest water I ever felt: 'tis very cleere, his plantations of Oakes etc is commendable: so we went this Evening to Oxford, lay at Dr. Hides Principal of Magdalen Hall (related to my L:) bro: to the Lord Ch: Justice, and that Sir Henry Hide that lost his head for his Loyalty: we were handsomly entertaind two dayes.

...

Commissioner for Wounded and Prisoners of War

[28] Being casualy in the Privy Gallery at White-hall, his Majestie gave me thanks (before divers Lords and noble men) for my Book of *Architecture* and *Sylva* againe: That they were the best designd and usefull for the matter and subject, the best printed and designd (meaning the Tallè doucès of the Paralelles) that he had seene: then caused me to follow him alone to one of the Windows, he asked me if I had any paper about me un-written, and a Crayon; I presented him with both, and then laying it on the Window stoole, he with his owne hands, designed to me the plot for the future building of White-hall, together with the Roomes of State, and other particulars, which royal draft, though not so accurately don, I reserve as a rarity by me: After this he talked with me of severall matters, and asking my advice, of many particulars, in which I find his Majestie had an extraordin[ar]y talent, becoming a magnificent Prince: The same day, at Council (there being Commissioners to be made, to take care of such sick and Wounded, and Prisoners at War, as might be expected upon occasion of a succeeding Warr, and Action at sea; a War being already declared against the Hollanders) his Majestie was pleasd to nominate me to be one; amongst three other Gent: of quality, Parliament Men: viz: Sir William D'oily knight and Baronet, Sir Tho: Clifford since L: Tressurer of England, and Bullein Rhemys Esquire, with a Sallary of 1200 pounds amongst us, besides extraordinares etc: for our care and attendance in time of Action, each of us appointed his particular District, and mine falling out to be Kent, and Sussex: with power to constitu[t]e Officers, Physitians, Chirurgeons, Provost Martials etc: dispose of halfe of the Hospitals thro England: after which I kissed his Majesties hand, as did the rest of

my Collegues when the Council was up: At this Council, I heard
Mr. Solicitor Finch since L: Chan plead most elegantly the
Merchants Cause, trading to the Canaries, that his Majestie would
grant them a new Charter. 29 Was the most magnificent triumph by
Water and Land of the Ld: Major, I dined at Guild-hall: the feast
said to cost 1000 pounds: at the upper Table, placed next to Sir H:
Bennet Secretary of State, just opposite to my L: Chancelor and
the Duke of Buckingham, who sate betweene Monsieur Comming-
es the Fr: Ambassador, Lord Tressurer, Dukes of Ormond, of
Albemarle, E: of Manchester Lord Chamberlaine and the rest of
the greate officers of State: My Lord Major came twice up to us,
first drinking in a Golden Goblett his Majesties health, then the
French Kings (as a Complement to the Ambassador). Then we
return'd my L: Majors health, the Trumpets, Drumms sounding:
for the rest, the Cheere was not to be imagind for the Plenty and
raritie, an infinitie of Persons at the rest of the Tables in that ample
hall: so I slip'd away in the crowd and came home late.

. . .

[1665. January] 4 I went in Coach (it being excessive sharp frost
and snow) towards Dover, and other parts of Kent, to settle
Physitians, Chirurgeons, Agents, Martials and other offices in all
the Sea-Ports, to take Care of such as should be set on shore,
Wounded, sick or Prisoner etc in pursuance of our Commission,
reaching from the North foreland in Kent, to Portsmouth in
hampshir: the rest of the Ports in England, from thence, to Sir Will:
D'oily, to Sir Tho Clifford afterward L: Tress: of England, Bulleyn
Rhemes: so that evening I came to Rochester, where I delivered the
Privy Councils letter to the Major to receive orders from me: 5. I
arived at Canterbury, 6 being Epiphanie, when I went to the
Cathedral, exceedingly well repaired since his Majesties returne:
[7]: To Dover, where Col: Stroode Lieutennant of the Castle,
(having receiv'd the Letter I brought him from the Duke of
Albemarle) invited me, and made me lodge in the Castle, and was
splendidly treated, assisting me from place to place: here I settled
my first Deputy: 8: I heard an excellent sermon in the chiefe
Church on[e] Dr. Hynd, on 12: Rom: 6. The Major, and Officers
of the Costomes were very civel to me:

. . .

St. James's Park: 'a Melancholy water foule'

[February 9] I went to St. Ja: Parke, where I examin'd the Throate of the Onocratylus or Pelecan, the tongue scarce appearing, the Peake above 2 foote long, crooked at the very point and a little red at the tip: the neck rough, a fowle betweene a Stork and Swan and neere as big as a Swan; a Melancholy water foule: brought from Astracan by the Russian Ambassador: it was diverting to see how he would tosse up and turne a flat-fish, plaice or flounder to get it right into its gullet, for it has one at the lower beake which being filmy stretches to a prodigious widenesse when it devours a greate fish etc: Here was also a small Water-fowle that went almost quite erect, like the Penguin of America: It would eat as much fish as its whole body weighed, I never saw so unsatiable a devourer, I admir'd how it could swallo[w] so much and swell no bigger: I believe it to be the most voracious creature in nature, it was not biger than a More hen . . . The Parke was at this time stored with infinite flocks of severall sorts of ordinary, and extraordinary Wild foule, breeding about the Decoy, which for being neere so greate a Citty, and among such a concourse of Souldier[s], Guards and people, is very diverting: There were also Deere of severall countries, W[h]ite, spotted like Leopards, Antelope: An Elke, Red deeres, Robucks, Staggs, Guinny Goates; Arabian sheepe etc: The supporting the Withy potts or nests for the Wild foule to lay in, a little above the surface of the water was very pretty . . .

. . .

The Second Dutch War: Charles II's Kindness

[April] 20: To White-hall, to the King, who call'd me into his Bed-Chamber as he was dressing, to whom I shew'd the Letter written to me from his R: Highness the Duke of York from the Fleete, giving me notice of Young Evertse, and some other considerable Commanders (newly taken in fight with the *Dartmouth* and *Diamond* fregats) whom he had sent me as Prisoners at Warr: I went to know of his Majestie how he would have me treat them: who commanded me to bring the Young Cap: to him, and, to take the Dutch Ambassadors Word (who yet remained here) for the other, that he should render himselfe to me when ever I cald, and not stir without leave . . .

. . .

24 I presented Young Cap: Everse, eldest sonn of Cornelius, Vice-Admirall of Zealand, and Nephew of John now Admiral, a most valiant person, to his Majestie, being in his bed-chamber: the K. gave his hand to kisse, gave him his liberty, asked many quest: concerning the fight (it being the first bloud drawne) his Majestie remembring the many civilities he had formerly received from his relations abroad, and had now so much Interest in that Consider-able Province: Then I was commanded to go with him to the Holl: Ambassador, where he was to stay for his pass-port, and ordered me to give him 50 pieces in broad gold: next day I had the Ambassadors Parole for the other Cap: taken in Cap: Allens fight [before] Cales etc: 26: I gave his Majestie Accompt of what I had don, and desired the same favour for another Cap: which his Majestie gave me: 27: went I home . . .

. . .

Lowestoft: An Inconclusive Victory

[June] 8: Came newes of his Highnesse Victory over the Enemie, and indeede it might have ben a compleate one, and at once ended the Warr, had it ben pursued: but the Cowardize of some, Tretchery, or both frustrated that: we had however bonfires, bells, and rejoicing in the Citty etc . . .

. . .

[June] 23 The Duke of Yorke told us, that his dog sought out absolutely the very securest place of all the vessel, when they were in fight . . .

'The most glorious fleete'

30 I went to Chattam: 1 July downe to the fleete, with my Lord San[d]wich now Admiral, with whom I went in a Pinnace to the Buy of the Noore where the whole fleete rod at anker: went on board the Prince a vessel of 90 brasse ordnance, (most whole canon) and happly the best ship in the world both for building and sailing: she had 700 men: They made a greate 'huzza' or shout at our approch 3 times: here we dined with many noble men, Gent: and Volunteeres; served in Plate, and excellent meate of all sorts: after dinner came his Majestie and the Duke and Prince Rupert; and here I saw him knight Cap: Cuttance, for behaving himselfe so bravely in the late fight: and was amaz'd to [behold] the good order,

decency, and plenty of all things, in a vessell so full of men: The ship received an hundred Canon shot in her body: Then I went on board the *Charles*, to which after a Gun was shot off, came all the flag-officers to his Majestie, who there held a generall Council, determining his R. Highness should adventure himselfe no more this summer: I spake with Sir Geo: Ayscogh, Sir William Pen etc: and Sir William Coventry (secretary to the Duke) about buisinesse, and so came away late, having seene the most glorious fleete, that ever spread saile: here was also among the rest the *Royal Sovraigne*: we returned in his Majesties Yacht with my L: Sandwich and Mr. V: Chamberlaine landing at Chattam on Sunday morning: In the afternoone I went to Church at Chatt: where the Minister preached on   Redeeming the time, because the daies are evil etc: 3. I tooke order for 150 men to be carried on board, (who had ben recovered of their wounds and sicknesse) the *Clove-tree*, *Carolus quintus* and *Zeland*, ships that had ben taken by us in the fight: and so returnd home.

The Plague

... [16] There died of the Plague in Lond: this Weeke 1100: 23. our Curat on 8 Rom: 18: There perished this weeke above 2000, and now were two houses shut up in our parish: 30: our Doctor as formerly 1. Pet. 2. 5.

Aug: 2. Was the Solemn Fast through England to deprecate Gods displeasure against the Land by Pestilence and War ...

...

28 The Contagion growing now all about us, I sent my Wife and whole family (two or three of my necessary Servants excepted) to Wotton to my Brothers, being resolved to stay at my house my selfe, and to looke after my Charge, trusting in the providence and goodnesse of God.

...

[September] 7 Came home, there perishing now neere ten-thousand poore Creatures weekely: however I went all along the Citty and suburbs from Kent streete to St. James's, a dismal passage and dangerous, to see so many Cofines exposd in the streetes and the streete thin of people, the shops shut up, and all in mournefull silence, as not knowing whose turne might be next: I went to the D: of Albemarle for a Pest-ship, to waite on our infected men, who were not a few: 10: Dr. Plume at Greenewich, on 3. Coloss: 5. 6. shewing how our sinns had drawne downe Gods Judgements: I dined with the Commissioners of the Navy, retreated hither, and with whom I had buisinesse:

14 I went to Wotton, to see my Wife and family: 16: To visite old Secretary Nicholas being now at his new Purchase of West Horsley, once Mortgaged to me by my L: VC. Montague: a pretty drie seate on the downe: returned to Wotton. 17: Receiving a Letter from his Excellency my L. Sandwich of a defeate given to the Dut[c]h, I was forc'd to travell all Sonday, when by the way calling in to see my other Bro: at Woodcot, as I was at dinner, I was surpriz'd with a fainting fit: which much a'larm'd the family, as well it might, I coming so lately from infected places; but I blesse God it went off, so as I got home that night; but was exceedingly [perplex'd], to find that there were sent me to dispose of neere 3000 Prisoners at Warr; so as on the 18, I was forc'd to go to Lond; and take orders from my Lord Gen: what I should do with them, they being more than I had places fit to receive and guard, he made me dine with him, and then we consulted about it:

. . .

[October 1] This afternoone as I was at Evening prayer, tidings were brought me, of my Wifes being brought to bed at Wotton of a Daughter [Mary] (after 6 sonns) borne this morning 1. Octob: in the same Chamber, I had first tooke breath in . . .

. . . 10 I returned to Lond: I went thro the whole Citty, having occasion to alight out of the Coach in severall places about buisinesse of mony, when I was invironed with multitudes of poore pestiferous creatures, begging almes; the shops universaly shut up, a dreadfull prospect: I dined with my L: Gen: was to receive 10000 pounds and had Guards to convey both my selfe and it, and so returned [home], through Gods infinite mercy . . .

17 I went to Gravesend, next day to Chattam, thence to Maidstone, in order to the march of 500 Prisoners to Leeds Castle which I had hired of my Lord Culpeper . . .

. . .

Plunder of Prizes
. . . [November 27] There was no small suspicion of my Lord Sandwiches permitting divers Commanders that were in the fight

and action, at the taking the E. India prizes, to break bulk, and take to their owne selves many rich things, Jewels, Silkes etc: though I believe some whom I could name, fill'd their pockets, my L: Sandwich himselfe had the least share: however he underwent the blame of it, and it created him Enemies, and prepossessed the L: Generall, for he spake to me of it with much zeale and concerne, and I believe laied load enough on Sandwich at Oxford.

. . .

The Contagion Abated

[1666. January] After much, and indeede extraordinary mirth and cheere, all my Brothers, our Wives and Children being together, and after much sorrow and trouble during this Contagion, which separated our families, as well as others, I returned to my house, but 12 my Wife went back to Wotton, I not as yet willing to adventure her, the Contagion, though exceedingly abated, not as yet wholy extinguish'd amongst us:

. . .

29 I went to waite on his Majestie (now return'd from Oxford to Hampton Court) where the Duke of Albemarle presenting me to him, he ran towards me, and in most gracious manner gave me his hand to kisse, with many thanks for my Care, and faithfullnesse in his service, in a time of that greate danger, when every body fled their Employments; he told me he was much oblig'd to me, and said he was severall times concern'd for me, and the peril I under-went, and did receive my service most acceptably: Though in truth I did but what was my duty, and ô that I had perform'd it as I ought: After this his Majestie was pleas'd to talke with me alone neere an houre, of severall particulars of my Employment, and ordred me to attend him againe the thursday following at White-hall: Then the Duke came towards me and embrac'd me with much kindnesse, and told me, if he had but thought my danger would have ben so greate, he would not have sufferd his Majestie to employ me in that Station . . .

. . .

[February] 6 My Wife and family return'd to me now out of the Country, where they had ben since August by reason of the Contagion, now almost universaly ceasing: Blessed be God for his infinite mercy in preserving us; I having gon through so much danger, and lost so many of my poore officers, escaping still my selfe, that I might live to recount and magnifie his goodnesse to me . . .

. . .

Repairs to Leeds Castle

[May] 7 I went to Rochester: 8 To Queenborow where finding the *Richmond* fregate I sailed to the Buy of the Noore to my L: Gen: and Prince Rupert where was the Rendezvous of the most glorious Fleete in the World, now preparing to meete the Hollander; having received orders and settled my buisinesse there, I return'd on the 9th to Chattham at night: next day I went to visite my Co: Hales at a sweetely watred place neere Bochton at Chilston: The next morning to Leedes-Castle, once a famous hold etc. now hired by me of my Lord Culpeper for a Prison: here I flowed the drie moate and made a new draw bridge, brought also Spring Water into the Court of the Castle to an old fountaine, and tooke order for the repaires: 10: returnd to Rochester, and next day home:

. . .

The First of June: A Shattering Sea Fight

June: 1. Being in my Garden and hearing the Greate gunns go thick off: I immediately tooke horse, and rod that night to Rochester it being 6 at Evening when I set out: 2 Thence next day towards the Downes and Sea-Coast: but meeting with the Lieutenant of the *Hantshire* fregat, who told me what pass'd, or rather not pass'd, I returned to Lond: (there being no noise, nor appearance at Deale or that Coast of any engagement) this recounting to his Majestie (whom I found at St. Jams's Park impatiently expecting) and I knowing that Prince Rupert was loose, about 3 at St. Hellens point at N. of Wight, it greately rejoic'd him; but was astonish'd when I assur'd him they heard nothing of the Gunns in the Downes, nor the Lieutenant who landed there by five that morning.

. . .

5 I went this morning to Lond: where came severall particulars of the fight: 6. came Sir Dan: Harvey from the Generall and related the dreadfull encounter, upon which his Majestie commanded me to dispatch away an extraordinary Physitian, and more Chirurgions:

'Twas on the solemn fast day, when the newes came, his Majestie being in the Chapell made a suddaine Stop, to heare the relation, which being with much advantage on our side, his Majestie commanded that Publique Thanks should immediately be given as for a Victory; The Deane of the Chapell going downe to give notice of it to the other Deane officiating; and so notice was likewise sent to St. Paules and Westminster abby: But this was no sooner over, but newes came that our losse was very greate both in ships and men: That the *Prince* fregat was burnt and so a noble vessel of 90 brasse Guns lost: together with the taking of Sir Geo: Ayscue and exceeding shattring of both fleetes, so as both being obstinate, both parted rather for want of amunition and tackle than Courage, our Generall retreating like a Lyon, which exceedingly abated of our former jolitie: There was however order given for bone-fires and bells, but God knows, it was rather a deliverance than a Triumph: so much it pleased God to humble our late over Confidence, that nothing could withstand the Duke of Albemarle: who in good truth made too forward a reckoning of his successe, now, because he had once beaten the Dutch in another quarrell: and being ambitious to out-do the Earle of Sandwich, whom he had prejudice [to] as defective of Courage:

. . .

12 To Lond: to our Commission. 13 To the R: Society, where was brought the new Pendulum:

A Sad Spectacle

14 Went home: 15 I went to Chattham: 16 in the Jemmy Yach't (an incomparable sailer) to sea, arived by noone at the Fleete in the B of Nore, dined with Pr: Rupert and Generall: 17: came his Majestie, Duke, and many Noblemen; after Council, we went to Prayers: having dispatch'd my buisinesse, I return'd to Chattham having layne but one night at sea, in the *Royal Charles*, we had a tempestuous sea; I went on shore at Sheere-Nesse, where they were building an Arsenal for the Fleete, and designing a royal Fort, with a receptable for greate ships to ride at Anker; but here I beheld that sad spectacle, namely more than halfe of that gallant bulwark of the Kingdome miserably shatterd, hardly a Vessell intire, but appearing rather so many wracks and hulls, so cruely had the Dutch mangled us: when the losse of the *Prince* (that gallant

Vessell) had ben a losse to be universaly deplor'd, none knowing for
what reason we first ingagd in this ungratefull warr: we lost besids 9
or 10 more, and neere 600 men slaine, and 1100 wounded 2000
Prisoners, to balance which perhaps we might destroy 18 or 20 of
the Enemies ships and 7 or 800 poore men: 18 weary of this sad
sight I returned home . . .

   . . .

Surveying Old St. Paul's

[August] 27 I went to St. Paules Church in Lond: where with Dr.
Wren, Mr. Prat, Mr. May, Mr. Tho: Chichley, Mr. Slingsby, the
Bish: of Lond., the Deane of S. Paule, and severall expert
Workmen, we went about, to survey the generall decays of that
antient and venerable Church, and to set downe the particulars in
writing, what was fit to be don, with the charge thereof: giving our
opinion from article to article: We found the maine building to
receede outward: It was Mr. Chichleys and Prats opinion that it
had ben so built ab origine for an effect in Perspective, in reguard
of the height; but I was with Dr. Wren quite of another judgement,
as indeede ridiculous, and so we entered it: We plumbed the
Uprights in severall places: When we came to the Steeple, it was
deliberated whither it were not well enought to repaire it onely
upon its old foundation, with reservation to the 4 Pillars: This Mr.
Chichley and Prat were also for; but we totaly rejected it and
persisted that it requird a new foundation, not onely in reguard of
the necessitie, but for that the shape of what stood was very meane,
and we had a mind to build it with a noble Cupola, a forme of
church building, not as yet knowne in England, but of wonderfull
grace: for this purpose we offerd to bring in a draught and estimate,
which (after much contest) was at last assented to, and that we
should nominate a Committè of able Workemen to examine the
present foundation: This concluded we drew all up in Writing, and
so going with my L: Bishop to the Deanes, after a little
refreshment, went home.

   . . .

The Great Fire of London

September 2: This fatal night about ten, began that deplorable
fire, neere Fish-streete in Lond: 2: I had pub: prayers at home:

after dinner the fire continuing, with my Wife and Sonn took Coach and went to the bank side in Southwark, where we beheld that dismal speectaccle, the whole Citty in dreadfull flames neere the Water side, and had now consumed all the houses from the bridge all Thames Streete and up-wards towards Cheape side, downe to the three Cranes, and so returned exceedingly astonishd, what would become of the rest: 3 The Fire having continud all this night (if I may call that night, which was as light as day for 10 miles round about after a dreadfull manner) when consp[ir]ing with a fierce Eastern Wind, in a very drie season, I went on foote to the same place, when I saw the whole South part of the Citty burning from Cheape side to the Thames, and all along Cornehill (for it likewise kindled back against the Wind, as well [as] forward) Tower-Streete, Fen-church-streete, Gracious Streete, and so along to Bainard Castle, and was now taking hold of St. Paules-Church, to which the Scaffalds contributed exceedingly: The Conflagration was so universal, and the people so astonish'd, that from the beginning (I know not by what desponding or fate), they hardly stirr'd to quench it, so as there was nothing heard or seene but crying out and lamentation, and running about like distracted creatures, without at all attempting to save even their goods; such a strange consternation there was upon them, so as it burned both in breadth and length, The Churches, Publique Halls, Exchange, Hospitals, Monuments, and ornaments, leaping after a prodigious manner from house to house and streete to streete, at greate distance one from the other, for the heate (with a long set of faire and warme weather) had even ignited the aire, and prepared the materials to conceive the fire, which devoured after a[n] incredible manner, houses, furniture and everything: Here we saw the Thames coverd with goods floating, all the barges and boates laden with what some had time and courage to save, as on the other, the Carts etc carrying out to the fields, which for many miles were strewed with moveables of all sorts, and Tents erecting to shelter both people and what goods they could get away: ô the miserable and calamitous speectacle, such as happly the whole world had not seene the like since the foundation of it, nor to be out don, 'til the universal Conflagration of it, all the skie were of a fiery aspect, like the top of a burning Oven, and the light seene above 40 miles round about for many nights: God grant mine eyes may never behold the like, who now saw above ten thousand houses all in one flame, the noise and crakling and thunder of the impetuous flames, the shreeking of Women and children, the hurry of people, the fall of towers, houses and churches was like an hideous storme, and the aire all about so hot and inflam'd that at the last one was not able to approch it, so as they were force'd [to] stand still, and let the flames consume on which they did for neere two whole mile[s] in length and one in bredth: The Clowds also of Smoke were dismall, and reached upon computation neere 50 miles in length: Thus I left it this afternoone burning, a resemblance of Sodome, or the last day: It call'd to mind that of 4 Heb: 'non enim hic habemus stabilem Civitatem': the ruines resembling the picture of Troy: London was, but is no more: Thus I return'd:

4. The burning still rages; I went now on horse back, and it was now gotten as far as the Inner Temple; all Fleetestreete, old baily, Ludgate hill, Warwick Lane, Newgate, Paules Chaine, Wattling-streete now flaming and most of it reduc'd to ashes, the stones of Paules flew like granados, the Lead mealting downe the streetes in a streame, and the very pavements of them glowing with fiery rednesse, so as nor horse nor man was able to tread on them, and the demolitions had stopped all the passages, so as no help could be applied; the Easter[n] Wind still more impetuously driving the flames forewards: Nothing but the almighty power of God was able to stop them, for vaine was the help of man: on the fift it crossed towards White-hall, but ô the Confusion was then at that Court: It pleased his Majestie to command me among the rest to looke after the quenching of fetter-lane end, to preserve (if possible) that part of Holborn, whilst the rest of the Gent: tooke their several posts, some at one part, some at another, for now they began to bestirr themselves, and not 'til now, who 'til now had stood as men interdict, with their hands a crosse, and began to consider that nothing was like to put a stop, but the blowing up of so many houses, as might make a [wider] gap, than any had yet ben made by the ordinary method of pulling them downe with Engines; This some stout Seamen proposd early enought to have saved the whole Citty; but some tenacious and avaritious Men, Aldermen etc. would not permitt, because their houses must have ben [of] the first: It was therefore now commanded to be practised, and my concerne being particularly for the Hospital of st. Bartholomeus neere

Smithfield, where I had many wounded and sick men, made me the more diligent to promote it; nor was my care for the Savoy lesse: So as it pleased Almighty God by abating of the Wind, and the industrie of people, now when all was lost, infusing a new Spirit into them (and such as had if exerted in time undoubtedly preserved the whole) that the furie of it began sensibly to abate, about noone, so as it came no farther than the Temple West-ward, nor than the enterance of Smithfield North; but continued all this day and night so impetuous toward Cripple-Gate, and The Tower, as made us even all despaire; It also brake out againe in the Temple: but the courage of the multitude persisting, and innumerable houses blown up with Gunpowder, such gaps and desolations were soone made, as also by the former three days consumption, as the back fire did not so vehemently urge upon the rest, as formerly: There was yet no standing neere the burning and glowing ruines neere a furlongs Space; The Coale and Wood wharfes and magazines of Oyle, rozine, chandler etc: did infinite mischiefe; so as the invective I but a little before dedicated to his Majestie and publish'd,* giving warning what might probably be the issue of suffering those shops to be in the Citty, was lookd on as prophetic: but there I left this smoking and sulltry heape, which mounted up in dismall clowds night and day, the poore Inhabitans dispersd all about St. Georges, Moore filds, as far as higate, and severall miles in Circle, Some under tents, others under miserab[l]e Hutts and Hovells, without a rag, or any necessary utinsils, bed or board, who from delicatnesse, riches and easy accommodations in stately and well furnishd houses, were now reduc'd to extreamest misery and poverty: In this Calamitous Condition I returnd with a sad heart to my house, blessing and adoring the distinguishing mercy of God, to me and mine, who in the midst of all this ruine, was like Lot, in my little Zoar, safe and sound:

6 Thursday, I represented to his Majestie the Case, of the French Prisoners at War in my Custodie, and besought him, there might be still the same care of Watching at all places contiguous to unseized houses: It is not indeede imaginable how extraordinary the vigilanc[e] and activity of the King and Duke was, even labouring in person, and being present, to command, order, reward, and encourage Workemen; by which he shewed his affection to his people, and gained theirs: Having then disposed of

some under Cure, at the Savoy, I return'd to white hall, where I dined at Mr. Offleys, Groome-porter, who was my relation, together with the Knight Martial, where I also lay that night.

Aftermath of the Great Fire

7 I went this morning on foote from White hall as far as London bridge, thro the Late fleete streete, Ludgate hill, by St. Paules, Cheape side, Exchange, Bishopsgate, Aldersgate, and out to Morefields, thence thro Cornehill, etc: with extraordinary difficulty, clambring over mountaines of yet smoking rubbish, and frequently mistaking where I was, the ground under my feete so hott, as made me not onely Sweate, but even burnt the soles of my shoes, and put me all over in Sweate: In the meane time his Majestie got to the Tower by Water, to demolish the houses about the Graft, which being built intirely about it, had they taken fire, and attaq'd the white Towre, where the Magazines of Powder lay, would undo[u]btedly have not onely beaten downe and destroyed all the bridge, but sunke and torne all the vessels in the river, and rendred the demolition beyond all expression for severall miles even about the Country at many miles distance: At my returne I was infinitly concern'd to find that goodly Chur[c]h St. Paules now a sad ruine, and that beautifull Portico (for structure comparable to any in Europ, as not long before repaird by the late King) now rent in pieces, flakes of vast Stone Split in sunder, and nothing remaining intire but the Inscription in the Architrave which shewing by whom it was built, had not one letter of it defac'd: which I could not but take notice of: It was astonishing to see what imense stones the heate had in a manner Calcin'd, so as all the ornaments, Columns, freezes, Capitels and proje[c]tures of massie Portland stone flew off, even to the very roofe, where a Sheete of Leade covering no lesse than 6 akers by measure, being totaly mealted, the ruines of the Vaulted roofe, falling brake into St. Faithes, which being filled with the magazines of bookes, belonging to the Stationer[s], and carried thither for safty, they were all consumed burning for a weeke following: It is also observable, that the lead over the Altar at the East end was untouch'd; and among the divers monuments, the body of one Bishop, remaind intire. Thus lay in ashes that most venerab[l]e Church, one of the [most ancient] Pieces of early Piety in the Christian World, beside neere

100 more; The lead, yronworke, bells, plate etc mealted; the exquisitely wrought Mercers Chapell, the Sumptuous Exchange, the august fabricque of Christ church, all the rest of the Companies Halls, sumptuous buildings, Arches, Enteries, all in dust. The fountaines dried up and ruind, whilst the very waters remained boiling; the Voragos of subterranean Cellars Wells and Dungeons, formerly Warehouses, still burning in stench and dark clowds of smoke like hell, so as in five or six miles traversing about, I did not see one loade of timber unconsum'd, nor many stones but what were calcind white as snow, so as the people who now walked about the ruines, appeard like men in some dismal desart, or rather in some greate Citty, lay'd wast by an impetuous and cruel Enemy, to which was added the stench that came from some poore Creaturs bodys, beds, and other combustible goods: Sir Tho: Gresshams Statue, though falln to the ground from its nich in the Ro: Exchange remain'd intire, when all those of the Kings since the Conquest were broken to pieces; also the Standard in Cornehill, and Q: Elizabeths Effigies, with some armes on Ludgate continud with but little detriment, whilst the vast yron Chaines of the Cittie streetes, vast hinges, barrs and gates of Prisons were many of them mealted, and reduc'd to cinders by the vehement heats: nor was I yet able to passe through any of the narrower streetes, but kept the widest, the ground and aire, smoake and fiery vapour, continud so intense, my haire being almost seinged, and my feete unsufferably surbated: The bielanes and narrower streetes were quite fill'd up with rubbish, nor could one have possibly knowne where he was, but by the ruines of some church, or hall, that had some remarkable towre or pinacle remaining: I then went towards Islington, and high-gate, where one might have seene two hundred thousand people of all ranks and degrees, dispersed, and laying along by their heapes of what they could save from the Incendium, deploring their losse, and though ready to perish for hunger and destitution, yet not asking one penny for reliefe, which to me appeard a stranger sight, than any I had yet beheld: His Majestie and Council indeeade tooke all imaginable care for their reliefe, by Proclamation, for the Country to come in and refresh them with provisions: when in the middst of all this Calamity and confusion, there was (I know not how) an Alarme begun, that the French and Dutch (with whom we were now in hostility) were not onely landed, but even

entring the Citty; there being in truth, greate suspicion some days before, of those two nations joyning, and even now, that they had ben the occasion of firing the Towne: This report did so terrifie, that on a suddaine there was such an uprore and tumult, that they ran from their goods, and taking what weapons they could come at, they could not be stop'd from falling on some of those nations whom they casualy met, without sense or reason, the clamor and perill growing so excessive, as made the whole Court amaz'd at it, and they did with infinite paines, and great difficulty reduce and apease the people, sending Guards and troopes of souldiers, to cause them to retire into the fields againe, where they were watched all this night when I left them pretty quiet, and came home to my house, sufficiently weary and broken: Their spirits thus a little sedated, and the affright abated, they now began to repaire into the suburbs about the Citty, where such as had friends or opportuni-t[i]e got shelter and harbour for the Present; to which his Majesties Proclamation also invited them. Still the Plage, continuing in our parish, I could not without danger adventure to our Church. 10: I went againe to the ruines, for it was now no longer a Citty: 11 Sat at Star Chamber, on the 13, I presented his Majestie with a Survey of the ruines, and a Plot for a new Citty, with a discourse on it, whereupon, after dinner his Majestie sent for me into the Queenes Bed-chamber, her Majestie and the Duke onely present, where they examind each particular, and discoursd upon them for neere a full houre, seeming to be extreamly pleasd with what I had so early thought on: The Queene was now in her Cavaliers riding habite, hat and feather and horsemans Coate, going to take the aire; so I tooke leave of his Majestie and visiting the Duke of Albemarle, now newly return'd from Sea, I went home . . .

. . .

[October] 10 This day was indicted a Generall fast through the nation, to humble us, upon the late dreadfull Conflagration, added to the Plage and Warr, the most dismall judgments could be inflicted, and indeede but what we highly deserved for our prodigious ingratitude, burning Lusts, disolute Court, profane and abominable lives, under such dispensations of Gods continued favour, in restoring Church, Prince, and people from our late intestine calamities, of which we were altogether unmindfull even to astonishment: This made me resolve to go to our Parish

Assemblie, where our Doctor preached on 19 Luke: 41 etc: piously applying it to the occasion, after which follow'd a Collection for the poore distress'd loose[r]s in the late fire, and their present reliefe. 14: He preach'd on 9: Dan: 14:

New Fashions at Court

18 To Lond: Star-Chamber: thence to Court, it being the first time of his Majesties putting himselfe solemnly into the Eastern fashion of Vest, changing doublet, stiff Collar, bands and Cloake etc: into a comely Vest, after the Persian mode with girdle or shash, and Shoe strings and Garters, into bouckles, of which some were set with precious stones, resolving never to alter it, and to leave the French mode, which had hitherto obtained to our greate expense and reproch: upon which divers Courtiers and Gent: gave his Ma[jesty] gold, by way of Wager, that he would not persist in this resolution: I had some time before indeede presented an Invective against that unconstancy, and our so much affecting the french fashion, to his Majestie in which [I] tooke occasion to describe the Comelinesse and usefullnesse of the Persian clothing in the very same manner, his Majestie clad himselfe; This Pamphlet I intituled *Tyrannus* or the mode, and gave it his Majestie to reade; I do not impute the change which soone happn'd to this discourse, but it was an identitie, that I could not but take notice of: This night was acted my Lord Brahals Tragedy cal'd *Mustapha* before their Majesties etc: at Court: at which I was present, very seldom at any time, going to the publique Theaters, for many reasons, now as they were abused, to an atheisticall liberty, fowle and undecent; Women now (and never 'til now) permitted to appeare and act, which inflaming severall young noble-men and gallants, became their whores, and to some their Wives, wittnesse the Earle of Oxford, Sir R: Howard, Pr: Rupert, the E: of Dorset, and another greater person than any of these, who fell into their snares, to the reproch of their noble families, and ruine both of body and Soule: I was invited to see this Tragedie, exceedingly well writ, by my Lord Chamberlain, though in my mind, I did not approve of any such passe time, in a season of such Judgements and Calamitie: 19 I return'd home;

21 Our Viccar on his former subject: This season (after so long and extraordinary a drowth in September, and Aug: as if

preparatory for the dreadfull fire) was so very wett and rainy, as many feared an ensuing famine: 23. To Star-Chamber.

. . . [30] To Lond. to our Office, and now had I on the Vest, and Surcoate, or Tunic as 'twas cald, after his Majestie had brought the whole Court to it; It being a comely, and manly habite: to[o] good to hold, it being impossible for us to leave the Monsieurs Vanitys in good earnest long . . .

. . .

The Prisoners Again

[November] 14 I went my Winter Circle through my district, Rochester and other places wher I had men quartered and in Custody: 15. To Leedes Castle. 16 I musterd them being about 600 Dutch and French, ordred their proportion of Bread to be augmented, and provided cloths and fuell: Monsieur Colbert Ambassador at the Court of England, having also this day sent mony from his Master the French King to every Prisoner of that nation under my Guards: I lay at Chilston at my Co: Hales's. 17: I return'd to Chattham, my Charriot overturning on the steepe of Boxley-hill, wounded me in two places in the head, but slightly, my sonn Jack being with me, and then but newly out of long Coates, was like to have ben Worse cutt, by the Glasse, of the Charriot dores, but I thank God, we both escaped without much hurt, though not without exceeding danger . . .

Arundel's Library

1667. January . . . 9 To the R: Soc:, which since the sad Conflagration, were now invited to sit at Arundel house in the strand, by Mr. Howard; who upon my instigation likewise bestowed on the Society that noble Library, which his Grandfath[er] especialy, and all his Ancesters had collected: this Gent: having so little inclination to bookes, that 'twas the preserving them from imbezilment . . .

Young John to Oxford

29 To Lond: in order to my sonns Oxford Journey, who being very early entered both in the Lat: and Greeke, and prompt to learne beyond most of his age, I was perswaded to trust him under the tutorage of Mr. Bohune fellow of New Coll: who had ben his

Præceptor in my house some years before; but at Oxford, under the inspection of Dr. Batthurst President of Trinity where I placed him: My son not as yet 13 years old . . .

. . .

A Blood Transfusion

. . . [March] 28: To Lond. at Ar: house the Society experimented the transfusion of bloud, out of one animal into another; it was successfuly don out of a sheepe into a dog, 'til the sheepe died, the dog well, and was ordered to be carefully looked to . . .

. . .

The Dutch at Chatham

. . . [June] 11: To Lond: alarm'd by the Dutch, who were falln on our Fleete, at Chattam by a most audacious enterprise entering the very river with part of their fleete, doing us not onely disgrace, but incredible mischiefe in burning severall of our best Men of Warr, lying at Anker and Moored there, and all this thro the unaccountable negligence of our negligence in setting out our fleete in due time: This alarme caused me (fearing the Enemie might adventure up the Thames even to Lond, which with ease they might have don, and fired all the Vessels in the river too) to send away my best goods, plate etc: from my house to another place; for this alarme was so greate, as put both County and Citty in to a pan[i]que feare and consternation, such as I hope I shall never see more: for every body were flying, none [knew] why or whither: Now then were Land forces dispatched with Lord Duke of Albemarle, L: Midleton, Pr: Rupert and the Duke to hinder the Dut[c]h comming to Chattham, fortifying Upnore Castle, and Laying chaines and bombs, but the resolute Enemy brake through all, and set fire on our ships, and retreated in spight, stopping up the Thames, the rest of their Fleete lying before the mouth of it: 14: I went to see the Work at Woolwich, a batterie for to defend them from coming up to Lond: which Pr: Rupert comanded, and sunk some ships in the river. 16: Our Viccar on 13. Hosea. 9.

17 This night about 2 a clock, some chipps and combustible matter prepared for some fireships, taking flame, in Deptford yard, made such a blace, and caused such an uprore in the Towne, it

being given out that the Dutch fleet were come up, and had landed their me[n], and fired the Towne, as had like to have don much mischiefe before people would be perswaded to the Contrary, and believe the accident: every body went to their armes, and all my family alarm'd with the extraordinarie light, and confusion etc: These were sad, and troublesome times:

... on the 28 I went to Chattham, and thence to view not onely what Mischiefe the Dutch had don, but how triumphantly their whole Fleete, lay within the very mouth of the Thames, all from North-foreland, Mergate, even to the Buoy of the Noore, a Dreadfull Spectacle as ever any English men saw, and a dishonour never to be wiped off: Those who advised his Majestie to prepare no fleete this Spring, deserv'd I know what! but –

Here in the river of Chattam, just before the Towne lay the Carkasse of the *Lond*: (now the 3d time burnt) the *Royal Oake*, the *James* etc yet Smoking, and now when the mischiefe was don, we were making trifling forts on the brink of the river: Here were yet forces both of horse and foote with Gen: Midleton, continualy expecting the motions of the Enemys fleete: I had much discourse with him, an experien[c]'d Commander: I told him I wondered the King did not fortifie Sheerenesse, since don: and the Ferry, both abandon'd: and so returned home:

. . .

[July] 17: dined with Sir Ed: Bowyer, Sir Anth: Auger and other friends: Then to Lond, returnd next day. 21. our Viccar finished his text: 23. To Lond: returned: 24 I went to Gravesend, (The Dutch fleete at anker still before the River) where I saw 5 ships of his Majesties men of Warr, encounter above 20 of the Dutch, in the bottome of the Hope, chacing them with many broad sides given and retur[n]ed, towa[r]ds the buoy of the Noore, where the body of their Fleete lay, which lasted til about midnight: There was one of their ships fired, suspected as don by the Enemie, she being run on ground: having seene this bold action, and their braving us so far up the river, I went home the next day, not without indignation at our negligence and nations reproch: 'Tis well knowne who of the Commissioners of the Treasury gave advice that the charge of setting forth a Fleete this yeare, might be spared . . .

. . .

A 'wicced and barbarous sport'

. . . [August 20] There was now a very gallant horse to be baited to death with doggs, but he fought them all, so as the fiercest of them, could not fasten on him, till they run him thro with their swords; This wicced and barbarous sport, deserv'd to have ben published in the cruel Contrivers, to get mony, under pretence the horse had killed a man, which was false: I would not be perswaded to be a Spectator . . .

. . .

A Dejected Lord Chancellor

27: Visited L: Chancellor to whom his Majestie had sent for the Seales a few daies before: I found him in his bed Chamber very Sad: The Parliament had accused him, and he had enemies at Court, especialy the boufoones and Ladys of Pl[e]asure, because he thwarted some of them and stood in their way, I could name some of the chiefe, The truth is he made few friends during his grandure among the royal Sufferers; but advanced the old rebells, that had mony enough to buy places: he was however (though no considerable Lawyer,) one who kept up the forme and substance of things in the nation with more solemnity than some would have, and was my particular kind friend on all occasions: but the Cabal prevailed, and that ingredient in Parliament: Greate division at Court concerning him, and divers greate persons interceeding for him . . .

An Inscrutable Muscovite

[28] Afternoone I went againe to the Lords Comm: for mony; and thence to the Audience of a Russian Envoÿe in the Queens Presence chamber: introduced with much State, the Souldiers, Pensionars, Guards in their order; his letter of Credence brought by his Secretary in a Scarfe of Sarsenett; their vests Sumptuous much embroid[er]ed with pearle. He delivered his Speech in the Russe language alowd, but without the least action or motion of his body (besides his tongue) which was immediately interpreted alowd also by a German that Spake good English; halfe of it consisted in repetition of the Zarrs titles which were very haughty and oriental; and the substance of the rest, that he onely sent to see the King and Queene and know how they did etc: with much compliment and

froth of Language, then they kissed their Majesties hands, and went as they came: but their real errand was to get mony:

. . .

[September] 13 'Twixt the houres of 12 and one at night, was borne my second daughter.

16 Came my Bro: and Sister of Woodcot to us. 17: My Daught[e]r was Christned Elizabeth by my Sister Evelyn, A: Pretyman, and Sir R: Bro. her Grandfather by Dr. Breton our Viccar, in my house at Says Court: 18 my Bro: and Sister returned home.

The Arundel Marbles

19 To Lond: and with Mr. Hen: Howard of Norfolck: of whom I obtained the gift of his Arundelian Marbles, Those celebrated and famous Inscriptions Greeke and Latine, with so much cost and Industrie gathered from Greece, by his illustrious Grandfather the magnificent Earle of Arundel, Thomas E. Marishall of England, my noble friend whilst he lived: These precious Monuments, when I saw miserably neglected, and scattred up and downe about the Gardens and other places of Arundell-house, and how exceedingly the corrosive aire of London impaired them, I procured him to bestow on the Universite of Oxford; This he was pleased to grant me, and now gave me the Key of the Gallery, with leave to marke all those stones, Urnes, Altars etc: and whatever I found had Inscriptions on them that were not Status: This I did, and getting them removed and piled together, with those which were incrusted in the Garden walles, I sent immediately letters to the Vice-Chancelor what I had procured, and that if they esteemed it a service to the University (of which I had ben a Member) they should take order for their transportation: This don, 21. I accompanied Mr. Howard to his Villa at Alburie, where I designed for him the plat for his Canale and Garden, with a Crypta thro the hill etc:

. . .

Vivisection

. . . [October] 10: To Lond: dined with the Swedish Resident: where was a disection of a dog, the poore curr, kept long alive after the Thorax was open, by blowing with bellows into his lungs, and that long after his heart was out, and the lungs both gashed and pierced, his eyes quick all the while: This was an experiment of more cruelty than pleased me . . .

. . .

The Departure of Clarendon

[December] 9: To Lond: to visite my late Lord Chancelor, I found him in his Garden at his new built Palace sitting in his Gowt wheele chayre, and seeing the Gates towards the North and fields setting up: he looked and spake very disconsolately, after some while deploring his condition to me, I tooke my leave, and the next morning heard he was gon: though I am perswaded had he gon sooner, though but to Cornbery and there lay quiet, it would have satisfied the Parliament: That which exasperated them was his presuming to stay, and contest the Accusation as long as twas possible, and that they were upon the point of sending him to the Tower etc:

. . .

Evelyn Shocked

. . . [1668. January] 8: Wednesday I saw deepe and prodigious gaming at the Groome-porters, vast heapes of Gold squandered away in a vaine and profuse manner: This I looked on as an horrid vice, and unsuitable to a Christian Court: 9: met at the R: So: went to see the Revells at the Middle Temple, which is also an old, but riotous Costome, and has relation to neither Virtue nor policy . . .

. . .

A Great Ship

. . . [March] 3. Was launched at Deptford that goodly Vessel the *Charles*: I was now neere his Majestie, she is longer than the *Sovraine*, and carries 110 brasse Canon: built by old Shish, a plaine honest Carpenter (Master builder of this Dock) yet one that can give very little account of his art by discourse, as hardly capable to reade, yet of greate abilitie in his calling: They [have] ben Ship-Carpenters in this Yard above 100 yeares . . .

11 To Lond. 12 Went to visite Sir Jo: Cotton who had me into his Library, full of good MSS: Gr: and Lat: but most famous for

those of the Saxon and English Antiquities collected by his
Grandfather:

. . .

A Rare Fruit

[August] 14 His Majestie was pleased to grant me a lease of a slip
of ground out of Brick-Close, to enlarge my fore Court; for which I
now gave him thanks; and then entering into other discourse, he
talked to me of a new Invention of a Vernish for ships, instead of
Pitch, and of the Guilding with which his new Yacht was beautified
with all: I also shew'd his Majestie the Perpetual motion sent me by
Dr. Stokes from Collen, and then came in Monsieur Colbert the
French Ambass: etc: 15 I returned home: 16 our Viccar as
formerly; against the Anabaptists, now swarming: 18 To Lond:
about my Lease: 19 I saw the magnificent Entrie of the Fr:
Ambassador Colbert received in the Banqueting house: I had never
seene a richer Coach than what he came in to Whitehall. Standing
by his Majestie at dinner in the Presence, There was of that rare
fruite called the King-Pine, (growing in Barbados and W. Indies),
the first of them I had ever seen; His Majestie having cut it up, was
pleasd to give me a piece off his owne plate to tast of, but in my
opinion it falls short of those ravishing varieties of deliciousnesse,
describ'd in Cap: Liggons history and others; but possibly it might
be, (and certainly was) much impaired in coming so farr: It has yet
a gratefull accidity, but tasts more of the Quince and Melon, than
of any other fruite he mentions: 20 I went home.

. . .

A Venetian Ambassador

[September] 17: I entertained Signor Muccinigo The Venetian
Ambassador and one of the noblest families of that State, this being
the day of making his Publique Enterie, setting forth from my
house, with severall Gent: of Venice and others in a very glorious
traine: With me he staied til the Earle of Anglesea, Sir Cha:
Cotterell (Master of the Ceremonie) etc came with the Kings
Barges to Carry him to the Tower, where the Gunns went off at his
Landing, and then entered his Majesties Coach, follow'd by many
others of the nobility: I accompanied him to his house, where there
was a most noble Supper to all the Companie of six Courses: After

the extraordinarie compliment to me and my Wife for the civilities he receiv'd at my house, I tooke leave of his Excellency and return'd: he is a very much accomplish'd person: since Ambassador at Rome.

. . .

'A pendule ball of solid Glasse'

[December] 17 At the Ro: Society, some experiments about the Principle of Motion, viz. Elastic, and that where was not spring, there could be no motion; tried by a pendule ball of solid Glasse, vibrating against wyre strings and catts-gutts; it making a much greater and quicker rebound from the Wyre, than from the fiddle strings, t[h]o equaly stretched: and died suddanly against wood, or Yron, where there was no Spring . . .

. . .

A Barbarous Custom

. . . [1669. March] 18, I went with my L: Howard of Norfolk to visite Sir William Ducy at Charleton, where we dined: The servants made our Coach-men so drunk that they both fell-off their boxes upon the heath, where we were faine to leave them, and were droven to Lond: by two Gent: of my Lords: This barbarous Costome of making their Masters Wellcome, by intoxicating the Servants had now the second time happn'd to my Coachman . . .

. . .

[May] 20 This Evening returning, I found my Wife in Labour, but was delivered within an houre at 10 a clock at night, being Ascension day, when was borne my third Daughter . . .

25 Was baptisd my Daughter Susanna (by the name of her Godmother her Aunt Hungerford of Cadenam): Godfather her Grandfather Sir R: Browne etc:

. . .

A Good Turn by Mr. Pepys

. . . [June 10] I went that evening to Lond: to carry Mr. Pepys to my Bro: (now exceedingly afflicted with the Stone in the bladder) who himselfe had ben successfully cut; and carried the Stone (which was as big as a tenis-ball) to shew him, and encourage his resolution to go thro the operation. 12 home: 16 To Lond:

and tooke leave of my Bro: going out of towne: 17: home ...

28 To Lond: and 30 return'd: My Wife being gon a journey of Pleasure downe the River as far as the Sea, with Mrs. Howard, and her daughters the Maids of Honor, amongst whom, that excellent creature Mrs. Blagge: I now built the long wall which separates my Court from the brick-close, newly granted me of the King:

. . .

An Encaenia at Oxford

[July] 7 I went towards Oxford, lay at little Wicckam, 8: at Oxford, lay at one of the Beadles.

9 In the morning was celebrated the Encenia of the New Theater, so magnificently built by the munificence of Dr. Gilbert Sheldon Arch-Bishop of Canterbery, in which was spent 25000 pounds, (as Sir Chr: Wren the Architect as I remember told me) and yet was never seene by the Benefactor, my L: A Bish: having upon occasion told me, that he never did, nor never would see it. It is in truth a fabrique comparable to any of this kind of former ages, and doubtlesse exceeding any of the present, as this Universitie dos, for Colledges, Libraries, Scholes, students and Order all the Universities in the World:

To the Theater is [joined] the famous Sheldonian Printing-house: This being at the Act, and the first time of opening the Theater (Acts being formerly kept in St. Maries-Church, which might be though undecent, as being soly set a part for the immediate worship of God, and was the inducement of building this noble Pile) it was now resolv'd, to celebrate its dedication with the greatest splendor and formalitie that might be, and therefore drew a world of strangers and other Companie to the University from all parts of the Nation: The Vice-Chancelor then, Heads of Houses, and Doctors being seated in magisterial seates, the Vice-Chancellors Chaire and Deske, Proctors etc: covered with Brocatell and Cloth of Gold: The Universitie Register read the Founders Grant and gift of it to the Universitie, for their Scholastic Exercises upon these solemn occasions: Then follow'd Dr. South the Universities Orators Eloquent Speech upon it; it was very long, and not without some malicious and undecent reflections on the Royal Society as underminers of the University, which was very foolish and untrue, as well as unseasonable, (but to let that passe, from an ill natured man) the rest was in praise of the Arch Bish: and the ingenious Architect: This Ended, after loud Musique, from the Corridor above, (where was placd an Organ) there follow'd divers Panegyric Speeches both in Prose and Verse interchangeably pronounc'd by the young students, plac'd in the Rostrum, Suggestum, Plutea's etc Some in Pindarics, Ecclogas, Heroics etc: mingled with excellent Musique both vocal, and Instrumental to entertaine the Ladys etc: then was a spech made in praise of Academical Learning; all which lasted from 11 in the morning till 7 at night, which was likewise concluded with Bells ringing, and universal joy and feasting:

10 The next day began the more solemn Lectures in all the Faculties which were perform'd in their several Scholes, where all the Inceptor Doctors did their Exercises, the Professors having first ended their reading: The Assembly now return'd to the Theater, the Terræ Filius or Universitie bouffoone, entertaind the Auditorie with a tedious, abusive, sarcastical rhapsodie, much unbecoming the gravity of the Universitie, and that so grossly, as that unlesse it be suppress'd, will be of ill consequence, as I plainly expressed my sense, both to the Vice Chancelor and severall heads of houses afterwards, who were perfectly ashamed of it, and resolv'd to take care of it for the future, for they had left the facetious old way of raillying upon the Questions: etc and fell wholy upon persons; so as in good earnest, 'twas rather licentious lying, and railing than genuine and noble witt: In my life was I never witnesse of so shamefull entertainement. After this ribauldry, The Proctors made their Speeches: Then began the Musick Act, Vocal, and Instrumental, above in the Balustred Corridore, opposite to the Vice-Chancelors seate: Then Dr. Wallis the Mathematical Professor made his Oration, and created one Doctor of Musique, according to the usual Ceremonies, of Gowne (which was white Damask) Cap: Ring, kiss etc: Next follow'd the Disputation of the Inceptor Doctors in Medicine, the Speech of their Professor Dr. Hyde, and so in Course their respective Creations: Then Disputed the Inceptors of Law, the Speech of their Professor and Creation: Lastly, Inceptors in Theologie, Dr. Compton (bro: to the Earle of Northampton) being Junior began, with greate modesty, and applause: and so the rest: After which Dr. Tillotson, Dr. Sprat etc: and then Dr. Alestreès (the Kings Professors) Speech, and their

respective Creations: Last of all the Vice-Chancelors shuting up all in a Panegyrical Oration celebrating their Benefactor, and the rest apposite to the occasion: Thus was the Theater Dedicated by the Scholastic Exercises in all the faculties with infinite solemnity, and the night (as the former) entertaining the new Doctors friends, in feasting and Musique: I being invited by Dr. Barlow, the worthy and learned Provost of Queenes Coll:

11 The Act Sermon was this forenoone preach'd by Dr. Hall in St. Marie's in an honest practical discourse against Atheisme on Rom.   In the afternoone, the Church was so crowded, that coming not so early, I could not approch to heare: 12 Moneday was held the Divinity Act in the Theater againe, where proceede[d] 17 Doctors in all the Faculties some: 13 I dined on Tuesday at the V. Chancelors, and spent the afternoone in seeing the rarities of the Pub: Librarie, and visiting the noble Marbles and Inscriptions now inserted in the Walles that compasse the Area of the Theater, which were 150 the most antient, and worthy treasure in the Learned World of that kind, procur'd by me for them some time before: now observing that people, approching them too neere, some Idle people began to Scratch and injure some of them, I advis'd that an hedge of holly, should be planted at the foote of the wall, to be kept breast-high onely, to protect them, which the V: Chancelor promisd to see don the next season:

An Honorary Doctorate

14 Came Dr. Fell (Deane of Christchurch) Vice-Chancellor, now Bish: of Oxon with Dr. Alestree, K[ing]s Professors; Beadles and Maces before them, to Visite me at my Lodging: Then I went to Visite My L: Howards sonns at Magdalen Coll: who also repaied me theirs: 15 Having two daies before notice that the Universitie intended me the honor of Doctor-ship, I was this morning attended by the Beadles belonging to the Law, who carried me to the Theater, where I found the Duke of Ormond (now Chancelor of the Universitie,) with the Earle of Chesterfild, and Mr. Spencer brother to the late Earle of Sunderland: Thence we marched to the Convocation house, a Convocation having ben cald on Purpose: Here being all of us rob'd in Scarlet, with Caps and hoods etc: in the Porch, we were led in by the Professor of Laws, and presented respectively by name and a short elogie etc: to the Vice-Chancelor

who sate in the Chaire, with all the Doctors and heads of houses and Masters about the roome, which was exceeding full: Then began the Publique Orator, his speech, directed chiefly to the Chancelore, the Duke of Ormond, in which I had also my Compliment in Course: This ended, we were called up, and Created Doctors according to the forme, and seated by the Vice-Chancelor amongst the Doctors, on his right hand: Then made the Vice-Chancelor a short spech, and so saluting our Bro: Doctors the Pageantry concluded, and the Convocation desolved: So formal a Creation of Honorarie Doctors, had seldome ben seene, that a Convocation should be cald on purpose, and Speeches made by the Orator etc: But they could do no lesse, their Chancelor being to receive, or rather do them this honour: I had ben made Doctor with the rest at the Publique Act; but their expectation of the Duke their Chancelor made them deferr it; and so I was led with my Bro: Doctors, to an extraordinary Entertainement at Dr. Mewes, head of St. Johns Coll: and after aboundance of feasting and complements, having visited the V: Chancelor and other Doctors and given them thanks for the honours don me, 16 I went towards home the next day, and got as far as Windsor, and to my house 17 the next.

. . .

A Cold Winter

. . . [December] 8: To Lond: upon the second Edition of my *Sylva*, which I presented to the R: Society. 10: Din'd at Goring house about a referrence, returned this Evening . . . Hardly was ever felt so greate cold in England of many yeares . . .

. . .

[1670. January] 26 I had much discourse with the Venetian Ambassador concerning the excessive Cold weather they often had in Italy, and especialy this Winter etc: 27: home.

. . .

Death of Richard Evelyn

March: 3 Finding my brother in such exceeding torture, and that he now began to fall into Convulsion fits, 4 I solemnly set the next-day a part, to beg of God to mitigate his sufferings, and prosper the onely meanes which yet remained for his recovery; or if otherwise; that it would please Almighty God to prepare him for himselfe, he not onely being very much wasted, but exceedingly, and all along averse from being cut, which he was advised to undergo from time to time, with extraordinary probability of successe: but when it came to the operation, and all things prepared, his spirit and resolution failed, and there was now lesse hopes than ever. 5. I went to visite my poore afflicted brother, whom I found almost in the last agonies:

6 . . . I participated of the blessed Sacrament, recomending the deplorable condition of my bro: his agonies still increasing: In the Afternoone, a stranger made an excellent sermon against Atheists: etc. I watched late with my Bro: this night, yet not imagining his end to be so neere; but so it pleased God, to deliver him out of this miserable life, towards five this moneday morning, to my unspeakeable griefe and sorrow, being a Bro: whom I most dearely loved for many Virtues; and that was but two yeares Younger than my-selfe, a sober, prudent, and worthy Gent: he had married a greate fortune, and left one onely daughter, and a most noble seate, at Woodcot neere, Epsom in Surrey etc: 7: I staied all the next day to comfort my sister in Law, his Wife: 8 On Tuesday he was ordred to be opened; but it was not a specctacle I desir'd to be present at; and therefore returned home this evening full of sadnesse, and to bemoane my losse: 10: To Lond: My Bro: being opened, a stone was taken out of his bladder, not much bigger than a nutmeg, somewhat flatt, and oval, not sharp, one part excepted, which was a little rugged: but his Livar so faulty, that in likelyhood [it could not] have lasted much longer, and his kidnis almost quite consum'd: all of this doubtlesse the effects of his intollerable paine proceeding from the stone; and that perhaps by his drinking too excessively of Epsom Waters, when in full health, and that he had no neede of them, being all his lifetime of a sound and healthy constitution, etc . . .

. . .

A Bear-Garden

. . . [June] 15 To Lond: 16 I was forc'd to accompanie some friends to the Bear-garden etc: Where was Cock fighting, Beare, Dog-fighting, Beare and Bull baiting, it being a famous day for all these butcherly Sports, or rather barbarous cruelties: The Bulls did exceedingly well but the Irish Wolfe dog exceeded, which was a tall Gray-hound, a stately creature in deede, who beate a cruell Mastife: One of the Bulls tossd a Dog full into a Ladys lap, as she sate in one of the boxes at a Considerable height from the Arena: There were two poore dogs killed; and so all ended with the Ape on horse-back, and I most heartily weary, of the rude and dirty passetime, which I had not seene I think in twenty yeares before:

...

Newmarket

... [July 22] passing through New-Market, we alighted, to see his Majesties house there now new building, the arches of the Cellers beneath, are exceedingly well turned, by the Architect Mr. Samuel, the rest meane enough, and hardly capable for a hunting house: Many of the roomes above had the Chimnies plac'd in the angles and Corners, a Mode now introduc'd by his Majestie which I do at no hand approve of, and predict it will Spoile many noble houses and roomes if followed; it dos onely well in very Small and trifling roomes, but takes from the state of greater: besids this house is plac'd in a dirty Streete; without any Court or avenue, like a common Burgers: whereas it might and ought to have ben built at either end of the Towne, upon the very Carpet, where the Sports are Celebrated; but it being the purchase of an old wretched house of my Lord Tumonds, his Majestie was perswaded to set it on that foundation, the most improper imaginable for an house of Sport and pleasure: We went to see the Stables and fine horses, of which many were here kept, at vast expense, with all the art and tendernesse Imaginable ...

...

Windsor Restored

[August 28] I went in the Evening to Eaton to visite the Provost Dr. Alestrie Professor Regius Oxon: 29 returned home. Note, that Windsor was now going to be repaired, being exceedingly ragged and ruinous: Prince Rupert Constable had begun to trim up the Keepe or high round Tower, and handsomly adorn'd his hall, with a furniture of Armes, which was very singular; by so disposing the Pikes, Muskets, Pistols, Bandilers, holster[s], Drumms, Back, brest and head pi[e]ces as was very extraordinary: and thus those huge steepe stayres ascending to it, had the Walls invested with this martial furniture, all new and bright, and set with such study, as to represent, Pillasters, Cornishes, Architraves, Freezes, by so disposing the bandalliers, holsters, and Drums, so as to represent festoones, and that with out any Confusion, Trophy like: from the Hall, we went into his Bedchamber and ample roomes which were hung with tapissrie, curious and effeminate Pictures, so extreamely different from the other, which presented nothing but Warr and horror, as was very Surprizing and Divertissant. The King passed most of his time in hunting the Stag, and walking in the Parke which he was now also planting with walks of Trees, etc:

. . .

William of Orange

. . . [November 4] Dined at the Groome-porters, return'd that Evening, having seene the Prince of Orange, newly come to see his Unkle the King: he has a manly couragious wise Countenance, resembling both his Mother, and Duke of Glocester both deceased: I now also saw that famed beauty (but in my opinion of a childish simple and baby face) Madamoiselle Quirreval,* lately maide of honour to Madame, and now to be so to the Queene:

. . .

26 I had a Tryall in Guild-Hall againest on[e] Cock who had exceedingly wronged me in an Accompt of monies going through his hands; but there being many Causes, 'twas* respited til Wednesday following . . .

. . .

Discovery of Grinling Gibbons

[1671. January] 18 I this day first acquainted his Majestie with that incomparable young man, Gibson* whom I had lately found in an Obscure place, and that by meere accident, as I was walking neere a poore solitary thatched house in a field in our Parish neere Says-Court: I found him shut in, but looking into the Window, I perceiv'd him carving that large Cartoone or Crucifix of Tintorets, a Copy of which I had also my selfe brought from Venice, where the original Painting remaines: I asked if I might come in, he opned the doore civily to me, and I saw him about such a work, as for the curiosity of handling, drawing, and studious exactnesse, I never in my life had seene before in all my travells: I asked why he worked in such an obscure and lonesome place; he told me, it was that he might apply himselfe to his profession without interruption; and wondred not a little how I came to find him out: I asked if he were unwilling to be made knowne to some Greate men; for that I believed it might turne to his profit; he answerd, he was yet but a beginner; but would yet not be sorry to sell off that piece; I asked him the price, he told me 100 pounds. In good earnest the very frame was worth the mony, there being nothing even in nature so tender, and delicate as the flowers and festoones about it, and yet the worke was very strong; but in the Piece above 100 figures of men etc: I found he was likewise Musical, and very Civil, sober and discreete in his discourse: There was onely an old Woman in the house, so desiring leave to visite him sometimes, I tooke my leave: Of this Young Artist, together with my manner of finding him out, I acquainted the King, and beged of his Majestie that he would give me leave to bring him and his Worke to White-hall, for that I would adventure my reputation with his Majestie that he had never seene any thing approch it, and that he would be exceedingly pleased, and employ him: The King sayd, he would himselfe go see him: This was the first notice his Majestie ever had of Mr. Gibbons.

. . .

Mar: 1. I caused Mr. Gibbon to bring to Whitehall his excellent piece of Carving where being come, I advertised his Majestie who asked me where it was, I told him, in Sir R: Brownes (my F. in Laws) Chamber, and that if it pleased his Majestie to appoint whither it should be brought (for 'twas large, and though of Wood, yet heavy) I would take care for it: No says the King; shew me the Way, Ile go to Sir Richards Chamber; which his Majestie immediately did, walking all along the Enteries after me as far as the Ewrie til he came up into the rome where I also lay: and no sooner was he entred, and cast his eye on the Worke but he was a stonish'd at the curiositie of it, and having considred it a long time, and discours'd with Mr. Gibbon, whom I brought to kisse his hand; he commanded it should be immediately carried to the Queenes side to shew her Majestie, so it was carried up into her bed-chamber, where she and the King looked on and admired it againe, the King thus leaving us with the Queene being now caled away, I think to Council, believing that she would have bought it, it being a Crucifix; but when his Majestie was gon, a French pedling woman, one Madame de Boord, that used to bring peticoates and fanns and baubles out of France to the Ladys, began to find faults with severall things in the worke, which she understood no more than an Asse or Monky; so as in a kind of Indignation, I caused the porters who brought it, to carry it to the Chamber againe, finding the Queene so much govern'd by an ignorant french woman: and this incomparable Artist [had] the labour onely for his paines, which not a little displeased me; so he was faine to send it downe to his cottage againe, though he not long after sold it for 80 pounds, which was realy, (even without the frame) worth an hundred: Sir Geo: Viner buying it of him, as his first Essay, and his Majesties Surveyor Mr. Wren faithfully promising me to employ him for the future; I having bespoke his Majestie also for his Worke at Windsore which my friend Mr. May (the Architect there) was going to alter and repaire universaly:

Charles II and Nell Gwyn

... on the next day, I had a faire opportunity of talking to his Majestie about it, in the Lobby next the Queenes side, where I presented him with some Sheetes of my historie, and thence walked with him thro St. James's Parke to the Garden, where I both saw and heard a very familiar discourse betweene – – and Mrs. Nellie* as they cal'd an impudent Comedian, she looking out of her Garden on a Tarrace at the top of the Wall, and – standing on the greene Walke under it: I was heartily sorry at this scene: Thence the King walked to the Dutches of Cleavelands,* another Lady of Pleasure and curse of our nation: It was on a Council day, and so I went back and on the 4th to my house. –

5 Our Viccar on his former subject: The holy Sacrament follow'd, I dined at Greenewich to take leave of Sir Tho: Linch now going Governer of Jamaica etc:

10 To Lond: about passing my Grant for my sallarie of 500 pounds per ann: as one of the standing Council for Plantations; a considerable honour ...

...

Captain Blood

[May] 10 To Lond: din'd at Mr. Treasurers where dined

Monsieur de Gramont and severall French noblemen: and one
Bloud that impudent bold fellow, who had not long before
attempted to steale the Imperial Crowne it selfe out of the Tower,
pretending onely curiositie of seeing the Regalia there, when
stabbing (though not mortaly) the keeper of them, he boldly went
away with it, thro all the guards, taken onely by the accident of his
horses falling. How he came to be pardoned, and even received to
favour, not onely after this, but severall other exploits almost as
daring, both in Ireland and here, I could never come to understand:
some believed he became a spie of severall Parties, being well with
the Sectaries and Enthusiasts, and did his Majestie services that
way, which none alive could so well as he: But it was certainely as
the boldest attempt, so the onely Treason of this nature that was
ever pardon'd: The Man had not onely a daring but a vilanous
un-mercifull looke, a false Countenance, but very well spoken, and
dangerously insinuating: 11 I went to Eltham to sit as one of the
Commission about the subsidie now given his Majestie by
Parliament: returnd . . .

. . .

The Condition of New England and Jamaica

26: Meeting all at Queenes streete at the Earle of Bristols house
(which we had lately taken, and furnish'd with rich hangings of the
Kings, 7 roomes on a floore with a long Gallery, Gardens etc:) The
Duke of Buckingham, E: of Lauderdail, L: Culpeper, Sir Geo:
Carteret Vice-Chamberlaine and my selfe, had our Oathes given us
by the Earle of Sandwich our President: To Advise and Counsel
his Majestie to the best of our abilities etc: for the well Governing
of his Majesties forraine Plantations etc. The forme very little
differing from what is given the Privy Council: Then we tooke all
our Places in the Council Chamber at the board: The roome very
large, and furnished with the Atlases, Mapps, Charts, Globes etc:
Then came the Lord Keeper Sir Orlando Bridgeman, E: of
Arlington Pr: Secretary of State: Lord Ashley, Mr. Treasurer, Sir
Jo: Trevor the other Pr: Secretary, Sir Jo: Duncomb, Lord
Allington, Mr. Grey, sonn to the Lord Grey, Mr. Hen: Broncher,
Sir Humfry Winch; Sir John Finch, Mr. Waller, Coll: Titus of the
Bed chamber, Mr. Slingsby the Secretary to the Council, and two
Clearks of the Council, who were all Sworne some dayes before:

being all set, our Patent was read, and then the additional Patent, in which was recited this new establishment: Then was delivered to every one of us a Copy of the Patent, and of our Instructions: after which we fell to debate matters; and first agreed on a forme for Circulating Letters to be immediately dispatched to all his Majesties Plantations and Territories in the West Indies and Ilands thereof; to give them notice to whom they should apply themselves on all occasions, and to render us an account of their present state, and Government; and therefore the Letters were directed to the respective Governors: but most we insisted on, was to know in what condition New-England was; which appearing to be very independent as to their reguard to old England, or his Majestie, rich and strong as now they were, greate were the debates, in what style to write to them: for the Condition of that Colonie was such, as they were able to contest with all our Plantations about them, and feare there was, of their altogether breaking from all dependance on this nation: His Majestie therefore recommended this afaire more expressly: We therefore thought fit, in the first place, to acquaint our selves as well as we could of the state of that place, by some who we heard of, that were newly come from thence, and to be informed of their present posture and Condition; because some of our Council were for sending them a menacing Letter which those who better understood the touchy and peevish humor of that Colonie, were utterly against. Then a letter was red which came from Sir Tho: Modiford Governor of Jamaica, and then the Council brake up: My agreement with Cock not succeeding, I went to take advise of that famous Lawyer Mr. Jones of Grays Inn: and 27: had a Trial before the L: C. Justice Hales for a summ of mony owing me; so after the Lawyers had wrangled sufficiently, It was againe referred to a new Arbitration: This being the very first Suite at Law, that ever I had with any Creature before and ô that it might be the Last: from hence I returned to my house:

. . .

Conciliation Backed by Force

. . . [June] 6: I went to Council, where was produc'd a most exact and ample Information of the state of Jamaica, and of the best expedients to reduce New-England, on which there was a long debate, and whether it were fit to send a Letter and certaine curious Queries relating to the seacrets of the Government: but 'twas concluded in the negative, and that if any, it should be onely a conciliating paper at first, or civil letter 'til we had better information of the present face of things; since we understood they were a people al most upon the very brink of renouncing any dependance of the Crowne ... 20: To carry Coll: Midleton to White hall to my L: Sandwich our President, for some information he was able to give the Council of the state of the Colonie in N. England, and return'd: Next day to Council againe, where one Coll: Cartrite a Notinghamshere man, (formerly in Commission with Coll: Nichols) gave us a considerable relation of that Country. Upon which the Council concluded, that if policy would not reduce the disaffected there, force should: that yet in the first place, a letter of amnestie should be dispatch'd, with an intention to fortifie a certaine Iland in the mouth of the chiefe river; and to purchase the maine of that part of the Plantation belonging to Ferdinando Gorges, which would inable the King to curb Boston ...

...

26 To Lond: to Council, where my Lo: Arlington being present, acquainted us that it was his Majesties Proposal, we should every one of us contribute 20 pounds a piece, towards the building of a Council-chamber and conveniences some where in White-hall, to the end, that his Majestie himselfe might come and sit amongst us and heare our debates; The mony we laied out to be reimbours'd us out of the contingent monies already set apart for us, viz: 1000 pounds yearley: To which we unanimously consented. There came also an uncertaine brute from Barbados, of some disorder there: so I went home, steping in at the Theater, to see the new Machines for the intended scenes, which were indeede very costly, and magnificent:

...

... [July] 24: To Lon: Council: Mr. Surveyor brought us a plot for the building of our Council-Chamber to be erected at the end of the Privy-Garden in White-hall which was all was don: I returned ...

...

[August] 3 To Lond: and to Council where was a full appearance: viz, The Lo: Keeper, Secretaries of State, Mr. Treasurer, and many of the Lords of the Privy Council: The matter in debate was, whether we should send a Deputy to New England requiring them of the Massachusets to restore such to their limits, and respective possessions, as had petitioned the Council: This to be the open Commission onely, but in truth with seacret Instructions to Informe the Council of the condition of those Colonies; and whether they were of such power as to be able to resist his Majestie and declare for themselves as Independent of the Crowne, as we were told, and which of late yeares made them refractorie: Coll: Midleton being called in assured us they might be curbed by a few of his Majesties 5t rate fregats, to spoile their Trade with the Ilands: but though of this my L: President was not satisfied, the rest were, and we did resolve to advise his Majestie to send Commissioners with a formal Commission for adjusting boundaries, etc: but under hand with seacret Instructions etc . . .

. . .

The Exploit at Panama

19 To Lond: and Council: The letters of Sir T: Mudiford were read, giving relation of the Exploit at Panamà, which was very brave: They tooke and burnt, and pilag'd the Towne of vast Treasures, but the best of the booty had ben ship'd off, and lay at anker in the South Sea, so as after our Men had ranged the Countriy 60 miles about, they went back to Nombre de Dios and embarq'd to Jamaica; Such an action had not ben don since the famous Drake: I dined at the Resident of Hambroghs, and after dinner at the Christning of Sir Sam: Tukes Son Charles which was don at Somerset house by a Popish Priest with many odd Ceremonies, Spittle and anointings: Godfathers the King: L: Arundell of Wardoer, etc Countesse of Huntington: after which I went home. 20: Viccar as above: 24: To Lond: returned.

. . .

. . . [September] 21. I dined in the Citty, at the fraternity feast in yron-mongers hall, where the 4 stewards chose their successors of the next yeare with a solemn procession, garlands about their heads and musique playing before them, so coming up to the uper Tables where the gentlemen sate, they drank to the new [stewards] etc: and so we parted . . .

. . .

The King at Euston

[October] 9 We set out on the 9th in [a] Coach of 6 brave horses, which we changed thrice: and first at Bishop Stratford, and last at Chesterford so as by night we got to N. Market, where Mr. Henry Jermin (Nephew to the Earle of St. Albans) lodged me very Civily: We went immediately to Court (the King and all the English Gallantes being here at their autumnal sports) supped at my L: Chamberlaines, and next day after dinner went on the heath, where I saw the greate match run betweene Wood-cock and Flat-foot the Kings, and Mr. Eliots of the Bedchamber, many thousands being spectators, a more signal race had not ben run of many yeares: This over, I went that night with Mr. Tressurer to Euston, a palace of my L: [Arlingtons] 10 where we found Monsieur Colbert (the French Ambassador) and the famous new french maid of honor, Mademoisell Quierovil now comeing to be in greate favour with the K—: here was also the Countesse of Sunderland, and severall Lords and Ladies more who lodged in the house: during my stay here with my Lord Arlington neere a fortnight; Came his Majestie almost every second day with the Duke, who commonly returnd againe to New-market; but the King lay often here, during which time I had twice the honor to sit at Dinner with him, with all freedome: It was universaly reported that the faire Lady — * was bedded one of these nights, and the stocking flung, after the manner of a married Bride: I acknowledge she was for the most part in her undresse all day, and that there was fondnesse, and toying, with that young wanton; nay 'twas said, I was at the former ceremonie, but tis utterly false, I neither saw, nor heard of any such thing whilst I was there, though I had ben in her Chamber and all over that appartment late enough; and was my selfe observing all passages with curiosity enough: however twas with confidence believed that she was first made a Misse as they cald these unhappy creatures, with solemnity, at this time etc:

. . .

16 Came all the greate Men from N: Market and other parts both of Suffolck, and Norfolck to make their Court; the whole house fill'd from one end to the other, with Lords, Ladys and Gallants, and such a furnished Table had I seldome seene, nor any thing more splendid and free: so as for 15 dayes there were entertain'd at the Least 200 people, and halfe as many horses,

besids Servants, Guards, at Infinite expense: In the mornings we went a hunting and hauking; In the afternoone 'til almost morning to Cards and dice etc yet I must say without noise, swearing, quarell or Confusion of any sort: I who was no Gamster, had often discourse with the French Ambassador Colbert, and went sometimes abroad on horse back with the Ladys to take the aire, and now and then to hunting; thus idly passing the time, but not without more often recesse to my prety apartment, where I was quite out of all this hurry, and had [leasure], when I would to converse with bookes; for there is no man more hospitably easy to be withall than my L: Arlington, of whose particular friendship and kindnesse I had ever a more than ordinary share:

My Lord Chamberlaines house is a very noble pile consisting of 4 greate pavilions after the french, beside a body of a large house, and though not built altogether, but form'd of additions to an old house (purchasd by his Lordship of one Sir T Rookwoods) yet with a vast expence, made not onely capable and roomesome, but very magnificent and commodious, as well within as without, nor lesse splendidly furnish'd: The Stayre case is very elegant, the Garden handsome, the Canale beautifull, but the soile drie, barren, and miserably sandy, which flies in drifts as the wind sets: Here my Lord was pleasd to advise with me about the ordering his Plantations of firs, Elmes, limes etc up his parke, and in all other places and Avenues; I perswaded him to bring his Park so neere, as to comprehend his house with in it, which now he resolved upon; it being now neere a mile to it: The Water furnishing the fountaines is raised by a pretty Engine or very slight plaine Wheele, which likewise serves to grind his Corne, from a small cascade of the Canale, the invention of Sir Sam: Moreland: In my Lords house, and especialy above the Stayre Case, the greate hall and some of the Chambers and roomes of State, is painted in fresca, by the hand of Signor Virrio the same who has painted all Winsor being the first worke which he did in England.

A Visit to Norwich

17 My Lord: Henry Howard coming this night to visite my Lord Chamberlain, and staying a day, would needes have me go along with him to Norwich; promising to convey me back againe after a day or two; This as I could not refuse, so I was not hardly

perswaded to, having a desire to see that famous Scholar and Physition Dr. T. Browne author of *Religio Medici* and *Vulgar Errors* etc: now lately knighted: Thither then went my Lord and I alone in his flying Charriat with 6 horses; and by the way discoursing to me of severall of his Concernes, he acquainted me of his going to marry his Eldest sonn to one of the Kings natural daughters, by the Dutchesse of Cleaveland; by which he reckon'd he shall come into might[y] favour: he also told me that though he kept that idle Creature and common — Mrs. B— and would leave 200 pounds a yeare to the sonne he had by her; he would never marry her, and that the King himselfe had caution'd him, against it: All the world knowes, how he kept this promise; and I was sorry at heart to hear what now in confidence he confessed to me; and that a person and a family (which I so much honou[re]d, for the sake of that noble and illustrious friend of mine, his Grandfathers) should dishonour and polute them both, with those base, and vicious Courses he of late had taken, and was falln into, since the death of Sir Sam: Tuke, and that of his owne virtuous Lady my L: Ann Somerset (sister to the Marquesse) who whilst they lived, preserv'd this Gentleman by their example and advice, from those many extravagances that impaird both his fortune and reputation:

Being come to the Ducal Palace, my Lord made very much of me, but I had little rest, so exceedingly desirous he was to shew me the contrivances he had made, for the entertainement of their Majesties and whole Court not long before, and which, though much of it, but temporary appartments fram'd of boards etc onely, were yet standing: As to the Palace, tis an old wretched building, and that part of it, newly built of brick, is very ill understood; so as I was of opinion, it had ben much better to have demolish'd all, and set it in a better place than to proceede any farther; for it stands in the very Market place, and though neere a river, yet a very narrow muddy one and without any extent: here before we went to bed, my Lord fell-out with his Carpenter, about measuring of a roome, and grew into such a passion, as in my life, I had never seene any mortal man; so much beneath his dignitie, and for so wretched a trifle; my Lord saying the dimension was so many foote, the Workman so many: This conflict lasting from 8 till 1 at night, was grievous to me:

Sir Thomas Browne

Next morning I went to see Sir Tho: Browne (with whom I had sometime corresponded by Letters tho never saw before) whose whole house and Garden being a Paradise and Cabinet of rarities, and that of the best collection, especialy Medails, books, Plants, natural things, did exceedingly refresh me after last nights confusion: Sir Thomas had amongst other curiosities, a collection of the Eggs of all the foule and birds he could procure, that Country (especialy the promontorys of Norfolck) being (as he said) frequented with severall kinds, which seldome or never, go farther into the Land, as Cranes, Storkes, Eagles etc: and variety of Water-foule: He likewise led me to see all the remarkeable places of this antient Citty, being one of the largest, and certainely (after London) one of the noblest of England, for its venerable Cathedrall, number of Stately Churches, Cleanesse of the streetes; and buildings of flint, so exquisitely headed and Squared, as I was much astonish'd at; Sir Tho: told me they had lost the art, of squaring the flint, which once they [were] so excellent in: and of which the Churches, best houses, and Walls are built: The Castle is an antique extent of ground, which now they call marsfield, and had ben a fitting area to have placed the Ducal Palace in: The suburbs are large, the prospect sweete, and other amoenities, not omiting the flower-gardens, which all the Inhabitans excell in of this Citty, the fabric of stuffs, which it affords the Merchants, and brings a vast trade to this populous Towne: Being return'd to my Lords, who had ben with me all this morning, he advis'd with me concerning a plot to rebuild his house, having already (as I said) erected a front next the streete, and a left wing, and now resolving to set up another wing, and pavilion next the Garden, and to convert the bowling greene into Stables: In summ, my advise was to desist from all, and to meditate wholy on the rebuilding an handsome Palace at Arundell house in the Strand, before he proceeded farther here; and then to place this in the Castle, that ground belonging to his Lordship: One thing I observ'd of remarkable in this Citty, that most of the Church-yards (though some of them large enough) were filled up with earth, or rather the congestion of dead bodys on[e] upon another, for want of Earth etc to the very top of the Walls, and many above the wales, so as the Churches seem'd to be built in pitts:

18 I return'd to Euston next day (leaving my Lord Howard at Norwich) in my Lords Coach . . .

. . .

Jolly Blades at Newmarket

[19] Leaving Euston, I lodged this night at Newmarket, where I found the jolly blades, Racing, Dauncing, feasting and revelling, more resembling a luxurious and abandon'd rout, than a Christian Court: The Duke of Buckingam was now in mighty favour, and had with him here that impudent woman, the Countesse of Shrewsbery, with his band of fidlars etc.

Next morning (in Company with Sir Bernard Gascoyne and my L: Hawly) I came in the Tressurers Coach, to Bish: Stratford, where the Tressurer gave us a noble supper, and next day to London and so home:

. . .

Convoys

. . . [1672. February] 12. At the Council of Plant: we entred upon enquiries about improving his Majesties American Dominions by Silk, Galls, Flax, Senna etc and considered how Nutmegs and Cinamon might be obtaind, and brought to Jamaica, that Soile and Climat promising successe; upon this Dr. Worsley being called in spake many considerable things to encourage it: We also tooke order to send to the Plantations, that none of their ships should adventure homeward single, but stay for company and Convoyes, in reguard of the late indicted War etc: we also deliberated of sending some fit Person to goe as Commissioner to Inspect their actions at New-England, and from time to time to make report by Letters, and to give us information how that Nation stood affected: This we had formerly in deliberation: Then adjourn'd for the future to meete at White-hall, and 13 I returned home.

An Excellent Preacher Expires

18 Dr. Breton, our excellent Minister, and my good friend unhappily dying, the young Curate preached on 4: Gal: 4. 5.

20 Dr. Parr (of Camerwell) made a most pathetical funeral discourse, and Panegyric at the Interrment of our late Pastor on 'Happy is that servant whom when his Lord cometh' etc: this good

man (among other expressions) professed he had never ben so touch'd and concern'd at any losse, as at this, unlesse it were the death of K. Charles our Martyr, and that of the Archbishop of Armagh, Usher, whose Chaplaine he had ben: he shewed how suddain Death (such as was our Doctors) was no malediction to the prepared, and those who die in the Lord: for on friday, having fasted all that day, making his provisionary Sermon for the Sonday following, he went well to bed, and being suddenly surpriz'd, expir'd before help could come to him, being of a plethoric habit of body, and seemingly over full, even of health it selfe: Never had Parish a greater losse, not onely as he was an Excellent Preacher, and fitted for our greate and vulgar Auditory, but for his excellent life and Charity, his meekenesse, and obliging nature, Industrious, help-full, and full of good workes; leaving neere 400 pounds to the poore in his Will, and that what children of his should happen to die in minority, their portion should be so employed: I lost in particular a special friend, and one that had an extraordinary love to me and mine: Gods will be don.

. . .

Leeward Islands

Mar. 1 To Lond: at our Council of Plant: where was present his Royal Highnesse the Duke: Pr: Rupert, D: of Buckingham, both the Secretaries of state etc: divers Lords of the Privy Council: Debating of our saving the Lee-ward Ilands, now in danger of the French, who had taken some of our Ships, and began to interrupt our trade; as also about the power of the new Governor of st. Christophers, whither he should be Subordinate to the Governor of Barbados etc: The Debates were serious and long:

. . .

'A quarel slenderly grounded'

12 To Lond: Now was the first blow given by us against the Dutch Convoy of the Smyrna fleete, by Sir Robert Holmes and my Lord Ossorie, in which we received little save blows, and a worthy reproch, for atacquing our neighbours ere any war was proclaim'd, and then pretending the occasion to be, that some time before, the *Merline Yacht* chancing to saile thro the whole Dutch fleete, their Admiral did not Strike to that trifling vessel: Surely this was a

quarel slenderly grounded, and not becoming Christian neighbours, and of a Religion: and we are like to thrive accordingly: My
Lord Ossory several times deploring his being ingaged in it to me,
and he had more justice and honour than in the least to approve of
it, though he had ben over perswaded to the expedition, and there
is no doubt, but we had surpriz'd this exceeding rich fleete, had not
the avarice and ambition of Holmes and Sprag, separated
themselv[e]s and willfully divided our fleete, on presumption that
either of them were strong enough to deale with the Dutch Convoy,
without joyning and mutual help; whilst the Dutch Convoy, so
warmly plied our divided fleete, that whilst they were in Conflict,
the Merchants saild away and got safe into Holland:

A Stop of the Exchequer

It was a few daies before this that the Treasurer of his Majesties
Howshould (Sir Tho: Clifford) hinted to me (as a Confident) that
his Majestie would shut up the Chequer, and accordingly his
Majestie made use of infinite Treasure there to prepare for an
intended rupture; but says he, it will soone be open againe, and
every body satisfied: for this bold man (who had ben the sole
adviser of the King, to invade that sacred stock, though some
pretend it was my Lord Ashleys counsel (Chancelor then of the
chequer) was so over confident of the successe of this unworthy
designe against the Smyrna Merchants; as to put his Majestie on an
action which not onely lost the hearts of his subjects, and ruined
many Widdows and Orphans whose stocks were lent him, but the
reputation of his Exchequer for ever, it being before in such Credit,
that his Majestie before this seizure, might have commanded halfe
the wealth of the nation: The Credit of this bank being thus
broken, did exceedingly discontent the people, and never did his
Majesties afaires prosper to any purpose after it, for as it did not
supply the expense of the meditated war, so it mealted away I know
not how.

'Warping to Rome'?

And to this succeded his Majesties declaration for an universal
Tolleration; Papists and Swarmes of sectaries now boldly shewing
themselves in their publique meetings; and this was imputed to the
same Council, Clifford warping to Rome, as was believe'd, nor was

my Lord Arlington cleare of suspicion, to gratifie that partie, but, as since it has prov'd and was then evidently fore-seene, to the extreame weakning the Church of England and its Episcopal Government; as 'twas projected: I speake not this as my owne sense, but what was the discourse and thoughts of others, who were lookers on: for I think, there might be some relaxations without the least prejudice to the present Establishment, discreetely limited, but to let go the reines in this manner, and then to imagine they could take them up againe as easily, was a false politique, and greately destructive; The truth is our Bishops slipt the occasion; since had they held a steady hand upon his Majesties restauration, as easily they might have don, The Church of England had emerg'd and flourish'd without interruption; but they were then remisse, and covetous after advantages of another kind, whilst his Majestie suffer'd them to come into an harvest, which without any injustice he might have remunerated innumerable gallant Gentlemen with for their services, who had ruin'd themselves for him in the late rebellion . . .

A Cruel Operation

24. I din'd with Mr. Commissioner Cox having seene that morning my Chirurgeon cut off a poore creaturs Leg, a little under the knee, first cutting the living and untainted flesh above the Gangreene with a sharp knife, and then sawing off the bone in an instant; then with searing and stoopes stanching the blood, which issued aboundantly; the stout and gallant man, enduring it with incredible patience, and that without being bound to his chaire, as is usual in such painefull operations, or hardly making a face or crying oh: I had hardly courage enough to be present, nor could I endure to se any more such cruel operations.

The leg was so rotten and gangreen'd, that one might have run a straw through it; but neither did this the cure, for it not being amputated high-enough, the gangreene prevaild upon the knee, and so a second amputation of the Thigh, cost the poore Creature his life, to my very greate sorrow: I do not remember that ever in my life I smelt so intollerable a stink as what issu'd from the part was cut off, and which I ordered should immediately be buried in the Garden: Lord, what miseries are mortal men obnoxious to, and what confusion and mischiefe dos the avarice, anger, and ambition of Princes cause in the world, who might be happier with halfe they possesse: This stoute man, was but a common sailer.

Kentish Scenery

... [27] I came back through a Country the best cultivated of any that in my life I had any where seene, every field lying as even as a bowling greene, and the fences, plantations, and husbandrie in such admirable order, as infinitely delighted me, after the sad and afflicting specctacles and objects I was come from: observing almost every tall tree, to have a Weather-cock on the top bough, and some trees halfe a dozen, I learned, that on a certain holy-day, the Farmers feast their Servants, at which solemnity they set up these Cocks in a kind of Triumph etc:

...

May: 2: My sonne John was specialy admitted of the Middle Temple by Sir Fra: North, his Majesties Solicitor general Since Lord Chancelor: I pray God blesse this begining, my intention being he should seriously apply himselfe to the study of the Law:

'In attendance of the Fleete'

5 A young man preached at the Abby etc: where I received the B: Sacrament: and dined with the Bishop of Rochester; Pomerid: Dr. Stradling on 2. Philip: 7: 6. I went home. 10. To Lond: din'd with Sir W: D'Oylie when came a Letter from the Council, that I was forthwith to repaire to his Majestie whom I found in the Pal-Mal in St. Ja: Park, where his Majestie coming to me from the companie, he commanded me to go immediately to the Sea-Coast, and to observe the motion of the Dutch Fleete and ours, the Duke, and so many of the flower of our Nation being now under saile coming from Portsmouth thro the Downes, where 'twas believed there might be an encounter; so as I went on the next day (11) to Chatham: 12 heard a sermon at the Cathedrall of Rochester, din'd at Coll: Midletons: 13 To Canterbury, Visited Dr. Bargrave my old fellow Travelor in Italy and greate Virtuoso. 14: To Dover where I staied in attendance of the Fleete from Portsmouth, but which appear'd not til the 16: Ascension day, when the Duke of York with his, and the French Squadron, in all 170 ships, of which above 100 Men of War, sailed by after the Dutch, who were newly withdrawn: Such a gallant and formidable Navy never I think spread saile upon

the seas, it was [a] goodly, yet tirrible sight, to behold them as I did passing by the straits, twixt Dover and Calis eastward, in a glorious day: The wind was yet so high, that I could not well go on board, and they were soone gotten out of sight: So the next day having visited our Prisoners at the Castle and saluted the Governor, I tooke horse 17 for Margate, where from North-foreland lighthouse top (which is a pharos built of Bricque, having on the top a Cradle of yron, in which one attends a greate Sea-Coale fire, all the yeare long when the nights are darke, for the safe-guard of Sailers) we could see our fleete as it lay at Anker; and the next morning weighing, sailed out of sight to the N: East: 19: I went to Margate church, where one Mr. Chunie the minister made an excellent sermon on 14: Apoc: 7:

. . .

The Third Dutch War: Lord Sandwich

. . . 31. I received another Command to repaire to the sea-side againe, so I went to Rochester, where I found many both Wounded, sick, and Prisoners newly put on shore, after the Engagement of the 28, in which the Earle of Sandwich, that incomparable person, and my particular friend and divers more whom I loved, were lost: My Lord (who was Admiral of the [Blew]) in the *Prince* which was burnt, being one of the best Men of War, that ever spread canvas on the sea: Lost likewise with this brave man, was Sir Charles Coterell['s] Sonn, whose Father was Master of the Ceremonies, and Sir Ch: Harbord sonn of his Majesties Surveyor generall, two valiant, and most accomplish[ed] youths, full of virtue and Courage, and that might have saved themselves, but would perish with my Lord, whom they honor'd and loved above their owne lives: And here I cannot but make some reflection upon things past: Since it was not above a day or two, that going at White-hall to take my leave of his Lordship (who had his Lodgings in the Privy Gardens) shaking me by the hand bid me god buy, he should he thought see me no more, and I saw to my thinking something boading in his Countenance; no says he, they will not have me live: Had I lost a Fleete (meaning on his returne from Bergen, when he tooke the E. India prise) I should have fared better; but be it as please God; I must do I know not what, to save my reputation; something to this effect, he had hinted to me; but thus I tooke my leave: and well I remember, that the Duke of Albemarle, and my now Lord Clifford, had I know not why, no greate opinion of his Courage, because in former Conflicts, being an able and experienc'd sea-man (which neither of them were) he allwayes brought of his Majesties ships, without losse, though not without as many markes of true Courage as the stoutest of them; and I am witnesse, that in the late War, his owne ship was pierced like a Culender: But the buisinesse was, he was utterly against the War from the beginning, and abhor'd the attacquing of the Smyrna fleete; He did not favour the brutish and heady expedition of Clifford at Bergin; nor was he so stupidly furious, and confident as was the D: of Albemarle, who believed he could vanquish the Hollander with one Squadron: My L: Sandwich was prudent as well as Valiant, and allways govern'd his afairs with successe, and little losse, he was for deliberation, and reason, they for action and slaughter without either; and for this, whisperd it, as if my L: of Sandwich were not so Gallant, because he was not rash, and knew how fatal it were to loose a Fleete, such as was that under his Conduct, and for which these very persons would have censurd him on the other side: This it was which I am confident griev'd him, and made him enter like a Lion, and fight like one too, in the middst of the hottest service, where the stoutest of the rest, seing him ingagd, and so many ships upon him, durst not, or would not, come into his succour, as some of them, whom I know, might have don: Thus this gallant Person perish'd to gratifie the pride and envy, of some I named: and deplorable was the losse, of one of the best accomplish[ed] persons, not onely of this Nation but of any other: He was learned in the Mathematics, in Musique, in Sea affaires, in Political: Had ben divers Embassies, was of a sweete obliging temper; Sober, Chast, infinitly ingenious, and a true noble man, an ornament to the Court, and his Prince, nor has he left any that approch his many Virtues behind him: He had I confesse serv'd the Tyrant Cromwell, when a young man, but 'twas without malice, and as a souldier of fortune, and readily submitted and that with joy, bringing an intire fleete with him from the Sound, at the very first tidings of his Majesties restauration: nor praise I him for what he did then amisse, but for the signal services he since had don, and verily believe him as faithfull a Subject as any that were not his Friends: I am yet heartily griev'd at this mighty losse, nor do I call it to my thoughts without emotion.

. . .

[June] 7 I went to see Upnore Castle, which I found pretty well defended, but of no greate moment: Nex[t] day I sailed to the Fleete now riding at the buoy of the Noore, where I met his Majestie, the Duke, L. Arlington and all the greate men in the *Charles*, lying miserably shatterd; but the misse of my Lord Sandwich redoubled the losse to me, as well as the folly of hazarding so brave a fleete, and loosing so many good men, for no provocation in the World but because the Hollander exceeded us in Industrie, and all things else but envy . . .

. . .

Mistresse Blagge

[October] 16 My Devout, and deare Friend declaring her condition to me for want of one she could trust, to govern and manage her competent stock; and earnestly desiring my poore assistance; I promised to do my best to serve her, and from that time forwards, I reckond her as my Child; for none did ever shew greater esteeme for a Father, than did this incomparable Creature to me, worthy of all the returnes I could ever make, for the many lasting obligations I received from her; a rare example of so much piety, and Virtue in so greate a Witt, beauty and perfection; This Miracle of a young Lady in a licentious Court and so deprav'd an age . . .

. . .

Young John Confirmed

[1673. March] 28 Preached coram rege the Bish: of Rochester on 23. Luke. 34. being Good-friday, in a most passionat and pathe[t]ic discourse, according to his usual way:

29 I carried my Sonn to the Bishop of Chichester that learned and pious man, Dr. Peter Gunning, to be instructed by him before he received the holy Sacrament, when he gave him most excellent advise, which I pray to God may influence, and remaine with him as long as he lives; and ô that I had ben so blessed, and instructed, when first I was admitted to that Sacred Ordinance! 30: Easter-day preached in the Morning one Mr. Field . . . a Resurrection sermon with much eloquence: The Blessed Communion followd, at which

both my selfe, and my Sonne received, it being his first time, and
with that whole weekes more extraordinary preparation, I besech
God make him a sincere good Christian, whilst I endeavor to instill
into him the feare and love of God, and discharge the Duty of a
Father . . .

. . .

A Curious 'Paradise'

[September] 23 To Lond; dining with Mrs. Bl: we went to see
Paradise, a roome in Hatton Garden furnished with the representations of all sorts of animals, handsomely painted on boards or
cloth, and so cut out and made to stand and move, fly, crawll, roare
and make their severall cries, as was not unpretty: though in it selfe
a meere bauble, whilst the man who shew'd, made us Laugh
heartily at his formal poetrie. 24 I went home . . .

. . .

Nineveh

[December] 20 I had some discourse with certaine strangers, not
unlearned, who had ben born not far from the old Niniveh: They
assur'd me the ruines being still extant, and vast, wonderfull was
the buildings, Vaults, Pillars, and magnificent fragments now
buried, and remaining: but little could they say of the Toure of
Babel that satisfied me: but the description of the amœnitie and
fragrancy of the Country for health, and cherefullnesse, did almost
ravish me; so sensibly the[y] spake of the excellent aire and climat,
in respect of our cloudy and splenetic Country:

. . .

A Careerist

[1674. July] 22 I went to Winsore with my Wife and sonn, to see
my Daughter Mary who was there with my Lady Tuke; and to do
my Duty to his Majestie: next day to a greate entertainment at Sir
Robert Holmes's at Cranburne Lodge in the forest: There were his
Majestie, Queene, Duke, Dutchesse and all the Court: I returned
in the Evening with Sir Jos: Wiliamson now declared Secretary of
state: Sir Jos: was sonn of a meane Clergyman some where in
Cumberlandshire, brought up at Queenes Coll: Oxon: of which he
came to be a fellow; Then traveled with . . . and returning when

the King was restord, was received as a Clerk under Mr. Secretary
Nicholas: Sir Hen: Bennet (now L. Arlington:) succeeding,
Williamson is transferred to Sir Henry: who loving his ease more
than buisinesse, (though sufficiently able had he applyed himselfe
to it) remitted all to his man Williamson, and in a short time let him
so into the seacret of affaires, that (as his Lordship himselfe told
me) there was a kind of necessity to advance him; and so by his
subtilty, dexterity and insinuation, he got now to be principal
Secretary; absolutely my L: Arlingtons Creature, and ungratefull
enough; for so it has ben the fate of this obliging favorite, to
advance those who soone forgot their original: Sir Joseph was a
Musitian, could play at *jëu de Goblets*, exceeding formal; a severe
Master to his Servants; but so inward with my Lord Obrian, that
after a few moneths of that Gent: death, he maried his Widdow,
who being daughter and heire of the Duke of Richmond, brought
him a noble fortune; but, twas thought, they lived not so kindly after
marriage as they did before: and she was infinitely censur'd for
marrying so meanely, being herselfe alyed to the royal family . . .
. . .

War Games at Windsor

[August] 21 There was approches, and a formal seige, against a
Work with Bastions, Bullwarks, Ramparts, Palizads, [Graft],
hornworks, Conter-scarps etc: in imitation of the Citty of
Maestrict, newly taken by the French: and this being artificialy
design'd and cast up in one of the Meadows at the foote of the long
Terrace below the Castle, was defended against the Duke of
Monmouth (newly come from that real seige) who with the Duke of
York attaqu'd it with a little army, to shew their skill in Tactics: so
on Saturday night, They made their approches, opened trenches,
raised batteries, took the Conter-scarp, Ravelin, after a stout
Defence. Greate Gunns fir'd on both sides, Granados shot, mines
Sprung, parties sent out, attempts of raising the seige, prisoners
taken, Parlies, and in short all the Circumstances of a formal seige
to appearance, and what is most strange, all without disorder, or ill
accident, but to the greate satisfaction of a thousand spectators,
when being night it made a formidable shew, and was realy very
divertisant: This mock seige being over, I went with Mr. Pepys
back to Lond: where we arived about 3 in the morning: and at St.

Martines heard a sermon [23] on 26: Matt: 74: The very same sermon, by the same preacher, I happn'd to heare againe at St. Jamess this Afternoone . . .

. . .

A 'greate lover of Musique'

[November] 19 I heard the stupendious Violin Signor Nicholao (with other rare Musitians) whom certainly never mortal man Exceeded on that Instrument: he had a stroak so sweete, and made it speake like the Voice of a man; and when he pleased, like a Consort of severall Instruments: he did wonders upon a note: was an excellent Composer also: here was also that rare Lutinist Dr. Wallgrave: but nothing approch'd the Violin in Nicholas hand: he seem'd to be spiritato'd and plaied such ravishing things on a ground as astonish'd us all: 20 I went home after Council:

. . .

. . . [December] 2: heard Signor Francisco on the Harpsichord, esteem'd on[e] of the most excellent masters in Europe on that Instrument: then came Nicholao with his Violin and struck all mute, but Mrs. Knight, who sung incomparably, and doubtlesse has the greatest reach of any English Woman: she had lately ben roming in Italy: and was much improv'd in that quality: There was other Musique, and this Consort was at Mr. Slingsbys Master of the Mint, my worthy friend, and greate lover of Musique: 4 A Council. 5 home:

. . .

Sir William Petty*

. . . [1675. March 24] I supped at Sir William Pettys, with The Bish: of Salisbury, and divers honorable persons: we had a noble entertainment, in a house gloriously furnished; The Master and Mistris of it extraordinary Persons: Sir Will: being the sonn of a meane man some where in Sussex, was sent from Schole to Oxon: where he studied Philos: but was most eminent in Mathematics and Mechanics, proceeded Doctor of Physick, and was growne famous as for his Learning, so for his recovering a poore wench that had ben hanged for felonie, the body being beged (as costome is) for the Anatomie lecture, he let bloud, put to bed to a warme woman, and with spirits and other meanes recovered her to life; The Young

Scholars joyn'd and made her a little portion, married her to a Man who had severall children by her, living 15 yeares after, as I have ben assured: He came from Oxon: to be [pedagogue] to a neighbour of mine; Thence when the Rebells were dividing their Conquests in Ireland, he was employed by them to measure and set out the Land, which he did upon an easy contract so much per Acker: which he effected so exactly, and so expeditiously, as not onely furnish'd him with a greate summ of mony, but enabled him to purchas an Estate worth 4000 pounds a yeare; he afterwards married the Daughter of Sir Hardresse Waller, she an extraordinary witt, as well as beauty, and a prudent Woman: Sir William amongst other inventions author of the Double-bottom'd ship; which though it perishd, and he censur'd for rashnesse; yet it was lost in the bay of Biscay in a storme when, I think 15 more Vessels misscarried: The Vessell was flat-bottom'd, of exceeding use to put into shallow Ports, and ride over small depths of water; It consisted of two distinct Keeles crampt together with huge timbers etc: so as a violent streame ran betweene: It bare a monstrous broad saile; and he still persists it practicable and of exceeding use, and has often told me he would adventure himselfe in such another, could he procure sailors, and his Majesties Permission to make a second Experiment, which name the King gave it at the Launching: The Map of Ireland made by Sir William is bilieved to be the most exact that ever was yet made of any Country: he did promise to publish it: and I am told it has cost him neere 1000 pounds to have it ingrav'd at Amsterdam. There is not a better Latine pöet living, when he gives himselfe that Diversion; nor is his Excellency lesse in Counsil, and prudent matters of state: :tc: but is so extraordinary nice in scifting, and examining all possible contingences, that he adventures at nothing, which is not Demonstration: There were not in the whole world his equal for a superintendent of Manufacturs, and improvement of Trade; or for to govern a Plantation: If I were a Prince, I should make him my second Counselor at least: There is nothing difficult to him; besids he is Coragious, on which account I cannot but note a true storie of him: That when Sir Aleyn Brodrick sent him a Challenge, upon a difference twixt them in Ireland: Sir Will: though, exceedingly purblind, accepted the challenge, and it being his part to propound the Weapon, defied his Antagonist, to meete him with an hatchet or Axe in a darke Cellar; which he refusing, was laught at, for challinging one whom every body knew was so short sighted: Sir William was with all this facetious, and of Easy Conversation, friendly, and Courteous and had such a faculty to imitate others, that he would take a Text, and preach now like a grave orthodox Divine, then fall-into the Presbyterian way, thence to the Phanatical, the Quaker, the Moonk, and frier, the Popish Priest, with such admirable action, and alteration of voice and tone, as it was not possible to abstaine from wonder, and one would sweare, to heare severall persons, or think he were not in good earnest an Enthusiast and almost beside himselfe, when he would fall out of it in to a serious discourse etc which was very divertisant: but it was very rarely he would be courted to oblige the company with this faculty, unlesse among most intimate friends: My Lord Duke of Ormond once obtain'd it of him, and was almost ravished with admiration of it; but by and by he fell upon a serious reprimand of the faults and miscarriages of some Princes and Governors, which though he named none, did so sensibly touch my L: Duke, who was then Lieutenant of Ireland; that my Lord began to be very uneasy, and wish'd the spirit alayed: for he was neither able to indure such truths, nor could he for his heart but be delighted; so at last he mealted his discourse to another more ridiculous subject and came done from the joyne stoole; but my Lord, would heare him preach no more. He could never get to be favoured at Court; because he outwitted all the projecturs that came neere him: In my life having never know[n] such a Genius, I cannot but mention these particulers, among multitude of others, which I could produce: When I have ben in his splendid Palace, who knew him in meaner Circumstances, he would be in admiration himselfe how he ariv'd to it; nor was it his value [or] inclination to splendid furnitur and the curiositie of the age: but his Elegant Lady, who could indure nothing meane, and that was not magnificent; whilst he was very negligent himselfe and of a Philosophic temper: Lord, would he say, what a deale of do is here; I can lie in straw with as much satisfaction: and was indeede rather negligent of his person etc: Sir William is the Author of the ingenious deductions from the bills of Mortality which go under the name of Mr. Graunt: also of that usefull discourse of the manufactur of Wooll, and severall other, in our Register of the R: Society: The Author of that Paraphrase on 104 Psal: in Latin

Verse, which gos about in MSS: and is inimitable: In a word, there is nothing impenetrable to him.

. . .

[May 17] This day was my deare friend Mrs. Blagg maried to Mr. Sidny Godolphin Groome of the Bed-Chamber to his Majestie at the Temple Church by Mr. Leake Chap: to the Duke:*

. . .

Mr. Quierwill and his Lady

[June 21] This afternoone came Monsieur Quierwill and his Lady Parents to the famous beauty and . . . favorite at Court, to see Sir Rich: Bro: my F. in Law, with whom they were intimately acquainted in Bretagne, what time Sir Richard was sent to Brest, to supervise his Majesties sea affaires during the later part of his Majesties banishment abroad: This Gent: house being not a mile from Brest; Sir Richard made an acquaintance there, and being used very Civily, was oblig'd to returne it here, which we did in a Collation: after which they returned to Lond: He seem'd a souldierly person, and a good fellow, as the Bretons generaly are, his Lady had ben very handsom, and seem'd a shrew'd understanding woman: Conversing with him in our Garden, I found severall words of the Breton language the same with our Welch: His daughter was now made Dutchesse of Portsmouth and in the height of favour; but we never made any use of it: etc:

. . .

Oxford Again

[July] 8 I went with Mrs. Howard and her two daughters towards Northampton Assises about a Tryal at Law, in which I was Concerned for them as a Trusteè. We lay this night at Henly on the Thames at our Attourney Mr. [Stephens's] who entertain'd us very handsomely: Thenc next day dining at Shotover at Sir Tim. Tyrills a sweete place, we lay at Oxford it being the Act: when Mr. Rob: Spencer Unkle to the Earle of Sunderland and my old acquaintance in France, entertain'd us at his appartment in Christ-Church (where he had hired one of the Canons Lodgings,) entertain'd us all the while, with exceeding generosity: 10: The Vice-Chancelor Dr. Bathurst, (who had formerly taken particular care of my Sonn) President of Trinity, invited me to Dinner, and did me greate honour all the time of my stay: The next day he also invited me and all my Company, though strangers to him, to a very noble Dinner: I was at all the Academique Exercises: Sondy, at St. Maries preached a fellow of Brasen nose on 2: Tit: 15., not a little magnifying the dignity of Church-men: In the afternoone one of New Coll: but the heate and presse was so greate I could not hear etc: and was faine to go out:

We heard the Speeches and saw the Ceremonie of Creating Doctors in Divinity, Law, Physique etc: I had in the morning early heard Dr. Morison Botanic Professor, reade on divers Plants in the Physic Garden; and saw that rare Collection of natural Curiosities, of Dr. Plots of Magdalen hall: Author of the Natural hist: of Oxford-shire; all of them collected in that shire, and indeede extraordinary, that in one County, there should be found such varietie of Plants, Shells, Stones, Minerals, Marcasites, foule, Insects, Models of works etc: Chrystals, Achates, Marbles: he was now intending to Visite Staffordshire and as he had of Oxfordshire to give us the Natural, Topical, Political, Mechani[c]al history: and pitty it is, more of this industrious mans genius were not employed so to describe every County of England, since it would be one of the most usefull and illustrious Workes that was ever produc'd in any age or nation: I visited also the Bodlean library and my old friend the Learned Obadia Walker head of Universitie Coll: which he had now almost quite rebuilt or repair'd: So taking leave of the V: Chancelor, Dr. Alestree the Kings Professor in Divinity, Deane of Christ Church Dr. Fell, we proceeded to Northampton where we arived next day:

In this journey went part of the way Mr. Ja: Grahame Since privy purse to the Duke, a Young Gent: exceedingly in love with Mrs. Dorothy Howard one of the Mayds of honor in our Company: I could not but pitty them both: The Mother not much favouring it: This Lady was not onely a greate beauty, but a most virtuous and excellent Creature, and worthy to have ben Wife to the best of men: My advice was required, and I spake to the advantage of the young gent: more out of pitty, than that I thought she deserv'd no better; for though he was a gent: of a good family, yet there was greate inequalitys etc:

Althorp

14 I went to see my Lord Sunderlands seat at Althorp, 4 miles from the ragged Towne of Northampton Since burned and well rebuilt: tis placed in a pretty open bottome, very finely watred and flanqued with stately woods and groves in a Parke with a Canale, yet the water is not running, which is a defect: The house a kind of modern building of Free stone: within most nobly furnishe'd: The Apartments very commodious, and Gallerie and noble hall: but the Kitching for being in the body of the house, and Chapell too small were defects: There is an old, yet honorable Gate house standing a wry, and out-housing meane, but design'd to be taken away: It was Moated round after the old manner, but it is now dry and turf'd with a sweete Carpet: above all are admirable and magnificent the severall ample Gardens furnish'd with the Choicest fruite in England, and exquisitely kept: Great plenty of Oranges, and other Curiosities: The Parke full of Fowle and especialy Hernes, and from it a prospect to Holmby house, which being demolished in the late Civil Warre, shews like a Roman ruine shaded by the trees about it, one of the most pleasing sights that ever I saw, of state and solemne:

15 Our Cause was pleaded in behalfe of the Mother Mrs. Howard and Daughters before baron Thurland, who had formerly been Steward of Courte for me: We carried our Cause, as there was reason; for here was an imprudent as well as disobedient sonn, against his Mother by instigation doubtlesse of his Wife, one Mrs. Ogle (an antient Maid) whom he had clandestinly married, and who brought him no fortune, he heire aparent of the Earle of Berkshire. After dinner we went toward Lond: Lay at Brickhill in Bedfordshire and came late next day to our journeys end.

All for Love

This was a journey of Adventure and knight errantry, one of the Ladys servants being as desperately in love with Mrs. Howards Woman, who riding on horsback behind his Rival, the amorous and jealous Youth, having a little drink in his pate, had certainly here killed himselfe, had he not ben prevented; for alighting from his horse and drawing his sword, he endeavored to fall upon it twise or thrice, but was interrupted; [by] our Coach-man and a stranger that passed by, after which running to his rival, and snatching another sword from his side (for we had beaten his owne out of his hand) and on the suddaine pulling downe his Mistriss, would have run both of them through; but we parted them, though not without some blood: This miserable Creature Poyson'd himselfe for her not many daies after they came to Lond:

. . .

[August] 9 My Coach-house was broken open this night, and the Glasses and Damaske Cushions, Curtaines etc: taken away . . .

. . .

An Expensive Duchess

[September] 10 I was Casualy shewed the Dutchesse of Portsmouths splendid Appartment at Whitehall, luxuriously furnished, and with ten times the richnesse and glory beyond the Queenes, such massy pieces of Plate, whole Tables, Stands etc: of incredible value etc . . .

. . .

An Apoplectic Ambassador

[October] 27 My Lord Berkeley* now in precinct for his departure into France, coming to the Council fell downe in the Gallery at White-hall of a fit of Apoplexie, and being carried into my L: Chamberlaines Lodgings employed all that night severall famous Doctors and with much adò was at last recovered to some sense by applying hot fire-pans and Spirit of Amber to his head, but nothing was found so effectual as cupping on the shoulders: an almost miraculous restauration: The next day he was carried to B: house. This stopped for the present his journey, and caused my stay in Towne, into whose hands he had put all his Affaires and whole estate in England during his absence, which though I was very unfit to undertake, in reguard of [many] buisinesses then which tooke me up; yet upon the greate importunity of my Lady, and Mrs. Godolphin (to whom I could refuse nothing) I did; It seemes when he was Deputy (not long before in Ireland) he had ben much wronged by one he left in trust with his affaires, and therefore wished for some unmercenary friend, who would take that trouble on him; which was to receive his Rents, looke after his Houses and Tennants, solicite for Supplies from the L: Tressurer etc: Correspond weekly with him, more than enough to employ any drudge in England: but what will not friendship and love make on[e] do!

31 The Anniversary of my Birthday and 55th of my Age being Sonday likewise I received the holy Sacrament at St. James's . . .

November 2 I went home: 7 our Viccar on: 7 Matt: 1. 2, the holy Sacrament followd: Curate on 1. Jo: 5. 8: 8. To Lond: in order to my Sonns journey, and to provide bills of Exchange for Mrs. Godolphin, whose whole Concernes were still in my hands:

9 I din'd at B: house, and went late home: the next day being the time appointed for my L: Ambassador to set forth, 10 I met them with my Coach at New-Crosse: There was with him my Lady his Wife, and my deare friend Mrs. Godolphin who, out of an extraordinary friendship, would needes accompany my Lady to Paris and stay with her some time, which was the chiefe inducement of my permitting my Sonn to Travell; but I knew him safe under her inspection, and in reguard my Lord himselfe had so promis'd me to take him into his special care, who had intrusted all he had to mine: Thus we set out 3 Coaches, 3 Wagons, and about 40 horse besides my Coach: It being late and my Lord but valetudinarie yet, we got but to Dartford the first day, and 11 the next to Citinburne; by the Way the Major of Rochester Mr. Cony, who was then an Officer of mine for the Sick and Wounded of that place etc, entertain'd the Ladys with an handsome present of refreshments, as we came by his house: 12 We came to Canterbery, where next morning Mrs. Godolphin and I went to the Cathedrall to prayers, and thence to Dover: There was in my Lady Ambassadors Company also my Lady Hammilton, a Spritefull young Lady, who was much in the good-graces of that family, and wife of that valiant and worthy Gent: Geo: Hammilton not long after slaine in the Warrs; she had ben a Maid of Honor to the Dutchesse, and now turn'd Papist:

13 At Dover Mrs. Godolphin delivered me her Will, which her Husband had given her leave to make, and absolutely to dispose of all her fortune, which was in value better than 4000 pounds: then after prayers, 14 the next morning my Lord having delivered me before his Letters of Attourney, Keyes, Seale, and his Will, (it being Sonday-morning and a glorious day) We tooke solemn leave of one another upon the Beach, the Coaches carrying them into the sea to the Boats, which delivered them to Cap: Gunmans Yacht the

Mary: and so I parted with my Lord, my sonn, and the person in the world whom I esteemed as my owne life Mrs. Godolphin; being under saile, the Castle gave them 17 Gunns, and Cap: Gunman answered with 11: Hence I went to Church to beg a blessing on their Voyage . . .

. . .

. . . [1676. April 4] I had now notice that Mrs. Godolphin was returning from Paris and landing the 3d at Dover; so I din'd with my L: Sunderland expecting her:

6 Came my dearest Friend to my greate joy; whom after I had welcom'd, I gave accompt to of her buisinesse, and return'd home . . .

. . .

A Surprise

26 Din'd with ☿,* discovered her Marriage by her sister:

27 My Wife entertaind her Majestie at Deptford, for which the Queene gave [me] thanks in the Withdrawing roome at White-hall.

. . .

[May] 3 Visited Mrs. Godolphin expostulated with her about the concealement, and was satisfied, it was not her intention . . .

. . .

12 Dind with my L: Arlington. 13 returned home, and found my sonn returned out of France, praised be God; for my deare friend Mrs. Godolphin coming thence I had no desire he should stay there any longer for many reason[s]:

. . .

The North West Passage

[August] 26 I din'd at the Admiralty, with Sec: Pepys: Supp'd at L: Chamberlaines, here was Cap: Baker, who had ben lately on the attempt of the Nor-west passage: he reported prodigious depth of yce, blew as a Saphire and as transparant: That the thick mists was their chiefe impediment, and cause of returne . . .

. . .

An Accident

[October] 9 I went with Mrs. Godolphin and my Wife to Black-wall to see some Indian Curiosities, and as I was walking thro a streete, the way being s[l]ipperie and misty, I fell against a piece of Timber, with such violence, as quite beate the breath out of my body, so as being taken up, I could not speake, nor fetch any breath, for some space, and then with greate difficulty, coming to my sense, after some applications, being carried into an house, and let bloud: I was carried to the water side, and so home, where after a daies rest, I recovered, though my bruse was not quite healed: This being one of the greatest deliverances that ever I had, The Lord Jesus make me ever mindfull, and thankfull . . .

. . .

An Apparition

. . . [30] Mrs. Ann Howard Mayd of honor to the Queene, whom I went to Visite, related to me the strang[e] Vision she saw: which was thus: One of her maides being lately dead and one whom I well knew, had in her life time told her Mistris, that when she died she would certainly appeare to her: This Wench, being deepely in love with a young man, dying, a little while after appeared to her Mistris, as she lay in [bed], drawing the Curtaine, siting downe by her, and beckning to her; her Mistris being broad awake, and sitting up at the affright, called alow'd for her maid to come to her, but no body came; The Vision, now going from her, she still continued to call her Maid, who lying in another chamber next to her, rose and came at last to her Mistris: begging her pardon that she did not come at her first call; for said shee, I have ben in a most deadly fright, and durst not stirr for Mistress Maundy (for so was her name) who has appear'd to me, and looked so wistly on me, at the foote of my bed, that I had not the power to rise or answer: These two, Mistris Howard and her Woman Davis, affirming it so positively and happning to see it, neere the same time, and in severall chambers, is a most remarkable thing: and I know not well how to discredit it, Mrs. Howard being so extraordinary a virtuous and religious Lady.

. . .

Business Concluded

[1677. June] 12 I went to Lond: to give the L. Ambassador Berkeley (now return'd from the Treaty at Nimegen) an accompt of the greate Trust repos'd in me during his absence, I having received and transmitted to him no lesse than 20000 pounds: to my no small trouble, and losse of time, that during his absence, and when the Lord Tressurer was no greate friend, I yet procur'd him greate Summs, very often soliciting his Majestie in his behalfe, looking after the rest of his Estate and concernes intirely; without once so much as accepting any kind of acknowledgement, purely upon the request of my deare friend Mrs. Godolphin.

13 I din'd with Mrs. Godolphin and return'd, with aboundance of thanks and professions 16 from my Lord Berkeley and Lady etc: 17: Viccar as before and so the Curate.

24 My Lord Berkeleys troublesome buisinesses being now at an end and I delivered from that intollerable servitude and Correspondence; I had leasure to be somewhat more at home, and to myselfe . . .

. . .

Bury St. Edmunds

. . . [September] 4. I went to visite my Lord Crofts, now dying at St. Edmonsbery, and tooke this opportunity to see this antient Towne, and the remaines of that famous Monasterie and Abby; There is little standing intire save the Gate-house, which shews it to have ben a vast and magnificent Gotique structure, and of greate extent: The Gates are Wood, but quite plated over with iron: There are also two stately Churches, one especialy. 5. I went to Thetford the Borrogh Towne, where stands likewise the ruines of another religious house; and there is a round mountaine artificialy raised, either for some Castle or Monument, which makes a pretty Landscape: As we went and return'd a Tumbler shew'd his extraordinary addresse in the Warren: I also saw the Decoy, much pleased with the stratagem etc: 9: A stranger preach'd at Euston Church on 1. Thess: 5. 21. Prove all things, that is examine your faith, your life, your actions, and that of others, to imitate the best; and then fell into an handsome Panegyric on my Lords new building the Church, which indeede for its Elegance and cherefullnesse is absolutely the prettiest Country Church in England: My Lord told me that his heart smote him, after he had bestow'd so much on his magnificent Palace there he should see Gods-house in the ruine it lay; he has also rebuilt the Parsonage house all of stone, very neately and ample:

Euston Again

... [10] we return'd late to Euston, having travelled above 50 miles this day:

Since first I was at this place, seated in a bottome betweene two gracefull swellings, I found things exceedingly improv'd: The maine building being now made in the figure of a Greeke π with 4 pavilions two at each corner and a breake in the front, rail'd and balustred at the top, where I caused huge jarrs of Earth to be plac'd full of Earth to keepe them steady [on] their [Piedestalls], betweene the statues, which make as good a shew, as if they were of stone; and though the building be of brick and but two stories, besides Cellars and Garrets, covered with blew Slate, yet there is roome enough for a full Court, the offices and out-houses being so ample and well disposed: The Kings appartment is both painted a fresca, and magnificently furnish'd: There are many excellent Pictures in the roomes of the greate Masters: The Gallery is a pleasant noble roome, and in the breake or middle, a Billiard Table; but the Wainscot being of firr, and painted dos not please me so well as Spanish Oake without painting: The Chapell is pretty, and Porch descending to the Gardens: The Orange-Garden is very fine, and leads into the Greene-house, at the end whereoff is a sall to eate in, and the Conservatory very long (some hundred feete) adorn'd with Mapps, as the other side is with the heads of Cæsars ill cut in alabaster: over head are severall appartments for my Lord, Lady, and Dutchesse, with Kitchins and other offices below in a lesser volume, with lodgings for servants, all distinct, for them to retire to when they please, and that he would be in private and have no communication with the Palace, which he tells me he will wholly resigne to his Sonn in Law, and Daughter, that Wise, and charming young Creature: The Canale running under my Ladys dressing chamber window, is full of Carps, and fowle, which come and are fed there with greate diversion: The Cascade at end of the Canale turnes a Corne-mill which finds the family, and raises water for the fountaines and offices: To passe this Chanal into the opposite Meadows, Sir Sam: Moreland has invented a Skrew Bridge, which being turned with a Key land[s] you 50 foote distant, at entrance of an ascending Walke of trees for a mile in length: as tis also on the front into the Park, of 4 rows of Ashes and reaches to the Parke Pale which is 9 miles in Compas, and the best for riding and meeting the game that ever I saw, There were now of red and fallow deere almost a thousand, with good Covert, but the soile barren and flying sand in which nothing will grow kindly: The Tufts of Firr and much of the other wood were planted by my direction some yeares before. In a word, this seate is admirably placed for field sports, hauking, hunting, racing: The mutton small but sweete: The stables are capable of 30 horses and 4 Coaches: The out offices make two large quadrangles, so as never servants liv'd with more ease and convenience, never Master more Civil; strangers are attended and accomodated as at their home in pretty apartments furnish'd with all manner of Conveniences and privacy: There are bathing roomes, Elaboratorie, Dispensatorie, what not: Decoy and places to keepe and fat foule etc: He had now in his new Church (neere the Garden) built a Dormitory or Vault with severall repositories to burie in for his family: In the expense of this pious structure, I meane the church, exceedingly laudable, most of the houses of God in this Country resembling rather stables and thatched Cottages than Temples to serve God in: He has also built a Lodge in the Park for the Keeper, which is a neate and sweete dwelling, and might become any gentleman of quality, the same has he don for the Parson, little deserving it, for his murmuring that my Lord put him for some time out of his wretched hovell, whilst it was building: he has also built a faire Inn at some distance from his Palace, a bridge of stone over a River neere it, and repaired all the Tennants houses, so as there is nothing but neatenesse, and accomodations about his estate, which yet I think is not above 1500 pounds a yeare: I believe he had now in his family 100 domestic servants. His Lady (being one of the Bredrodes daughters, grandchild to a natural sonn of Henry Fred: Prince of Orange) is a good natured, and obliging woman. They love fine things, and to live easily, pompously, but very hospitable; but with so vast expense as plunges my Lord into debt exceedingly:

Lord Arlington

My Lord himselfe is given to no expensive vise but building and to have all things rich, polite, and Princely: he never plays, but reades much, having both the Latine, French and Spanish tongues in perfection: has traveled much, and is absolutely the best bred and Courtly person his Majestie has about him; so as the publique

Ministers more frequent him than any of the rest of the nobility: Whilst he was secretary of state and prime Minister he had gotten vastly, but spent it as hastily, even before he had established a funds to maintaine his greatenesse, and now beginning to decline in favour (the Duke being no great friend of his) he knows not how to retrench: He was the sonn of a Doctor of Laws whom I have seene, and being sent from Westminster Schole to Oxon: with intention to be a divine, and parson of Arlington a Village neere Brainford, when Master of Arts, the Rebellion falling out, he followd the Kings Army, and receiving an honorable wound in the face, grew into favour and was advanc'd from a meane fortune at his Majesties restauration, to an Earle, and knight of the Garter: L: Chamb: of the Household, and first favorite for a long time, during which the King married his Natural Sonn the Duke of Grafton, to his onely Daughter and heiresse: worthy for her beauty and vertue of the greatest Prince in Christendom: My Lord is besids all this a prudent and understanding person, in buisinesse, speakes very well: Unfortunate yet in those he has advanc'd, proving ungratefull most of them: The many obligations and civilities I have to this noble gent: exacts from me this Character, and I am sorry he is in no better Circumstances. Having now pass'd neere three weekes at Euston, to my greate Satisfaction, with much difficulty he sufferd me to looke homewards; being very earnest with me to stay longer, and to engage me, would himselfe have carried and accompanied me to Lynn regis, a Towne of important Trafique about 20 miles beyond, which I had never seene, as also the Travelling Sands, about 10 miles wide of Euston, that have so damaged the Country, rouling from place to place, and like the Sands in the desarts of Lybia, quite overwhelmed some gentlemens whole Estates, as the relation extant in print, and brought to our Society describes at large:

The 13 of September my Lords-Coach conveyed me to Berry: and thence baiting at New Market, stepping in at Audly end, to see that house againe, I lay at Bishops Stratford, and the next day home, accompanied in my Jorney with one Major Fairfax of a Younger house of the Lord Fairfax, a Souldier, a Traveller, an excellent Musitian, good natured, well bred gent:

16 Our Viccar preach'd on 5. Matt: 20: Curat on 4: Eph: 29: I preferred Mr. Philips to the service of my L: Chamb: who wanted a

scholar to reade to and entertaine him some times: My Lord has a library at Euston full of excellent bookes: 18 To Lond: dind with Mrs. Godolphin. 20 with my Lord Treasurer . . .

. . .

Marden, Surrey

. . . [October] 11. To Lond: 12 With Sir Robert Clayton to Marden, an estate he had lately bought of my kindsman Sir John Evelyn of Godstone in Surry: which from a despicable farme house Sir Robert had erected into a Seate with extraordinary expense: Tis seated in such a solitude among hills, as being not above 16 miles from Lond, seemes almost incredible, the ways also to it so winding and intricate: The Gardens are large and walled nobly, and the husbandry part made so convenient, and perfectly understood, as the like I had not seene: The barnes, the stacks of Corne, the Stalls for Cattell, Pidgeon house, etc of most laudable example: Innumerable are his plantations of Trees, espe[c]ialy Wallnuts, the Orangerie and Gardens very curious; large and noble roomes in the house. He and his Lady (very curious in Distilling etc) entertain'd me 3 or 4 dayes very freely: I earnestly suggested to him, the repairing of an old desolate delapidated Church, standing on the hill above the house, which I left him in good disposition to do, and endow it better, there not being above 4 or 5 inhabitants in the Parish besids this prodigious rich Scrivenor: This place is exceeding sharp in Winter, by reason of the serpenting of the hills, and wants running water, but the solitude exceedingly pleased me: all the ground is so full of wild Time, Majoram and other sweete plants, as is not to be overStock'd with Bees, so as I think he had neere 40 hives of that industrious Insect . . .

. . .

A Crucial Question Resolved

[1678. February] 5 Dind at ☿: 6. I had a private audience of the Duke in his Closet about my pretence to the Fee of Sayes-Court: Being in some dispute with my Lord Gerhard of Brandon, concerning the Corporal presence of Christ in the holy Sacrament, and that I told him, the impossibility of it, for that his body as man was after his Ascension to be and remaine in Heaven, my Lord desiring to see the Text: (we being both in the little privat chapell at

White-hall) we went to the desk, and asked Dr. Pierce who [was] then officiating to shew us the words; he said, such a Text there was, but he could not readily turne to it; upon which I opning the greate Bible at adventure put my finger exactly on 3. Acts: 21: which did both exceedingly astonish and satisfie my Lord . . .

. . .

Mrs Godolphin's Last Visit

[May] 16 Being the Wedding Anniversarie of my excellent friend Mrs. Godolphin, she, with my Lady Sylvius and her sister Grahame came to visite, and dine with me; returning in the Evening, and was the last time, that blessed Creature ever came to my house, now being also great with Child, and seldome stirring abroad:

. . .

Curiosities at Lambeth

[July] 23 Return'd, having ben to see Mr. Elias Ashmoles Library and Curiosities at Lambeth, he has divers MSS, but most of them Astrological, to which study he is addicted, though I believe not learned; but very Industrious, as his history of the Order of the Gartir shews, he shewed me a Toade included in Amber: The prospect from a Turret is very fine, it being so neere Lond: and yet not discovering any house about the Country. The famous John Tradescant, bequeath'd his Repositary to this Gent: who has given them to the University of Oxford, and erected a Lecture on them etc: over the Laboratorie, in imitation of the R: Society . . .

. . .

The Norfolk Inheritance

[August] 23 Upon Sir Rob: Readings importunity, I went to Visite the Duke of Norfolck at his new Palace by Way bridge; where he has laied out in building neere 10000 pounds, on a Copyhold, and in a miserable barren sandy place by the streeete side, never in my daies had I seene such expense to so small purpose: The roomes are Wainscoted, and some of them richly parquetted with Cedar, Yew, Cypresse etc. There are some good Pictures, especialy, that [incomparable] painting of Holbens where The Duke of Norfolck, Charles Brandon, and Hen: the 8: are daucing with the three Ladys, such amorous countenances, and spritefull motion did I never see expressed: 'Tis a thousand pitties (as I told my Lord of Arundel his sonn) that Jewell should be given away to the present broode, and not be fixed to the incontaminate issue:

. . .

29 I was cald againe to London to waite againe on the Duke of Norfolck who having at my request onely, bestow'd the Aru[n]delian Library on the Royal Society, sent to me to take charge of the Bookes and remove them; onely that I would suffer the Heraulds Chiefe Officer Sir W: Dugdale to have such of them as concernd Herauldry and Martials Office As bokes of Armorie and Geneologies; the Duke being Earle Marishal of England: I procured for our Society besides Printed bookes, neere 700 MSS: some in Greeke of greate concernement; The Printed books being of the oldest Impressions, are not the lesse valuable; I esteeme them almost equal with MSS: Most of the Fathers printed at Basil etc: before the Jesuites, abused them with their Expurgatorie Indexes: There is a noble MSS: of Vitruvius: Many of these Bookes had ben presented by Popes, Cardinals and greate Persons to the Earles of Arundell and Dukes of Norfolck; and the late magnificent Tho: E: of Arundel bought a noble Library in Germanie, which is in this Collection; nor should I for the honour I beare the family, have perswaded the Duke to part with these, had I not seene how negligent he was of them, in suffering the Priests, and every body to carry away and dispose of what they pleased: so as aboundance of rare things are gon, and irrecoverable:

Having taken Order here, I went to the R: Society, to give them an account of what I had procured, that they might call a Council, and appoint a day to waite on the Duke to thank him for this munificent gift:

. . .

Death of Mrs. Godolphin

[September] 3 I went to Lond: to dine at Mrs. Godolphins according to my custome every Tuesday, and found her in Labour; and staye'd 'til they brought me word the infant was borne, a lovely boy, the Mother exceeding well laied to all appearance, Mr. G: (the Father) being at Windsore with the Court: 5 It was christned, The

Susceptors being Sir Will: Godolphin (head of the family) Mr. Jo: Hervey Tresurer to the Queene, and Mrs. Boscawen (sister to Sir William and the Father); and named after the Gra[n]dfathers name Francis: It was baptiz'd in the Chamber where it was borne, in the mothers presence, at White-hall, by the Chaplaine who used to officiate in her pretty family; so I returned this evening home with my Wife, who was also come up to see her and congratulate. 8: our Curate (in absence of the Viccar) preaching on his former Text, whilst I was at Church this morning, came a Letter from Mr. Godolphin (who had ben sent for from Winsore the night before) to give me notice that my deare friend, his Lady, was exceedingly ill, and desiring my Prayers and assistance, his affliction being so extreame: so my Wife and I tooke boate immediately, and went to White-hall, where to mine unexpressable sorrow I found she had ben atacqu'd with the new feavor then reigning, this excessive hot Autumne, which being of a most malignant nature, and prevailing on her now weakned and tender body, eluded all the skill and help of the most eminent Physitians; and [surprizing] her head, so as she fell into deliriums, and that so vilontly and frequent, that unlesse some (almost mira[c]ulous) remedy were applied, it was impossible she should hold out; nor did the Doctors dare prescribe such remedies as might have ben proper in other cases, by reason of her condition, then so lately brought to bed; so as the paroxysmes increasing to greater height, it was now despair'd that she should last many houres, nor did she continue many minutes, without repeated fitts, with much paine and agonie, which carried her off 9 the next day, being moneday, betweene the houres of one and two in the afternoone, in the 26t yeare of her Age: to the unexpressable affliction of her deare Husband, and all her Relations; but of none in this world, more than my selfe, who lost the most excellent, and most estimable Friend, that ever liv'd: I cannot but say, my very Soule was united to hers, and that this stroake did pierce me to the utmost depth: for never was there a more virtuous, and inviolable friendship, never a more religious, discreete, and admirable creature; beloved of all, admir'd of all, for all the possible perfections of her sex: But she is gon, to receave the reward of her signal Charity, and all other her Christian graces, too blessed a Creature to converse with mortals, fitted (as she was) by a most holy Life, to be receiv'd into the mansions above: But it is not here, that

I pretend to give her Character, who have design'd, to consecrate her worthy life to posterity: I must yet say, she was for witt, beauty, good-nature, fidelitie, discretion and all accomplishments, the most choice and agreable person, that ever I was acquainted with: and a losse to be more sensibly deplord by me, as she had more particularly honord me with a friendship of the most religious bands, and such, as she has often protested she would even die for with cherefullnesse: The small services I was able to do her in some of her secular concernes, was immensly recompenc'd with her acceptance onely; but how! ah how! shall I ever repay my obligations to her for the infinite good offices she did my soule, by so o'ft ingaging me to make religion the termes and tie of the friendship which was betweene us: She was certainely the best Wife, the best Mother, the best Mistris, the best friend that ever Husband, Child, Servant, friend or that ever any creature had, nor am I able to enumerate her vertues: Her husband fell downe flat like a dead man, struck with unspeakeable affliction, all her Relations partooke of the losse; The King himselfe and all the Court express'd their sorrow, and to the poore and most miserable it was irreparable; for there was no degree, but had some obligation to her memorie: So virtuous and sweete a life she lead, that in all her fitts, (even those which tooke away her discernement); she never was heard to utter any syllable unbecoming a Christian, or uninnocent, which is extraordinary in delirious persons: So carefull, and provident she was to prepare for all possible accidents, that (as if she fore-saw her end), she received the heavenly Viaticum but the Sunday before, after a most solemn recollection; and putting all her domestic Concerns in the exactest order, left a Letter directed to her Husband (to be opened in case she died in Child-bed) in which, with the most pathetic and indearing expressions of a most loyal and virtuous wife, she begs his kindnesse to her Memorie, might be continu'd; by his care and esteeme of those she left behind, even to her very domestic servants, to the meanest of which she left considerable Legac[i]es, desiring she might be buried in the Dormitorie of his family neere 300 miles from all her other friends; And as she made use of me to convey innumerable and greate Charities all her lifetime, so I paied 100 pounds to her chiefe woman, 100 to a kindswoman in declining circumstances: To her sister[?s] the value of 1000 pounds: In diamond rings to other of her friends, 500 pounds: and to severall poore people, widows, fatherlesse, Prisoners and indigents, pensions to continue: ô the passionate, humble, mealting disposition of this blessed Friend; how am I afflicted for thee! my heavenly friend . . . The excessive affliction of this losse did so exceedingly affect her husband, and other neere Relations, that knowing in what profession of a most signal Friendship, she ever own'd me; The Fees to the Physitians, The intire Care of her funeral, was wholy comitted to me; so as having closed the Eyes, and drop'd a teare upon the Cheeke of my blessed Saint, Lovely in death, and like an Angel; I caused her Corps to be embaulmed, and wrap'd in Lead, with a plate of Brasse sothered on it, with an Inscription and other Circumstanc[e]s due to her worth, with as much dilligence and care as my grieved heart would permitt me; being so full of sorrow, and tir'd with it, that retiring home for two daies, I spent it in solitude, and sad reflections:

. . .

16 I went to Lond: in order to the funeral of my deare Friend: so as on the 17th in an herse with 6 horses, and two other Coaches of as many, and with about 30 people of her relations and servants, we as privately, and without the least pomp (as expressly required by her) proceeded towards the place, where she would be buried: There accompanied her hearse her husbands Bro: Sir Will. and two more of his Bro: and 3 Sisters: Mr. G: her husband, so surcharg'd with griefe, that he was wholy unfitt to Travell so long a journey 'til he should be more composed, and for this reason, after I had waited on the companie as far as Hounslow heath, with a sad heart, I was oblig'd to returne, upon some indispensable affaires: The Corps was ordred to be taken out of the hearse and decently placed in the house, with tapers about it, and her servants attending, every night during all the way to the foote of Cornewell, neere 300 miles, and then as honorably interred in the Parish Church of Godolphin. This funerall, as private as it was, costing her deare husband not much lesse than 1000 pounds; and ô that ten thousand more might have redeemed her life! . . .

. . .

The Popish Plot

Octob: 1 I went with my Wife to Lond: The Parliament being now alarm'd with the whole Nation, about a conspiracy of some

Eminent Papists, for the destruction of the King and introducing Popery; discovered by one Oates and Dr. Tongue, which last, I knew, being the Translator of the Jesuites Morals: I went to see and converse with him, now being at White-hall, with Mr. Oates, one that was lately an Apostate to the Church of Rome, and now return'd againe with this discovery: he seem'd to be a bold man, and in my thoughts furiously indiscreete; but everybody believed what he said; and it quite chang'd the genius and motions of the Parliament, growing now corrupt and intrested with long sitting, and Court practises; but with all this Poperie would not go downe: This discovery turn'd them all as one man against it, and nothing was don but in order to finding out the depth of this etc: Oates was encourag'd, and every thing he affirm'd [taken] for Gospel: The truth is, The Roman Chath: were Exceeding bold, and busy every where, since the D: forbore to go any longer to the Chapell etc . . .

. . .

21 The barbarous murder of Sir Edmund Bery-Godfry, found strangled about this time, as was manifest by the Papists, (he being a Justice of the Peace, and one who knew much of their practises, as conversant with Coleman, a Servant of the . . . now accus'd) put the whole nation in a new fermentation against them . . .

. . .

[November] 4 To Lond: 5. Dr. Tillotson before the house of Commons at St. Margarits: 'Tis since Printed: 'Twas now he sayed, the Papists were ariv'd to that impudence, as to deny there was ever any such thing as the Gun-powder Conspiresy: To this he affirm'd, he had himselfe severall letters written by Sir Everard Digby (one of the Traytors) in which he glories that he was to suffer for it; and that it was so contriv'd, that of the Papists, not above 2 or 3 should have ben blown-up, and they such, as were not worth the saving:

10 I went to St. Jamess in the morning Synax: Cor: Rege at W:hall Dr. Butler on 5. Gal: 1, shewing by way of Paralell, the Case of the Protestants, wavering betweene us and the Papists: he spake very home to his Majestie, exhorting to stedfastnesse in the Faith, and Liberty, in which Christ had made us free in this Land especialy, reckning up the heavy Yoake of Popish bondage etc.

13 Was an Universal Fast; That God would avert his Judge-

ments, and bring to naught the Conspirators against the K: and Government: In the morning preach'd to The Lords, the A:Bishop of Cant: in the Abby on 57: Psal: 1. shewing how safe the Church and People of God were in the midst of the most iminent dangers, under the wings of the Almighty: This was also Printed.

15 The Queenes birthday etc: I never saw the Court more brave, nor the nation in more apprehension, and Consternation etc: It was also my Baptismal Anniversary:

. . .

'Oates so presumptuous'

[24] Now had Coleman ben try'd, and one Staly, both Condemn'd and Executed: Oates on this grew so presumptuous as to accuse the Queene for intending to Poyson the King; which certainely that pious and vertuous Lady abhorred the thought off, and Oates his Circumstances, made it utterly unlikely in my opinion: 'Tis likely he thought to gratifie some, who would have ben glad his Majestie should have married a more fruitfull Lady: but the King was too kind an husband to let any of these make impression on him. However, Divers of the Popish Peres sent to the Toure, as accused by Oates, all the Ro: Cath: Lords were by a new Act, for ever Excluded the Parliament: which was a mighty blow: The Kings, Queenes and Dukes servants banished, and a Test to be taken by every body, who pretended to enjoy any Office of publique Trust, or not be suspected of Popery: This was so Worded That severall good Protestants scrupled; and I went with Sir W: Codolphin (a Member of the Commons house) to Bish: of Ely (Dr. Pet: Gunning) to be resolved, whether Masse were Idolatry, as the Test expressed it: for Sir William (though a most learned Gent: and excellent Divine himselfe) made some doubt of it: but the Bishops opinion was he might take it, and that the Papists could not excuse themselves from Idolatry; though he wished it had ben otherwise worded in the Test:

[December] 29 Being very ill of Gripings I was faine to keepe my bed: Divers of my Neighbours invited etc: according to Costome: 31 I gave God thanks for his goodnesse to me the yeare past, and begg'd that I might make a sanctified use of those Afflictions I had pass'd thro for the losse of a deare friend.

A Menacing Cloud

1679. Jan: 1 I implord Gods blessing for the Yeare now entred: 5. our Viccar as before: The holy Comm: followed: Pomerid: Curate on 21 Luke 27: 28: 12: Viccar on his former; When so strange a Clowd of darknesse came over, and especialy, the Citty of London, that they were faine to give-over the publique service for some time, being about 11 in the forenoone, which affrited many, who consider'd not the cause, (it being a greate Snow, and very sharp weather,) which was an huge cloud of Snow, supposed to be frozen together, and descending lower than ordinary, the Eastern wind, driving it forwards:

. . .

Parliament Dissolved

25 Was the Long Parliament (which now had sate ever-since his Majesties restauration) disolv'd by perswasion of the L: Tressurer: though divers of them were believed to be his Pensioners; at which all the polititians were at a stand: they being very eager in pursuite of the late plot of the Papists . . .

Inveighing Against Hobbes

Feb: White-hall, Candlemas day Dr. Durell D: of Winsore preach'd to the household on: 1: Cor: 16. 22: The Doctor read the whole sermon out of his notes, which I had never seene Frenchman (he being of Jersey, and altogether bred at Paris etc) do before. The holy Communion follow'd. Coram Rege Dr. Pierce D: of Salisbury on 1. John: 4: 1. 'Try the Spirite' – there being so many delusorie ones gon forth of late into the world, he inveied against the pernicious doctrines of Mr. Hobbs:

. . .

Mr. Pepys in the Tower

[June] 4. To Lond: Din'd with Mr. Pepys at the Tower, whither he was committed by the house of Commons, for misdemeanors in the Admiralty, where he was Secretary; but I believe unjustly: Here I saluted my Lord Stafford and Peters who were also committed for the Popish Plot: 7: I saw the magnificent Cavalcade and Entery of the Portugal Ambassador: din'd at L: Chamberlaines: 7: went home.

. . .

July 1 I din'd at Sir William Godolphins, and with that most learned Gent: to take the aire in Hyde-park; where was a glorious Cortege: 3. Sending a piece of Venison to Mr. Pepys Sec: of the Admiralty, still a Prisoner, I went and dined with him . . .

. . .

Cliveden

. . . [July 23] I went to Clifden that stupendious natural Rock, Wood, and Prospect of the Duke of Buckinghams, and building of extraordinary Expense: The Grotts in the Chalky rock are pretty, 'tis a romantic object, and the place alltogether answers the most poetical description that can be made of a solitude, precipice, prospects and whatever can contribute to a thing so very like their imaginations: The [house] stands somewhat like Frascati as to its front, and on the platforme is a circular View to the uttmost verge of the Horison, which with the serpenting of the Thames is admirably surprising: The Staire Case, is for its materials, singular: The Cloisters, Descents, Gardens, and avenue through the wood august and stately: but the land all about wretchedly barren, producing nothing but ferne: and indeede, as I told his Majestie that evening, (asking me how I liked Clifden?) without flattery: that it did not please me yet so well as Windsore, for the Prospect and the Park, which is without compare; There being but one onely opening, and that but narrow, which let one to any Variety, where as That of Winsore is every where greate and unconfin'd:

. . .

The Duke of Grafton Married

[November] 6 Dind at the Co: of Sunderlands, and was this evening at the re-marriage of the Dutchesse of Grafton to the Duke (his Majesties natural son) she being now 12 yeares old: The Ceremonie was perform'd in my Lord Chamberlaines (her fathers Lodgings) at Whitehall below, by the Bish: of Rochester, his Majestie Present: a suddaine, and unexpected thing (when every body believed the first marriage, would have come to nothing:) But the thing being Determined, I was privately invited by my Lady her mother, to be present: but I confesse I could give her little joy, and so I plainely told her; but she told me, the King would have it so, and there was no going back: and this sweetest, hopfullest, most beautifull child, and most vertuous too, was Sacrific'd to a boy, that had ben rudely bred, without any thing to encourage them, but his Majesties pleasure: I pray God the sweete Child find it to her advantage; who if my augurie deceave me not, will in few yeares be such a paragon, as were fit to make the Wife of the greatest Prince in Europe: I staied Supper, where his Majestie sate betweene the Dutchesse of Cleaveland (the incontinent mother of the Duke of Grafton) and the sweete Dutchesse the Bride, with severall greate Persons and Ladies, without Pomp; my Love to my Lord Arlingtons family, and the sweete Child made me behold all this with regret: Though as the Duke of Grafton affects the Sea, to which I find his father intends to use him; he may emerge a plaine, usefull, robust officer; and were he polish'd, a tollerable person, for he is exceedingly handsome, by far surpassing any of the Kings other naturall Issue . . .

. . .

A Prince of Citizens

18 I dined at my Lo: Majors, being desired by the Countesse of Sunderland to carry her thither on a Solemn Day, that she might see the pomp and ceremonie of this Prince of Citizens, there never having ben any, who for the statlinesse of his Palace, prodigious feasting and magnificence exceeded him: This Lord Majors acquaintance had ben from the time of his being Apprentice to one Mr. Abbot (his Unkle) who being a Scrivenor, and an honnest worthy man, (one who was condemn'd to die (but escaped) at the beginning of the Troubles 40 years past, as concerned in the Commission of Aray, for K. Char: 1:) I often used his assistance in mony matters: Rob: Clayton (now Major) his Nephew, then a boy, became after his Unkle Abbotts death, so prodigiously rich and opulent, that he was reckoned on[e] of the welthiest Citizens: he married a freehearted Woman, who also became his hospitable disposition, and having no Children, with the accession of his Partner and fellow Apprentice, who also left him his Estate; he grew Excessively rich, was a discreete Magistrate, and though, envied, I thinke without much cause: some believ'd him gilty of hard-dealing, especialy with the Duke of Buckingham, much of whose estate he had swallow'd: but I never saw any ill by him, considering the trade he was off: The reputation, and known

integrity of his Unkle Abbot, brought all the Royal party to him, by which he got not onely greate credite, but vast riches; so as he passed this Office with infinite magnificence and honor:

. . .

'The Protestant Duke'

. . . 28: Came over the Duke of Munmoth from Holland unexpectedly to his Majestie whilst the D: of Yorke was on his Journey to Scotland, whither the King sent him to preside, and governe etc: The Bells and Bone-fires of the Citty at this arival of D:M: publishing their joy to the no small regret of some at Court; This Duke (whom for distinction they cal'd the Protestant Duke, though the sonn of an abandoned woman) the people made their Idol of: I returned home . . .

. . .

Billiards

[December] 4 I dined (together with my L: Ossorie and E: of Chesterfild) at the Portugal Ambassadors now newly come, at Cleaveland house: a noble Palace, too good for that infamous——: The Staire Case is sumptuous and Gallerie: with the Garden: but above all the costly furniture belonging to the Ambassador, especialy the rich [Japan] Cabinets of which I think there were a dosen; and a Billiard table with as many more hazards as ours commonly have: the game being onely to prosecute the ball til hazarded, without passing the port or touching the pin: If one misse hitting the ball every time, the game is lost, or if hazarded: and 'tis more difficult to hazard a ball though so many, than in our Tables, by reason the board is made so exactly Even, and the Edges not stuff'd: The balls also bigger, and they for the most part use the sharp and small end of the billiard-stick, which is shod with brasse or silver: The Entertainement was exceeding Civile, but besids a good olio, the dishes were trifling, hash'd and Condited after their way, not at all fit for an English stomac, which is for solid meate: There was yet good fowle, but roasted to Coale; nor were the sweetemeates good: I had much discourse with the Secretary, who seem'd an understanding person.

. . .

30 I went to Lond, to meete Sir John Stonehouse, and give him a

particular of the settlement on my Sonn, who now made his addresses to the Young Lady his Daughter in Law; and so returned home:

. . .

Young John Married

[1680. February] 19 Were the Writings for the Settling Joynture, and other Contracts of Marriage of my Sonn finish'd and sealed etc: at White-hall Mr. Thursby and Melldecot being our Counsel, Sir John Stonehouse and Nephew Glanvill being Trustees: The Lady was to bring 5000 pounds in consideration of a settlement of 500 pounds a yeare present maintenance,——Which was likewise to be her joynture, and 500 pounds, after myne and my Wifes decease: though with Gods blessing it will be at the least 1000 pounds a yeare more in few yeares; I pray God make him worthy of it, and a Comfort to his excellent Mother, who deserves much from him: 20: I dined at a Servant of my Wifes, with the Earle of Ossory, whose servant had married her, and so home: 22: Viccar on 5. Eph: 15: I went in the Evening againe to Lond:

24 It being Shrove tuesday was my Sonne Married to Mrs. Martha Spencer Daughter to my Lady Stonehouse by a former Gent: at St. Andrews in Holborn by our Viccar, (borrowing the Church of Dr. Stillingfleete Deane of St. Paules who was the present incumbent) and afterward dined [at] an House in Holborn; and after the solemnity and Dauncing was don, They were beded at Sir Jo: Stonehouses Lodging in Bow streete Covent garden: I would very faine have had the marriage deferr'd til after the Lent; but severall accidents requiring it now, it was left to the disposall of her friends, and their convenience:

. . .

[March] 4 I went home, to receive my new Daughter in Law and her husband my sonn, with his Wifes Relations, who all dined with us, and returning to Lond: in the Evening, left my Daughter in Law with us for altogether.

. . .

An Electric Eel or Mortiferous Torpedo

18 At the Ro: Society was a letter from Surenam of a certaine small Eele that being taken with hooke and line at 100 foote length,

did so benumb, and stupifie the limbs of the Fisher, that had not the line suddainly beene cutt, by one of the Iland (who was acquainted with its effects) the poore man had immediately died: There is a certaine wood growing in the Country, which put into a Waire or Eele-pot, dos as much intoxicate the fish as Nux Vomica dos other fish, by which this mortiferous Torpedo is not onely caught, but becomes both harmelesse, and excellent meate . . .

A Dull Preacher

26 To Lond: the D: of Sarum on a Text he entred on 5. Feb: viz: 45 Jer: 5. Not to seeke great things to our selves, Gods counsel to Baruc, in the time of distresse: In which he assembled so many Instances out of heathen histories, and greate persons, who had quitted the Splendor and opulence of their births, fortunes, and grandures, that he seemed for an houre and halfe to do nothing else but reade Common-places, without any thing of Scripture almost in his whole sermon, which was not well: I went home next day:
. . .

An Honest and Remarkable Shipwright

. . . [May] 13: I was at the funerall of old Mr. Shish Master Shipwrite of the Kings Yard here in this Parish, an honest and remarkable man, and his death a publique losse, for his excellent successe in building Ships, (though illiterate altogether) and for the breeding up so many of his Children to be able Artists: I held up the Pall, with three knights who did him that honour, and he was worthy of it: our Viccar preaching on a Text of the good-mans choice out of 12 Isa: 2. shewing his Trust, and faith in God, and thankfullnesse for his mercies: It was the Costome of this good man, to rise in the night, and to pray kneeling in his owne Cofin; which many yeares he had lying by him: he was borne that famous yeare of the Gunpowder Plot 1605:
. . .

'The paine of Hell-fire'

[July] 11 A stranger on 9: Mar: 43. 44. The advantage of parting with the greatest pleasure to secure Eternal life: He spake of the Death they put Malefactors to in Egypt, the cutting them asunder, and [setting] the upper halfe of the body on a hot plate: the

suffering mans paine expressed in weeping teares, and gnashing of
teeth, which he applyed to the paine of Hell-fire . . .

. . .

Lord Ossory's Fate

26 my most noble and illustrious friend, the Earle of Ossorie
espying me this morning after sermon, in the Privy-Gallerie, calling
to me, told me he was now going his journey; (meaning to Tangier,
whither he was designed Governor, and Generall of the Forces, to
regaine the losses we had lately suffer'd from the Moores, when
Inchequeene was Governor): I asked his Lordship if he would not
call at my house (as he allways did when ever he went out of
England on any exploit) I feare I shall not said his Lordship, for I
foresee I must embarque at Portsmouth; wherefore I pray, let you
and I dine together to day, I am quite alone, and have something to
impart to you: I am not well, and have taken a little Physick this
morning; and so shall be private, and I desire your Company: Being
retird to his Lodgings and sat downe on the Couch, he sent to his
secretary for the Copy of a Letter, which he had written to my Lo:
Sunderland (secretary of state) wishing me to reade it; and it was to
take notice, how ill he resented it, That he should tell the King
before my L: Ossories face, That Tangier was not to be kept, but
would certainly be lost; and yet added, that twas fit, my L: Ossorie
should be sent, that they might give some account of it to the world,
meaning (as supposed,) the next Parliament, when all such
miscarriages would probably be examin'd, This my L: O: tooke
very ill of my L: S: a not kindly of his Majestie, who resolving to
send him with an incompetent force, seem'd (as his Lordship tooke
it) to be willing to ast him away upon not onely an hazardous
Adventure, but, in most mens opinions Impossible; seing there was
not to be above 3 or 400 horse and 4000 foote, for the Garison and
all, both to defend the Towne, forme a Camp, repulse the Enemie,
and fortifie what ground they should get in: This touch'd my Lord
deeply, that he should be so little consider'd, as to put him on a
buisinesse, in which he should probably, not onely loose his
reputation, but be charg'd with all the miscarriages and ill successe;
where as at the first they promis'd him 6000 foote and 600 horse
effective: My Lord, being an exceeding brave and valiant person,

and that had so approv'd himselfe in divers signal batailes, both at Sea, and Land; so beloved, so esteem'd by the people, as one they depended on upon all occasions worthy such a Captaine; looked on this as too greate an indifference in his Majestie after all his services (and the merits of his father the Duke of Ormond) and a designe of some who envied his Virtue; And it certainly, tooke so deepe roote in his mind, that he who was the most voide of feare in the world (and assur'd me he would go to Tangier with ten men, if his Majestie Commanded him) could not beare up against this unkindnesse: Having disburdned himselfe of this to me after dinner, he went with his Majestie to The Sherifs, at a greate supper in Fishmongres Hall; but my Lord, finding himselfe ill, tooke his leave immediately of his Majestie and came back to his Lodging, without staying at all at the Sherifs: Not resting well this night, he was perswaded to remove to Arlington house for better accommodation; where being no longer able to sustaine his indisposition, it manifestly turn'd to a Malignant feavor; which increasing to violence, after all that six of the most able Physitians could do to save him, beginning now and then to be somewhat delirious, at other times with intervalls of better sense: Dr. LLoyd, (now Bish: of St. Asaph) administring then to him the holy Sacrament, (of which I also participated) he died the friday after, about 7 in the Evening, being the 30th of July, to the universal griefe of all that either knew, or ever heard of his greate worth: nor had any a greater losse than my selfe, he being so much my friend; Oft would he say I was the oldest acquaintance he had in England (when, his Father was in Ireland) it being now of above 30 yeares, contracted abroad, when he rid at the Academie in Paris, and that we were seldome asunder: Surely his Majestie never lost a worthier Subject; nor Father, a better, and more dutifull sonn, a loving, goodnatured, generous and perfectly obliging friend, and one who had don innumerable kindnesses to severall persons, before they so much as kn[e]w it; nor advanc'd he any but such as were worthy; None more brave, more modest, none more humble, sober, and every way virtuous: Ô unhapy England! in this illustrious persons losse: Universal was the Mourning for him, the Elogies on him, nor can I sufficiently deplore him: I staied night and day by his bed-side to his last gasp to close his deare Eyes . . .

. . .

A French Traveller

[August] 27 To Lond: return'd that Evening: 29 Viccar as before: 30: Lond: I went to visite a French Stranger, one Monsieur Jardine* since Knighted by his Majestie and made Denison of England who having ben thrice at the East Indias, Persia and other remote Countries, came hither in our returne ships from those parts; and it being reported he was a very curious man, and knowing, I was desir'd by the Ro: Society in their name, to salute him, and to let him know how glad they should be to receive him, if he pleased to do them that honour: etc. There were appointed to accompanie me Sir Jo: Hoskins and Sir Chr: Wren etc. We found him at his lodging, in his Eastern habite, a very handsòm person, extreamely affable, not inclin'd to talke Wonders, but exceedingly modest, and a well bred man: It seemes he traveld in search of Jewels, and was become extreamely rich: He spake Latine, understood the Greeke, Arabic and Persian by 11 yeares Conversation in those Parts, yet seem'd he not to be above 36 years of age: After the usual Civilities, we told him, we much desired an account of the extraordinary things he must have seene; having (as we understood) trav[e]ld over land, those places, where few, if any northern Europeans used to go, as about the Black and Caspian Sea, Mingrelia, Bagdat, Ninive, [Persepolis] etc: He told us the things most worthy of our sight, would be, the draughts he had caused to be made of some noble ruines etc: for that (besides his little talent that way) he had carried two very good Painters along with him, to draw Landskips, Measure, and designe the remainders of the Palace which Alexander burnt in his frolique at Persepolis, with divers Temples, Columns, Relievos, and statues, yet extant, which he affirm'd were Sculptures far exceeding, any thing he had observ'd either at Rome, Greece or any other part of the World, where Magnificence was in estimation: That there was there an Inscription, of Letters not intelligible, though exceedingly intire; but was extreamely sorry he could not gratifie the Curiosity of the Society, at present, his things, not being yet out of the ship; but would take the first opportunity to waite on us with them, at his returne from Paris, whither he was hastning the very next morning, but with intention, to be suddenly back againe, and stay longer in our Country, the persecution in France not suffering Protestants, and such he was, to be quiet: so we failed of seeing his Papers; but it was told us by others, that he durst indeede not open or shew them, 'til he had first shew'd them to the French King; though of this he himselfe said notthing: On farther discourse, he told us that Nineveh was a vast Citty, all now buried in her ruines, and the Inhabitants building on the subterranean Vaults, which were (as appeared) the first stories of the old Cittie; That there were frequently [found], huge Vasas of fine Earth, Columns, and other Antiquities etc: That the straw which the Egyptian Pharoah so tyrannicaly requir'd of the Israelites, was not to burne, or Cover their rowes of brick, as we use; but being chopp'd small, to mingle with the Clay, which drying in the Sunn (for they bake not in the furnaces) would else cleave asunder: That in Persia are yet a race of Igniculi, that still Worship the Sunn, and the fire as Gods: That the Women of Georgia and Mingrelia were Universaly, and without any compare, the most beautifull Creatures for shape, features, and figure in the whole world, and that therefore The Grand Signor, and Bashaws etc had thence most of their Wives and Concubines: That there had within these 100 yeares ben Amazons amongst them (that is) a sort or race of Valiant Women, given to Warr: That Persia was infinitely fertile. He spake also of Japon, and China, and of the many greate errours of our late Geographers etc: as we suggested occasion to discourse; and so we tooke our leaves, and made report to our Society: and I returned home:

The King's Library

September 2: I went to Lond: because of an Opportunity I had of his Majesties being yet at Winsor, to see his private Library at Whitehall, which I now did at my full Ease; and went with expectation of finding some Curiosities: But tho there were about a thousand Volumes, there were few of any greate importance, or which I had not perused before; they consisting chiefely of such books as had from time to time ben dedicated, or presented him: Few Histories, some Traveles, and french bookes, Aboundance of Mapps and Sea-[Charts]: Entertainements, and Pomps; buildings, and Pieces relating to the Navy: some Mathematical Instruments etc: But what was most rare were 3 or 4 Romish Breviaries with a greate deale of Miniature and Monkish Painting and Gilding; one of which is most exquisitely don, both as to the figures, Grotescs and Compartments, to the uttmost of that curious art: There's another in which I find written by the hand of Henry the 7th, his giving it to his deare Daughter Margarite, afterwards Queene of Scots (Greate mother of our K. James, and greate greate Grandmother to the successive Kings, uniting the two Kingdomes) in which he desires her to pray for his soule, subscribing his Name at length: There is also the Processe of the Philosophe[r]s greate Elixir, represented in divers pieces of incomparable miniature; but the Discourse is in high-Dut[c]h and a MSS: Also another MS. in quarto of above 300 yeares old in French, being an Institution of Physic, and in the Botanical part, the Plants are curiously painted in Miniature: There is likewise a Folio Manu-script of a good thicknesse, being the severall exercises, as Theames, Orationes, Translations etc: of K. Edward the sixt, all written and subscrib'd by his owne hand, and with his name very legibly, and divers of the Greeke, interlin'd, and corrected, after the manner of Schole-boys exercises, and that exceedingly well and proper, with some Epistles to his Præceptor etc, which shews that Young Prince to have ben extraordinarily advanc'd in learning, and as Cardan that greate Wit etc (who had ben in Englan'd) affirmed, stupendiously knowing for his age: There is likewise his Journal, no lesse testif[y]ing his earely ripenesse and care about the affaires of state: Dr. Burnet has transcribd many remarks out of this in his Hist of the Reformation.

There are besides many other pompous Volumes, some emboss'd with Gold, and Intaglios on Achats, Medailes etc: I spent 3 or 4 intire daies locked up, and alone amongst these bookes etc: There is in the rest of the Private Lodgings contiguous to this, divers of the best pictures of the greate Masters, Raphael, Titian etc (and in my esteeme) above all the *Noli me tangere* of our B: Saviour to M: Magdalen, after his Resurrection, of Hans Holbeins, than which, in my life, I never saw so much reverence and kind of Heavenly astonishment, expressed in Picture: There are also divers Curious Clocks, Watches and Penduls of exquisite work, and other Curiosities: An antient Woman, who made these lodgings Cleane, and had all the Keyes, let me in at pleasure, for a small reward, by the meanes of a friend:

A Fantastical Curate

5 I found our late affected fantastical Curate Mr. Al——preaching in the Chapel at W:hall on 119 Psal: 175 ver: that mens

soules were certainely immortal, distinct from the animal life etc: It was not [possible] to heare him without astonishment at his Confidence and formalitie: He was a boy of our Parish, that from a poore grammar schole, turn'd Preacher; and at last got the degree of Batchelor of Art, by a Mandamus, at Cambridge, where he had ben 2 or 3 daies, in his whole life: when he came back, that people might take notice of his degree, he ware his lamb-skin not onely two whole Sundays in the Church, but going all over the Towne, and Every streete, with a wonderfull traine of boys and girles running after him, (as they do when the Baeres are led about) came to give me a visite in his formalities, at which I could not [possibly] containe my Countenance: This yet I must say of Mr. A. . . . that he has together with a vast stock of Confidence, a prodigious Memorie, and strong lungs, and some are taken with his Preachment, that know not the man out of the Pulpet: In a word he is a most singular person, and exceedingly conceited of his abillities: The blessed Sacrament follow'd: Pomerid: Co: Garden the Lecturer, on 1. Joh: 2. 23. an heavenly discourse:

*Sir Stephen Fox**

6 I din'd with Sir St: Fox, now one of the Lords Commissioners of the Treasury: This Gent: came first a poore boy from the Quire of Salisbury, then was taken notice of by Bish: Duppa, and afterwards waited on my Lord Percy (bro: to Algernon E: of Northumberland) who procured for him an inferior place amongst the Clearks of the Kitchin and Greene-Cloth side: Where he was found so humble, dilligent, industrious, and prudently to behave himselfe, that his Majestie being in Exile, and Mr. Fox waiting, both the King and Lords about him, frequently Employed him about their affaires, trusted him both with receiving and paying the little mony, they had: Returning with his Majestie into England after greate Wants, and greate sufferings: . . . so honest and industrious, and withall so capable and ready; that being advanced, from Cl: of the Kitchin to that of the Greene-Cloth etc: he procured to be pay-Master to the Whole Army, and by his dexterity, and punctual dealing [obtained] such credit amongst the Banquers, that he was in short time, able to borrow vast summs of them, upon any exigence; The continud Turning thus of mony, and the souldiers moderate allowance to him, for his keeping touch with

them, did so inrich him; that he is believed to be worth at the least
200000 pounds honestly [gotten], and unenvied, which is next to
Miracle, and that with all this he still continues as humble, and
ready to do a Courtesie, as ever he was; nay he is generous, and
lives very honorably, of a sweete nature, well spoken, and well bred,
and so very highly in his Majesties Esteeme, and usefull, that being
long-since made a Knight, he is also advanc'd to be one of the
Lords Commissioners of the Treasury: and has the reversion of the
Coferers place after Harry Brounckar: He has married his Eldest
Daughter to my Lord Cornwallis, and gave her 12000 pounds and
restored that intangled family besides: Match'd his Eldest Sonn to
Mrs. Trallop who brings with her (besides a greate summ) neere, if
not altogether 2000 pounds per annum: Sir Stephens Lady (an
excellent Woman) is sister to Mr. Whittle one of the Kings
Chirurgions: In a word, never was man more fortunate than Sir
Stephen; and with all this he is an handsom person, Vertuous and
very religious, and for whom I have an extraordinary esteeme:

. . .

Queen Christina of Sweden

23 Came to my house some German strangers, and Signor
Pietro a famous Musitian, who had ben long in Sweden in Queene
Christinas Court: he sung admirably to a Guitarr and has a perfect
good tenor and base etc: and had set to Italian composure, many of
Abraham Cowleys Pieces which shew'd extreamely well: He told
me the heate some part in summer was as excessive as the Cold in
winter in Sweden; so cold he affirm'd, that the streetes of all the
townes are desolate, no creature stirring in them for many moneths,
all the inhabitans retiring to their stoves: He spake high things of
that romantic Queene, her Learning, skill in Languages, the
Majestie of her behaviour, her Exceeding Wit, and that the
Histories she had read of other Counteries, especialy of Italy and
Rome made her despize her owne: That the real occasion of her
resignation of the Crowne to her Cousin, was the Noblemens
importuning her to Marie, and the Promise which the Pope had
made her of procuring her to be Queene of Naples, which also
caused her to change her Religion, but she was cheated by his
crafty holinesse, working on her ambition: That the reason of her
Killing her secretarie at Fontain Beleaw, was his revealing that

Intrigue with the Pope: But after all this, I rather believe it was her mad prodigality and extreame Vanity, which had Consum'd all those vast treasures, the greate Adolphus (her father) had brought out of Germany, during his enterance there, and wonderfull successes; and that if she had not voluntarily resign'd (as forseeing the Event) the States of her Kingdome would have compell'd her.

. . .

A Solemn Survey

[October] 30 I went to Lond: to be private: My Birth-day being the next; and I now arived to the sixtieth yeare of Age; 31 upon which, I began a more solemn survey of my whole Life, in order to the making, and confirming my peace with God, by an accurate Scrutinie of all my actions past, as far as I was able to call them to min'd: And oh, how difficult, and uncertaine, yet most necessarie worke; The Lord be mercifull to me and accept me. Who can tell how oft he offendeth? Teach me therefore so to Number my daies, that I may apply my heart to wisdome, make my calling and election sure . . .

. . .

The Trial of Lord Stafford

[November] 30 The Anniversary Elections at the Ro. Society brought me to Lond: where was chosen Præsident, that excellent person, and greate Philosopher Mr. Robert Boyle who indeed, ought to have ben the very first; but neither his infirmitie, nor modestie could now any longer excuse him: I desir'd I might for this yeare be left out of the Council, by reason my dwelling was in the Country; The Society, according to Costome, din'd together: This signal day, began the Trial of my Lord Vicount Stafford for conspiring the Death of the King, and was likewise his Birth-day.

December 2. I was curious to see and heare the famous Triale of my L: Stafford second sonn to my Lord Thomas Howard, Earle of Arundel and Surry, Earle Marishall of England, and Grandfather to the present Duke of Norfolck, whom I so well knew, and from which excellent person, I received so many favours: The Trial was in Westminster Hall, before the King, Lords and Commons, just in the same manner as just 40 yeares past, the greate and wisé Earle of Strafford (there being but one letter differing their names) received his Tryal (for pretended ill government in Ireland) in that famous Parliament and same place: This Lord Staffords Father being High-Steward etc: Onely the Place of sitting was now exhalted some considerable height from the Paved flore of the Hall, with a stage of boards, His Majesties Throne or state, the Woolsacks for the Judges, long formes for the Peeres, Chaire of the Lord Steward *pro tempore*, exactly ranged as in the house of Lords: All the sides on both hands Scaffolded to the very roofe, for the Members of the H: of Commons: At the upper end, and right side of the Kings satte, was a box for his Majestie, others for the Greate Ladys on the left hand; and over head a gallerie for Ambassadors and Pub: Ministers: At the lower-end or Enterance was a Barr, and place for the Prisoner, The Lieutennant of the Toure of London, the Axe-bearer and Guards, My Lord Staffords two Daughters, the Marchionesse of Winchester being one. There was likewise a Box for my Lord to retire into; At the right hand in another box some what higher, stood the Witnesses, at the left, the Manegers, who were to produce and manege the Evidence and whole processe in the name of the Commons of England: viz: Serjeant Maynard, (the greate lawyer, the same who prosecuted the Cause against the Earle of Strafford 40 yeares before in the same place, being now neere 80 yeares of age) Sir William Jones, (late Attourney Gen:) Sir Fran: Winnington (a famous Pleader) and Mr. Treby (now Recorder of Lond:) not appearing in their gownes as Lawyers, but in their cloakes and swords, as representing the Commons of England. To these were joyn'd Mr. Hamden, Mr. Sechevarell, Mr. Poule, Coll: Titus, Sir Tho: Lee all Gentlemen of Qualitie and noted Parliament men: The two first dayes (in which was read, the Commission, and Impeacchment) was but a very tedious enterance into Matter of fact, the Charge, at which I was little present: But on Thursday being commodiously seated amongst the Commons, when the wittnesses were sworn, and deposed, of which the principle were Mr. Oates (who cal'd himselfe Doctor) Mr. Dugdale and Turberville: Oates tooke his Oath, that he delivered a Commission to V. Count Stafford from the Pope, to be Pay-Master Generall, to an Army intended to be raised etc: Dugdale, that being at my Lord Astons, the [Prisoner] dealt with him plainely to Murder his Majestie, and Turbervile, that at Paris also he proposed the same to him etc.

3 Friday was spent in Depositions of my Lords Wittnesses, to invalidate the Testimonie of the Kings Witnesses, which being very slight persons, though many, viz, 15 or 16: tooke up all that day: and in truth they rather did my Lord injurie than service, and made but little for him. 4: Saturday came other Witnesses of the Commons, to corroborate the Kings, of which some were Peeres, and some Commons, with other of good qualitie, who tooke off all the former days objections, and set the Kings Witnesses *recti in Curia*, and then adjourn'd 'til moneday:

. . .

Oates Discredited: But in Vain

6 Moneday, being the 6 of December I went againe to the Trial, where I heard the Evidences summ'd up by Sir William Jones, which was very large; and when he had don, and said all he could to exaggerate the charge succeeded all the rest of the Lawyers Manegers; Then began Mr Hen: Poule in a vehement Oration, as to the profes of the Jesuitical doctrine, of holding it not onely lawfull, but meritorious to Murder an Heretic King; which my Lord, had in his plea denyed: After this my Lord (as upon all occasions, and very often he did during the whole Trial) spake in his owne defence, denying the Charge altogether; that he never in his life saw either Turbervile or Oates at the time, and manner affirmed; and in truth their Testimonie did little weigh with me; Dugdales onely seemed to presse hardest: To which my Lord spake a greate while, but without any method, and confus'dly: One thing my Lord said, which I confesse did exceedingly affect me, as to Titus Oates, That a Person, who, during his depositions, should so vauntingly as he did, brag that though he went over to the Church of Rome, yet he was never a Papist, nor of their Religion, all the time that he seem'd to Apostatize from the Protestant; but onely as a spie; Though he confess'd he tooke their Sacraments, Worship'd Images, went through all the Oathes and discipline of their Proselytes, swearing seacrecy, and to be faithfull, but with intention to come over againe and betray them: That such an Hypocrite, that had so deepely prevaricated, as to turne even Idolater, (for so we of the Church of England esteem'd it) attesting God so solemnly, that he was intirely theirs, and devoted to their interests, and consequently (as he pretended) trusted; I say that the

Witnesse of such a proflygate wretch should be admitted, against
the life of a Pere; This my Lord, looked upon as a monstrous thing,
and such as must needes redown'd to the dishonor both of our
Religion and Nation: And verily, I am of his Lordships opinion;
Such a mans Testimonie should not be taken against the life of a
Dog: 'Tis true, many Protestants had defected, and return'd
againe; but we know of none, (nor if any, can approve them) who
when they turned Papists, did not heartily believe they were in the
right, 'til they were convinc'd to the Contrary: But this is not Oates
his case, he went thro all the mysteries of their Religion, thro all
their Oat[h]es, Execrations on himselfe, Sacraments etc, whilst by
his owne Confession, he disembl'd all; This he affirmed and I know
not on what occasion it escaped from him, no lesse impiously: than
foolishly: From this moment foreward, I had quite lost my opinion
of Mr. Oates. But the merite and service of something material
which he discovered against Coleman at first, put him in such
esteeme with the Parliament etc: that now I fancy, he stooke at
nothing, and thought every body was to take what he said for
Gospel afterwards: The Consideration of this, and some other
Circumstances began to stagger me; particularly, how 'twas
possible, that one who went amongst the Papists with such a
designe, and pretended to be intrusted with so many letters, and
Commissions from the Pope and party, nay and delivered them to
so many greate Persons, should not reserve one of them to shew, or
produce, nor so much as one Copie of any Commission; which he
who had such dexterity in opening letters etc, might certainly have
don, to the undenyable Conviction of those whom he accus'd: But,
as I said, he gained Credit upon Coleman, but as to others whom
he so madly flew upon, I am little inclined to believe his testimonie;
he being so slight a person, so passionate, ill-bred, and of impudent
behaviour: nor is it at all likely, such piercing politicians as the
Jesuites should trust him with so high, and so dangerous seacrets. 7
On Tuesday I was againe at the Trial, when Judgement was
demanded, and after my Lord had spoken what he could in denying
of the fact etc: The Manegers answering the objections etc: The
Peeres adjourned to their House, and within two houres, return'd
againe: There was in the meane time this farther question put,
whither there being but one witnesse to any single Crime or act, it
could amount to convict a man; upon this, the Judges being cald on

to give their opinion, unanimously declar'd, that in case of Treason
they all were overt acts; for though no man should be condemn'd by
one witnesse for any one act, yet for severall acts to the same intent,
it was valid, which was my Lord Staffords Case; for one sware he
practised him to Kill his Majestie at Paris, another at my L: Astons,
a Third that he delivered him a Commission from Rome, but to
neither of these were [there] above one Witnesse, so it was
overruled: This being past, and The Peres in their seates againe,
my Lord Chancelor Finch (who was this day High Steward)
removing to the Wool-sack next his Majesties state, after summoning the Lieutennant of the Tower to bring forth his Prisoner, and
Proclamation made for silence; demanded of every Peere (who
were in all 86) whither William Lord Vicount Stafford were Guilty
of the Treason Laied to his Charge, or not Guilty: Then the Peere
(spoken to) standing up, and laying his right hand upon his breast,
sayed Guilty, or Not Guilty Upon his honour; and then sate downe:
and so another 'til all were asked: the L: Steward noting their
severall Suffrages as they answered upon a paper: When all had
don, the number of not Guilties being but 31, the Guiltys 55, after
Proclamation for silence againe; The Steward directing his speech
to the Prisoner (against whom the Axe was turn'd edge ways
towards him, and not before) in aggravation of his Crime, he being
enobled by his Majesties Father, and since received many favours
and grace from his present Majestie: That came of such a stock,
and noble family, had appeared in his defence in time of the late
rebellion etc: and all that could signifie to the charge of his
ingratitude and disloyalty: Then inlarged on the honor and justice
of their Proceedings against him with a Christian exhortation to
Repentance, and Confession, deploring first his owne unhapinisse,
that he who never Condemned any man before, should now be
necessitated to begin with him, etc: and then Pronounced Sentence
of Death, by Hanging, Drawing and Quartering (according to
forme) with greate solemnity, and dreadfull gravity; last of all, after
a short pause; Told the Prisoner, That he believed the Lords would
interceede with his Majestie that some Circumstances of his
sentence, might be omitted, beheading onely excepted and then
breaking his White-staff, the Court disolved. My Lord Stafford
during all this later part spake very little, and onely Gave their
Lordships thanks, after the sentence was pronounc'd; and indeede

behav'd himselfe modestly, and as became him: 'Twas observ'd, that all his owne Relations, and of his Name and family Condemn'd him, excepting onely his Nephew the Earle of Arundel: sonn to the D: of Norfolck: and it must be acknowledg'd that the whole Trial was carried on from first to last, with exceeding gravity, and so stately and august appearance I had never seene; for besides innumerable spectators of Gent: and forraine Ministers etc: who saw and heard all the proceedings, the Prisoner had the Consciences of all the Commons of England for his Accusers, and all the Peeres to be his Judges and Jury: He had likewise the assistance of what Counsel he would to direct him in his plea, that stood by him: And yet I can hardly think, a person of his age and experience, should engage men, whom he never saw before, (and one of them that came to visite him as a stranger, at Paris), point blanque to Murder the King: God onely, who searches hearts, can discover the Truth, and to him it must be left: My Lord Stafford, was not a man belov'd, Especialy of his owne family, and had ben suspected, and in danger to by it, of a Vice in Germanie, which neede not be nam'd, and I doubt not but he had seriously repented.

11 I returned home:

A Comet

12 Our Viccar and Curate proceeded on their former Texts: This Evening looking out of my Chamber Window towards the West, I first saw a Meteor, (or what ever other Phænomenon it was) of an obscure bright Colour (if so I may call it without a solecisme) resembling the brightnesse of the Moone when under a thin Clow'd, very much in shape like the blade of a sword, whose point to the starre in appearance, bending Northwards towards London, not seeming at the Horizon to be above a yard in bredth, and so pyramidal, the rest of the skie, very serene and cleere; The Moone new, but not appearing, the Weather exceeding sharp, hard frost with some snow falling 2 daies before: What this may Portend (for it was very extraordinarie) God onely knows; but such another Phænomen[on] I remember I saw, which went from North to South, and was much brighter, and larger, but not so Ensiforme in the yeare 1640, about the Triall of the greate Earle of Strafford, præceeding our bloudy Rebellion: I pray God avert his Judgements; we have had of late severall Comets, which though I believe

appeare from natural Causes, and of themselves operate not, yet I cannot despise them; They may be warnings from God, as they commonly are for-runners of his Annimadversions . . .

. . .

. . . 29, was the unhappy Vi-Count Stafford beheaded on Tower hill. 31 after recollection etc: I humbly gave thanks to God, for his mercies to me this past Yeare:

. . .

The Monument

[1681. May] 5 Came to visite and dine with me Sir William Fermor, of N:hamptonshire, and Sir Chr: Wren, his Majesties Architect and Surveyor, now building the Cathedrall of St. Paules, and the Columne in memorie of the Citties Conflagration, and was in hand with the building of 50 Parish Churches: a [wonderfull] genius had this incomparable Person:

. . .

Sermons

20 I went home. 22: our Viccar on Whitsonday pr: on: 4: Eph: 30: The Bl: Sacrament followed: Pomerid: the new Curate, a pretty hopefull young man, yet somewhat raw, and newly come from the Colledge, full of latine sentences etc: which in time will weare off: He read prayers very well, and preached on 6: Matt. 33 of the preference of Heaven before Earthly fruitions; etc:

There had scarce fallen yet any raine since Christmas:

. . .

[June] 12 Our Viccar on 4 Eph: as before: Curate on 5. Matt: 3. My exceeding drowsinesse hindred my attention, which I feare proceeded from Eating too much, or the drinesse of the season and heate, it still continuing so greate a drowth, as was never knowne in Eng: and was said to be universal . . .

16 returned home: 19 our Viccar proceeded: The Curate also went on: The dry weather had now withered every thing, and threatned some universal dirth etc:

. . .

Neat Agriculture Near Wotton

[August] 30 I went to visite Mr. Hussey a neere neighbour of my Bro: who has a very pretty seate, delicately watred, and he certainely

the neatest husband for curious ordering his Domestic and field
Accomodations, and what pertaines to husbandry, that in my life I
have ever seene, as to his several Graneries, Tackling, Tooles and
Utensils, Ploughs, Carts, Stables, Woodpiles, Woork house, even
to the hen rosts and hog troughs: so as mithought I saw old Cato or
Varro in him: all substantial, all in exact order, which exceedingly
delighted me: The sole inconvenience he lies under, is the greate
quantities of sand, which his streames bring along with them, which
fills his chanales and receptacles of fish too soone: The rest of my
time of stay at Wotton was spent in walking about the grounds and
goodly Woods, where I have in my Youth entertained my solitude
etc: and so on the 2d of September I returned to my home, being
two daies after my Wife etc was returned from Tunbridge, where
they had ben, I blesse God, with good successe, now neere five
weekes:

                    . . .

Chelsea Hospital

   . . . 14. Din'd with Sir Step: Fox: Who proposed to me the
purchasing of Chelsey Coll; which his Majestie had some time
since given to our Society, and would now purchase it of us againe,
to build an Hospital Infirmary for Souldiers there; in which he
desired my assistance as one of the Council of the R: Society: 15 I
had another opportunity of perusing his Majesties private Library
at White-hall . . .

                    . . .

A Moroccan Embassy

[1682. January] 11 To Lond: Saw the Audience of the Morroco
Ambassador: his retinue not numerous, was receivd in the
Banqueting-house both their Majesties present: he came up to the
Throne without making any sort of Reverence, bowing so much as
his head or body: he spake by a Renegado English man, for whose
safe returne there was a promise: They were all Clad in the
Moorish habite Cassocks of Colour Cloth or silk with buttons and
loopes, over this an Alhaga or white wollan mantle, so large as to
wrap both head and body, a shash or small Turban, naked leg'd and
arm'd, but with lether socks like the Turks, rich Symeters, large
Calico sleev'd shirts etc: The Ambassador had a string of Pearls

odly woven in his Turbant; I fancy the old Roman habite was little
different as to the Mantle and naked limbs: The Ambassador was
an handsom person, well featur'd, and of a wise looke, subtile, and
extreamely Civile: Their Presents were Lions and Estridges etc:
Their Errant, about a Peace at Tangire etc: But the Concourse and
Tumult of the People was intollerable, so as the Officers could
keepe no order; which they were astonish'd at at first; There being
nothing so regular exact and perform'd with such silence etc, as in
all these publique occasions of their Country, and indeede over all
the Turkish dominions . . .

A Civil Heathen

. . . [24] This Evening I was at the Entertainement of the
Morroco [Ambassador] at the Dut: of Portsmouths glorious
Appartment at W.hall, where was a greate banquet of Sweetemeates, and Musique etc but at which both the Ambassador and
Retinue behaved themselves with extraordinary Moderation and
modestie, though placed about a long Table a Lady betweene two
Moores: viz: a Moore, then a Woman, then a Moore etc: and most
of these were the Kings natural Children, viz: the Lady Lichfield,
Sussex, DD of Portsmouth, Nelly etc: Concubines, and catell of
that sort, as splendid as Jewells, and Excesse of bravery could make
them: The Moores neither admiring or seeming to reguard any
thing, furniture or the like with any earnestnesse; and but decently
tasting of the banquet: They dranke a little Milk and Water, but not
a drop of Wine, also they drank of a sorbett and Jacolatte: did not
looke about nor stare on the Ladys, or express the least of surprize,
but with a Courtly negligence in pace, Countenance, and whole
behaviour, answering onely to such questions as were asked, with a
greate deale of Wit and Gallantrie, and so gravely tooke leave, with
this Compliment That God would blesse the D: of P: and the
Prince her sonn, meaning the little Duke of Richmon'd: The King
came in at the latter end, just as the Ambassador was going away: In
this manner was this Slave (for he was no more at home)
entertained by most of the Nobility in Towne; and went often to
Hide-Park on horse back, where he and his retinue shewed their
extraordinary activity in Horsmanship, and the flinging and
Catching their launces at full speede; They rid very short, and
could stand up right in full speede, managing their speares with

incredible agility. He also went sometimes to our Theaters, where when upon any foolish or fantastical action he could not forbeare laughing, he endeavored to hide it with extraordinary modesty and gravity: In a word, the Russian Ambassador still at Court behaved himselfe like a Clowne, compar'd to this Civil Heathen:

. . .

Organizing Chelsea Hospital

[27] This Evening Sir St. Fox acquainted me againe with his Majesties resolutions of proceeding in his Erection of a Royal Hospital for Emerited Souldiers on that spot of ground The Ro: Society had sold his Majestie for 1300 pounds and that he would settle 5000 pounds per Annum on it, and build to the value of 20000 pounds for the reliefe and reception of 4 Companies, viz. 400 men, to be as in a Coledge or Monastrie: I was therefore desired by Sir Stephen (who had not onely the whole menaging of this, but was (as I perceiv'd) himselfe to be a grand benefactor, as well it became him, who had gotten so vast an Estate by the Souldiers etc) to assist him and Consult what Method to Cast it in, as to the Government: So in his Study, we set downe the Governor, Chaplaine, Steward, Housekeeper, Chirurgion, Cooke, Butler, Gardner, Porter and other Officers, with their severall salaries and entertainements: I would needes have a Librarie, and mentioned severall books etc. since some souldiers might possibly be studious, when they were at this leasure to recolect: Thus we made the first Calculations, and set downe our thoughts to be considered and digested better to shew his Majestie and the Archbishop: He also engaged me to consider of what Laws and Orders were fit for the Government, which was to be in every respect as strickt as in any religious Convent etc: After supper, came in the famous Trebble Mr. Abel newly return'd from Italy, and indeede I never heard a more excellent voice, one would have sworne it had ben a Womans it was so high, and so well and skillfully manag'd: being accompanied with Signor Francesco on the Harpsichord:

. . .

Uses of Hot Milk

[February] 7. I went home: My Daughter Mary now first began to learne Musick of Signor Bartholomeo, and Dauncing of

Monsieur Isaac, both reputed the best Masters etc: I continu'd ill
for 2 fitts after, and then bathing my leggs to the knees in Milk
made as hott as I could endure it, and sitting so in it, in a deepe
Churn or Vessell, Covered with blanquets and drinking Carduus
posset, then going to bed and sweating, I not onely missed that
expected fit, but had no more; onely continued so weake that I
could not go to church 'til Ash-wednesday, which I had not missed
I think so long in twenty yeares, so long had God ben gracious to
me:

...

Grandson Jack Born

March 1 Was my second Grand-child borne, exactly at
Sunn-rising; and Christned the next day by our Viccar at
Sayes-Court, his Susceptors being My Selfe with my Nephew Jo:
Evelyn of Wotton, by the Name of John: his God-mother was Mrs.
Anderson, sister to his mother: I beseech God to blesse him.

...

Chelsea Hospital Again

[May] 25 Dies Ascentionis: I was desired by Sir St: Fox, and Sir
Chr: Wren, his Majesties Surveior, and Architect, to accompanie
them to Lambeth, with the plot, and designe of the College to be
built at Chelsey for emerited Souldiers, to have the Archbishops
approbation: It was a quadrangle of 200 foote square, after the
dimensions of the larger quadrangle of Christ Church in Oxon for
the accommodation of 440 Persons with Governor and Officers:
This being fix'd, and agreed upon, we went to dinner, and then
returned ...

...

Indonesian Envoys

[June 20] The Bantame or East India Ambassadors (for we had
at this time in Lond together The Russian, Morrocan, and Indian
Ambassador) being invited to dine at my Lord Geo: Berekeleys
(now created Earle) I went to the entertainment, to Consider the
exotic guests: They were both very hard favour'd, and much
resembling in Countenance to some sort of Munkeys: We eate at
two Tables, The Ambassador and Interpreter by themselves: Their

Garments were rich Indian silks flowred with gold, viz, a Close Wast-Coate to their knees, Drawers, Naked leggs; and on their heads Capps made just in fashion like fruit baskets; They Ware poison'd Daggers at their boosome, the haft carved with some ougly serpents or devils head, exceeding keene, and of damasco mettal: they wore no sword: The second Ambassador (sent it seemes to succeede, in case the first should die by the Way in so tedious a journey) having ben at Méca (for they were Mahumetans) ware a Turkish or rather Arab Shash, a little part of the linnen hanging downe behind his neck, With some other diference of habite; and was halfe a negro; bare legg'd and naked feete; esteem'd a very holy man: They sate Crosse-legd like Turks, and sometimes in the postures of Apes and Munkys; Their nailes and [Teeth] black as any jeat and shining, which being the effect of perpetual chewing betell, to preserve them from the Toothatch more raging in their Country, is esteem'd beautifull: The first Ambassador was of an Olive hue, had a flatter face and narrow eyes, squat nose and morish lips, haire none appeared: Wore severall rings of silver, gold, coper on their finger, which was a toaken of Knighthood or nobility: They were of Java major, whose Princes have ben turn'd Mahumetans not above 50 yeares since, The Inhabitans stil Pagans and Idolaters: They seem'd of a dul and heavy Constitution, not wondering at any thing they saw; but exceedingly astonish[ed] to understand, how our Law's gave us propriety in our Estates, and so thinking we were all Kings; for they could not be made to Comprehend, how subjects could possesse any thing but at the pleasure of their Prince, they being all slaves, but infinitly surprized at it, and pleased with the notion, and admiring our happinesse; They were very sober, and I believe subtile in their way: Their meate was cook'd, carried up, and they attended on, by severall fat slaves, who had no Covering save drawes, their whole body from the girdle upward stark naked, as well as their leggs, which appeared very uncouth, and lothsom; They eate their pilaw and other spoone-meate without spoones, taking up their pottage in the hollow of [their] fingers, and very dextrously flung it into their mouthes, without spilling a drop:

. . .

Chinese Curiosities

[July] 30 A stranger on the 5t of Matt: 20 Pomerid at Lee the Lecturer on: 1. Pet: 55, of the grace of humility, danger of traducing of this age: spiritual pride and prejudices among the dissenters etc:— We went after to visite our good neighbour Mr. Bohune, whose whole house is a Cabinet of all elegancies, especialy Indian, and the Contrivement of the [Japan] Skreenes instead of Wainscot in the Hall, where an excellent Pendule-Clock inclosed in the curious flower-work of Mr. Gibbons in the middst of the Vestibule, is very remarkable; and so are the Landskips of the Skreenes, representing the manner of living, and Country of the Chinezes etc: but above all his Ladys Cabinet, adorn'd on the fret, Ceiling and chimny-piece with Mr. Gib: best Carving; there is also some of Streeters best painting, and many rich Curiosities of Gold and sil: growing in the Mine: etc: Besides the Gardens are exactly kept, and the whole place very agreable and well watred: The Owners good and worthy neighbours, and he has also builded, and endowed an Hospital for Eight poore people, with a pretty Chapell, and all accommodations:

. . .

A Singular Worm

[August] 9 To Lond: R: Society, where Dr. Tyson produced a Lumbricus Latus, which a Patient of his voided, of 24 foote in length, it had severall joynts, at lesse than one inch asunder, which on examination prov'd so many mouthes and stomachs in number 400 by which it adhered to and sucked the nutrition and juice of the Gutts, and by impairing health, fills itselfe with a white Chyle, which it spewed-out, upon diping the worme in spirit of Wine; nor was it otherwise possible a Creature of that prodigious length should be nourish'd, and so turgid, with but one mouth at that distance: The part or joynt towards the head was exceeding small: We ordered the Doctor to print the discourse made upon it: The Person who voided it, indured such torment in his bowels, that he thought of killing himselfe . . . Then Dr. King presented a sharp pointed stone that a day or two before had ben taken out of the Ureters of a Gent, who [had] no kidney at all: The Council this day had recommended to them the being Trusteès and Visiters or Supervisers of the Academie which Monsieur Faubert did hope to procure to be builded by the subscription of worthy Gent: and noblemen, for the Education of Youth, and to lessen the vast expense the nation is yearely at, by sending their Children into France, to be taught these militarie Exercises: We thought therefore good, to give him all the Encouragement our recommendation could procure: After this we Adjourned our meetings 'til Michaelmas according to Costome at this season: so I went home where I found my Aunt Hungerford come to Visite us:

. . .

A Swedish Banquet

[November] 25 I was invited by Monsieur Lionberg The Swedish Resident, who made a magnificent Entertainement it being the Birth-day of his King: There dined the Duke of Albemarle, D: Hamilton, Earle of Bathe, E: of Alesbery, Lord Arran, Lord Castlehaven, the sonn of him who was executed 50 yeares before for Enormous Lusts etc: and sevveral greate persons: I was exceedingly afraide of Drinking, (it being a Dutch feast) but the Duke of Albemarle being that night to waite on his Majestie Excesse was prohibited; and to prevent all, I stole away and left the Company as soone as we rose from Table . . .

. . .

[December] 18 I sold my East India Adventure of 250 pounds, Principal for 750 pounds after it had ben in that Companie 25 yeares, to my extraordinary Advantage: and by the blessing of God . . .

. . .

Death of Sir Richard Browne

[1683. February] 12 This morning being at Mr. Packers, I received the newes of the death of my Father in Law, Sir Rich: Browne knight and Baronet, who dyed at my house at Says-Court this 12th of Feb: at 10 in the morning, after he had labour'd under the Gowt, and Dropsie for neere 6 monethes, in the 78th yeare of his Age, upon which I returned home to comfort my disconsolate Wife; and take order about his Funerall.

18 I went not to Church, obeying the Custome of keeping at home 'til the Ceremonies of the Funerall were over: which were solemniz'd, on the 19th at Deptford with as much Decency, as the

Dignity of the Person, and our Relation, required: There being invited the Bishop of Rochester, severall Noble Men, knights, and all the fraternity of the Trinity Companie (of which he had ben Master) and others of the Country etc: The Viccar preaching on 39: Psal: 10, a short, but Proper discourse upon the frailty of our mortal Condition, Concluding with an ample, and well deserving Elogie upon the Defunct, relating to his honorable Birth, and Ancestors, Education, Learning in Gre: and Latin, Modern Languages, Travells, Publique Employments, Signal Loyaltie, Character abroad, and particularly the honour of supporting the Church of England in its publique Worship, during its pers[e]cution by the late Rebells Usurpation, and Regicide, by the Suffrages of divers Bishops, Doctors of the church and others, who with it, found such an Asylum in his house and family at Paris, that in their disputes with the Papists etc (now triumphing over it, as utterly lost) they us'd to argue for its Visibility and Existence from Sir R: Brownes Chapell and Assembly there . . . By an especial Clause in his last Will, he ordered to be buried in the Church-Yard under the South-East Window of the Chancel, joyning to the burying places of his Ancestors, since they came out of Essex to Says-Court: being much offended at the novel Costome of burying every body within the body of the Church and chancel, as a favour hertofore granted onely to Martyrs, and greate Princes, this excesse of making Churches Charnel-houses being of ill and irreverent example, and prejudicial to the health of the living: besides the continual disturbance of the Pavement, and seates, the ground sinking as the Carcases consume, and severall other undecencies: Dr. Hall, the pious Bish: of Norwich would also so be interr'd, as may be read in his Testament:

. . .

Sir Josiah Child

[March] 16 I went to see Sir Josiah Childs prodigious Cost in planting of Walnut trees, about his seate, and making fish-ponds, for many miles in Circuite, in Eping-forest, in a Cursed and barren spot; as commonly these over growne and suddainly monied men for the most part seate themselves: He from an ordinary Merchants Apprentice, and managements of the E. India Comp: Stock, being arived to an Estate of (tis said) 200000 pounds: and lately married his daughter to the Eldest sonn of the Duke of Beaufort, late Marques of Worcester, with 30000 pounds portion at present, and various expectations: This Merchant, most sordidly avaricious etc . . .

. . .

A New Tavern

[May]: 1. Our Viccar on 7: Matt: 21: The Foefees for the Poore met, with whom I was, and then went to Black-heath, to see the new faire, being the first, procured by the L: Dartmoth, this being the first day, pretended for the sale of Cattell; but, I think in truth to inrich the new Tavern at the bowling-greene, erected by Snape his Majesties farrier, a man full of projects: There appeared nothing but an innumerable assemblie of drinking people from Lond, Pedlers etc: and I suppose it too neere Lond; to be of any greate use for the Country: March was unaccostomably hott and drie this spring and all April hitherto, excessively Wet; I planted all the out limites of the Garden, and long Walks, with Holly:

. . .

An Unkind Thought

7 To Lond: about affaires. 8. To our Society. 9: Din'd at Sir Gab: Sylvius, and thence went to visite the Duke of Norfolck, and to know whither he would part with any of his Cartoones and other Drawings of Raphael and the greate masters: He answered me, he would part with and sell any thing for mony, but his Wife (the Dutchesse etc) who stood neere him; and I thought with my selfe, That if I were in his condition, it should be the first thing I would be glad to part with . . .

. . .

Popish and Protestant Plots

[June 18] The Popish Plot also (which had hitherto made such a noise) began now sensibly to dwindle, through the folly, knavery, impudence and giddynesse of Oates; so as the Papists began now to hold up their heads higher than ever, and those who were fled flock'd to Lond: from abroad: Such suddaine Changes and eager doings there had ben, without any thing of steady, or prudent for these last seaven yeares: 19: I returned in Coach with the Earle of Clarendon, when passing by the glorious Palace his father built, but few years before, which they were now demolishing, being sold to certaine undertakers etc: I turn'd my head the Contrary way til the Coach was gon past it, least I might minister occasion of speaking of it, which must needes have grieved his Lordship that in so short a time, their pomp was fallen etc: I went 20 next day to my house:

. . .

28 After the Popish-plot etc there was now a new (and as they call'd it,) Protestant-Plot discover'd, that certaine Lords, and others should design the Assacination of his Majestie and Duke, as they were to come from New-Market, with a general rising of several of the Nation, and especialy the Citty of Lond: disafected to the present Government etc: Upon which were committed to the Tower the Lord Russel, Eldest sonn of the Earle of Bedford: Earle of Essex, Mr. Algernon Sydnie, sonn to the old Earle of Licester; Mr. Trenchard, Hambden: Lord Howard of Eskrick and others; with Proclamation out against my Lord Grey, the Duke of Munmouth, Sir Tho: Arme-Strong, and one Ferguson who had escaped beyond sea etc: of which some were said to be for the Killing of his Majestie, others for onely seasing on him, and perswading him to new Counsils, on pretence of the danger of Poperie, should the Duke live to succeede etc: who was now admitted to the Councils, and Cabinet seacrets againe etc: Much deplor'd were my Lords Essex and Russell, few believing they had any evil Intention against his Majestie or the Church, and some that they were cunningly drawn in by their Enemies, for not approving some late Councils, and manegement of affaire[s], in relation to France, to Popery, to the prosecution of the Dissenters etc. They were discovered by the Lord Howard, and some false breathren of the Clubb, and the designe happily broken; since had all taken effect; it would in all appearance have indangered the Government to unknowne and dangerous Events: which God avert:

. . .

Suicide in the Tower

[July] 13 [Friday], as I was visiting Sir Tho: Yarbrow and Lady in Covent Garden, that astonishing newes of the Earle of Essex having Cut his owne Throat was brought to us, having now ben but three dayes prisoner in the Tower, and this happning on the very day and instant that the Lord Russel was on his Trial, and had sentence of death . . . This fatal newes coming to Hicks-hall upon the article of my L: Russels Trial, was said to have no little influenc'd the Jury, and all the bench, to his prejudice: Others said, he had himselfe upon some occasions hinted, that in case he should [be] in danger of having his life taken from him, by any publique misfortune, those who thirsted for his Estate, should misse of their aime, and that he should long since speake favourably of that D: of Northumberland and some others who made away themselves: But these are discourses so very unlike his sober and prudent Conversation, that I have no inclination to credit them: what might instigate him to this develish fact I am not able to conjecture; since (as my Lord Clarendon his bro: in Law, who was with him but the day before assur'd me) he was then so very cherefull, and declared it to be the Effect of his innocence and loyalty: and most believe his Majestie had no severe intentions against him; however, he was altogether inexorable as to my Lord Russell and some of the rest: For my owne part I believe the crafty and ambitious Earle of Shaftsbery had brought them into some dislike of the present carriage of matters at Court, not with any designe of destroying the Monarchy (which Shaftesbery has in Confidence and for un-answerable reasons, told me, he would support, to his last breath, as having seene and felt the miserie of being under a Mechanic Tyrannie etc) but perhaps of seting up some other, whom he might govern, and frame to his owne Platonic fancie, without much reguard to the Religion establish'd under the Hierarchie, for which he had no esteeme: But when he perceiv'd those whom he had engag'd to rise, faile of his expectations, and the day past, reproching his Complices, that a second day for an Exploit of this nature, was never successfull, he gave them the slip, and got into Holland, where the fox died, three moneths before these unhappy Lords and others were discovered or suspected: Every creature deplored Essex, and Russell, especialy the last, as being thought to be drawn in on pretence onely of endeavoring to rescue the King from his present Counselors, and secure Religion, from Popery, and the Nation from Arbitrary government, now so much apprehended; whilst the rest of those who were fled, especialy Ferguson and his gang, had doubtlesse some bloudy designe, set up

a Commonwealth, and turne all things topsie turvy; of the same
tragical principles is Sidney etc:

...

Old-Fashioned Eloquence

15 A stranger preached on 6. Jer: 8: The old man preached
much after Bish: Andrews's method, full of Logical divisions, in
short, and broken periods, and latine sentences, now quite out of
fashion in the pulpet; grown into a far more profitable way, of
plaine and practical, of which sort this Nation nor any other ever
had greater plenty, and more profitable (I am confident) since the
Apostles time: so much has it to answer for thriving no better on it:

...

A Sinful Nation

The whole Nation was now in greate Consternation, upon the
late Plot and Conspiracy; his Majestie very Melancholic, and not
stirring without redoubled Guards, all the Avenue and private
dores about White-hall and the Park shut up; few admitted to walke
in it: The Papists in the meane while very jocond, and indeede they
had reason, seeing their owne plot brought to nothing, and turn'd
to ridicule and now a Conspiracy of Protestants, as they cald them:
The Turk likewise in hostility against the German Emperor, almost
Master of the upper Hungarie and drawing towards Vienna; on the
other side the French (who tis believed brought in the Infidel)
disturbing their Spanish, and Dutch Neighbours, and almost
swallowed, all Flanders, pursuing his ambition of a fift and
Universal Monarchy; and all this blood, and dissorder in Christendome had evidently its rise from our defections at home, in a
Wanton peace, minding nothing but Luxurie, Ambition, and to
procure Mony for our Vices: To this add our irreligion and
Atheisme, greate ingratitude and selfe Interest: the Apostacie of
some, and the Suffering the French to grow so Greate, and the
Hollanders so Weake. In a word we were Wanton, madd, and
surfeiting with prosperity, every moment unsettling the old
foundations, and never constant to any thing. The Lord in mercy
avert the sad Omen; and that we do not provoke him farther, 'til he
beare it no longer:

...

20 Severall of the Conspirators, of the lower forme, were
Executed at Tyburn—

21 And the next day was the Lord Russell decapitated in Lincolns in fields, the Executioner giving him 3 butcherly strokes: The Speech he made and Paper he gave the Sherif, declaring his Innocence, the noblenesse of the family, the piety and worthynesse of the unhappy Gent: wrought effects of much pitty, and various discourses on the plot etc:

...

George of Denmark

25 I went to Lond: saw againe Prince George, he had the Danish Countenance, blound; a young gent of few words, spake French but ill, seemed somewhat heavy; but reported Valiant, and indeede had bravely rescued and brought off his brother the K. of Denmarke in a battaile against the Swede, when both those Kings, were engaged very smartly:

...

28 Prince Geo: was married to the Lady Ann at White-hall: Her Court and household to be moduled just as the Dukes her fathers etc: and to continue in England:

...

An Unrepentant Gambler

[September] 18 I went to Lond: to visite and waite on the Dutchesse of Grafton now greate with Child, a most vertuous and beautifull Lady, and dining with her at my Lord Chamberlains met my Lo: of St. Albans, now growne so blind, that he could not see to the taking his meate: It is incredible how easy a life this Gent: has lived, and in what plenty even abroad, whilst his Majestie was a sufferer; nor lesse, the immense summs he has lost at play, which yet at about 80 yeares old he continues, having one that sets by him to name the spot in the Chards: He eate and dranke with extraordinary appetite. He is with all this a prudent old Courtier, and much inrich'd since his Majesties returne.

After dinner I walked to survey the sad demolitions of Clarendon house that costly and onely sumptuous Palace of the late L. Chancelor Hydes, where I have often ben so cherefull with him, and so sad ...

...

Vienna Relieved

23 We had now the wellcome tidings of the K: of Polands etc raising the siege before Vienna, which gave terror to all Europe, and uttmost reproch to the French, who 'tis believed brought him in, for diversion, that he might the more easilie swallow Flanders, and pursue his unjust conquests on the Empire etc, whilst we sate unconcerned, and under a deadly charme from somebody: There was this day a Collection for the rebuilding of New-Market Consum'd by an accidental fire, which removing his Majestie thence sooner than was intended, put by the Assassinates, who were dissapointed of their Rendezvous and expectation, by a wonderfull providence: This made the King more earnest to render Wi[n]chester the seate of his Autum[n]al field diversions for the future, designing a Palace there, where the antient Castle stood, infinitely indeede preferrable to New-Market, for Prospect, aire, pleasure, and provisions; The Surveior having already begun the foundations for a palace of 35000 pounds and his Majestie purchasing ground about it, to make a Parke etc:

. . .

Wages of Sin

[October 4] Following his Majestie this morning through the Gallerie, [I] went (with the few who attended him) into the Dutchesse of Portsmouths dressing roome, within her bed-chamber, where she was in her morning loose garment, her maides Combing her, newly out of her bed: his Majestie and the Gallants standing about her: but that which ingag'd my curiositie, was the rich and splendid furniture of this woman's Appartment, now twice or thrice, puld downe, and rebuilt, to satisfie her prodigal and expensive pleasures, whilst her Majestie dos not exceede, some gentlemens Ladies furniture and accommodation: Here I saw the new fabrique of French Tapissry, for designe, tendernesse of worke, and incomparable imitation of the best paintings; beyond any thing, I had ever beheld: some pieces had Versailles, St. Germans and other Palaces of the French King with Huntings, figures, and Landscips, Exotique fowle and all to the life rarely don: Then for Japon Cabinets, Skreenes, Pendule Clocks, huge Vasas of wrought plate, Tables, Stands, Chimny furniture, Sconces, branches, Braseras etc they were all of massive silver, and without number, besides of his Majesties best paintings: Surfeiting of this, I din'd yet at Sir Steph: Foxes, and 5 went contentedly home to my poore, but quiet Villa. Lord what contentment can there be in the riches and splendor of this world, purchas'd with vice and dishonor:

...

Judge Jeffreys

[December] 5 I was this day invited to a Weding of one Mrs. Castle ... There was at the Wedding the Lord Major, the Sherif, severall Aldermen and persons of quality, and above all Sir Geo: Jeoffries newly made Lord Chiefe Justice of England, with Mr. Justice Withings, daunced with the Bride, and were exceeding Merrie: These greate men spent the rest of the afternoone til 11 at night in drinking healths, taking Tobacco, and talking much beneath the gravity of Judges, that had but a day or two before Condemn'd Mr. Algernoon Sidny, who was executed on the 7th on Tower hill upon the single Wittnesse of that monster of a man the L: Howard of Eskrick, and some sheetes of paper taken in Mr. Sidnys study, pretended to be writen by him, but not fully proov'd, nor the time when, but appearing to have ben written before his Majesties restauration, and then pardon'd by the Act of Oblivion: So as though Mr. Sidny was known to be a person obstinately averse to government by a Monarch (the subject of the paper, in answer to one of Sir E: Filmer) yet it was thought he had very hard measure: There is this yet observable, that he had ben an inveterate enemy to the last King, and in actual rebellion against him: a man of greate Courage, greate sense, greate parts, which he shew'd both at his trial and death; for when he came on the scaffold, in stead of a speech, he told them onely, that he had made his peace with God; that he came not thither to talk but to die, put a paper into the Sherifs hand, and another into a friends, sayed one prayer as short as a grace, laied downe his neck, and bid the Executioner do his office: The Duke of Monmouth now having his pardon, refuses to accknowledge there was any Treasonable plot, for which he is banish'd White-hall: This was a greate dissappointment to some, who had prosecuted the rest, namely Trenchard, Hampden etc: that for want of a second wittnesse were come out of the Tower upon their Habeas Corpus. The King had now augmented his

guards with a new sort of dragoons, who carried also granados and
were habited after the polish manner with long picked Caps very
fierce and fantastical; and was very exotic:

. . .

The Thames Frozen

[1684. January 1] My Daughter Susan had some few small pox
come forth on her, so as I sent her out of the Family; The Weather
continuing intollerably severe, so as streetes of Boothes were set up
upon the Thames etc: and the aire so very cold and thick, as of
many yeares there had not ben the like: The small pox being very
mortal, many feared a worse Contagion to follow etc:

2 I dined at Sir St: Foxes, aftcr dinner came a fellow that eate
live charcoale glowingly ignited, quenching them in his mouth, and
then champing and swallowing them downe: There was a dog also
that seemd to do many rational actions.

. . .

6 I went home to Says-Court to see my Grandson, it being
extreame hard weather, and return'd the next-day by Coach the
river being quite frozen up:

. . . 9 I went crosse the Thames upon the Ice (which was now
become so incredibly thick, as to beare not onely whole streetes of
boothes in which the[y] roasted meate, and had divers shops of
wares, quite crosse as in a Towne, but Coaches and carts and
horses passed over): So I went from Westminster stayers to
Lambeth and dined with my L. Archbishop, where I met my Lord
Bruce, Sir Geo. Wheeler, Coll: Coock and severall Divines; after
dinner, and discourse with his Grace 'til Evening prayer, Sir Geo:
and I returnd, walking over the Ice from Lambeth stayres to the
Horse Ferry, and thence walked on foote to our Lodgings: 10: I
visited Sir Rob: Reading, where after supper we had musique, but
none comparable to that which Mrs. Bridgeman made us upon the
Gittar, which she master'd with such extraordinary skill, and
dexterity, as I hardly ever heard any lute exceed for sweetnesse.

. . .

Bull-Baiting on Ice

24 The frost still continuing more and more severe, the Thames
before London was planted with bothes in formal streetes, as in a

Citty, or Continual faire, all sorts of Trades and shops furnished, and full of Commodities, even to a Printing presse, where the People and Ladys tooke a fansy to have their names Printed and the day and yeare set downe, when printed on the Thames: This humour tooke so universaly, that 'twas estimated the Printer gained five pound a day, for printing a line onely, at six-pence a Name, besides what he gott by Ballads etc: Coaches now plied from Westminster to the Temple, and from severall other staires too and froo, as in the streetes; also on sleds, sliding with skeetes; There was likewise Bull-baiting, Horse and Coach races, Pupet-plays and interludes, Cookes and Tipling, and lewder places; so as it seem'd to be a bacchanalia, Triumph or Carnoval on the Water, whilst it was a severe Judgement upon the Land: the Trees not onely splitting as if lightning-strock, but Men and Cattell perishing in divers places, and the very seas so locked up with yce, that no vessells could stirr out, or come in: The fowle Fish and birds, and all our exotique Plants and Greenes universaly perishing; many Parks of deere destroied, and all sorts of fuell so deare that there were greate Contributions to preserve the poore alive; nor was this severe weather much lesse intense in most parts of Europe even as far as Spaine, and the most southern tracts: London, by reason of the excessive coldnesse of the aire, hindring the ascent of the smoke, was so filld with the fuliginous streame of the Sea-Coale, that hardly could one see crosse the streete, and this filling the lungs with its grosse particles exceedingly obstructed the breast, so as one could scarce breath: There was no water to be had from the Pipes and Engines, nor could the Brewers, and divers other Tradesmen work, and every moment was full of disastrous accidents etc:

. . .

[February] 4 I went to Says-Court to see how the frost and rigorous weather had dealt with my Garden, where I found many of the Greenes and rare plants utterly destroied; The Oranges and Myrtils very sick, the Rosemary and Lawrell dead to all appearance, but the Cypresse like to indure it out: I came to Lond: the next day when it fir[s]t of all began to Thaw, and pass'd-over without alighting in my Coach from Lambeth to the Horse-ferry at Mill-bank at Westminster; the Weather growing lesse severe, it yet began to freeze againe, but the boothes were allmost-all taken downe; but there was first a Map or Landskip cut in copper representing all the manner of the Camp, and the several actions, sports and passe-times thereon in memory of this signal Frost:

. . .

A Public Library Intended

[13] Dr. Tenison communicating to me his intention of Erecting a Library in St. Martines parish, for the publique use, desird my assistance with Sir Chr: Wren about the placing and structure thereof: a worthy and laudable designe: He told me there were 30 or 40 Young Men in Orders in his Parish, either, Governors to young Gent: or Chaplains to Noble-men, who being reprov'd by him upon occasion, for frequenting Taverns or Coffè-houses, told him, they would study and employ their time better, if they had books: This put the pious Doctor upon this designe, which I could not but approve of, and indeede a greate reproch it is, that so great a Citty as Lond: should have never a publique Library becoming it: There ought to be one at St. Paules, the West end of that Church, (if ever finish'd), would be a convenient place . . .

. . .

[March 28] There was so greate and eager a concourse of people with their children, to be touch'd of the Evil, that 6 or 7: were crush'd to death by pressing at the Chirurgions doore for Tickets. etc. The weather began now onely to be more mild and tollerable, but there was not the least appearance of any Spring.

Three Royal Dukes

30 Easter-day, I received the B: Sacrament at white-hall early, with the Lords and household: the B: of Lond: officiating: Then went to St. Martines wher Dr. Tenison (now first coming abroad after his recovery of the small-pox) preached on 16: Psal: 11:— Hence I went againe to White Hall, where coram Rege, preach'd the B: of Rochester on a Text out of Hosea 6. 2. touching the subject of the day: After which his Majestie, accompanied with 3 of his natural Sonns, (viz. the Dukes of Northumb: Richmond and St. Albans, base sonns of Portsmouth, Cleaveland, Nelly, prostitute Creatures) went up to the Altar: The three Boyes entering before the King within the railes, at the right hand, and 3 Bishops on the left: viz: Lond: (who officiated) Durham, Rochester, with the

sub-Deane Dr. Holder: The King kneeling before the Altar, making his offering, the Bishops first received, and then his Majestie, after which, he retir'd to a Canopied seate on the right hand etc: note, there was perfume burnt before the office began: Pomeridiano, preached at St. Mart: the Lecturer Dr. Meriton on 6: Rom: 4:

Aprill 4 After 5 monethes being in Lond: this severe winter, I return'd home with my family this day: My sonn with his wife etc: continuing behind, upon pretence of his applying himselfe more seriously to his studying the Law, but wholy without my approbation: — hardly the least appearance of any Spring.

. . .

The Dimensions of Noah's Ark

[May] 26 Being Trinity monday Dr. Can, preached before the Trinity Company (my L: Dartmouth being first chosen and continued Master for the Ensuing Yeare, now newly return'd with the fleete from blowing up, and demolishing Tangier) Text 107 Psal: 31. After a very learned discourse about the dimensions of the Ark, compar'd with other Vessells of antient and later times, to obviate severall objections of Atheistical persons; he shewed the prophanesse of others, in the usual sarcasme, of calling an ignorant sayler on[e] of St. Paules seamen, for that description in 27 St. Luke Acts Apost: where 'tis said they cast Ankers out of the fore-ship, to proceede from utter ignorance, that because we do not so in our seas, in stresse of Weather, and as our Vessels are built; so they did in other seas; whereas it is at this day, and allways has bin the practise so to do in the Mediterranean seas, as St. Luke describes it: he also most rhetoricaly inlarg'd on the severall perils of sea Adventurers, and Mariners, by Tempests, leakes, casual fires, Wracks; fights, slavery, diseases etc: thereby exciting those sort of men, to be above all others most religious, who were found usualy the most prophane: and what cause they had also above all others, to praise God for their deliverances; He preached with much action: Then we went to Lond: where we were magnificently feasted at the Trinity house, My L: of Dartmouth, Earles of Cravon and Berkely etc to the number of at the least of 100 at one table as I conjectur'd etc:

. . .

A Rhinoceros or Unicorn

[October] 22 Sir William Godolphin and I went to see the Rhinocerous (or Unicorne) being the first that I suppose was ever brought into England: It more ressembled a huge enormous Swine, than any other Beast amongst us; That which was most particular and extraordinary, was the placing of her small Eyes in the very center of her cheekes and head, her Eares in her neck, and very much pointed: her Leggs neere as big about as an ordinarie mans wast, the feete divided into claws, not cloven, but somewhat resembling the Elephants, and very round and flatt, her taile slender and hanging downe over her Sex, which had some long haires at the End of it like a Cowes, and was all the haire about the whole Creature, but what was the most wonderfull, was the extraordinary bulke and Circumference of her body, which though very Young, (they told us as I remember not above 4 yeares old) could not be lesse than 20 foote in compasse: she had a set of most dreadfull teeth, which were extraordinarily broad, and deepe in her Throate, she was led by a ring in her nose like a Buffalo, but the horne upon it was but newly Sprowting, and hardly shaped to any considerable point, but in my opinion nothing was so extravagant as the Skin of the beast, which hung downe on her hanches, both behind and before to her knees, loose like so much Coach leather, and not adhering at all to the body, which had another skin, so as one might take up this, as one would do a Cloake or horse-Cloth to a greate depth, it adhering onely at the upper parts: and these lappets of stiff skin, began to be studdied with impenetrable Scales, like a Target of coate of maile, loricated like Armor, much after the manner this Animal is usualy depicted: she was of a mouse Colour, the skin Elephantine; Tame enough, and suffering her mouth to be open'd by her keeper, who caus'd her to lie downe, when she appeared like a greate Coach overthrowne, for she was much of that bulke, yet would rise as nimbly as ever I saw an horse: T'was certainly a very wonderfull creature, of immense strength in the neck, and nose especialy, the snout resembling a boares but much longer; to what stature she may arive if she live long, I cannot tell; but if she grow proportionable to her present age, she will be a Mountaine: They fed her with Hay, and Oates, and gave her bread.

She belonged to Certaine E. Indian Merchants, and was sold for (as I remember) above two-thousand pounds:

And a Crocodile

At the same time I went to see a living Crocodile, brought from some of the W: Indian Ilands, in every respect resembling the Egyptian Crocodile, it was not yet fully 2 yards from head to taile, very curiously scaled and beset with impenetrable studds of a hard horny substance, and most beautifully ranged in works especialy on the ridge of the back and sides, of a dusky green Colour, save the belly, which being tender, and onely vulnerable, was of a lively and lovely greene, as lizards are, whose shape it exactly kept: The Eyes were sharp and piercing, over which it could at pleasure draw up a thin cobweb skinn: The rictus was exceeding deepe set with a tirrible rank of sharp and long teeth: We could not discerne any tongue, but a small lump of flesh at the very bottome of its throate, which I suppose helped his swallowing: the feete were divided into long fingers as the Lizards, and he went forward wadling, having a chaine about the neck: seemed to be very tame; I made its keeper take up his upper jaw which he affirmed did onely move, and so Pliny and others confidently report; but it did not appeare so plaine to me, whither his keeper did not use some dexterity in opening his mouth and placing his head so as to make it seeme that the upper chap, was loose; since in that most ample and perfect sceleton in our Repositarie at the R: Society, it is manifestly fixed to the neck and Vertebræ: the nether jaw onely loose: They kept the beast or Serpent in a longish Tub of warme Water, and fed him with flesh etc: If he grow, it will be a dangerous Creature.

More Royal Dukes

Octob: 23 I dined at Sir Stephen Foxes with the Duke of Nor[t]humberland another of his Majesties natural sonns, by that strumpet Cleaveland: He seemed to be a Young gent, of good capacity, well bred, civile, and modest, had ben newly come from Travell, and had made his Campagne at the siege of Luxemburg: Of all his Majesties Children, (of which he had now 6 Dukes) this seemed the most accomplished, and worth the owning; he is likewise extraordinary handsome and perfectly shaped: what the Dukes of Richmond, and St. Albans, base sonns of the Dutchesse of Portsmouth a French Lasse, and of Nelly, the Comedian and Apple-woma[n]s daughter, will prove their youth dos not yet discover, farther than that they are both very pretty boys, and seeme to have more Witt than most of the rest:

. . .

The English Climate

[November] 2 Our Viccar proceeded on his former Text: the holy Comm: followed at which I was participant: So suddaine an alteration from temperate warme weather to an excessive cold, raine, frost, snow and storme, as had seldome ben knowne, this Winter weather beginning as early and firce, as the past did late, and neere christmas, till which there had hardly ben any winter at all:

. . .

Superb Turkish Horses

[December] 17 Early in the morning I went into St. James's Park to see three Turkish or Asian Horses, brought newly over, and now first shewed his Majestie: There were 4 of them it seemes in all, but one of them died at sea, being 9 weekes coming from Hamborow: They were taken from a Bashaw at the seige of Vienna in Austria, the late famous raising that Leaguer: and with mine Eyes never did I behold so delicate a Creature as was one of them, of somwhat a bright bay, two white feete, a blaze; such an head, Eye, eares, neck, breast, belly, buttock, Gaskins, leggs, pasterns, and feete in all reguards beautifull and proportion'd to admiration, spiritous and prowd, nimble, making halt, turning with that sweiftnesse and in so small a compasse as was incomparable, with all this so gentle and tractable, as called to mind what I remember Busbequius speakes of them; to the reproch of our Groomes in Europ who bring them up so churlishly, as makes our horse most of them to retaine so many ill habits etc: They trotted like Does, as if they did not feele the Ground; for this first Creature was demanded 500 Ginnies, for the 2d 300, which was of a brighter bay, for the 3d 200 pound, which was browne, all of them choicely shaped, but not altogether so perfect as the first. In a word, it was judg'd by the Spectators, (among whom was the King, Prince of Denmark, the Duke of Yorke, and severall of the Court Noble persons skilled in Horses, especialy Monsieur Faubert and his sonn and Prevost, Masters of the Accademie and esteemed of the best in Europe), that there were never seene any horses in these parts, to be compared with them: Add to all this, the Furniture which consisting of Embrodrie on the Saddle, Housse, Quiver, bow, Arrows, Symeter, Sword, Mace or Battel ax a la Tur[c]isque: the Bashaws Velvet Mantle furr'd with the most perfect Ermine I ever beheld, all the Yron worke in other furnitur being here of silver curiously wrought and double gilt, to an incredible value: Such, and so extraordinary was the Embroidery, as I never before saw any thing approching it, the reines and headstall crimson silk, covered with Chaines of silver gilt: There was also a Turkish royal standard of an horses taile, together with all sorts of other Caparison belonging to a Generals horse: by which one may estimate how gallantly and [magnificently] those Infidels appeare in the fild, for nothing could certainely be seene more glorious, The Gent: (a German) who rid the horse, being in all this garb: They were shood with yron made round and closed at the heele, with an hole in the middle about as wide as a shilling; the hoofes most intire:

I dined with severall Gent: of the R: Society, going to Gr: Colledge after, where was the experiment of Dr. Papins Syphon: etc:

Gallants at Exercise

18 Mr. Faubert having newly railed in a Manage and fitted it for the Academy, I went with my Lord Cornwallis to see the Young Gallants do their Exercise: There were the Dukes of Norfolck and Northumberland, Lord Newburge, and a Nephew of the Earle of Feversham: The exercises were first running at the ring, next flinging a Javlin at a Mores head, 3d, discharging a Pistol at a Mark, lastly, the taking up a [Gauntlet] with the point of the Sword, all these [Exercises] performed in full speede: The D: of Northumberland, hardly miss'd succeeding in every one a douzen times as I think: Next the D: of Norfolck did exceeding bravely: Newburge and Duras seemed to be nothing so dextrous: here I saw the difference of what the French call *bell-homme a Cheval*, and *bonn homme a Chevall*, the D: of Norfolck being the first, that is rather a fine person on an horse; The D: of Northumberland being both, in perfection, namely a most gracefull person, and excellent rider: But the Duke of Norfolck told me he had not ben at this exercise this twelve yeare before: There were in the fild the Prince

of Denmark and the L: Landsdown, sonn of the Earle of Bath, who had ben made a Count of the Empire last summer for his service before Vienna.

. . .

Death of Charles II

[1685. February] 4 I went to Lond, hearing his Majestie had ben the moneday before surpriz'd in his bed chamber with an Apoplectical fit, and so, as if by Gods providence, Dr. King (that excellent chirurgeon as well as Physitian) had not ben accidentaly present to let him bloud with his lancet in his pocket) his Majestie had certainly died that moment, which might have ben of direfull consequence, there being no body else with the King save this doctor and one more, as I am assured: It was a mark of the extraordinary dexterity, resolution, and presentnesse of Judgment in the Doctor to let him bloud in the very paroxysme, without staying the coming of other physitians, which regularly should have ben don, and the not doing so, must have a formal pardon as they tell me: This rescued his Majestie for that instant, but it prov'd onely a reprieve for a little time; he still complain'd and was relapsing and often fainting and sometimes in Epileptical symptoms 'til Wednesday, for which he was cupp'd, let bloud againe in both jugularies, had both vomit and purges etc: which so relieved him, that on the Thursday hops of recovery were signified in the publique Gazett; but that day about noone the Physitians conjectur'd him somewhat feavorish; This they seem'd glad of, as being more easily alaied, and methodicaly to be dealt with, than his former fits, so as they prescrib'd the famous Jesuits powder; but it made his Majestie worse; and some very able Doctors present, did not think it a feavor, but the effect of his frequent bleeding, and other sharp operations used by them about his head: so as probably the powder might stop the Circulation, and renew his former fitts, which now made him very weake: Thus he pass'd Thursday night with greate difficulty, when complaining of a paine in his side, the[y] drew 12 ounces more of blood from him, this was by 6 in the morning on friday, and it gave him reliefe, but it did not continue; for being now in much paine and strugling for breath, he lay doz'd, and after some conflicts, the Physitians desparing of him, he gave up the Ghost at halfe an houre-after Eleeven in the morning, being the 6 of Feb: in the 36t yeare of his reigne, and 54 of his age: Feb: 6 'Tis not to be express'd the teares and sorrows of Court, Citty and Country: Prayers were solemnly made in all the Churches, especialy in both the Court Chapells, where the Chaplaines relieved one another every halfe quarter of an houre, from the time he began to be in danger, til he expir'd: according to the forme prescribed in the Church office: Those who assisted his Majesties devotion were the A: Bish: of Cant: of London, Durrham and Ely; but more especialy the B: of Bath and Wells. It is sayd they exceedingly urged the receiving the H: Sacrament but that his Majestie told them he would Consider of it, which he did so long, 'til it was too late: others whispered, that the Bishops being bid withdraw some time the night before, (except the Earls of Bath, and Feversham), Hurlston the Priest, had presum'd to administer the popish Offices; I hope it is not true; but these buisie emissaries are very forewarde upon such occasions . . . He gave his breeches and Keys to the Duke, who was almost continualy kneeling by his bed side, and in teares; he also recommended to him the care of his natural Children, all except the D: of Monmoth, now in Holland, and in his displeasure; he intreated the Queene to pardon him, (nor without cause) who a little before had sent a Bishop to excuse her not more frequently visiting him, in reguard of her excessive griefe, and with all, that his Majestie would forgive it, if at any time she had offended him: He spake to the Duke to be kind to his Concubines the DD: of Cleveland, and especialy Portsmouth, and that Nelly might not sterve; I do not heare he said any thing of the Church or his people, now falling under the government of a Prince suspected for his Religion, after above 100 yeares the Church and Nation had ben departed from Rome:

Character of Charles II

Thus died K. Charles the 2d, of a Vigorous and robust constitution, and in all appearance capable of a longer life. A prince of many Virtues, and many greate Imperfections, Debonaire, Easy of accesse, not bloudy or Cruel: his Countenance fierce, his voice greate, proper of person, every motion became him, a lover of the sea, and skillfull in shipping, not affecting other studys, yet he had a laboratory and knew of many Empyrical Medicines, and the easier Mechanical Mathematics: Loved Planting, building, and brought in a politer way of living, which passed to Luxurie and intollerable expense: He had a particular Talent in telling stories and facetious passages of which he had innumerable, which made some bouffoones and vitious wretches too presumptuous, and familiar, not worthy the favours they abused: He tooke delight to have a number of little spaniels follow him, and lie in his bed-Chamber, where often times he suffered the bitches to puppy and give suck, which rendred it very offensive, and indeede made the whole Court nasty and stinking: An excellent prince doubtlesse had he ben lesse addicted to Women, which made him uneasy and allways in Want to supply their unmeasurable profusion, and to the detriment of many indigent persons who had signaly serv'd both him and his father: Easily, and frequently he changed favorites to his greate prejudice etc: As to other publique transactions and unhappy miscarriages, 'tis not here I intend to number them; but certainely never had King more glorious opportunities to have made himselfe, his people and all Europ happy, and prevented innumerable mischiefs, had not his too Easy nature resign'd him to be menag'd by crafty men, and some abandoned and prophane wretches, who corrupted his otherwise sufficient parts, disciplin'd as he had ben by many afflictions, during his banishment: which gave him much experience, and knowledge of men and things; but those wiccked creatures tooke him off from all application becoming so greate a King: the History of his Reigne will certainely be the most wonderfull for the variety of matter and accidents above any extant of many former ages: The sad tragical death of his father, his banishment, and hardships, his miraculous restauration, conjurations against him; Parliaments, Warrs, Plagues, Fires, Comets; revolutions abroad happning in his time with a thousand other particulars: He was ever kind to me and very gracious upon all occasions, and therefore I cannot without ingratitude but deplore his losse, which for many respects (as well as duty) I do with all my soule . . .

King James II

His Majestie dead, The Duke (now K. James the 2d) went immediately to Council, and before entering into any buisinesse, passionately declaring his sorrow, Told their Lordships, That since the succession had falln to him, he would endeavor to follow the

example of his predecessor in his Clemency and tendernesse to his
people: That however he had ben misrepresented as affecting
arbitrary power, they should find the contrary, for that the Laws of
England had made the King as greate a Monarch as he could
desire; That he would endeavour to maintaine the Government
both in Church and state as by Law establish'd, its Principles being
so firme for Monarchy, and the members of it shewing themselves
so good and Loyal subjects; and that as he would never depart from
the just rights and prerogative of the Crown, so would he never
Invade any mans propriety: but as he had often adventured his life
in defence of the Nation, so he would still proceede, and preserve it
in all its lawfull rites and libertyes:

This being the substance of what he said, the Lords desired it
might be published as containing matter of greate satisfaction to a
jealous people, upon this change: which his Majestie consented to:
Then were the Counsel sworn, and a proclamation ordered to be
publish'd, that all officers should continue in their station; that
there might be no failure of publique Justice, 'til his farther
pleasure should be known: Then the King rose, the Lords
accompanying him to his bed Chamber, where, whilst he reposed
himselfe (tired indeede as he was with griefe and watching) They
immediately returned againe into the Council-Chamber to take
order for the Proclayming of his Majestie which (after some debate)
they consented should be in the very forme, his Grandfather K.
James the first was, after the death of Q: Elizabeth, as likewise that
the Lords etc: should proceede in their Coaches through the Citty
for the more solemnity of it; upon this was I and severall other
Gent: (waiting in the privy Gallerie), admitted into the Council
Chamb: to be wittnesse of what was resolv'd on: and Thence with
the Lords (the Lord Martial and the Herraulds and other Crowne
Officers being ready) we first went to Whitehall gate, where the
Lords stood on foote beareheaded, whilst the Herauld proclaimed
His Majesties Titles to the Imperial Crowne, and succession
according to the forme: The Trumpets and Kettle drumms having
first sounded 3 times, which after also ended with the peoples
acclamations: Then an Herauld called the Lords Coaches according to ranke, my selfe accompanying the solemnity in my Lord
Cornwallis Coach, first to Temple barr, where the Lord Major and
his breathren etc met us on horseback in all their formalities, and

proclaymed the King; Thence to the Exchange in Cornhill, and so we returned in the order we set forth: being come to White-hall, we all went and kissed the King and Queenes hands, he had ben on the bed, but was now risen, and in his Undresse. The Queene was in bed in her appartment, but put forth her hand; seeming to be much afflicted, as I believe she was, having deported herselfe so decently upon all occasions since she came first into England, which made her universally beloved: Thus concluded this sad, and yet Joyfull day: I am never to forget the unexpressable luxury, and prophanesse, gaming, and all dissolution, and as it were total forgetfullnesse of God (it being Sunday Evening) which this day sennight, I was witnesse of; the King, sitting and toying with his Concubines Portsmouth, Cleaveland, and Mazarine: etc: A french boy singing love songs, in that glorious Gallery, whilst about 20 of the greate Courtiers and other dissolute persons were at Basset round a large table, a bank of at least 2000 in Gold before them, upon which two Gent: that were with me made reflexions with astonishment, it being a sceane of uttmost vanity; and surely as they thought would never have an End: six days after was all in the dust.

. . .

The Reign of James II
1685–1688

9 I went home the next day to refresh, it being injoyned, that those who put on mourning, should weare it as for a father, in the most solemn and lugubrous manner:

10 Being sent to by the Sherif of the County, to appeare, and assist the Proclayming the King; 11 I went the next day to Bromely, where I met the Sherif, and the Commander of the Kentish Troope, with an appearance of (I suppose) above 500 horse, and innumerable people: Two of his Majesties Trumpets, and a searjeant, with other officers, who having drawn up the horse in a large field neere to towne, march'd thence with swords drawn to the Market place, where making a ring, after sound of Trumpets, and silence made, the high Sherif read the Proclaming Titles, to his Bailife, who repeated it alow'd, and then after many shouts of the people etc: his Majesties health being drunk in a flint glasse of a yard-long, of the Sherif, Commanders, Officers and chiefe Gent: they all disperc'd and I returned:

. . .

The Face of the Court Changed

14 The King was this night very obscurely buried in a Vault under Hen: 7th Chapell in Westminster, without any manner of pomp, and soone forgotten after all this vainity, and the face of the whole Court exceedingly changed into a more solemne and moral behaviour: The new King affecting neither Prophanesse, nor bouffonry: All the Greate Officers broke their white-Staves on the Grave etc: according to forme:

. . .

The 2d sermon (which should have ben before the King, who to the greate griefe of his subjects, did now the first time go to Masse publicly in the little Oratorie at the Dukes lodgings, the doores set wide open) was by Mr. Fox, a young quaint Preacher, who made a

very profitable sermon on Pro: 'Fooles make a mock at sin',
against prophanes and Atheisme; now reigning more than ever
through the late dissolutenesse of the Court:

...

Death of Daughter Mary

[March] 7 Newes coming to me that my Daughter Mary was
falln ill of the Small Pox, I hastned home full of apprehensions, and
indeede found her very ill, still coming-forth in aboundance, a
wonderfull affliction to me, not onely for her beauty, which was
very lovely, but for the danger of loosing one of extraordinary parts
and virtue. etc: Gods holy will be don.

8 A stranger preach'd at our Parish on 4. Gal: 18, very solidly.

My Deare Child continuing ill, by reason of the Disseases fixing
in the Lungs, it was not in the power of physick without more
plentifull expectoration to recover her, insomuch as 9 Dr. Short
(the most approved and famous Physition of all his Majesties
Doctors) gave us his opinion, that she could not escape, upon the
Tuesday; so as on Wednesday she desired to have the B:
Sacrament given her (of which yet she had participated the Weeke
before) after which disposing her selfe to suffer what God should
determine to inflict, she bore the remainder of her sicknesse with
extraordinary patience, and piety and with more than ordinary
resignation, and marks of a sanctified and blessed frame of mind,
rendred up her soule to the Lord Jesus on Saturday the 14 of
March, exactly at halfe-an houre after Eleaven in the fore noone, to
our unspeakable sorrow and Affliction, and this not to ours (her
parents) onely, but all who knew her, who were many of the best
quality, greatest and most vertuous persons: How unexpressable
losse I and my Wife sustain'd, the Virtues and perfections she was
endow'd with best would shew; of which the justnesse of her
stature, person, comelinesse of her Countenance and gracefullnesse of motion, naturall, and unaffected (though more than
ordinaryly beautifull), was one of the least, compar'd with the
Ornaments of her mind, which was truely extraordinary, especialy the
better part: Of early piety, and singularly Religious, so as spending a
considerable part of every day in private devotion, Reading and
other vertuous exercises, she had collected, and written out
aboundance of the most usefull and judicious periods of the Books

she read, in a kind of Common place; as out of Dr. Hammonds N. Test: and most of the best practical Treatises extant in our tonge: She had read and digested a considerable deale of History, and of Places, the french Tongue being as familiar to her as English, she understood Italian, and was able to render a laudable Account of what she read and observed, to which assisted a most faithfull memory, and discernement, and she did make very prudent and discreete reflections upon what she had observe'd of the Conversations among which she had at any time ben (which being continualy of persons of the best quality), she improved: She had to all this an incomparable sweete Voice, to which she play'd a through-base on the Harpsichord, in both which she ariv'd to that perfection, that of all the Schollars of those Two famous Masters, Signor Pietro and Bartolomeo: she was esteem'd the best; for the sweetenesse of her voice, and manegement of it, adding such an agreablenesse to her Countenance, without any constraint and concerne, that when she sung, it was as charming to the Eye, as to the Eare; this I rather note, because it was a universal remarke, and for which so many noble and judicious persons in Musique, desir'd to heare her; the last, being at my Lord Arundels of Wardours, where was a solemn Meeting of about twenty persons of quality, some of them greate judges and Masters of Musique; where she sung with the famous Mr. Pordage, Signor Joh: Battist touching the Harpsichord etc: with exceeding applause: What shall I say, or rather not say, of the cherefullnesse and agreablenesse of her humor, that she condescending to the meanest servant in the family, or others, she kept still her respect without the least pride: These she would reade to, examine, instruct and often pray with, if they were sick; so as she was extreamely beloved of every body: Piety was so prevalent an ingredient in her constitution (as I may say) that even amongst superiors, as equals, she no sooner became intimately acquainted; but she would endeavour to improve them by insinuating something of Religious, and that tended to bring them to a love of Devotion; and she had one or two Confidents, with whom she used to passe whole dayes, in fasting, reading and prayers, especialy before the monethly Communions, and other solemn occasions: She could not indure that which they call courtship, among the Gallants, abhorred flattery, and tho she had aboundance of witt, the raillery was so innocent and ingenuous, as was most agreable; She sometimes would see a play, but since the stage grew licentious, tooke greate scandal at them, and express'd her being weary of them, and that the time spent at the Theater was an unaccountable vanity, nor did she at any time play at Cards, without extreame importunity and for the Company; but this was so very seldome, that I cannot number it among any thing she could name a fault: No body living read prose, or Verse better and with more judgement, and as she read, so she writ not onely most correct orthography, but with that maturitie of judgement, and exactnesse of the periods, choice expressions, and familiarity of style, as that some letters of hers have astonish'd me, and others to whom she has occasionaly written: Among other agreablenesses she had a talent of rehersing any Comical part or poeme, as was to them she might decently be free with, more pleasing than the Theater: She daunc'd with the most grace that in my whole life I had ever seene, and so would her Master say, who was Monsieur Isaac; but she very seldome shew'd that perfection, save in the gracefullnesse of her Carriage, which was with an aire of spritefull modestie, not easily to be described . . . She was kind to her Sisters, and was still improving them, by her constant Course of Piety: Ô deare, sweete and desireable Child, how shall I part with all this goodnesse, all this Vertue, without the bitternesse of sorrow, and reluctancy of a tender Parent! Thy Affection, duty and love to me was that of a friend, as well as of a Child, passing even the love of Women, the Affection of a Child: nor lesse dearer to thy Mother, whose example and tender care of Thee was unparalleled; nor was Thy returnes to her lesse conspicuous: Ô how she mourns thy losse! ô how desolate hast Thou left us, Sweete, obliging, happy Creature! . . .

It was in the nineteenth yeare of her Age, that this sicknesse happn'd to her, at which period Dr. Harvy somewhere writes, all young people should be let blood; and to this we advised her; whilst to all who beheld her she looked so well, as her extraordinary beauty was taken notice of, the last time she appeared at Church: but she had so great an aversion to breathing a veine, as we did not so much insist upon it as we should: being in this exceeding height of health, she was the more propence to change, and had ever ben subject to feavors; but there was yet another accident that contributed to the fixing it in this dissease; The apprehension she had of it in particular, and which struck her but two days before she came home, by an imprudent Gentlewomans telling my Lady Faulkland (with whom my daughter went to give a Visite) after she had entertained them a good while in the house, that she had a servant sick of the small pox above, who died the next day; This my poore Child accknowledged made an impression on her spirits, it being with all of a mortal and spreading kind at this time about the towne:

There were now no lesse than foure Gent: of Quality offering to treate with me about Marriage; and I freely gave her her owne Choice, knowing she was discreete: One (against which I had no exceptions) and who most passionately lov'd her, but was for a certaine natural blemish that rendered him very disagreable, she would in complyance to me have married, if I did injoyne her; but telling me she should never be happy with him (observing it seemes a neerenesse in his nature, and a little under-breeding) I would not impose it; for which she often expressed her satisfaction, and thanks to me in the most obliging and respectfull manner: The other was one Weston a Stafford shire Gent: of the family, and I thinke heire (within one) to the Earles of Portland: This was but now just beginning: But the person who first made love to her, was Mr. Wilbraham a Chesshire Gent: of a noble Family, whose extreamely rich and sordid Fathers demands of Portion, I could by no meanes reach, without injury to the rest of my daughters, which this pious, and good natured Creature, would never have suffered, and so that match stood in suspense; I say in suspense, for the young Gent: still pursu'd, and would have married her in private, if either my Daughter, or We had don so disingenuously: She and we had principles that would by no meanes suffer us to harken to it: At last he's sent for home, continues his Affection, hop[e]s to bring his father to reasonable termes: My Child is taken with his Constancy, his Virtuous breeding, and good nature, and discretion, having beene a fortnight together in my house: This, made us not forward to embrace any other offers, together with the extraordinary indifferency she ever shewed of Marrying at all; for truely says shee to her Mother, (the other day), were I assur'd of your lives and my deare Fathers, never would I part from you, I love you, and this home, where we serve God, above all things in the world, nor ever shall I be so happy . . .

. . .

Coronation of James II

[April] 23 Was the day of his Majesties Coronation, the Queene was also crown'd, the solemnity very magnificent, as the particulars are set forth in print: The Bish: of Ely preached, but (to the greate sorrow of the people) no Sacrament, as ought to have ben: However the King beginns his reigne with greate expectations and hopes of much reformation as to the former vices, and prophanesse both of Court and Country:

Having ben present at our late Kings Coronation, I was not ambitious of seing this Ceremonie; nor did I think fit to leave my poore Wife alone, who was yet in greate sorrow:

. . .

Retribution for Oates

[May] 5 To Lond: 7th: I was in Westminster Hall when Oates (who had made such a stirr in the whole Kingdome, (upon his revealing a plot of the Papists) as alarm'd several Parliaments, and had occasion'd the execution of divers persons, priests, noble men etc:) was tried for Perjurie at the Kings-bench; but it being exceedingly tedious, I did not much endeavor to see the issue of it, considering that it would certainly be publish'd: Aboundance of R: Cath: were now in the Hall, in expectation of the most gratefull conviction and ruine of a person who had ben so obnoxious to them; and as I verily believe had don much mischiefe and greate injurie to several by his violent and ill grounded proceedings, whilst he was at first so unreasonably blowne-up, and encourag'd, that his insolence was no longer sufferable:

6 I went to the R: Society, Dr. Wallis presenting his booke of Algebra etc:

. . .

16 Was sentenc'd Oates to be whip'd and pilloried with uttmost severity: etc:

. . .

Sir William Dugdale

20 To Lond: R. Soc: 21. Din'd at my Lord Privy-Seales, with Sir Will: Dugdale the [Garter] K: at Armes, Author of the *Monasticon*, and greate Antiquarie; with whom I had much discourse: he told me he was 82 yeares of age, had his sight and

memory perfect etc: There was shew'd a draght of the exact shape
and dimensions of the Crowne the Queene had ben crown'd
withall, together with the Jewells and Pearles, their weight and
value, which amounted to 100650 pounds sterling, an immense
summ: attested at the foote of the paper by the Jeweller and
Gooldsmith who set the Jewells etc:

The King's Promise

22 In the morning, I went (together with a French gent, a person
of quality) with my Lord Pr: Seale to the house of Lords, where we
were both plac'd by his Lordship next the barr just below the
Bishops very commodiously both for hearing and seeing: After a
short space came in the Queene and Princesse of Denmark, and
stood next above the Arch-Bishops, at the side of the house on the
right hand of his Majesties Throne: In the interim divers of the
Lords (who had not finish'd before) tooke the Test, and usual
Oathes, so as her Majestie (Spanish Ambassador and other
forraine Ministers who stood behind the state) heard the Pope, and
worship of the Virg: Mary etc: renounc'd very decently, as likewise
the following Prayers, standing all the while: Then came in the
King, the Crowne on his head etc and being sate, The Commons
were let in, so the house being fill'd, he drew forth a Paper,
containing his speech, which he [read] distinctly enough to this
effect: That he resolved to call a Parliament from the moment of
his brothers decease, as the best meanes to settle all the concernes
of the Nation so as might be most easy and happy to himselfe and
his subjects: That he would confirme what ever he had said in his
declaration at the first Council, concerning his opinion of the
principles of the Church of England, for their Loyaltie, and would
defend and support it, and preserve its government, as by Law now
establish'd: That as he would Invade no mans property, so he
would never depart from his owne prerogative: and as he had
[ventur'd] his life in defence of the nation so he would proceede to
do still: That having given this assurance of his Care of our
Religion (his word was your Religion) and propertie, (which he had
not said by chance, but solemnly) so he doubted not of suitable
returnes of his subjects duty and kindnesse, especialy as to the
settling his Revenue for life for the many weighty necessities of the
government which he would not suffer to be precarious: That some

might possibly suggest that it were better to feede and supply him from time to time onely, out of their inclination to frequent Parliaments; but that that, would be but a very improper Method to take with him; since the best way to engage him to meete oftener, would be allways to use him well; and therefore expected their compliance speedily, that this session being but short, they might meete again to satisfaction: At every period of this, the house gave lowd shouts etc: Then he acquainted them with that mornings news of Argiles being landed in the West-highlands of Scotland from Holland, and the Treasonous declaration he had published, which he would communicate to them, and that he should take the best care he could it should meete with the reward it deserv'd, not questioning of the parliaments Zeale and readinesse to assist him, as he desired: At which There followed another *Vive le roy*, and so his Majestie retired: etc: and I went into the Court of Requests etc:

Revenue for Life

So soone as the Commons were return'd, and put themselves, into a grand Committè, they immediately put the Question, and unanimously voted the Revenue to his Majestie during life: Mr. Seamour made a bold speech against many Elections, and would have had those Members who (he pretended) were obnoxious, to withdraw, 'til they had cleared their being legaly return'd, but no body seconded him: The truth is there were very many of the new Members, whose Elections and returnes were universaly censur'd; being divers of them persons of no manner of condition or Interest in the nation, and places for which they served, especialy in the Counties of Devon, Cornwell, Norfolck, etc, said to have ben recommended from the Court, and effect of the new charters, changing the Electors: It was reported my L: of Bath, carried-down with him no fewer than 15 Charters, so as some cald him the Prince Elector: whence Seaymor told the house in his speech, that if this were digested, they might introduce what Religion and Lawes they pleased, and that though he never gave heede to the feares and jealosies of the people before, he now was realy apprehensive of Popery etc: The truth is, by the printed List of Members of 505, there did not appear to be above 135 who had ben in former Parliaments, especialy that lately held at Oxon:

. . .

The Popish Lords (who had some time before ben released from their Confinement about the Plot) were now discharg'd of their Impeachment: of which I gave my L. Arundel of Wardoer joy:

Oates Whipped

Oates, who had but two days before ben pilloried at severall places, and whip't at the Carts taile from New-gate to Algate; was this day placed in a sledge (being not able to go by reason of his so late scourging) and dragd from prison to Tyburn, and whip'd againe all the way, which some thought to be very severe and extraordinary; but in case he were gilty of the perjuries, and so of the death of many innocents, as I feare he was; his punishment was but what he well deserv'd: I chanc'd to passe in my Coach, just as Execution was doing on him: A strange revolution.

. . .

Drought

[24] We had hithertoo not any raine for many monethes, insomuch as the Caterpillar had already devoured all the Winter fruite through the whole land, and even killed severall greate and old trees; such two Winters, and Summers I had never known:

. . .

Persecution of Protestants in France

June 4. Came to visite, and take leave of me Sir Gab: Sylvius now going Envoyè Extraordinary into Denmark: with his secretary, and chaplaine, a french-man who related the miserable persecution of the Protestants in Fr: not above ten Churches left them, and they threatned to be also demolish'd: That they were commanded to christen their children within 24 houres after birth, or else a Popish-priest was to be call'd, and then the Infant brought-up in popery: and that in some places they were 30 leagues from any Minister or opportunity: That this persecution had dispeopled the most industrious part of the nation and dispers'd them into Swisse, Burgundy, Hollond, Ger: Denmark, England, Plantations and where not. There were with Sir Gab: his Lady, Sir William Godolphin, and sisters, and my Lord Godolphins little son, (my Charge): I brought them to the water side, where Sir Gab: embarked for his Voyage, and the rest return'd to Lond:

. . .

The Monmouth Rebellion

[June 14] There was now certaine Intelligence of the Duke of Monmoths landing at Lyn in Dorset shire, and of his having set up his standart, as K. of England: I pray God deliver us from the confusions which these beginings threaten:

Such a drowth for want of raine, was never in my memory:

17 To Lond: at which time the D: of Monmoth invaded this nation landing with but 150 men at Lyme in Dorsetshire, which wonderfully alarm'd the whole Kingdome, fearing the joyning of dissafected people; many of the train'd bands flocking to him: he had at his landing publish'd a Declaration, charging his Majestie with Usurpation, and severall horrid crimes, upon pretence of his owne title, and the calling of a free-Parliament: This Decl: was condemn'd to be burnt by the hang-man, the Duke proclaim'd Traytor, a reward of 5000 pounds to him that should kill him etc: Now were also those words in the Inscription about the Pillar (intimating the Papists firing the Citty) erased and cut out etc:

The exceeding Drouth still continued: God grant a successfull conclusion to these ill-boding beginnings: I tooke the Chaire as Vice-President at the R: Society.

28 We had now plentifull Raine after two yeares excessive drowth, and severe winters. A stranger preached on 1: Jam: 25:—Argile taken in Scotland and executed; his party desperssed:

July 2 . . . No considerable account of the forces sent against the D: of Mon: though greate forces sent: there was a small ski[r]mish, but he would not be provok'd to come to an encounter, but still kept in the fastnesses: The Parliament prorogu'd til 4: Aug: Dangerfild whip'd and like Oates for perjurie:

. . .

Monmouth Taken

8 To Lond: Came now the newes of Monmouths Utter defeate, and the next day of his being taken by Sir William Portman and Lord Lumley, with the Militia of their Counties. It seemes the horse commanded by my Lord Grey, being newly raised, and undisciplin'd, were not to be brought in so short a time to indure the Fire, which exposed the foote to the Kings: so as when Monmoth had led the foote in greate silence and order thinking to surprise my Lord Feversham Lieutenant Generall newly incamped,

and given him a small charge, interchanging both greate and small shot; The horse breaking theire owne ranks; monmoth gave it over, and fled with Grey, leaving their party to be cut in pieces: to the number of 2000: the whole number reported to be about 8000: The Kings but 2700: The slaine were most of them Mendip-miners, who did greate Execution with their tooles, and sold their lives very dearely: whilst their leaders flying were pursu'd and taken the next morning, not far from one another: Mon: had walked 16 miles on foote changing his habite with a poore coate, and was found by L. Lumley in [a] dry-ditch cover'd with fern-braken, but neither with sword, pistol, or so much as any Weapon, and so might happly have passed for some country man, his beard being grown so long, and so gray, as hardly to be known, had not his George discovered him, which was found in his Pocket: Tis said he trembled exceedingly all over not able to speake: Grey was taken not far from him: Most of his party were Anabaptists, and poore Cloth-workers of the Country, no Gent: of account being come into him: The Arch-bouttefew Ferguson, Mathews etc: were not yet found: The 5000 pounds to be given to whomsoever should bring Monmouth in by Proclamation, was to be distributed among the Militia by agreement twixt Sir William Portman and Lumley: The battail ended, some words first in jeast then in heate passing twixt Sherrington Talbot a worthy Gent, (son to Sir Jo: Talbot, and who had behav'd himselfe very handsomly) and one Capt: Love, both commanders of the Militia forces of the Country, whose souldiers fought best: both drawing their Swords, and passing at one another Sherrington was wounded to death upon the spot; to the greate regrett of those who knew him, being also his fathers onely son:

Tension at Court

9 Just as I was coming into the Lodgings at Whitehall a little before dinner my Lord of Devonshire standing very neere his Majesties bed-Chamber-doore in the lobby: came Coll: Culpeper and in a rude manner looking my Lord in the face, Asked whether this were a time and place for Excluders to appeare, my Lord tooke little notice of what he said at first, knowing him to be a hot-headed fellow; but reiterating it againe, Asked Culpeper whether he meant him? he said, yes, he meant his Lordship: My Lord told him he was

no Excluder (as indeede he was not) the other affirms it againe: My
Lord told him he Lied; on which Culpeper struck him a box
o'th'Eare, my Lord him another and fell'd him downe; upon which
being soone parted: Culpeper was seiz'd and commanded by his
Majestie (who was all the while in the B: Chamber) to be carried
downe to the Greenecloth Officer, who sent him to the Martialsea,
as he deserv'd: My L: Devon had nothing said to him.

. . .

Monmouth's Fate

[15] This day was Monmoth brought to Lond: examin'd before
the King to whom he made great submission, accknowledg'd his
seduction by Fergusson the Scot, whom he named the bloudy
Villain: thence sent to the Tower, had an enterview with his late
Dutchesse, whom he received coldly, having lived dishonestly with
the Lady Hen: Wentworth for two yeares; from obstinatly asserting
his conversation with that debauched woman to be no sin, seing he
could not be perswaded to his last breath, the Divines, who were
sent to assist him, thought not fit to administer the holy
Communion to him: for the rest of his faults he professed greate
sorrow, and so died without any apparent feare, would make use of
no cap, or other circumstance, but lying downe bid the fellow do his
office better than to my late Lord Russell, and gave him gold: but
the wretch made five Chopps before he had his head off, which so
incens'd the people, that had he not ben guarded and got away they
would have torne him in pieces: He made no Speech on the
Scaffold (which was on Tower-hill) but gave a paper (containing
not above 5 or 6 lines) for the King, in which he disclaimes all Title
to the Crowne, accknowledges that the late King (his Father) had
indeede told him, he was but his base sonn, and so desire'd his
Majestie to be kind to his Wife and Children: This Relation I had
from the Mouth of Dr. Tenison Rector of St. Martines, who with
the Bishops of Ely and Bath and Wells, was one of the divines his
Majestie sent to him, and were at the execution: Thus ended this
quondam Duke, darling of his Father, and the Ladys, being
extraordi[na]rily handsome, and adroit: an excellent souldier, and
dauncer, a favorite of the people, of an Easy nature, debauched by
lust, seduc'd by crafty knaves who would have set him up onely to
make a property; tooke this opportunity of his Majestie being of

another Religion, to gather a party of discontented; failed of it, and perished: He was a lovely person, had a vertuous and excellent Lady that brought him greate riches and a second Dukedome in Scotland; Was Master of the Horse, Gen. of the K. his fathers Army, Gent: of the Bed chamber: Knight of the Garter, Chancellor of Camb: in a Word had accumulations without end: Se what Ambition and want of principles brought him to. He was beheaded on Tuesday the 14th July: His mother (whose name was Barlow, daughter of some very meane Creatures) was a beautifull strumpet, whom I had often seene at Paris, and died miserably, without anything to bury her: Yet had this Perkin ben made believe, the King had married her: which was a monstrous forgerie, and ridiculous: and to satisfie the world the iniquitie of the report, the King his father (if his Father he realy were, for he most resembld one Sidny familiar with his mother) publiquely and most solemnly renounced it, and caused it to be so entred in the Council booke some yeares since, with the Privy Counsel[o]rs attestation.

. . .

19 Our Viccar absent, preached a stranger on 1: Cor: 16. 13 shewing the necessity of Armour and Christian vigilancy, with a long narrative of the Disloyaltie of our late Rebellions and the mischiefe of their principles:—

. . .

Troops from Holland

I went the Saturday before to see the Muster of the 6 Scotch and Eng: Regiments, whom the Pr: of Orange had lately sent his Majestie out of Holland, upon this rebellion, but were now returning, having had no occasion to make use of them: They were all excellently clad, and perfectly disciplined, and were incamped on Black-heath most formaly with their Tents: The King and Queene etc: being come to see them exercise and the manner of Encamping, which was very neate and magnificent.

By a grosse mistake of the Secretary of his Majesties forces, they had ben ordred to quarter in private Houses (which was contrary to an Act of Parliament) but upon my informing his Majestie timely of it, it was prevented:

The two horse-men which My Son and myselfe sent into the County Troopes, were now come home, after neere a moneths being out, to our extraordinary charge . . .

. . .

Elizabeth Evelyn's Escapade

27 This night when we were all asleepe went my Daughter Eliz: away, to meete a young fellow, nephew to Sir Jo: Tippet (Surveyor of the Navy: and one of the Commissioners) whom she married the next day being Tuesday; without in the least acquainting either her parents, or any soule in the house: I was the more afflicted and [astonish'd] at it, in reguard, we had never given this Child the least cause to be thus dissobedient, and being now my Eldest, might reasonably have expected a double Blessing: But it afterward appeared, that this Intrigue had ben transacted by letters long before, and [when] she was with my Lady Burton in Licester shire, and by private meetings neere my house: She of all our Children had hitherto given us least cause of suspicion; not onely for that she was yet young, but seemed the most flattering, souple and observant; of a silent and particular humor; in no sort [betraying] the levity and Inclination which is commonly apparent in Children who fall into these snares; having ben bred-up with the uttmost Circumspection, as to principles of severest honour and Piety: But so far it seemes, had her passion for this Young fellow made her forget her duty, and all that most Indulgent Parents expected from her, as not to consider the Consequence of her folly and dissobedience, 'til it was too late: This Affliction went very neere me and my Wife, neither of us yet well compos'd for the untimely losse of that incomparable and excellent Child, which it pleased God to take from us by the small pox a few moneths before: But this farther Chastizement was to be humbly submitted to, as a part of the burden God was pleased to lay farther upon us; in this yet the lesse afflictive, That we had not ben wanting in giving her an Education every way becoming us: We were most of all astonish'd at the suddainesse of this action, and the privatenesse of its manegement; the Circumstances also Consider'd and quality, how it was possible she should be flattered so to her dissadvantage: He being in no condition sortable to hers, and the Blessing we intended her: The thing has given us much disquiet, I pray God

direct us, how to govern our Resentments of her dissobedience; and if it be his will, bring good out of all this Ill:

Aug: 2 So had this Affliction descompos'd us, that I could not be well at Church the next Lords day; though I had prepared for the B: Sacrament: I hope God will be more gracious to my onely remaining Child, whom I take to be of a more discreete, sober and religious temper: that we may have that comfort from her, which is deny'd us in the other:

This Accident caus'd me to alter my Will; as was reasonable; for though there may be a reconciliation upon her repentance, and that she has suffer'd for her folly; yet I must let her see what her undutifullnesse in this action, deprives her of; as to the provision she else might have expected; solicitous as she knew I now was of bestowing her very worthily:

. . .

Its Tragic Sequel

16 Came newes to us that my undutifull daughter was visited with the small-pox, now universaly very contagious: I was yet willing my Wife should go visite and take care of her:

. . .

22 I went to Lond, to see my unhappy Child, now in greate danger, and carried our Viccar with me, that according to her earnest desire, (being very sensible and penitent for her fault) he might administer to her the H: Sacrament, which he did; and after some time, and her greate submissions and agonies, leaving her to the mercys of God, and her mother with her I returned in the Evening . . .

. . .

28 My poore unhappy Daughters sickness increasing, a violent feavor succeeding when her other distemper appeared to be past danger; I went up againe to see, and comfort her, together with our Minister: My disconsolate Wife I left with her, who had ben almost all her sicknesse with her; so I return'd home in greate doubt how God would deale with her, whom the next morning he was pleased to take out of this vale of misery, I humbly trust, to his infinite mercy, though to our unspeakeable affliction, loosing another Child in the flower of her age, who had never 'til now given us cause of any displeasure, but many hopes of Comfort: and thus in lesse than

6 moneths were we depriv'd of two Children for our unworthin-esse, and causes best known to God, whom I beseech from the bottome of my heart that he will give us grace to make that right use of all these chastisements that we may become better, and intirely submitt in all things to his infinite wise disposal. She departed this life on [Saturday] 29: Aug: at 8 in the Morning: fell sick and died on the same day of the weeke, that my other most deare and dutifull daughter did, and as also one of my servants (a very pious youth) had don the yeare before: I beseech God of his mercy Sanctifie this and all other Afflictions and dispensations to me. His holy will be don Amen.

30 This sad accident kept me from the publique service this day being Sonday.

My Child was buried by her sister on 2d September in the Church of Deptford:

Commissioner of the Privy Seal

The 3 of Sep: I went to Lond, being sent to by a Letter from my Lord Clarendon (Lord privy-seale) to let me know that his majestie being pleased to send him Lord Lieutennant into Ireland, was also pleased to Nominate me one of the Commissioners to execute the office of Privy-Seale during his Lieutenancy there: It behoving me 4 to waite upon his Majestie and to give him thanks for his greate honor (returning home that Evening) I accompanied his Lordship 5 the next morning to Windsore (dining by the Way at Sir Hen: Capels at Cue) where his Majestie receiving me with extraordinary kindnesse, I kissed his hands: I told him how sensible I was of his Majesties gracious favour to me: that I would endeavour to serve him with all sincerity, dilligence and loyalty, not more out of my duty, than Inclinations: He said, he doubted not of it, and was glad he had this opportunity to shew the kindnesse he had for me: After this came aboundance of the greate Men to give me Joy, particularly L: Tressurer, L: Sunderland, L. Peterborrow, L: Godolphin, L: Falkland and every body at Court who knew me . . .
. . .

With Pepys to Portsmouth

15 I went to Lond: accomp[a]nied Mr. Pepys (Secretary of the Admiralty) to Portsmouth, Whither his Majestie was going the first

time since his coming to the Crowne, to see in what state the Fortifications were. Wee tooke Coach and 6 horses, late after din[n]er, yet got to Bagshot that night: whilst supper was making ready I went and made a Visite to Mrs. Grahames, some time Maide of honor to the queen Dowager, now wife to Ja: Gr: Esquire of the Privie-purse to the King: her house being a Walke in the Forest, within a little quarter of a mile from Bagshot Towne: very importunate she was that I would sup, and abide there that night; but being oblig'd by my companion, I return'd to our Inn, after she had shew'd me her house which was very commodious, and well furnish'd, as she was an excellent housewife, a prudent and vertuous Lady: There is a parke full of red deare about it: Her eldest son, was now sick there of the small pox, but in a likely way of recovery; and other of her Children ran about, and among the infected, which she said she let them do on purpose that they might whilst young, passe that fatal disseasse, which she fancied they were to undergo one time or other, and that this would be the best: The severity of this cruel disseasse so lately in my poore family confirming much of what she affirm'd:

The King at Winchester: Pepys's Tact

16 The next morning early seting out, we ariv'd early enough at Winchester to waite on the King, who was lodg'd at the Deanes, (Dr. Megot) I found very few with him besides my Lord Feversham, Arran, Newport, and the Bishop of Bath and Wells to whom his Majestie was discoursing concerning Miracles, and what strange things the Saludadors would do in Spaine, as by creeping into heated ovens without hurt etc: and that they had a black Crosse in the roofe of their mouthes: but yet were commonly, notorious and prophane wretches: upon which his Majestie farther said, that he was so extreamely difficult of Miracles, for feare of being impos'd on, that if he should chance to see one himselfe, without some other wittnesse, he should apprehend it some delusion of his senses: Then they spake of the boy who was pretended to have had a wanting leg restor'd him, so confidently asserted by Fr: de Santa Clara, and others: To all which the Bishop added a greate Miracle happning in that Citty of Winchester to his certaine knowledge, of a poore miserably sick and decrepit Child, (as I remember long kept un-baptized) who immediately on his Baptisme, recover'd; as also

of the sanatory effect of K. Charles his Majesties fathers blood, in
healing one that was blind: As to that of the Saludador (of which
likewise I remember Sir Arthir Hopton, formerly Ambassador at
Madrid had told me many like wonders) Mr. Pepys passing through
Spaine, and being extreamely Inquisitive of the truth of these
pretended miracles of the Saludadors; found a very famous one of
them at last, whom he offered a considerable reward to, if he would
make a trial of the Oven, or any other thing of that kind, before
him: The fellow ingenuously told him, that, finding he was a more
than ordinary curious person, he would not deceive him, and so
accknowledg'd that he could do none of those feates, realy; but that
what they pretended, was all a cheate, which he would easily
discover, though the poore superstitious people were imposed
upon: yet have these Impostors, an allowance of the Bishops, to
practise th[e]ir Juggleings: This Mr. Pepys affirm'd to me; but said
he, I did not conceive it fit, to interrupt his Majestie, who told what
they pretended to do, so solemnly: Then there was something said
of the second-sight, happning to some persons, especialy Scotch:
Upon which both his Majestie and (I think) my Ld: Arran, told us,
that Monsieur   a French Nobleman lately here in
England, seeing the late Duke of Monmoth, come into the
Play-house at Lond: suddainly cryed out to some sitting in the
same box: 'Voila Messieurs comme il entre sans tete':

Charles II a Crypto-Catholic?

After this his Majestie speaking of some Reliques, that had effected
strange cures, particularly a Thorne of our B: S: Crosse; that
healed a Gentlewomans rotten nose by onely touching; and
speaking of the Golden Crosse and Chaine taken out of the Coffin
of St. Edward the Confessor at Westminster, by one of the
singing-men, who as the scaffolds were taking-down, after his
Majesties Coronation, espying an hole in the Tomb, and something
glisten; put his hand in, and brought it to the Deane, and he to the
King: his Majestie began to put the Bishop in mind, how earnestly
the late King (his brother) call'd upon him, during his Agonie, to
take out what he had in his pocckett: See Feb: 6: I had thought
(says the King) it had ben for some keys, which might lead to some
Cabinets, which his Majestie would have me secure; but (says he)
you well remember that I found nothing in any of his pockets but

onely a Crosse of Gold, and a few insignificant papers; and thereupon shewed us the Crosse, and was pleased to put it into my hand; it was of Gold about 3 Inches long, having on one side a Crucifix enameled and embossed, the rest was graved and garnished with gold-smith worke and two pretty broad table Amethists (as I conceived) and at the bottome a pendant pearle; within was inchas'd a little fragment (as was thought) of the true Crosse: and a latine Inscription, in Gotic and roman letters: How his Majestie came by it I do not remember; for more company coming in this discourse ended: Onely I may not forget, a Resolution which his Majestie there made, and had a little before entered upon it, at the Counsel board at Windsor or White-hal: That the Negros in the Plantations should all be Baptized, exceedingly declaiming against that impiety, of their Masters prohibiting it, out of a mistaken opinion, that they were then *ipso facto* free: But his Majestie persists in his resolution to have them Christn'd, which piety the Bishop, deservedly blessed him for; and so I went out, to see the New Palace his late Majestie had began, and brought almost to the Covering: It was placed on the side of the Hill, where formerly stood the old Castle; a stately fabrique of 3 sides, and a Corridor, all built of brique, and Cornished, windoes, Columns at the break and Entrance, of freestone: intended for a Hunting House, when his Majestie came to those parts, and having an incomparable prospect: I believe there had already ben 20000 pounds and more expended; but his now Majestie did not seeme to encourage the finishing of it; at least for a while; and it is like to stand: Hence I went to see the Cathedrall, a reverend pile, and in good repaire: There is still the Coffines of the 6 Saxon kings, whose bones had ben scattered by the sacrilegious Rebells of 1641, in expectation (I suppose) of finding some valuable Reliques; and afterward gather'd-up againe and put into new chests, which stand above the stalls of the Quire: Here lies the body of their Founder, of Card: and severall other Bishops etc: and so I went to my Lodging, very wett, it having rained the whole day:

The King at Portsmouth

17 Early next morning we went to Portsmouth, some thing before his Majestie arived: we found all the way full of people, the Women in their best dresse, multitudes of all sorts, in expectance of

seeing his Majestie passe by, which he did, riding on horse-back, a good part of the way: We found the Major, his Aldermen with their Mace, and in their formalities standing at the Entrance of the Fort, a Mile on this side the Towne, where he made a speech to the King, and then went off the Guns of the fort, as did all those of the Garison, so soone as he was come into Portsmouth, all the souldiers (which were neere 3000) drawn up, and lining the streetes, and platforme to Gods-house (which is the name of the Governors house) where (after his Majestie had viewed the new Fortifications, and Ship-yard) he was Entertained at a Magnificent dinner, by Sir   Slingsby, the Lieutenant Governor; all the Gent: of any quality, in his traine setting downe at Table with him, and which I also had don, had I not ben before engag'd to Sir Robert Holmes (Governor of the Isle of Wight) to dine with him at a private house, where likewise we had a very sumptuous and plentifull repast of excellent Venison, Fowle, Fish, fruit, and what not: After dinner I went to waite on his Majestie againe, who was pulling on his boots in the Towne hall joyning to the house where he dined, and then having saluted some Ladys etc: that came to kisse his hand; he tooke horse for Winchester, whither he returned that night: This hall is artificialy hung round, with Armes of all sorts, like the Hall and keepe of Windsor, which looks very finely:

I went hence to see the Ship-yard, and Dock, the Fortifications, and other things; What I learned was, the facility of an armies taking the Ile of Wight, should an attempt be made by any Enemy, for want of due care in fortifying some places of it, and the plenty of the Iland, able to nourish 20000 men, besides its inhabitants: Portsmouth when finished will be very strong, and a Noble Key: There were now 32 Men of war in the Harbour: I was invited by Sir R: Beach, the [Commissioner] where after a greate supper, Mr. Secretary and my selfe lay-all that night: and the next morning set out for Gildford 18 where we arived in goode houre, and so the day after to Lond: whence 19 taking leave of Mr. Pepys, I came home to my house, after a journey of 140 miles:

I had twice before ben at Portsmouth, Ile of Wight etc: many yeares since: I found this part of Hampshire bravely wooded; especialy about the house and estate of Coll: Norton, who (though now in being, having formerly made his peace by meanes of Coll Legg) was formerly a very fierce Commander in the first

Rebellion: His house is large, and standing low, as one goes from Winchester to [Portsmouth]:

By what I observed in this Journey; I find that infinite industry, sedulity, gravity, and greate understanding and experience of affaires in his Majestie, that I cannot but predict much happinesse to the Nation, as to its political Government, and if he so persist (as I am confident he will) there could nothing be more desired, to accomplish our prosperity, but that he were of the national Religion: for certainely such a Prince never had this Nation since it was one:

. . .

Pepys Makes a Revelation

[October] 2 I spent this morning in Devotion, preparing for the Communion, when having a letter sent me by Mr. Pepys, with this expression at the foote of it: 'I have something to shew you, that I may not have againe another time': etc and that I would not faile to dine with him: I went accordingly: After dinner he had me, and one Mr. Houblon (a very rich and considerable Merchant, whose Fathers had fled out of Flanders upon the persecution of the Duke of Alva) into a private roome: and being sate downe, told us that being lately alone with his Majestie and upon some occasion of speaking concerning my late Lord Arlingtons dying a R: Cath, who had all along seemed to professe himselfe a Protestant, taken all the Tests etc: 'til the day (I think) of his death: His Majestie say'd, that as to his inclinations he had known him long wavering, but [for] feare of loosing his places he did not think convenient to declare himselfe: There are (says the King) who believe the Ch: of R: gives Dispensations, for going to church, and many like things; but that it was not so; for if that might have ben had, he himselfe had most reason to make use of it: Indeede he said, As to some Matrimonial Cases, there are now and then Dispensations, but hardly in any Cases else: This familiar discourse encourag'd Mr. P: to beg of his Majestie (if he might aske it, without offence, and for that his Majestie could not but observe how it was whispered among many), whither his Late Majestie had ben reconcil'd to the C. of Rome: He againe humbly besought his Majestie to pardon his presumption, if he had touch'd upon a thing, did not befit him to looke into etc: The King ingenuously told him, That he both was, and died a

R: Cath: and that he had not long since declared it was upon some politic and state reasons, best known to himself (meaning the King his Brother) but that he was of that persuasion, he bid him follow him into his Closett, where opening a Cabinet, he shew'd him two papers, containing about a quarter of a sheete on both sides, written in the late Kings owne hand, severall Arguments opposite to the Doctrine of the Church of Eng: Charging her with heresy, novelty, and the phan[tas]ticisme of other Protestants: The chiefe whereoff (as I remember) were, our refusing to accknowledge the Primacy and Infallibility etc of the Church of Rome, how impossible it was so many Ages should never dispute it, til of late; how unlikely our B: Saviour would leave his Church without a Visible Head and guide to resort to during his absence, with the like usual Topics; so well penn'd as to the discourse, as did by no means seeme to me, to have ben put together by the Late King: Yet written all with his owne hand, blotted, and interlin'd, so as if indeede, it were not given him by some Priest; they happly might be such Arguments and reasons as had ben inculcated from time to time, and here recollected, and in the conclusion shewing his looking on the Protestant Religion, (and by name the Church of Eng:) to be without foundation, and consequently false and unsafe: When his Majestie had shew'd him these Originals, he was pleas'd to lend him the Copies of those two Papers, attested at the bottome in 4 or 5 lines, under his owne hand: These were the papers I saw and read: This nice and curious passage I thought fit to set down;

A Doubtful Conclusion

Though all the Arguments, and objections were altogether weake, and have a thousand times ben Answerd irreplicably by our Divines; though such as their Priests insinuate among their Proselytes, as if nothing were Catholique but the C. of Rome, no salvation out of that, no Reformation sufferable etc: botoming all their Errors on St. Peters Successors unerrable dictatorship; but proving nothing with any sort of Reason, or the taking notice of any Objection which could be made against it: Here was all taken for granted, and upon it a Resolution and preference implied: I was heartily sorry to see all this; though it were no other, than what was long suspected, by his late Majesties too greate indifference, neglect and course of Life, that he had ben perverted, and for secular respects onely, profess'd to be of another beliefe . . . and thereby giving infinite advantage to our Adversaries, both the Court, and generaly the Youth, and greate persons of the nation becoming dissolute and highly prophane; God was incensed to make his Reigne very troublesome and improsperous, by Warrs, plagues, fires, losse of reputation by a universal neglect of the publique, for the love of a voluptuous and sensual life, which a vitious Court had brought into credit. I thinke of it with sorrow and pitty, when I consider of how good and debonaire a nature that unhappy prince was, what opportunities he had to have made himselfe the most renouned King, that ever sway'd the British Scepter; had he ben firme to that Church, for which his Martyred and Bl: Father suffer'd; and gratefull to Almighty God, who so miraculously Restor'd him, with so excellent a Religion had he endeavored to owne and propagate it, as he should, not onely for the good of his Kingdomes, but all the Reformed Churches in Christendome, now weaken'd, and neere utterly ruind, through our remissnesse, and suffering them to be supplanted, persecuted and destroyed; as in France, which we tooke no notice of: The Consequence of this time will shew, and I wish it may proceede no farther: The Emissaries and Instruments of the C. of R: will never rest, 'til they have crush'd the Church of Eng: as knowing that alone able to cope with them: and that they can never answer her fairely, but lie aboundantly open to [irresistible] force of her Arguments, Antiquity, and purity of her doctrine: so that albeit it may move God (for the punishment of a Nation so unworthy) to eclipse againe the profession of her here; and darknesse and superstition prevaile; I am most confident the Doctrine of the Church of Eng: will never be extinguish'd, but remaine Visible, though not Eminent, to the consummation of the World: I have innumerable reasons that confirme me in this opinion, which I forbeare to mention here: In the meane time, as to This discourse of his Majestie with Mr. Pepys, and those Papers; as I do exceedingly preferr his Majesties free and ingenuous profession, of what his owne Religion is, beyond all Concealements upon any politique accounts what so ever; so I thinke him of a most sincere, and honest nature, one upon whose word, one may relie, and that he makes a Conscience of what he promises, to performe it: In this Confidence I hope, the Church of England may yet subsist; and when it shall please God, to open his Eyes, and turne his heart (for that is peculiarly in the Lords hands) to flourish also: In all events, whatever do become of the C. of Eng: It is certainely of all the Christian Professions on the Earth, the most Primitive, Apostolical, and Excellent:

. . .

Swallowfield, Berkshire

[October] 22 I accompanied my Lady Clarendon to her house at Swallowfield in Berkeshire, dining by the way at Mr. Grahams's Lodge at Bagshot: Where his Lady (my excellent and long acquaintance when maide of honour) entertain'd us at a plentifull dinner: The house, new repaired, and capacious of a good family, stands in a Park: Hence we went to Swallow-fild the house is after the antient building of honourable gent: houses where they kept up the antient hospitality: but the Gardens and Waters as elegant as 'tis possible to make a flat, with art and Industrie and no meane Expenses, my Lady being so extraordinarily skilld in the flowry part: and the dilligence of my Lord in the planting: so that I have hardly seene a seate which shews more toakens of it, then what is here to be found, not onely in the delicious and rarest fruits of a Garden, but in those innumerable and plentifull furniture of the grounds about the seate of timber trees to the incredible ornament and benefit of the place: There is one Ortchard of a 1000 Golden and other cider Pepins: Walks and groves of Elms, Limes, Oake: and other trees: and the Garden so beset with all manner of sweete shrubbs, as perfumes the aire marvelously: The distribution also of the Quarters, Walks, Parterre etc is excellent: The Nurseries, Kitchin-garden, full of the most desireable plants; two very noble Orangeries well furnish'd; but above all, The Canale, and fishponds, the one fed with a white, the other with a black-running water, fed by a swift and quick river: so well and plentifully stor'd with fish, that for Pike, Carp, Breame, and Tench; I had never seene any thing approching it: We had Carps and Pike etc of size fit for the table of a Prince, every meale, and what added to the delight, the seeing hundreds taken in the drag, out of which the Cooke standing by, we pointed what we had most mind to, and had Carps every meale, that had ben worth at London twenty shill a piece: The Waters are all flag'd about with Calamus arromaticus;

of which my Lady has hung a Closset, that retaines the smell very perfectly: Also a certaine sweete willow and other exotics: There is to this a very fine bowling-greene; Meadow, pasture, Wood, in a word all that can render a Country seate delightfull:

. . .

An Unpractical Chariot

28 I went to the R: Society, being the first meeting after our Summer recesse, and was very full: An Urn full of bones, was presented, for the repository, dug up in an high way, by the repairers of it: in a field in Camberwell in Surry: This Urn and cover was found intire among many others, believed to be truely Roman and antient: Sir Ri: Bulkeley, described to us a model of a Charriot he had invented, which it was not possible to overthrow, in whatsoever uneven way it was drawn: giving us a stupendious relation, of what it had perform'd in that kind; for Ease, expedition, and Safty: There was onely these inconveniences yet to be remedied; that it would not containe above one person; That it was ready to fire every 10 miles, and being plac'd and playing on no fewer than 10 rollers, made so prodigious noise, as was almost intollerable: These particulars the Virtuosi were desir'd to excogitate the remedies, to render the Engine of extraordinary Use: etc:

Judge Jeffreys Again

31 I dind at our great Lord Chancellors, who us'd me with greate respect: This was the late L: C. Justice Jeofries, who had ben newly the Western Circuite, to trie the Monmoth Conspirators; and had formerly don such severe Justice amongst the obnoxious in Westminster Hall etc for which his Majestie dignified him with creating him first a Baron, and now L. Chancellor: He had some yeares past, ben conversant at Deptford: is of an assur'd and undaunted spirit, and has serv'd the Court Interest upon all the hardiest occasions: of nature cruell and a slave of this Court.

. . .

Huguenots Persecuted

[November] 3 I returned home: The French persecution of the Protestants, raging with uttmost barbarity, exceeding what the very heathens used: Innumerable persons of the greatest birth, and riches, leaving all their earthly substance and hardly escaping with their lives, dispers'd thro' all the Countries of Europe: The Fr: Tyrant, abrogating the Edicts of Nants etc in favour of them, and without any Cause on the suddaine, demolishing all their Churches, banishing, Imprisoning, sending to the Gallies all the Ministers: plundring the common people, and exposing them to all sorts of barbarous usage, by souldiers sent to ruine and prey upon them; taking away their children; forcing people to the Masse, and then executing them as Relapsers: They burnt the libraries, pillag'd their goods, eate up their filds and sustenance, banish'd or sent to the Gallies the people, and seiz'd on their Estates: There had now ben numbred to passe through Geneva onely, from time to time by stealth onely (for all the usual passages were strictly guarded by sea and land) fourty thousand, towards Swisserland: In Holland, Denmark, and all about Germany, were dispersed some hundred thousands besids here in England, where though multitude of all degrees sought for shelter, and wellcome, as distressed Christians and Confessors, they found least encouragement; by a fatality of the times we were fall'n into, and the incharity and indifference of such, as should have embrac'd them: and I pray, it be not laied to our Charge: The famous Claude fled to Holland: Alex and severall more came to Lond: and persons of mighty estates came over who had forsaken all: But France was almost dispeopled, the bankers so broaken that the Tyrants revenue exceedingly diminished: Manufacture ceased, and every body there save the Jesuites etc. abhorring what was don: nor the Papists themselves approving it; what the intention farther is time will shew, but doubtlesse portending some extraordinary revolution: I was now shew'd the Harangue that the Bishop of Valentia on Rhone, made in the name of the Cleargie, celebrating the Fr: King (as if he were a God) for his persecuting the poore protestants; with this Expression in it: That as his Victories over Heresy was greater than all the Conquests of Alexander and Cæsars etc: it was but what was wished in England: and that God seem'd to raise the French King to this power and magnanimous action, that he might be in capacity to assist the doing of the same here: This paragraph is very bold and remarkable; severall reflecting on Æ: Ushers Prophecy as now begun in France, and approching the orthodox in all other reformed Churches: etc: One thing was much taken notice of, That the Gazetts which were still constantly printed twice a weeke, and informing us what was don all Europ over etc: never all this time, spake one syllable of this wonderfull proceeding in France, nor was any Relation of it published by any, save what private letters and the persecuted fugitives brought: Whence this silence, I list not to conjecture, but it appeared very extraordinary in a Protestant Countrie, that we should know nothing of what Protestants suffered etc: whilst greate Collections were made for them in forraine places more hospitable and Christian to appearance.

5 It being an extraordinary wett morning, and I indisposed by a very greate rheume, I could not go to Church this day, to my greate sorrow, it being the first Gunpouder conspiracy Anniversary, that had ben kept now this 80 yeares, under a Prince of the Roman Religion: Bonfires forbidden etc: What dos this portend?

. . .

A Standing Army

9 Began the Parliament; The King in his Speech requiring continuance of a standing force in stead of a Militia, and indemnity and dispensation to Popish Officers from the Test; Demands very unexpected and unpleasing to the Commons; He also requir'd a Supply of Revenue, which they granted; but returned no thanks to the King for his Speech 'til farther consideration:

. . .

12 The Commons postpon'd the finishing the bill for the Supply, to consider of the Test, and popish Officers: this was carried but by one voice:

. . .

20 Was the Parliament adjourn'd to ffeb: Severall both of Lords and Commons, excepting against some passage of his Majesties Speech, relating to the Test, and continuance of Popish Officers in Command: This was a greate surprize to a Parliament, which people believed would have complied in all things:

. . .

Pepys Continues President of the Royal Society

30 To Lond: it being St. Andrews the Patron of the R: Societies day: to choose Officers for the ensewing yeare: which we did,

continuing our former President Mr. Pepys, who had ben a bountifull benefactor to us: There was a very full meeting: . . .

A Venetian Embassy

[December] 18 I dind at the greate entertainement his Majestie gave the Venetian Ambassadors Signors Zenno and Justiniani, accompanied with 10 more Noble Venetians of their most illustrious families Cornaro, Maccenigo etc, who came to Congratulate their Majesties coming to the Crowne etc: The dinner was one of the most magnificent and plentifull that I have ever seene, at 4 severall Tables with Music, Trumpets, Ketle-drums etc which sounded upon a whistle at every health: The banquet was 12 vast Chargers pild up so high, as those who sat one against another could hardly see one another, of these Sweetemeates which doub[t]lesse were some dayes piling up in that exquisite manner, the Ambassadors touched not, but leaving them to the Spectators who came in Curiosity to see the dinner, etc were exceedingly pleas'd to see in what a moment of time, all that curious work was demolish'd, and the Comfitures etc voided and table clear'd: Thus his Majestie entertain'd them 3 dayes, which (for the table onely) cost him 600 pounds as the Cleark of the Greene-Cloth Sir W: Boreman, assur'd me: Dinner ended, I saw their procession or Cavalcade to W:hall, inumerable Coaches attending: The 2 Ambassadors had 4. Coaches of their owne and 50 footemen, as I remember, besides other Equipage as splended as the occasion would permitt, the Court being still in mourning . . .

Duelling

[1686. February 20] Many bloody and notorious duels were fought about this time, The D: of Grafton kill'd Mr. Stanley, bro: to the E: of Shrewsbery, indeede upon an almost unsufferable provocation: It is hop'd his Majestie will now at last, severely remedy this unchristian Custome: . . .

A Marriage Proposal Fails

March 1 Came Sir Gilb: Gerrard to treate with me about his

sonns marying my Daughter Susanna; The father being obnoxious, and in some suspicion and displeasure of the King, I would receive no proposal, 'til his Majestie had given me leave, which he was pleas'd to do: but after severall meetings, we brake off, upon his not being willing to secure any thing competant for my daughter[s] Children: besides that I found his estate to be most of it in the Coale-pits as far as N. Castle, and leases from the Bishop of Durrham, who had power to make concurrent Leases with other difficulties, so as we did not proceede to any conclusion:

. . .

Anglican Censorship

[May 9] The Duke of Savoy, instigated by the French [king], put to the sword many of his protestant subjects: No faith in Princes.

12 To Lond: Memorand, I refus'd to put the P: Seale to Dr. Walker[s] licence for the printing and publishing divers Popish Books etc: of which I complain'd both to my L: of Canterbury (whom I went to advise with, which was in the Council-chamber) and to my Lord Treasurer that evening at his lodging: My Lord of Cantorburies advise was that I should follow my owne Conscience therein; my L: Tressurer, that if in Conscience I could dispence with it; for any other hazard, he believed there was none: Notwithstanding which I persisted not to do it:

. . .

'Unhappy, unthankfull people!'

16 A stranger on: 2: Zeph: 1. 2. 3. Afternoone, on: 2. Tit: 11. 12 etc: both practical sermons exhorting to Repentance upon prospect of the ruines threating the Church, and drawing on for our prodigious Ingratitude, and doubtlesse Never was England so perverted, through an almost universal face of prophanesse, perjury, luxurie, unjustice, violence, hypocrisie, Atheisme, and dissolution: A kingdome and people so obliged to God, for its long prosperity, both in Church and state: so signaly delivered, and preserved: and now threatn'd to be destroyed, by our owne folly and wickednesse: How strangely is this nation fallen from its antient zeale and Integritie! ô unhappy, unthankfull people!

. . .

Lawyers' Tricks

[November] 26 I din'ed at my L. Chancelors, where being 3 other Serjants at Law, after dinner being cherefull and free, they told their severall stories, how long they had detained their clients in tedious processes, by their tricks, as if so many highway thieves should have met and discovered the severall purses they had taken: This they made but a jeast of: but God is not mocked:
...

Louis XIV 'patch'd up'

[1687. January] 5 The French K. now sayd to be healed or rather patch'd up of the fistula in Ano, for which he had ben severall times cutt: etc: The persecution still raging:

'A world of mysterious Ceremony'

I was to heare the Musique of the Italians in the new Chapel, now first of all opned at White-hall publiquely for the Popish Service: Nothing can be finer than the magnificent Marble work and Architecture at the End, where are 4 statues representing st. Joh: st. Petre, st. Paule, and the Church, statues in white marble, the worke of Mr. Gibbons, with all the carving and Pillars of exquisite art and greate cost: The history or Altar piece is the Salutation, The Volto, in *fresca*, the Asumption of the blessed Virgin according to their Traditions with our B: Saviour, and a world of figures, painted by Verio. The Thrones where the K. and Q: sits is very glorious in a Closset above just opposite to the Altar: Here we saw the Bishop in his Miter, and rich Copes, with 6 or 7: Jesuits and others in Rich Copes richly habited, often taking off, and putting on the Bishops Miter, who sate in a Chaire with Armes pontificaly, was adored, and censed by 3 Jesuits in their Copes, then he went to the Altar and made divers Cringes there, censing the Images, and glorious Tabernacle placed upon the Altar, and now and then changing place; The Crosier (which was of silver) put into his hand, with a world of mysterious Ceremony the Musique pla[y]ing and singing: and so I came away: not believing I should ever have lived to see such things in the K. of Englands palace, after it had pleas'd God to inlighten this nation; but our greate sinn, has (for the present) Eclips'd the Blessing, which I hope he will in mercy and his good time restore to its purity. This was on the 29 of December:

. . .

Jesus Defend his little flock

[17] Greate expectations of severall greate-mens declaring themselves Papists: and L: Tyrconell gon to succeede my Lord Lieutennant in Ireland, to the astonishment of all sober men, and to the evident ruine of the Protestants in that Kingdome, as well as of its greate Improvement: Much discourse that all the White-staff-Officers and others should be dismissed for adhering to their Religion: Popish Justices of Peace established in all Counties of the meanest of the people: Judges ignorant of the Law, and perverting it: so furiously does the Jesuite drive, and even compell Princes to violent courses, and distruction of an excellent Government both in Church and State: God of his infinite mercy open our Eyes, and turne our hearts, Establish his Truth, with peace: the L: Jesus Defend his little flock, and preserve this threatned church and Nation.

. . .

Christ's Hospital Flourishing

[March 13] I went this Evening to see the order of the Boys and children at Christs hospital, there was neere 800 of them, Boys and Girles: so decently clad, cleanely lodged, so wholesomly fed, so admirably taught, some the Mathematics, Especialy the 40 of the late Kings foundation; that I was plainly astonished to see the progresse some little youths of 13 and 14 years of age, had made: I saw them at supper, visited their dormitories, admired the order, Oeconomie, and excellent government of this most charitable seminary: The rest, some are tought for the Universitie, others designed for seamen, all for Trades and Callings: The Girles instructed in all such worke as became their Sex, and as might fit them to make good Wives, Mistresses, and a blessing to their generation: They sung a Psalme before they sat downe to supper in the greate hall, to an Organ which played all the time, and sung with that cherefull harmony, as seem'd to me a vision of heavenly Angels: and I came from the place with infinite Satisfaction, having never in my life seene a more noble, pious, and admirable Charity:

All these consisting of Orphans onely: The foundation (which has also had and still has many Benefactors) was of that pious Prince, K. Edward the 6: whose picture, (held to be an Original of Holbeins) is in the Court, where the Governors meete to consult of the affaires of the Hospital, and his stat[u]e in White-marble stands in a Nich of the Wall below, as you go to the Church which is a modern noble and ample fabric.

'Mischiefe-doing engines'

16 I made a step home, 10th Saw the trial of those devlish murdering mischiefe-doing engines Bombs, shot out of the Morter piece on black-heath: The distance that they are cast, the destruction they make where ever they fall is most prodigious:

. . .

Music with Mr Pepys

[April] 19 I heard the famous Singer the Eunuch Cifacca, esteemed the best in Europe and indeede his holding out and delicatenesse in extending and loosing a note with that incomparable softnesse, and sweetenesse was admirable: For the rest, I found him a meere wanton, effeminate child; very Coy, and prowdly conceited to my apprehension: He touch'd the Harpsichord to his Voice rarely well, and this was before a select number of some particular persons whom Mr. Pepys (Secretary of the Admiralty and a greate lover of Musick) invited to his house, where the meeting was, and this obtained by peculiar favour and much difficulty of the Singer, who much disdained to shew his talent to any but Princes:

. . .

'Patheticaly perswading to patience'

[24] Pomerid: at Greenewich the Curate on 5. Mat: 5: After this, I staied to heare the French sermon, which succeded (in the same place, and after use of the English Liturgie translated into French) the congregation consisting of about 100 French Protestants refugiès from the Persecution, of which Monsieur de Rouvigny (present) was the chiefe, and had obtain'd the use of the Church after the Parish had ended their owne Service etc: The Preachers text was 16: Psal: 11, patheticaly perswading to patience, constancy

and relyance on God, for the comfort of his Grace, amidst all their Sufferings, and the infinite reward to come:

...

'Stupid folly'

[May] 2 I dined at Myn heere Dickvelts the Holland Ambassadors: a prudent and worthy person: There din'd, my Lord Middleton Prin[ci]pal Secretary of state; Lord Pembrock, L: Lumly, L. Preston, Coll Fitz-Patrick, Sir J: Chardin: After dinner the Ambassador discoursed of and deplored the stupid folly of our Politics, in suffering the French to take Luxembourg: it being a place of the most concerne to have ben defended for the Interest of not onely the Netherlands, but of England also:

...

A Rich Prize

[June 12] There was about this time brought into the Downes, a Vast treasure which after 45 yeares being sunk in a Spanish Galioon, which perish'd somewhere neere Hispaniola or B[a]hama Ilands coming home; was now weighed up, by certaine Gentlemen and others, who were at the Charge of Divers etc: to the suddaine enriching of them, beyond all expectation: The Duke of Albemarles share came (tis believed) to 50000, and some private Gent: who adventured but 100 pounds and little more, to ten, 18000 pounds, and proportionably; his Majesties tenth to 10000 pounds:

The Camp was now againe pitch'd at Hounslow, The Commanders profusely vying in the expense and magnificence of Tents:

Toleration for Dissenters: 'refined Quakers'

16 I went to Lond: thence to Hampton-Court . . . Whilst I was in the Council-chamber came in a formal person, with a large roll of Parchment in his hand, being an Addresse . . . The Addresse was short, but much to the substance of the speech of their foreman: To whom the K. (pulling off his hatt,) sayed; That what he had don in giving liberty of Conscience, was, what was ever his judgement ought to be don, and that as he would preserve them in their injoyment of it during his reigne; so he would indeavor so to settle it by Law, that it should never be alter'd by his successors: After this he gave them his hand to kisse: It was reported the subscribers

were above 1000: But this is not so remarkeable as an Addresse of the Weeke before (as I was assured by one present) of some of the Family of Love; His Majestie asked them what their Worship consisted in, and how-many their party might consist of: They told him, their costome was to reade the Scriptures, and then to preach, but did not give any farther account, onely sayed, that for the rest, they were a sort of refined Quakers, but their number very small, not consisting (as they sayed) of above threescore in all, and those chiefly belonging to the Ile of Ely:

. . .

And Catholics
   . . . [October 29] The K: Q: Invited to feast at Guild-hall, together with Dadi, the Popes Nuncio—ô strange turne of affaires, That these who scandaliz'd the Church of England, as favourers of Popery (the Dissenters) should publiqly invite an Emissary from Rome, one who represented the very person of their Antichrist!

. . .

The French Tyrant
   [1688. March] The Fr: Tyrant, now finding he could make no proselytes amongst those Protestants of quality and others whom he had caused to be shut up in Dungeo[ns] and confin'd to Nunneries and Monastries; gave them after so long Tryal a general releasement, and leave to go out of the Kingdom, but Utterly taking away their Estates, and their Children; so as greate numbers came daily into England and other places, where they were received and relieved with very Considerable Christian Charity: This providence and goodnesse of God to those who thus constantly held out; did so work upon those miserable poore soules, who to avoy'd the persecution, sign'd their renuntiation, and to save their estates, went to Masse; That reflecting on what they had don, grew so afflicted in their Consciences, as not being longer able to support it; They Unanimously in infinite number thro all the french provinces; Acquaint the Magistrats and Lieutenants that being sorry for their Apostacy; They were resolved to returne to their old Religion, that they would go no more to Masse, but peaceably assemble where they could, to beg pardon and worship God, but so without weapons, as not to give the least umbrage of Rebellion or sedition,

imploring their pitty and commisseration: And accordingly meeting so from time to time, The Dragoon Missioners, popish Officers and Priests, fall upon them, murder and put to death who ever they could lay hold on, who without the least resistance embrace death, torture and hanging, with singing [psalmes] and praying for their persecutors to the last breath; yet still continuing the former Assembly of themselves in desert places, suffering with incredible Constancy, that through Gods mercy they might obtaine pardon for this Lapse: Such Examples of Christian behaviour has not been seene, since the primitive Persecution, by the Heathen: and doub[t]lesse God will do some signall worke in the end, if we can with patience and christian resolution hold out, and depend on his Providence:

...

An Ingenious Orangery

... [29] we went to Kew, to Visite Sir Hen: Capels, whose Orangerie and Myrtetum, are most beautifull, and perfectly well kept: He was contriving very high palisados of reedes, to shade his Oranges in during the Summer, and painting those reedes in oyle: We return'd to Lond: in the Evening:

...

[May 13] The Hollanders did now al'arme his Majestie with their fleete, so well prepar'd and out before we were in any readinesse, or had any considerable number to have encounter'd them had there ben occasion, to the greate reproch of the nation, whilst being in profound peace, there was a mighty Land Army, which there was no neede of, and no force by Sea, where onely was the apprehension; at present, but was doub[t]lesse kept and increased in order to bring in and Countenance Popery, the K beginning to discover his intention by many Instances, perverted by the Jesuites against his first seeming resolution to alter nothing in the Church Established, so as it appeared that there can be no relyance [o]n Popish promises.

A Scandalous Fraud

17 I went to Lond, to meete my Bro: G. Evelyn about our mutual concerne in the will of my Bro: Richard, by which, my Niepce Montague dying without issue, a considerable Estate ought to have

returned to our Family, after the decease of her husband: but thro the fraude and unworthy dealing of her mother, (my sister in-Law), the intaile had ben cut off and a recovery pass'd and consequently the Estate given to her husband Montag[u]e, through the perswasion of my sister contrary to the intent of her husband my brother, and that to a son-in law who had lived dissolutly and Scandalously with another woman, and his dishonesty made publiquely notorious: What should move my sister in Law, professing so greate love to the memory of her husband, to cause my Niepce to give away not onely this, but considerably more, to a son in law, who had no Issue, from all her husbands relations, was strangely spoken off, especialy to one who had so scandalously and so basely abused her da[u]ghter:

The Bishops' Revolt

18 The King injoyning the ministers the Reading his declaration for giving liberty of Conscience (as it was styled) in all the Churches of England: This Evening six Bishops, Bath and Wells, Peterborow, Ely, Chichester, St. Asaph, and Bristol, (in the name of all the rest) came to his Majestie to petition him that he would not impose the reading of it to the severall Congregations under their diocesse: not that they were averse to the publishing of it, for want of due tendernes towards dissenters, in relation to whom they should be willing to come to such a temper, as should be thought fit, when that matter might come to be consider'd and settled in parliament and Convocation: But that the 'declaration being founded upon such a dispencing power, as might at pleasure set aside all Lawes Ecclesiastical and Civil', it appeared to them Illegal, as doing so to the parliaments in –61 and 72; and that it was a point of such Consequence, as they could not so far make themselves parties to it, as the Reading of it in the Church in the time of divine service amounted to.

The King was so far incensed at this Addresse, that he with threatning expressions commanded them to obey him in reading of it at their perils; and so dismis'd them:

. . .

25 I visited Dr. Tenison, Secretary Pepys, of the Admiralty, Mr. Boile, Coll: Philips and severall of my Friends, all the discourse now being about the Bishops refusing to reade the injunction for

the abbrogation of the Test etc: It seemes the Injunction came so crudely from the Secretarys office, that it was neither sealed nor sign'd in forme, nor had any Lawyer ben consulted; so as the Bishops who tooke all imaginable advice, put the Court to greate difficulties how to proceede against them: Greate were the Consults, and a Proclamation expected all this day; but no thing don: The action of the Bishop[s] universaly applauded, and reconciling many adverse parties, Papists onely excepted, who were now exceedingly perplex'd, and violent courses every moment expected: Report was the Protestant Secular Lords and nobility would abett the Cleargy: God knows onely the event.

. . .

Seven Bishops in the Tower

[June] 8 This day were the Arch-Bishop of Canterbery together with the Bishops of Ely, Chichester, St. Asaph, Bristol, Peterborow and Bath and Wells, sent from the Privy Council, Prisoners to the Tower, for refusing to give baile for their appearance (upon their not reading the Declaration for Liberty of Conscience) because in giving baile, they had prejudiced their Peerage: Wonderfull was the concerne of the people for them, infinite crowds of people on their knees, beging their blessing and praying for them as they passed out of the Barge; along the Tower wharfe etc:

10 A young Prince borne etc. which will cost dispute.

10 Dr. Bohune preached this Trinity-Sonday on 2. Rom: 15:

About two a clock, we heard the Toure Ordnance discharge, and the Bells ringing; for the Birth of a Prince of Wales; This was very surprizing; it being universaly given-out, that her Majestie did not looke til the next moneth:

. . .

13 I went to the Tower to see the Bishops now there in Prison, for not complying with his Majesties commands to Cause his declaration to be read in their Diocesse; where I visited the A: Bish: B: of Ely, Asaph, and Bath and Wells:

14 Dined with my L. Chancelor—

15 The Bish: came from the Tower to Westminster upon their Habeas Corpus and after divers houres dispute before the Judges, by their Counsel, upon security to appeare friday fortnight, were dismiss'd: Their Counsel alledged false Imprisonment and abate-

ment of their Committment for want of some words: Denyed the
paper given privately to the K. to be a seditious libel or that it was
ever published: but all was over-ruled: W[r]ight, Alibon, Hollowell
and Powell were the Judges: Finch, Sawyer, Pollixfen and
Pemberton, their Counsel, who pleaded incomparably, so as the
Jury quitted them. There was a lane of people from the Kings
Bench to the water-side, upon their knees as the Bishops passed
and repassed to beg their blessing: Bon fires made that night, and
bells ringing, which was taken very ill at Court and an appearance
of neere 60 Earles and Lords etc upon the bench in honor of the
Bishops, and which did not a little comfort them: but indeede they
were all along full of Courage and cherefull:

Note that they denyed to pay the Lieutennant of the Tower:
(Hales who us'd them very surlily) any Fees, denying any to be due:

. . .

Royal Fireworks

[July] 17 I went to Lond: with my Wife etc: and This night were
the fireworks plaied, which were prepar'd for the Queenes
up-sitting: We stood at Mr. Pepys's Secretary of the Admiralty to
greate advantage for the sight, and indeede they were very fine, and
had cost some thousands of pounds about the pyramids and statues
etc: but were spent too soone, for so long a preparation:

. . .

[August 24] After long trials of the Doctors, to bring up the little
P: of Wales by hand (so-many of her Majesties Children having
died Infants) not succeeding: A country Nurse (the wife of a
Tile-maker) is taken to give it suck:

. . .

Panic in Whitehall

[September] 18 I went to Lond: where I found the Court in the
uttmost consternation upon report of the Pr: of Oranges landing,
which put White-hall into so panic a feare, that I could hardly
believe it possible to find such a change:

Writs issued now in order to the Parliament, and a declaration to
back the good order of Elections, with greate professions of
maintaining the Ch: of England: but without giving any sort of
satisfaction to people, who now began to shew their high discontent

at several things in the Government: how this will end, God onely can tell:

. . .

[October 7] Hourely dreate on expectation of the Pr: of Oranges Invasion still heightned to that degree, as his Majestie thought fit to recall the Writes of Summons of Parliament; to abbrogate the Commission for the dispencing power, but retaining his owne right still to dispense with all Laws and restore the ejected Fellows of Magdalen College Oxon: But in the meane time called over 5000 Irish, 4000 Scots; continue[s] to remove protestants and put papists in to Portsmouth and other places of Trust: and retaines the Jesuites about him, which gave no satisfaction to the nation, but increasing the universal discontent, brought people to so desperate a passe as with uttmost expressions even passionately seeme to long for and desire the landing of that Prince, whom they looked on as their deliverer from popish Tyrannie, praying uncessantly for an Easterly Wind, which was said to be the onely remora of his expedition, with a numerous Army ready to make a descent; To such a strange temper and unheard of in any former age, was this poore nation reduc'd, and of which I was an Eye witnesse: The apprehension was (and with reason) that his Majesties Forces, would neither at land or sea oppose them with that viggour requisite to repell Invaders:

The late Imprisoned Bishops, were now called to reconcile matters, and the Jesuites hard at worke to foment confusions amongst the Protestants, by their usual tricks etc: Leter sent the AB. of Cant informing from a good hand what was contriving by the Jesuits: etc

9 I return'd the 9th—A paper of what the Bishops advised his Majestie was publish'd

A forme of prayer, the Bishops were injoy[n]'d to prepare an office against the feared Invasion.

. . .

A Signal Anniversary

14 The Kings Birth-day, no Gunns from the Tower, as usualy: The sunn Eclips'd at its rising: This day signal for the Victory of William the Conqueror against Herold neere Battel in Sussex: The

wind (which had hitherto ben West) all this day East, wonderfull expectation of the Dutch fleete.

Our Viccar proceeds [on] his former Text: a stranger in the afternoone on 1. Cor: 15. ult: exhorting to an unmoveablenesse in our Re[l]ligion, these difficult times, etc:

Continual apprehensions of the Dutch Invasion, there were pub: prayers ordered to be read in the Church against it.

. . .

[29] There was a Council now cald, to which were summon'd the A:Bish of Cant. etc: Judges, Lord Major etc: Q: Dowager, all the Ladies and Lords, who were present at the Q: Consorts labour, upon oath to give testimonie of the Pr: of Wales's birth, which was recorded, both at the Council board, and at the Chancery a day or two after: This procedure was censur'd by some, as below his Majestie to condescend to, upon the talke of Idle people: Remarkable on this occasion, was the refusal of the A Bish: Marq: Halifax, Earles of Clarendon and Notinghams refusing to sit at the Council Table in their places, amongst Papists, and their bold telling his Majestie that what ever was don whilst such sate amongst them was unlawfull, and incurr'd præmunire: if at least, it be true, what I heard:

. . .

'A sad revolution to this sinfull Nation'

31. My Birthday, being the 68 yeare of my age: ô Blessed Lord, grant, that as I advance in yeare[s], so I may improve in Grace: Be thou my protector this following yeare, and preserve me and mine from these dangers and greate confusions, which threaten a sad revolution to this sinfull Nation: Defend thy Church, our holy Religion, and just Lawes, disposing his Majestie to harken to sober and healing Counsels, that yet if it be thy blessed will we may still enjoy that happy Tranquility which hitherto thou hast continued to us. Amen: Amen:

I din'd at my sonns:

November 1. Dined with my L: Preston againe, with other company, at Sir St: Foxes:

The Prince of Orange's Invasion

Continual al'armes of the Pr: of Oranges landing, but no

certainty: reports of his greate losses of horse in the storme; but without any assurance. A Man was taken with divers papers and printed Manifests, and carried to Newgate after examination at the Cabinet-Council: There was likewise a declaration of the States, for satisfaction of all publique Ministers in their Dominions, the reason of their furnishing the Prince with their Vessels and Militia on this Expedition, which was delivered to all the Ambassadors and publique Ministers at the Hague except to the English and French:

There was in that of the Princes, an expression as if the Lords both Spiritual and Temporal etc had invited him over, with a deduction of the Causes of his enterprise: This made his Majestie Convene my L: of Cant: and the other Bishops now in Towne, to give them an account of what was in the Manifesto: and to enjoyne them to cleare themselves by [some] publique writing of this disloyal charge.

2 It was now certainly reported by some who saw the Pr: imbarke, and the fleete, That they sailed from Brill on Wednesday Morning, and that the Princesse of Orange was there, to take leave of her Husband, 3 and so I returned home.

. . .

[4] Fresh reports of the Pr: being landed somewhere about Portsmouth or Ile of Wight: wheras it was thought, it would have ben north ward: The Court in greate hurry—

5 Being the Anniversary of the powder plot, our Viccar preach'd on 76. Psal. 10. by divers Instances: shewing the disasters and punishments overtaking perfidious designes.

8 I went to Lond: heard the newes of the Prince of Oranges being landed at Tor-bay, with a fleete of neere 700 saile, so dreadfull a sight passing through the Channell with so favorable a Wind, as our Navy could by no meanes intercept or molest them: This put the King and Court into greate Consternation, now employed in forming an Army to incounter their farther progresse: for they were gotten already into Excester, and the season, and wayes very improper for his Majesties forces to march so greate a distance:

The A Bish of Cant, and some few of the other Bishops, and Lords in Lond. were sent for to White-hall, and required to set forth their abhorrency of this Invasion; They assured his Majestie they had never invited any of the Princes party or were in the least privy to this Invasion, and would be ready to shew all testimonies of their Loyalty etc: but as to a publique declaration, they being so few, desired that his majestie would call the rest of their brethren and peeres, that they might consult what was fit to do on this occasion, not thinking it convenient to publish any thing without them, and untill they had themselves seene the Princes Manifest, in which it was pretended he was invited in by the Lords Sp: and temporal: This did not please his Majestie: So they departed: There came now out a Declaration, prohibiting all people to see or reade the Princes Manifest; in which was at large set-forth the cause of his Expedition, as there had ben on[c]e before one from the States: These are the beginnings of Sorrows, unlesse God in his Mercy prevent it, by some happy reconciliation of all dissentions amongst us, which nothing in likelihood can Effect but a free Parliament, but which we cannot hope to see, whilst there are any forces on either side: I pray God protect, and direct the King for the best, and truest Interest of his People: I saw his Majestie touch for the Evil, Piters the Jesuit and F. Warner officiating in the Banqueting house

. . .

[11] The Pr. of Orange increases every day in forces, several Lords go in to him; The King gos towards Salisbery with his Army; doubtfull of their standing by him, Lord Cornbery carrys some Regiments from him, marches to Honiton, the Princes head quarters; The Citty of Lond: in dissorder by the rabble etc who pull-downe the Nunery at St. Johns, newly bought by the Papists of my Lord Berkeley: The Queene prepare[s] to [go] to Portsmouth for safty: to attend the issue of this commotion, which has a dreadfull aspect:

18 Our Viccar on his former Text, shewing the wonderfull deliverances of Gods church in its greatest necessities:

. . .

It was now very hard frost:

The King gos to Salisbery to rendevouze the Army, and returning back to Lond: Lord De la Mare appears for the Pr: in Cheshire: The nobility meete in Yorkshire: The ABish and some Bishops, and such peeres as were in Lond: addresse to his Majestie to call a Parliament: The King invites all forraine nations to come over: The French take all the Palatinat, and alarme the Germans more than ever:

. . .

29 I went to the R: Society, we adjourn'd Election of Præsident til 23. Aprill by reason of the publique commotions, yet dined together as of custome on this day:

. . .

Protestant Religion and Laws

[December 2] Visited my L. Godolphin,* then going with the Marquis of Halifax, and E: of Notingham as Commissioner to the Prince of Orange: He told me, they had little power: Plymoth declared for the Prince and L: Bath: Yorke, Hull, Bristoll, all the eminent nobility and persons of quality throout England declare for the Protestant Rel[i]gion and Laws, and go to meete the Prince; who every day sets forth new declarations etc: against the Papists: The Greate favorits at Court, priest[s] and Jesuites, flie or abscond: Every thing (til now conceiled) flies abroad in publique print, and is Cryed about the streetes: Expectations of the Pr: coming to Oxon: Pr: of Wales and greate Treasure sent daily to Portsmouth, Earle of Dover Governor: Addresse from the Fleete not gratefull to his Majestie: The Popists in offices lay down their Commissions and flie: Universal Consternation amongst them: it lookes like a Revolution: Herbert, beates a french fleete:

7 My son went towards Oxon: I returned home:

. . .

13 I went to Lond: The rabble people demolish all Papists Chapells and severall popish Lords and Gent: house[s], especialy that of the Spanish Ambassador, which they pillaged and burnt his Library etc: 16 Dr. Tenison at St. Martins on: 8: Isay: 11:

I din'd at my L. Clarendons: The King flies to sea, putts in at Feversham for ballast is rudely detained by the people: comes back to W[hite]hall.

The Pr: of Orange now advanc'd to Windsor, is invited by the King to St. James, the messenger sent was the E. of Feversham the general of the forces: who going without Trumpet or passeport is detained prisoner by the Prince: The Prince accepts the Invitation, but requires his Majestie to retire to some distant place, that his owne Guards may be quartered about the palace and Citty: This is taken heinously, so the King gos away privately to Rochester: Is perswaded to come back: comes on the Sunday; Goes to masse and dines in publique, a Jesuite says grace: I was present That night a Council, 17 his Majestie refuses to assent to all proposals; gos away againe to Rochester:

The Prince at St. James's

18 The Pr: comes to St. James, fills W-hall (the King taking barge to Gravesend at 12 a Clock) with Dut[c]h Guard: A Council of Peres meete about an Expedient to call a parliament: Adjourne to the House of Lords: The Chancelor, E. of Peterbor, and divers Priests and other taken: E: of Sunderland flies and divers others, Sir E: Hales, Walker and other taken and secured: All the world go to see the Prince at St. Jamess where is a greate Court, there I saw him and severall of my Acquaintance that come over with him: He is very stately, serious, and reserved: The Eng: souldiers etc. sent out of Towne to distant quarters: not well pleased: Divers reports and opinions, what all this will end in; Ambition and faction feared:

21 I visited L. Clarendon where was the Bishops of Ely and St. Asaph: we had much discourse of Afairs: I returned home:

. . .

24 The King passes into France, whither the queen and child wer gon a few days before.

. . .

'The greate Question about the Government'

26 The Peeres and such Commons as were members of the Parliament at Oxford, being the last of Charles the first: meeting, desire the Pr: of Orange to take on him the Government, and dispose of the publique Revenue 'til a Convention of Lords and Commons should meete in full body, appointed by his Circulary Letters to the Shires and Borrowghs 22. Jan:

. . .

[1689. January] 7 I returned home: on foote, it having ben a long frost and deepe snow, [so] as the Thames was almost quite frozen over.

. . .

Divided Opinions

15 I went to visite my Lord Archbish of Cant: where I found the Bishops of St. Asaph, Ely, Bath and Wells, Peterborow and Chichester; The Earle of Alesbery and Clarendon, Sir Geo: Makenzy Lord Advocate of Scotland, and then came in a Scotch Archbishop: etc. After prayers and dinner, were discoursed divers serious matters concerning the present state of the publique: and sorry I was to find, there was as yet no accord in the judgements of those who both of the Lords and Commons were to convene: Some would have the princesse made Queene without any more dispute, others were for a Regency, There was a Torie part (as then called so) who were for [inviting] his Majestie againe upon Conditions, and there were Republicarians, who would make the Prince of Orange like a State-holder: The Romanists were also buisy among all these severall parties to bring them into Confusion; most for Ambition, or other Interest, few for Conscience and moderate resolutions: I found nothing of all this in this Assembly of Bishops, who were pleas'd to admitt me into their Discourses: They were all for a Regency, thereby to salve their Oathes, and so all publique matters to proceede in his Majesties name, thereby to facilitate the calling of a Parliament according to the Laws in being; this was the result of this meeting: My Lord of Cant: gave me greate thanks for the advertisement I sent his Grace in October, and assur'd me they tooke my counsel in that particular, and that it came very seasonable:

I found by the Lord Advocate of Scotland that the Bishops of Scotland, who were indeede very unworthy that Character and had don much mischiefe in that Church, were now coming about to the True Interest, more to save themselves in this conjuncture, which threatned the abolishing the whole Hierarchy in that Kingdome, than for Conscience: and therefore the Scotish Archbish: and Lord Advocate requested my L. of Cant: to use his best endeavors with the Prince, to maintaine the Church there in the same state as by Law at present settled: It now growing late, I after some private discourse, tooke my leave of his Grace, most of the Lords being gon: I beseech God of his infinite mercy to settle truth and peace amongst us againe:

. . .

The Convention Gives a Lead

23 I went to Lond, The great Convention being assembled the day before, falling upon the greate Question about the Government, Resolved that K. Jam: 2d, having by the advise of Jesuites and other wicked persons, endeavored to subvert the Lawes of church and state, and Deserting the Kingdome carrying away the Seales etc without taking any care for the manegement of the Government, had by demise, abdicated himselfe, and wholy vacated his right: and They did therefore desire the Lords Concurrence to their Vote, to place the Crowne upon the next heires: The Prince of Orange for his life, then to the Princesse his wife, and if she died without Issue to the Princesse of Denmark, and she failing to the heires of the Pr: Excluding for ever all possibility of admitting any Ro: Cath:

. . .

A Narrow Vote: 'Some fixt and sober establishment'

28 The Votes of the House of Comm: being Carried up, by their chaire-man Mr. Hamden, to the Lords, 29 I got a station by the Princes lodgings at the doore of the Lobby to the House, to heare much of the debate which held very long; The Lord Danby being in the chaire (for the Peres were resolved into a grand Committee of the whole house) after all had spoken, it comming to the question: It was carried out by 3 voices, again[s]t a Regency, which 51 of 54 were for, aledging the danger of dethroning   Kings, and scrupuling many passages and expressions of the Commons Votes; too long to set downe particularly, some were for sending to his Majestie with Conditions, others, that the K. could do no wrong, and that the maladministration was chargeable on his Ministers. There were not above 8 or 9 Bish: and but two, against the Regency; The Arch Bishop was absent: and the Cleargie now began a new to change their note, both in pulpet and discourse, upon their old passive Obedience: so as people began to talke of the Bishops being cast out of the House: In short, things tended to dissatisfaction on both sides, add to this the morose temper of the Pr: of Orange, who shewed so little Countenance to the Noblemen and others, expecting a more gracious and cherefull reception, when they made their Court: The English Army likewise, not so in order, and firme to his Interest, nor so weaken'd, but that it might,

give interruption: Ireland in a very ill posture, as well as Scotland; nothing yet towards any settlement: God of his infinite mercy, Compose these [things], that we may at lastt be a Nation and a church under some fixt and sober establishment:

. . .

[February] 6 The Kings Coronation day was ordred not to be observed, as hitherto it yearely had.

The Reign of William and Mary
1689–1695

The Convention of L: and Comm: now declare the Pr: and princesse of Or: Q: and K of England, Fr: and Ireland (Scotland being an Independent Kingdome) The Pr and Princesse to enjoy it jointly during their lives, but the executive Authority to be vested in the Prince during life, though all proceedings to run in both names: and that it descend to the heires of both, and for want of such Issue to the Princesse Ann of Denmark, and in want of such to the heires of the body of the Pr: of Or: if he survive, and for defect, to devolve to the Parliament to choose as they think fit: These produc'd a Conference with the Lords, when also there was presented heads of such new laws as were to be enacted: and upon those Conditions they tis thought will be proclaim'd: There was much contest about the Kings abdication, and whether he had vacated the Government: E. of Notingham and about 20 Lords and many Bishops, entred their protests etc, but the Concurrence was greater against them— The Princesse hourely Expected: Forces sending to Ireland that K[ing]dome being in greate danger, by the E. of Tyrconnells Armie, and expectations from France: which K. is buisy to invade Flanders, and encounter the German Princes comming now to their Assistance: so as this is likely to be one of the most remarkable summers for action, as has happed for many Ages:

. . .

William and Mary Proclaimed
[February 22] I saw the new Queene and King, so proclaim'd, the very next day of her coming to White-hall, Wednesday 13. Feb. with wonderfull acclamation and general reception, Bonfires, bells, Gunns etc: It was believed that they both, especialy the Princesse, would have shewed some (seeming) reluctancy at least, of assuming her Fathers Crowne and made some Apologie, testifying her regret, that he should by his misgovernment necessitat the Nation to so

extraordinary a proceeding, which would have shewed very handsomly to the world, (and according to the Character give[n] of her piety etc) and consonant to her husbands first Declaration, that there was no intention of Deposing the King, but of Succoring the Nation; But, nothing of all this appeared; she came into W-hall as to Wedding, riant and jolly, so as seeming to be quite Transported: rose early on the next morning of her arival, and in her undresse (as reported) before her women were up; went about from roome to roome, to see the Convenience of White-hall: Lay in the same bed and appartment where the late Queene lay: and within a night or two, sate downe to play at Basset, as the Q. her predecessor us'd to do: smiled upon and talked to every body; so as no manner of change seem'd in Court, since his Majesties last going away, save that the infinite crowds of people thronged to see her, and that she went to our prayers: This carriage was censured by many: she seemes to be of a good nature, and that takes nothing to heart whilst the Pr: her husband has a thoughtfull Countenance, is wonderfull serious and silent, seemes to treate all persons alike gravely: and to be very intent on affaires, both Holland, and Ireland and France calling for his care: Divers Bishops, and Noble men are not at all satisfied with this so suddain Assumption of the Crown, without any previous, sending and offering some Conditions to the absent King: or, upon his not returning and assenting to those Conditions within such a day: to have proclaim'd him Regent etc. But the major part of both houses, prevailed to make them King and Q: immediately, and a Crowne was tempting etc— This was opposed and spoke against with such vehemency by my L. Clarendon (her owne Unkle) as putt him by all preferments, which must doubtlesse, [have] been as greate, as could have ben given him: My L: of Rochester his bro: overshot himselfe by the same carriage and stiffnesse, which, their friends thought, they might have well spared, when they saw how it was like to be over-ruled, and that it had ben sufficient to have declared their dissent with lesse passion, acquiescing in due time: The ÆB of Cant, and some of the rest, upon scruple of Conscience, and to salve the Oathes they had taken, entred their protests, and hung off: Especially the Arch-Bishop, who had not all this while so much as appeared out of Lambeth: all which incurred the wonder of many, who observed with what zeale they contributed to the Princes Expedition, and all this while also, rejecting any proposals of sending againe [for] the absented King: That they should now boggle and raise scrupuls, and such as created much division among people, greatly rejoicing the old Courtiers, and Papist[s] especialy:

...

More Trouble Threatening

... [March 8] The new Parliament now being furiously about Impeaching those who were obnoxious: and as their custome has ever ben going on violently, without reserve or moderation: whilst wise men were of opinion that the most notorious Offenders being named and excepted, an Act of Amnesty were more seasonable, to paciffie the minds of men, in so generall a discontent of the nation, especialy of those who did not expect to see the Government assum'd without any reguard to the absent King, or proving a spontaneous abdication, or that the Pr: of Wales was an Imposture, etc: 5 of the Bishops also still refusing to take the new Oath: In the interim to gratifie and sweeten the people, The Hearth Tax was remitted for ever: but what intended to supply it, besids present greate Taxes on land: is not named: The King abroad furnished with mony and officers by the French King going now for Ireland, Their wonderfull neglect of more timely preventing that from hence, and disturbances in Scotland, gives men apprehension of greate difficulties before any settlement can be perfected here: whilst The Parliament men dispose of the greate Offices amongst themselves: The Gr: Seale, Treasury, Admiralty put into commission, of many unexperienc'd persons to gratifie the more: So as, by the present prospect of things (unlesse God Almighty graciously interpose, and give successe in Ireland, and settle Scotland) more Trouble seemes to threaten this nation, than could be expected: In the Interim, the New K. referrs all to the Parliament in the most popular manner imaginable: but is very slow in providing against all these menaces, besides finding difficulties in raising men to send abroad, The former army (who had never don any service hitherto, but received pay, and passed the summers in an idle scene of a Camp at Hounslow) unwilling to engage, and many of them dissaffected, and scarce to be trusted:

...

Things far from Settlement

[29] The new King, much blamed for neglecting Ireland, now like to be ruined by the L. Tyrconnel, and his popish party; too strong for the Protestants; wonderfull uncertainty where King James was, whether in France or Ireland: The Scotts seeme as yet to favor King William, rejecting K James letter to them: yet declaring nothing positively: Souldiers in England, discontented: Parliament preparing the Coronation Oath: Presbyterians and Dissenters displeased at the vote to preserve the protestant Religion as established by Law; without mentioning what they were to have as to Indulgence: The Arch-Bishop of Cant, and the other 4: refusing to come to Parliament, it was deliberated whether they should incurr premunire: but this was thought fit to be let fall, and connived at, for feare of the people, to w[h]om these prelates were very deare, for their opposing poper[y]: Court Offices, distributed among the Parliament men: no Considerable fleete as yet set forth: in summe: Things far from the settlement was expected by reason of the slothfull sickly temper of the new King: and unmindfullnesse of the Parliament, as to Ireland, which is like to prove a sad omission. The Confederats, beate the French out of the Palatinate, which they had most barbarously ruined:

. . .

The Coronation

[April] 11 I saw the procession both to, and from the Abby church of Westminster, with the greate feast in Westminster Hall etc: at the Coronation of the new K William and Q. Mary: That which was different from former Coronations, was, something altered in the Coronation Oath, concerning maintaining the Prot: Religion: etc: Dr. Burnet (now made L.B. of Sarum) preached on   with infinite applause: The parliament men had Scaffolds and places which tooke up one whole side of the Hall: and when the K and Q. had din'd. The Ceremonie of the Champion, and other services upon Tenures: The Parliament men were also feasted in the Exchequer Chamber: and had each of them a Medaile of Gold given them worth five and fourty shill: the K. and Q: effigies inclining one to another, on one side, the Reverse Jupiter throwing a bolt at Phaeton, the Word   which was but dull seing they might have had out of the poet something as apposite   The sculpture also very meane: Much of the splendor of the proceeding was abated, by the absence of divers who should have made it up: There being but as yet 5 Bish: 4. Judges, (no more at present, it seemes as yet sworn) and severall noblemen and great Ladys wanting: But indeede the Feast was magnificent: The next day, went the H of Commons and kissed their new Majesties hands in the Banqueting house:

12 I went the next day afternoone with the B: of St. Asaph to visite my L. of Canterbery at Lambeth, who had excused himselfe from officiating at the Coronation, (which the Bishop of Lond: performed assisted by the A.B: of Yorke) we had much private and free discourse with his Grace, concerning severall things, relating to the Church, there being now a Bill of Comprehension to be brought to the Commons from the Lords: I urg'd, that when they went about to reforme some particulars in the Liturgie, Church discipline, Canons etc: The Baptising in private Houses, without necessity, might be reformd: as likewise the Burying dead bodies so frequently in the Churches: The one proceeding meerely from the pride of the Women, bringing that into Custome, which was onely indulged in case of iminent danger: and out of necessity, during the Rebellion and persecution of the Cleargy, in our late Civil Warres etc: The other from the Avarice of the Minister, who made in some opulent parishes, almost as much of permissions to bury in the chancels and churches, as of their livings, and were paid with considerable advantage and gifts, for baptising in Chambers: To this the two Bishops, heartily assented: and promised their indeavors to get it reformed: utterly disliking both practice[s], as novel, and undecent: We discoursed likewise concerning the greate disturbance and prejudice it might cause should the new oath (now upon the anvile) be imposed upon any, save such as were in new office; without any retrospect to such as either had no office; or had ben long in office, who likely had some scruples about taking a new othe, having already sworn fidelity to the Government, as established by Law: and this we all knew to be the case of my L. Arch Bishop and some other worthy persons, who were not so fully satisfied with the Conventions abdicating the late K James, To whom they had sworn alegiance etc: So I went back to Whit hall, and thence home:

. . .

Scots Caution and Prudence

Scotland declare for K. William and Q: Mary, with the Reasons of their laying K James aside not as Abdicating but forfaiting his right by maladministrat[ion], the particulars mentioned which being published, I repeate not: proceeding with much more caution and prudence than we did; who precipitated all things to the great reproch of the Nation, but all that was plainly menaged by some crafty, ill principled men: The new Pr: Council having a Republican Spirit, and manifestly undermining all future Succession of the Crown, and prosperity of the Church of England: which yet, I hope, they will not be able to accomplish so soone as they hope: though they get into all places of Trust and profit:

. . .

James II in Ireland

[26] There now came certaine newes of K: James's being not onely landed in Ireland, but that by surprizing London Derry, he was become absolute Master of all that Kingdome: to the greate shame of our new King and Assembly at Westminster, who had ben so often solicited to provide against it, by timely succors, and which so easily they might have don: This is a terrible beginning of more troubles, especialy should an Armie come thence into Scotland; People being so generaly dissafected here and every where else; so as scarse would sea, or Landmen serve without compulsion:

. . .

Irish Distress

[May] Matters publique went very ill in Ireland, Confusion and dissention amongst ourselves, stupidity, unconstancy, emulation, in the Governours, employing unskillful men in greatest offices: No person of publique spirit, and ability appearing etc: threaten us with a very sad prospect what may be the conclusion: without Gods Infinite mercy: A fight by Admiral Herbert with the French, imprudently setting on them in a Creeke as they were landing men etc in Ireland: by which we came off with greate slaughter, and little honor: so strangely negligent, and remisse in preparing a timely and sufficient fleete. The S[c]ots Commissioners offer the Crowne etc to the new King, and Queene, upon Condition . . .

. . .

Art and Nature

[July] 8 To Lond: 9 I sat for my Picture to Mr. Kneller, for Mr. Pepys late Secretary of the Admiralty, holding my *Sylva* in my right hand: It was upon his long and earnest request; and is plac'd in his Library: nor did Kneller ever paint better and more masterly work:

11 I dind at my L: Clarendons, it being his Ladys Weding day: when about 3 in the afternoone, so great and unusual a storme of Thunder, raine and wind suddainly fell, as had not ben known in an age: many boates on the Thames were over wh[e]lmed, and such was the impetuosity of the wind, as carried up the waves in pillars and spouts, most dreadfull to behold, rooting up Trees, ruining some houses, and was indeede no other than an Hurocan:

The Co: of Sunderland told me, that it extended as far as Althorp, that very moment, which is about 70 miles from Lond . . .

. . .

The Succession to The Crown

19 I returned home: The Marishall de Scomberge, went now Generall towards Ireland, to the reliefe of Lond: Derry: Our Fleete lie before Brest: The Confederates, now passing the Rhyne, beseege Bonn, and Maence to obtaine a passage into France: A greate Victory gotten by the Muscovite, taking and burning Procop: A new Rebell against the Turks, unkle to Yegen Bassha threatens the destruction of that Tyrannie: All Europe in armes against France; and hardly in memory of an[y] Historie, so universal a face of Warr: The Convention (or Parliament as some called it) sitting, exempt the Duke of Hanover from the Succession to the Crowne, which they seeme to confine to the present New King, his Wife, and Princesse Ann of Denmark, who is so monstroustly s[w]ollen, that its doubted, her being thought with child, may proove a Tympane onely: so as the unhappy family of Steuarts, seemes to be extinguishing: and then what government next, is likely to be set up, whether Regal and by Election, or otherwise, The Republicaries and Dissenters from the C. of England looking evidently that way: The Scots having now againe newly, voted downe Episcopacy there: Greate discontent still through the nation, at the slow proceedings of the King, and the incompetent Instruments and Officers he advances to the greatest and most necessary charges:

. . .

Thanks be to God

[October] 31: My Birthday, being now 69 years old: Blessed Father who hast prolonged my years to this greate Age, and given me to see so greate and wonderfull Revolutions, preserved me amidst them, to this moment; accept I beseech thee the continuance of my Prayers and thankfull accknowledgements, and graunt to me the Grace to be working out my Salvation, and redeeme the Time, that thou mayst be glorified by me here, and my immortal Soule saved ...

. . .

[November] 27 I went to Lond with my family to Winter at Soho in the greate Square.

30 I went to the R: Society, where I was chosen one of the Council, my Lord Penbrok president, we dined together:

. . .

A Notorious Scandal

[1690. January] 24: The famous Infamous Tryal of my unworthy Nephew Montague at the Kings-bench, which indeede I heard with much regrett, that so vile and scandalous a Cause should have ben [published], the dammages being 6500 pounds: The immense wrong this proflygate wretch did my Niepce, drawing justly on him this disgrace: so vile a Cause had never ben brought to so publique an example:

. . .

Universal Discontent

[30] The Parliament, unexpectedly Prorogued til 2 Aprill, to the discontent and surprizal of many members, who being exceeding averse from settling anything, proceeding with animosities, multiplying exceptions, against those whom they pronounc'd obnoxious, produc'd as universal a discontent, against K. William and themselves, as was before against K: James: The new King, also having with so much reproch lost now above a yeare, resolving an expedition into Ireland in person; Thought best to proroge this troublesome Session, now they had given him so much mony, and had no more use of them for the Present: it being also believed they should hardly meete againe, but in a new, and more authenticque Parliament:

. . .

[February] 19 I dined with the Marqu[i]s of Caermarthen (late Lord Danby) where was Lieutenant Gen: Duglas, a very considerable and sober Commander, going for Ireland, and related to us the exceeding neglect of the English Souldiers, perishing for want of Clothing and necessarys this winter; and exceedingly magnifying their Courage and bravery during all their hardships: There dined also my Lord Lucas Lieutenant of The Towre, and The Bish: of St. Asaph etc:

...

Preaching Against Sin

23 Dr. Tenison in the fornoone at St. Martins, and the same sermon before the Queene at Wh:Hall in the afternoone: upon 1: Thess: 4: 7: against the sin of lust and uncleanesse, The Impudence of both sex, being now become so greate and universal, Persons of all ranks, keeping their Courtesans so publiqly, that the King had lately directed a Letter to the Bishops, to order their Cleargy to preach against that sin, swearing etc and to put the Laws Ecclesiastical in execution without any indulgence:

...

Kensington Palace

25 I went on foote to Kinsington, which K. Will: had bought of my Lord of Notingham, and new altered, but it was yet a patch'd building, yet with the Gardens a very sweete Villa, having to it the Parke, and the straite new way through the park: I din'd with the Bish: of St. Asaph, Dr. Tenison and Stradling, return'd that evening: News of some victory in Ireland.

...

The Condition of the Navy: Fireships

[March] 7: I din'd with Mr. Pepys, late Secretary of the Admiralty, where was that excellent Shipwright, and sea-man (for so had he ben, as also Commissioner of the navy) Sir Anthony Deane, who amongst other discourses, and deploring the sad condition of our Navy, as now Govern'd by unexperienc'd men etc since this Revolution: Related to us, what exceeding advantage we of this [nation] had, by being the first who built Fregats: the first that was ever made, being that Vessel, which was afterward called the Constant Warwick; which Pet: of Chattham built for a tryal of making a Vessel that would saile swiftly, it was built with low Decks, the Gunns lying neere the water; and was so light and swift of sailing, that in a short time, he told us, she had ere the Dut[c]h-War was ended, taken as much mony from Privateers as would have laden her, and that more such being built, did in a year or two scoure our Channels, from being exceedingly infested by those of Dynkirk and others: And added that it were the best and onely infallible expedient, to be masters at sea, and able to destroy the greatest Navy of any enemy whatsoever, if instead of building huge greate ships, and 2d and 3d rates etc: they quite left off building them with such high decks, which he said was nothing but to gratifie Gentlemen Commanders who must have all their Effeminate accommodations, and for pomp, which would be the ruine of our Fleetes, if such persons were continued to command, they neither having Experience, nor being capable of learning, because they would not submitt to the fatigue and inconveniences, which bred seamen, could do, in those so otherwise usefull swift fregats: Which he made appeare, being to encounter the greatest ships, would be able to protect, set on, and bring off, those who should manege the Fireships, and that whatsoever Prince should first store himself with numbers of such (viz. Fireships) would thro the help and countenance of such Fregats, be certainly able to ruine, the greatest force, that, of never so vast ships, could be put to sea for fight, and that by reason of the dexterity of working those light and swift-sailing vessels, to guard the Fireships: and this he made so evident, that he concluded there would shortly be no other method of sea fight: and that our greate ships and Men of Warr, however stored with Gunns and men, must submitt to whosoever should encounter them with far lesse number: He thereupon represented to us, the dreadfullnesse of these Fireships; and that he continualy observed in our last maritime warr with the Dut[c]h, that when ever an Enemys fireship, approch'd, the most valiant both of Commanders and common Sea-men and sailers, were in such feare and Consternation, that, though of all times, there was then most neede of the Gunns, boomes, and other Instruments, to keepe the misch[ie]f off; they grew pale and astonish'd, and as if possessed with a quite other meane soule, slung about, forsooke their gunns and worke, as in dispaire, everyone looking about, which way they might get out of their ship, though sure to be drown'd if they did so, or to be burnt to death if they staied: This he said was likly to prove hereafter the method of sea fights and that whatever King, got provision of this before his Neighbour potentats, must demonstrably destroy the other, and did therefore wish, it might not be the misfortune of England: especialy, if they continued to put the Gentlemen Commanders over experienced sea-men, upon accounte of their ignorance, effeminacy and Insolencie:

. . .

Pepys's Remonstrance

[June] 10 I went to Lond: Mr. Pepys read to me his Remonstrance, shewed with what malice and [injustice] he was suspected, with Sir Ant: Deane, about the Timber of which the 30 ships were built by a late Act of Parliament: with the exceeding danger the present Fle[e]t would be shortly in by reason of the Ignorance and incompetency of those who now manag'd the Admiralty and affaires of the Navy, of which he gave an accurate state, and shewed his greate abilitie: I retur[n]ed in the Evening:

. . .

24 Dined with and Visited me Mr. Pepys, Mr. Stuart and other friends. Mr. P: sent the next day to the Gate-house, and severall greate persons to the Towre, on suspicion of being affected to K. James: amongst which was my Lord Earle of Clarendon, unkle to the Queene.

Mr. Pepys was the next morning imprisoned etc:

. . .

King William : Veni, Vidi, Vici after the Battle of the Boyne

[July 13] King William having vanquished K James in Ireland, there was much publique rejoicing: It seemes K. J: army would not stand, namely the Irish, but the English Irish and French made greate resistance: Shomberg was slaine, and Dr. Wa[l]ker, who so bravely defended L.derry: K.W: received a slight wound by the grazing of a cannon bullet on his shouldier, which yet he endured with very little interruption of his pursuit: Hamilton, who brake his word, about Tyrconells, was taken: K. J. is reported gon back to France: Droghedah and Dublin surrendered: and if K.W. be returning, one may say of him as of Cæsar, Veni, vidi, vici, for never was such a Kingdome won in so short an Expedition; But to alay much of this the French fleete having exceedingly beaten the Dutch fleete, and ours not daring to interpose, ride at present in our Chanell, threatning to Land, which causes an extraordinary alarme etc:

16 The publique fast: our Viccar preached on 18 Jer: 7. 8:

17 I went to London to visite some friends in the Toure, where asking for my Lord Clarendon (now with divers other Noble persons imprisoned upon suspicion of a plot) by mistake they directed me to the E. of Torrington who about 3 days before had ben sent for from the Fleete, was put into the Toure for his Cowardize and not fighting the French Fleete, which having beaten a Squadron of the Hollanders (whilst Torrington did nothing) did now ride masters at sea with that power as gave terror to the whole nation, in daily expectation of a descent, which God Almighty avert:

. . .

[August 3] The French domineering still at sea, landed some souldiers at Tinmoth in Devon: and burned some poore houses:

. . .

[10] The K: William having taken in Waterford, Duncannon and other places marches to Limrick, which Tyrconell seemes with 4000 french etc to hold out; etc. The French F[l]eete still hovering about the Western Coast, (we having 300 saile of rich Merchant Ships in the bay of Plimoth,) our Fleete begin to move towards them under 3 Admiralls in Commission: The Country in the West all on their Guard, A camp of about 4000 still on Blak-heath . . .

. . .

[13] The French King having newes that King William was slaine, and his Army defeated in Ireland, causes such a Triumph at Paris and all over France, as was never heard of or almost read in any history, when in the midst of it, the unhappy K. James being vanquished, brought himselfe (by a speedy flight and escape) the sad tidings of his owne defeate, to the greate reproch of the French who made such unseasonable boasting:

. . .

Cork Delivered

[October 12] Corke Delivered: upon discretion; The Duke of

Grafton mortaly wounded: dies Churchil: before Kingsale, which he takes, our Ships (most of them) come into Harbor: The Parliament siting and voting vast summs for the next yeares Warr . . .

. . .

[1691. April] 10 This night, a suddaine and terible Fire burnt downe all the buildings over the stone Gallery at W-hall, to the waterside, begining at the Appartments of the late Dut[c]hesse of Portsmouth (which had ben pulled down and rebuilt to please her no lesse than 3 times) and Consuming other Lodgings of such lewd Creatures, who debauched both K Char: 2d and others and were his destr[u]ction:

. . .

Non-Juring Bishops

[May] 7 I went to visite the A:B: of Cant: yet at Lambeth: I found him alone, and discoursing of the Times, especialy of the new Bishops design'd, he told me that by no Canon, or Law divine etc: they could justifie the removing the present Incumbents: That Dr. Beverwich, designed Bishop of Bath and Wells, came to aske his Advice, The AB:told him, That though he should give it, he believed he would not take it: The Doctor said he would: Why then says the AB: When they come to aske you, say 'Nolo!' and say it from your heart: there's nothing Easier, than to resolve your selfe, what is to be don in the Case: The Doctor seem'd to Deliberate: what he will do, I know not; but Bishop Ken, who is to be put out, is exceedingly beloved of his D[i]ocesses: and if he (and the rest) should insist upon it, and plead their Interest as Freeholders, 'tis believed, there would be difficulty in their Case, and may indanger a Schisme and much disturbance: so as wise men thinke it had ben better to have let them alone, than to have proceeded with this rigour, to turne them out for refusing to sweare against their Conscience. I asked, at Parting, when his Grace removed, he sayd, that he had not yet received any summons: But I found the house altogether Disfurnished and his Bookes packing up:

. . .

Chelsea Hospital Complete

12 I went to see the Hospital and Infirmarie for Emerited

Souldiers lately built at Chelsey, which is indeede a very Magnificent, Compleat and excellent Foundation, the two Cutts from the Thames, Courts, and other accommodations wonderfull fine: The several wards for the souldiers, Infirmary for the sick, Dispensatory, Governors house and other officers, especialy the Refectory for 400 men, and Chapell; In the Refectory is a noble Picture of heroic argument in honor of Char: 2d painted by Virrio: also the Kings James Statue in Brasse, of the worke of Gibbons in the Court next the Cloister etc:

15 I returned with my family, home to my house in the Country, for the Summer:

...

Evelyn Heir to Wotton

[21] This day died my Nephew John Evelyn of Wotton, onely son and heire of my Eldest Bro: Geo: who sent me word of it the next day: He had ben long, and so dangerously sick, a greate part of the Winter, that Physitians despaired of his Recovery; but on the suddaine he began so to mend, that though his limbs were weake, his Appetite, (before lost) Spirit, and cherefullnesse returned, so as he was thought past danger, and went not onely downe about the house but tooke the aire abroad in the Coach, when unexpectedly, a Veine breaking carried him away, nothing being able to stop the flux, so greate was the sharpnesse of his blood, and weake the vessells, which inconveniences accompanied with a Palsy, was contracted by an habit of drinking much wine and strong waters to comply with other young intemperate men: He had else a very strong and robust body, and was a person of very good sense and parts: He died about 35 years of age, to the greate griefe of my Bro: and Joy (I believe) of his Wife, who never behaved herselfe so discreetely, as to give him any greate comfort, which made him at last, almost wish himselfe out of the World: he had had severall Children born, and lately a Son, a very pretty Child, and likely to live, but God was pleased to take them all to himselfe: So as now (there remaining onely Daughters, women grown, and of an Elder sons of my Bro:) according to the Intailement; I became the next heire to my Bro: and our Paternal Estate, exceedingly far from my least expectation, or desert: The Lord God render me and mine

worthy of this Providence, and that I may be a comfort to my Bro: whose prosperity I did ever wish and pray for:

. . .

A New Archbishop

[July 11] Now also was possession given at Lambeth to Dr. Tillotson, by the Sherif, the Arch-Bishop Sancroft being gon, but leaving his Nephew to keepe possession, who refusing to do it upon the Queenes message, was dispossesed by the Sherif, and imprisoned: This stout demeanor of the few Bishops refusing to take the oaths to K: William etc: animated a greate party, to forsake the Churches, so as to threaten a Schisme: Though those who looked farther into the antient practise, found, that when (as formerly) there were Bishops displac'ᵈ, upon secular accounts, the people never refused to acc[k]nowledge the new Bishops, provided they were not heretics: The truth is, the whole Cleargy had till now stretched the duty of Passive Obedience, that their now proceedings against these Bishops, gave no little occasion of exceptions: But this not amounting to Heresy, there was a necessity of receiving the new Bishops, to prevent a failure of that Order in the Church:

. . .

Southern Ireland Totally Reduced

[19] The greate Victory of K: Williams Army in Ireland was now fresh and looked upon as decisive of that Warr, for the total reduction of that Iland: The Irish foote had 'tis sayd, much advantage by being intrenched, over numbered us in horse, but they forsaking the foote, a total route, greate slaughter, and losse of all the Canon and baggage followed: The French Gen: St. Ruth, (who had ben so cruel a slaughter man to the poore protestants in France,) slaine with divers of the best Commanders: nor was it cheape to us, neere 1000 kild, but of them 4 or 5000:

The Smyrna fleete arrived safe in K. sale, very naro[w]ly escaping the French; and put to extraordinary suffering, by foule Weather carrying the[m] far to the West: which yet was by Gods providence, the cause of their safty:

Greate rejoicing in Lond:

. . .

Death of Robert Boyle

[1692.] Jan: 1: N-yeares day, Dr. Birch at St. James's on 5: Gal: 6: The B: Sacrament follow'd at which I communicated.

This last week died that pious admirable Christian, excellent Philosopher, and my worthy Friend Mr. Boyle, a greate losse to the publique, and to all who knew that vertuous person: aged about 65:

3 Bishop Elect of Lincoln at St. Martins on 1. John 11. The holy Sacrament followed, at which I participated: Dined at Sir W: Godolphins:

6 At the Funeral of Mr. Boile, at St. Martins preached Dr. Burnet Bishop of Salisbery on 2: Eccles: 26: To a man that is good God giveth Knowledge and Wisedome and Joy: on which he made a Philosophical Discourse, Concerning the Acquisitions of Mans knowledge, by the example of Salomon, who had made so many experiments of what this World, and the opportunities of his glorious Circumstances could attaine, and after all that there could be no Joy or true satisfaction in this knowledge, without its being applied to the Glory of God: Thence passed to Elogie due to Mr. Boyle, who made God and Religion the object and scope of all his excellent Tallents in the knowledge of Nature, who had arived to so high a degree in it, accompanied with such zeale and extraordinary piety, which he continualy shewed in the whole Course of his life: and particularly in his exemplary charity upon all occasions: That he gave 1000 pounds yearly to the distressed Refugies of France and Ireland, was at the Charge of Translating the Scripture into Irish, and Indian Tongues, and was now promoting a Turkish Translation, as he had formerly of Grotius de Veritate R.C. into Arabic, which he caused to be dispersed in those Eastern Countries; That he had setled a funds for Preachers who should preach expressly against Atheists, Libertins, Socinians [and] Jewes: besids given 8000 pounds now in his Will to Charitable uses, but that his private Charitys which no man knew of save himselfe were Extraordinary: He delated also of his greate learning in the Tongues, Heb: Greeke, his reading of the Fathers, and solid knowledge in Theologie, once deliberating about taking holy Orders, and that at a time when he might have made a greate figure in the Nation as to secular honor and Title, namely at he restauration of his Majestie Char: 2d: his feare of not being able to discharge so weighty a duty as the first made him decline the first,

and his humility the other: He spake of his wonderfull comity and Civility to strangers, the greate Good he did by his experience in Medicine, and Chymistry, and to what noble ends he applied himselfe to that his darling studies, The works both pious and Usefull which he published, the exact life he led, and the happy End which he made: something was touched of his sister the Lady Ranelagh, who died but very few days before him: And truly all this was but his due, without any grain of flattery: It is certainly not onely England, but all the learned world suffred a publique losse in this greate and good man, and my particular worthy friend:

This Weeke was committed a most execrable Murder on Dr. Clench, by Villans, who under [pretence] of carrying him in a Coach to see a Patient strangled him in the Coach, and under pretence of sending the Coach-man a litle distance, left the poore man dead, and escaped themselves in the dusk of the Evening: This is that Doctor, father of that extraordinary learned Child, whom he brought me sometime to my house etc:

. . .

Lord Marlborough Disgraced

[24] The Lord of Marboro, L: Gen: of K Williams Army in England, Gent of Bedchamber, etc. dismissed from all his Charges Military and other; and given to divers others: for his excessive taking bribes and Covetousnesse and Extortion upon all occasions from his inferior officers: Note this was the Lord who being intirely advanced by K James, the merit of his father being the prostitution of his Daughter (this Lords sister) to that King: Is now disgraced; and by none pittied, being also the first who betrayed and forsooke his Master K: James, who advanced him from the son of Sir Wi[nston] Churchill, an officer of the Greene-Cloth.

An Unkind Return

29 Died my Sister Evelyn of Woodcot, who had made our family so unkind a returne of so neere Relation, by violating my Brothers Will, in causing her daughter my Niepce, to cut of an Intailement and give it to her husband Montague, a Vicious young man, who leaving no children, defrauded my Bro: George of Baynards an Estate worth neere 500 pounds per Ann: etc: I pray God forgive her:

. . .

Bentley as Boyle Lecturer

[February] 13 Being by the late Mr. Boile, made one of the Trustees for his Charitable Bequests, I went this morning to a Meeting of the Bishop of Lincolne, Sir Robert Ashwood,* and Serjeant Roderith; to settle that Clause in Mr. Boyles will, which he had left for Charitable Uses, and Especialy for the Appointing and Electing a Minister to preach one sermon the first Sonday every moneth [except] the 4 summer monethes, June, July, Aug: [September]: expressly against Atheists, [Deists], Libertins, Jewes etc, without descending to any other Controversy whatever; for which is a fund left of 50 pounds per annum to be paid the Preacher quarterly and at the end of 3 years, to proceede to a new Election of some other able Divine, or to continue the same, according as we shold judge convenient; so we made choice of one Mr. Bently, a Chaplain to the Bishop of Worcester: Dr. Stilling-fleete for our first preacher; and that the first sermon shold begin on the first Moneday of March, at St. Martins Church, Westminster, and the 2d [on the first] Monday of Aprill, at Bow-Church in the Citty and so *alternis vicibus*:

. . .

Young John for Ireland

[March 20] My son was made one of the Commissioners of the Revenue and Tressury of Ireland, to which Imployment he had a mind, farr from my wishes, had it consisted with his Circumstances:

. . .

Bentley Against Atheism

[April] 4 Mr. Bentley at St. Mary le Bow, being the church appointed by us, every first Moneday of the Eight Monethes, for the Lecture establish'd by Mr. Boyle:

On: 17: Acts: 14: ad: 30th: So excellent a discourse, against the Epicurean Systeeme, as is not in few words to be recapitulated, shewing the extreame folly and weakenesse of those who question the existance of a Deity, or at least theire concerne for Mankind: He came to me to know whether I thought fit it should be published, or that there was any thing I desired should be altered therein: I tooke it for a Civilitye, and earnestly desired it might forthwith be printed, as one indeede of the most noble, learned, and Convincing discourses, that I had ever heard:

. . .

An Invasion Threatened

[24] Greate talke of the French Invading; and of an universal rising: our Fleete begins to joyne with the Dutch, Souldiers march towards the Coasts etc:

. . .

[May 5] The Reports of an Invasion being now so hott, alarmed the Citty, Court and People exceedingly, nothing but securing and Imprisoning suspected persons; sending downe forces to the sea side, hastening out the Fleete, and an universal consternation what would be the event of all this expectation:

. . .

[8] Continual discourse of the French Invasion, and no lesse of ours in France. The Eastern Winds, so constantly blowing, gave our Fleet time to unite, who were so tardy in preparation, that had not God thus wonderfully favored, they had in all probabillity ben upon us: Many daily secured, and proclamations out for more conspirator[s], so called:

. . .

And Thwarted

22: Trinity Sonday, I heard a sermon at Greenewich of the Curate on: 1: Pet: 5: 7: Exhorting us to cast all our Care upon the Providence of God, doing our owne duty, illustrated by many Instances: and Indeede confirm'd by the Event which happened this very weeke following: for within a day or two after (after all our apprehensions of being invaded, and doubtfull of the event at sea); it pleased Almighty God, to give us such a Victory at sea to the utter ruine of the French Fleete, Admirall and all their best men of Warr, Transport shipps etc: as perhaps never was greater in this part of the World . . . The King being yet with the Confederate Army in Flanders: The next expectation is what God will determine as to the Event of those forces being on both [sides] so dreadfully greate etc:

. . .

Eton

[June] 9 I went to Windsor to carry my Grandson to Eaton Schoole, where I met with My Lady Stonehouse and other of my daughter in Laws relations, who came on purpose to see her before her Journey into Ireland: We went to see the Castle, which we found furnish'd, and very neately kept as formerly, onely the Armes in the Gard Chambers and Keepe were removed and carried away:

. . .

[July] 23 I went with my Wife, Son and Daughter etc: to Eaton to see my Grandson and thence to Cranburne my Lord Godolphins house, where we lay and were most honorably entertained; next day 24 being Sunday, we went to Winsore, to St. Georges Chapell, where we heard a chaplain of the Duke of St. Albans preach, on 1. Pet: 2. 6: the whole discourse was against the Socinians etc:

. . .

Mr. Pepys's Clerk

25 We went to Mr. Hewers's to Clappham, who has a very excellent, usefull and Capacious House upon the Common: built by Sir Den: Gauden, and by him sold to Mr. Ewers, who got a very considerable Estate in the Navy, in which, (from being Mr. Pepys's Cleark) he came to be one of the principal Officers, but was put out of all Employment upon the Revolution, as were all the best Officers, upon suspicion of being no friends to the change: and such put in their place, as were most shamefully Ignorant: and unfit: Mr. Hewers lives very handsomly and friendly to every body etc.

. . .

An Earth Tremor

[September] 15 Happn'd an Earthquake, which though not so greate as to do any harme in England, was yet universal in all these parts of Europe; It shoke the House at Wotton, but was not perceived by any save a servant or two, who were making my bed, and another in a Garret, but I and the rest being at dinner below in the Parlor was not sensible of it. There had ben one in Jamaica this summer, which destroyed a world of people and almost ruin'd the whole Iland: God of his mercy, avert these Judgements, and make them to incite us to Repentance: This, of Jamaica, being prophanely and Ludicrously represented in a puppet play or some such lewd pass-time in the Faire at Southwarke, caused the Queene to put-downe and abolish that idle and vicious mock-shew.

. . .

Highway Robbery

[November 20] A signal Robbery of the Tax mony brought out of the North Country towards Lond; set upon by severall desperat persons, who dismounted and stopt all Travellers on the Ro[a]de, and guarding them in a field, when the exploit was don, and The Treasure taken, killed all the Horses of those they had stay'd, to hinder the pursuit of them: 16 Horses they stabbed and then dismis'd those that they had dismounted etc: This done in Hartfordshire . . .

. . .

A Peer not Culpable

[1693.] Feb: 4 After 5 days Trial, and extraordinary Contest, was the Lord Mohune acquitted by the Lords of the Murder of Montford the Player, notwithstanding that the Judges (from the pregnant witnesses of the fact) had declared him guilty: but whether in commiseration of his youth, being not 18 years old, though exceedingly dissolute, or upon what other reason (the King himselfe present, some part of the Trial, and satisfied they report, that he was culpable): 69 Lords acquitted him and onely 14: Condemn'd him.

Unheard of stories of the universal increase of Witches, men women Children devoting themselves to the Devil, in such numbers in New-England, That it threatened the subversion of the Government:

At the same time a Conspiracy among the Negros in the Barbados, to cut all the Throtes of their Masters, wonderfully detected by the over-hearing two of these slaves discourse of it to one another, and so preventing the execution:

. . .

Evelyn's Daughter Married

[April] 27 This day my Daughter Susanna was Married to William Draper Esquire, in the Chapell of Ely-house by my Lord

Bishop of Lincoln Dr. Tenison, since Arch Bishop of Cant: I gave her in portion 4000 pounds: Her Joynture is 500 pounds a yeare: Which Marriage I pray Almighty God to give his Blessing to: She is a good Child, religious, discreete, Ingenious, and qualified with all the ornaments of her sex: especialy has a peculiar talent in Designe and Painting both in oyle and Miniature, and a genious extraordinary, for whatever hands can pretend to do with the Needle: Has the French Toung, has read most of the Greek and Roman Authors, Poets, using her talents with greate Modesty, Exquisitely shap'd, and of an agreable Countenance: This Character is due to her, though coming from her Father.

. . .

[May] 11 My Daughter we accompanied to her Husbands house, where with many of his and our Relations we were magnificently treated and there we left her in an Appartment very richly addorned and furnish'd, and I hope in as happy a Condition as could be wished: and with the greate satisfaction of all our friends for which God be praised:

. . .

A Royal Collection

[July] 17 I saw the Queenes rare Cabinets and China Collection, which was wonderfull rich and plentifull, but especialy a huge Cabinet, looking Glasse frame and stands all of Amber much of it white, with historical Basrelie[vos] and statues with Medals carved in them, esteemed worth 4000 pounds, sent by the D. of Brandenburg, whose Country Prussia abounds with Amber, cast up by the sea etc: Divers other China, and Indian Cabinets, Schreens and Hangings: also her Library in which were many Bookes in English, French, Dutch, of all Sorts: also a Cuppord of Gold Plate, a Cabinet of silver Fillgrene which I think was our Q. Marys, and in my opinion with other Things, Cabinet pieces, should have ben generously sent her Majestie.

. . .

[August 6] Very lovely Harvest weather and an wholesome season: but no Hortulan fruite:

. . .

Captain Benbow's Exploit

[November 26] Newes of Cap: Benbows exploit and seting fire on St. Malows, in manys opinion not well don, for the small damage we did them may infinitely indanger our Coasts, by their numerous Vessels   our Rivages lying so much more open to them, and many Gentlemens houses well furnish[ed] etc within so few miles of the Coast: whereas all the French Townes and every small Dorp, is Walled, and so not obnoxious to sudden Incursions, I pray God we do not feele it reveng'd on us in the Summer:

. . .

A Convoy Perishes

[1694. March 22] Came the dismal newes of the disaster befalen our Turky merchants Fleete by Tempest, to the almost utter ruine of that Trade: The Convoy of 3 or 4 men of War, and divers Merchant ships with all their Men and Lading perishing; so vast a losse as had hardly ever ben known; and worse than all that both our Warres and Conflicts with any Enemy had don us these hundred years:

Unreasonable Taxes and Impositions layed on us by the Parliament to maintaine an hithertoo successles Warr with France, maneged hitherto with so little discretion etc:

. . .

A Dangerous Highlander

[April 22] Some Regiments of Highlande Dragoons, in their march thro England, men of huge stature and extremely well appointed, and disciplined: One of them being pursued by a Dutchman, whom it seemes he had reproch'd for cowardlinesse in our late fight when in church: The Highlander with his sword struck of his head with one blow, and cleft the scull of another Dutchman with him down to the chin;

. . .

Millenarian Riots

[24] A greate Rising of People in Buckinghamshire, upon the declaration of a famous Preacher (and til now, reputed sober and religious man) that our Lord Christ appearing to him on the 16 of

this moneth, told him he was now come downe, and would appeare publicly at Pentecost and gather all the Saints Jew and Gentile, and leade them to Jerusalem, and begin the Millenium, and destroying and Judging the wiccked, deliver the government of the world to them etc. This bringing great multitude of people to follow this Preacher, divers of the Zelous brought their Goods, and considerable summs of mony, and began to live in imitation of the primitive Saints; minding no private concernes, but were continualy dancing and singing Alalujas night and day; what the end of it may be, I know not, if there be not timely care taken to disperse them before they get to Lond: where there are such multitudes of disscenters and sects, and a mobile so dangerous: and so many discontents, so loose Government, in summ a whole nation so unsettled and distracted . . .

. . .

The Evelyns Leave Sayes Court

May 4th. I went this day, with my Wife and 3 Servants from Says-Court, and removing much furniture of all sorts, books, Pictures, Hangings, bedding etc: to furnish the Appartment my Brother assign'd me; and now after more than 40 yeares, to spend the rest of my dayes with him at Wotton, where I was borne; leaving my House, and 3 servants at my house at Deptford (full furnished) to my Son in Law Draper, to passe the summer in and what longer time he thought good to make use of it: I pray God this solemn Remove may be to the Glory of his mercy, and the good of my family:

. . .

[6] It being far to Church, and no sermon, my Bro: weaknesse obliged us to use the Evening Prayer at home:

This being the first Sunday of the Moneth, the B:Sacrament of the Lords Supper ought to have ben celebrated; but in this Parish exceedingly neglected, so as unlesse at the 4. greate feasts etc no Communion hereabouts, which is a greate fault both in Minister and people; I have spoken to my Brother who is the Patron to discourse the Minister about it.

This is an extraordinary dry season, scarsely one showre since the beginning of Aprill:

27 Whitsonday Wotton Mr. Morus: 26 John: 14: The holy

Communion followed at which I received, the Lord make me mindfull and thankfull:

There was no offering, and very few Communicants, of both which I complained, and desired it might be reformed if possible; The truth is, The present Incumbent, put in by my good natured Brother, upon the importunity of Relations, was one who having another fat living, tooke very little care of this parish, puting it under an hireling tho' I believe a good man, but one altogether without spirit or Vigour: The same did my Bro: to the next Parish in his Gift also, to a Relative of his Ladys, slothfull, and fitter to have ben any thing than a divine: The Lord pardon this fault and reforme it in his good time:

. . .

The Bank of England Founded

[July 8] The first greate Banke for a fund of Mony, being now established by Acct of Parliament was now filled and compleated to the summ of 120000 pounds, and put under the government of the most able and wealthy Citizens of Lond, by which all who adventured any summs had 4 per Centum, so long as it lay in the banke, and had power either to take it out againe at pleasure or Transferr it:

Never more glorious and steady Summer weather, Corne and all other fruits in extraordinary plenty generaly:

. . .

The Barbarity of Bombs

[15] My Lord Berkley burnt Dieppe and Haverdegrace with the bombs in revenge of the defeate at Brest: This manner of destructive warring begun every where by the French, tho' it be exceeding ruinous, especialy falling on the poorer people, and is very barbarous, dos not seeme to tend to make any sooner end of the Warr but rather to exasperate, and incite to revenge:

. . .

Clipping Money

Many Executed at London etc: for Clipping mony, which was now don to that intollerable degree, that there was hardly any mony stiring that was intrinsi[c]aly worth above halfe the value, to such a

strange exorbitance things were arived, beyond that any age can
shew example:

. . .

A Dangerous Accouchement

[September] 13 Hearing that my daughter Draper began to
Complaine and be uneasy of her greate belly, we went on the 13th
towards Deptford, hoping to get thither some competent time
before there would be neede of a Midwife: But were met upon the
way about Meecham, with the good newes of her being delivered of
a Boy the night before, about betweene 7 and 8 a clocke: and so
found her, after it seemes, a very sharp Conflict, very well layd to all
appearance, and so continuing without any unusual Accident for 2
or 3 days; but after that seized with a feavour, loosenesse, vapours
and other evil symptoms which increased upon her to that degree,
that on [21] the friday senight after, we had very little hopes of life:
so as receiving the B: Sacrament, we recomended her condition to
Almighty God, not expecting her to continue many hours after: But
it pleased God (of his infinite mercy) that escaping that night, Sir
Tho Melington and Dr. Cade (the physitians) gave us so[me]
hopes, and so from thence day to day, her feavor, and fits abating,
tho' very slowly, exceeding thirst, and no sort of rest, put us into
many doubts what would be the issue of it: She is now God be
praised in some more ease, lesse thirsty, now and then sleepes; but
still so exceeding Weake and low in Spirits, as puts us in feare: God
of his infinite mercy restore her:

I never saw a finer or goodlier Child: The Baptisme is, against
my will, deferr'd, expecting when Sir T: Draper (who is to be one
of the Godfathers) can come downe, who it seemes is gon a
journey, and returnes not til some days:

. . .

St. Paul's Rebuilt

[October] 5 I went to Paules to see the Choire now finished, as to
the stone work and that part both without and within the scaffolds
struck: some exceptions might yet perhaps be taken without [as] the
placing Columns upon Pilasters, at the East Tribunal: As to the rest
certainly a piece of Architecture without reproch: The pulling out

of the Formes, like drawers from under the stalles, is very ingenious:

...

The Uses of Quinine

[November 30] I visited L: Marques of Normanby, and had much discourse concerning the King Chas 2d being poisoned: also concerning the Quinquean which the Physitians would not give the King, at a time when in a dangerous Ague it was the onely thing could ever cure him, out of envy, because it had ben brought into vogue by Mr. Tabore an Apothecary; Til Dr. Short (to whom the K. sent to have his opinion of it privately, he being reputed a papist, but was in troth a very honest good Christian): he sent him word, it was the onely thing could save his life, and then the King, injoyn'd his physitians to give it him, and was recovered: Being asked by this Lord why they would not prescribe it: Dr. Lower said, it would spoile their practise or some such expression: and at last confessed it was a Remedy fit onely for Kings:

...

A Singular Misfortune

[December 16] Mr. Wells Curate at Abinger had a letter from me to the A Bishop of Cant to procure him a living in Surrey neere Gildford, in place of one Mr. Gerey, who was unhappily killed, by reaching a Gun to his son in a Tree, watching to shoote some rabbets, the Cock being up as he delivered the but end of the piece to his son it went of and hitting the father in the forehead miserably slew him:

...

Death of Queen Mary II

29 I went together with my Wife to Wotton, for the rest of the Winter; which with long frost and snow was I think the very sharpest I ever past: The small pox increasing and exceedingl[y] mortal: Queene Mary died theroff, full of Spotts: Died the 28: and I think was buried 2 or 3 days after: What this unexpected Accident may produce as to the present Government, many are the discourses, and a little time may shew: The K. seemed mightily afflicted, as indeede it behoved him:

...

[1695. January] 13 So very fierce was the frost, as kept us still from church: The Thames frozen over; the Infection of the small pox etc: increased to 500 more this weeke than the former:

20 The frost and continual snows has now lasted neere 5 weekes, with that severity, as hindered me yet from going to our distant parish church to my no small sorrow: The small pox still raging: Greate expressions in most parts of England, and in Holland exceeding, for the death of the late Queene: The King and Princesse Ann (til now displeased with the Court, upon some suggestions, which made the two sisters strang to one another) now so fully reconciled, that she is invited to keepe her Court at White-hall (till now living privately at Berkely-house) and desired to take into her family divers servants of the Queene, to maintain which the King had assign'd her 5000 a quarter: Greate preparation in the meane time for a most magnificent funeral: All people in Mourning; Addresse[s] of Condolence from all parts both at home, and from abroad:

Feb: 3 The weather and season had hitherto continued so very severe and the snow so deepe, and now so slabby, s[l]ippery and cold; as we could not be at church without danger: I do not know I have ben so many Sondays absent from it, above these 40 yeares, to my greate sorrow:

. . .

[March] 5 Was the Queens funeral infinitely expensive, never so universal a Mourning, all the Parliament men had Cloaks given them: 400 poore women, all the streets hung, and the middle of the streets boarded and covered with black cloth: there was all the Nobility, Mayor and Aldermen, Judges etc:

. . .

Her Virtues

8 I tooke leave of my L. of Canterbery: and supped at the B: of Lichfild and Co: who related me the pious behaviour of the Queene in all her sicknesse which was admirable and the noble designe she had in hand, her expensive Charity, never enquiring of the opinion of the partys if objects of charity: that a Cabinet [being] opened some time after her decease, a paper was found wherein she had desired her body might not be opned or any expense on her funerall extraordinary when ever she should happen to dye; both

which were not perform'd, finding this paper too late after all was already prepared: Other excellent things under her owne hand to the very least of her debts, which were very small, and every thing in that exact method as seldom is found in any private persons ...

...

The Reign of William III
1695–1702

Great Cheer at Lambeth

[July] 6 I din'd at Lambeth making my first Visit to my L A Bishop, where was much company and greate cheere: After Prayers in the Evening, my Lord, made me stay, to shew me his house, furniture, and Garden, which was all very fine, and far beyond the usual A Bishops: not as affected by this A.B: but as being bought ready furnished of his predecessor: we discoursed of severall publique matters, particularly of the Princesse of Denmark, who made so little a figure, and now after greate expectation, not with child etc: so I returned to Lond:

. . .

A Misadventure

[September 16] My good and worthy friend Cap: Gifford, who that he might get some competency to live decently, adventured all he had in a Voyage of 2 years to the E. Indies, was with another greate ship, taken by some French Men-of-Warr, almost within sight of England, to the los[s]e of neere 700000 pounds: to my greate sorrow, and pity of his Wife: he being also a valiant and Industrious man: The losses of this sort to the Nation has ben immense; and all thro the negligence and little care of the Government, to secure the same neere our owne Coasts, of infinite more concernment to the publique than spending their time in bombing and ruining two or three paltry Towns, Calais, St. Malo etc in which so many poore Creatures are destroyed, without any benefit, or weakening our Enemys, who, tho' they began, ought not to have ben imitated by an hostility totally averse to humanity, and especialy to Christianity.

. . .

A Catholic Plot

[1696. February] 26 There was this weeke a Conspiracy of about 30 Knights, Gent, Captaines, many of them Irish and English Papists and non Jurors or Jacobites (as calld) to murder K. William, upon the first opportunity of his going either from Kensington, to hunting, or the Chappell, and upon a signal of fire to be given from Dover C[l]iffe to Calis, an Invasion designed, where there were in order to it, a very greate Army in readinesse, Men-of Warr and transport ships innumerable to joyne with a general Insurrection here, The Duke of Barwick being seacretly come to London to head them, and K. James attending at Calis with the French Army: but it being discovered by I think the Duke of   and other of the Confederats, and by one of their owne party; and a 1000 pounds, to who soever could apprehend any of the 30 named: The whole designe was frustrated, most of the Ingaged taken and secur'd: The Parliament, Citty and all the nation congratulating the deliverance and Votings and Resolutions, that if ever K. William should be Assassinated, it should be revenged upon the Papists and Party throut the nation, an Act of Association drawing up to impower the Parliament to sit upon any such Accident, til the Crowne should be dispos'd of according to the late settlement at the Revolution; All Papists in the meane time to be banished 10 miles from London; which put this nation into an incredible disturbance and general Animosity against the Fr: King, and K. James: The Militia of the Nation raised, several Regiments sent for out of Flanders, and all things put into a posture to encounter a descent: which was so timed abroad, that, whilst we were already much confused, and discontented upon the greatnesse of the Taxes, and corruption of the mony etc, we had likely to have had very few Men of Warr neere our Coasts; but so it pleased God, the V Admiral Rooke wanting a Wind to pursue his Voyage to the Straites, That Squadron, with what other forces at Portsmouth and other places, were still in the Channell, and soone brought up to joyne with the rest of the Ships which could be gotten together: so as there is hope this Plot may be broken; It is certaine it had likely have ben very fatal to the danger of the whole Nation, had it taken Effect; so as I looke on it as a very greate deliverance and prevention by the Providence of God; for tho many did formerly pitty K. James's Condition, this designe of Assasination, and bringing over a French Army, did much alienate many of his Friends, and was like to produce a more perfect establishment of K. William, it likewise so much concerning the whole Confederacy . . .

. . .

[March 15] Three of the unhappy wretches (whereoff one a Priest) executed this weeke for intending to assassinate the King; accknowledging their intention, but acquitting K. James, of instigating them to it in that manner, and dying very penetently: Divers more in danger and some very Considerable persons:

Greate frost and cold:

. . .

Eton and Kensington Palace

[April] 23 I went to Eaton, din'd with Dr. Godolphin the Provost. The Scholemaster assured me that there had not ben in 20 yeares a more pregnant youth in that Place than my Grandson: I return'd that evening with Lady Jane Leueson and her daughter etc, who went to place Sir William Windham at that Schole:

I went to see the Kings house at Kensington with some Ladys: The House is very noble, tho not greate; the Gallerys furnished with all the best Pictures of all the Houses, of Titian, Raphel, Corregio, Holben, Julio Romano, Bassan, V: Dyke: Tintoret, and others, with a world of Porcelain; a pretty private Library; the Gardens about it very delicious:

. . .

Deptford and Greenwich Hospital

June 1. I went to Deptford to dispose of our Goods, being in order to lett it for 3 years to V. Admiral Benbow, with Conditions to keepe the Garden etc:

4: A Comitty meeting at W-hall, about the Hospital at Greenewich at Sir Chr: Wrenn, his Majesties Surveyor Gen: We made the first agreement with divers Workemen and for Materials, and gave the first Order for the proceding on the foundations, ordering payments to be Weekly to the Workmen and a general Accompt to be monethly:

I then received Orders from the Lords of the Tressury for the Kings 2000 pounds to be employed on that work:

. . .

[11] I let my House at Deptford to V: Admiral Benbow for 3 years etc

The Spaniards receive an overthr[ow] in Catalonia:

Financial Fears

Want of current money to carry on not onely the smalest concernes, but for daily provisions in the Common Markets: Ginnys lowered to 22s: and greate summs daily transported into Holland, where it yeelds more, which with other Treasure sent thither to pay the Armies, nothing considerable coined of the new and now onely current stamp, breeding such a scarsity, that tumults are every day feared; no body either paying or receiving any mony; so Imprudent was the late Parliament, to damne the old (tho clip't and corrupted) 'til they had provided supplies. To this add the fraud of the Bankers and Goldsmiths who having gotten immense riches by extortion, keepe up their Treasure, in Expectation of a necessity of advancing its Value. Duncumb not long since, a meane Goldsmith, having made a purchase of neere 90000 pounds of the late D. of Buckinghams Estate, and reputed to have neere as much in Cash etc: Banks and Lotteries every day set up, besides Taxes intollerable, and what is worse and cause of all this, Want of Publique Spirite, in a Nation daily sinking under soe many Calamities.

. . .

With Wren to Greenwich

30 I went with a select committee of the Commissioners for the fabri[c]k of Greenewich Hospital, and with Sir Chr: Wren the Surveyor, where with him I laied the first stone of that intended foundation; precisely at 5 a clock in the Evening after we had dined together: Mr. Flamsted the Kings Astronomical Profes[s]or observing the punctual time by Instruments . . .

. . .

The Bank to the Rescue

[August 9] I drank Epsom waters some days: nothing of publique this weeke save the Bank lending the King 200000 pounds for the Army in Flanders, that having don nothing against the Enemy, had so exhausted the Treasure of the Nation that one could not have

borrowed mony under 14 or 15 per Cent on bills nor Exchequer
Tallies [on] the best funds for 30 per Cent, so miserably had we
lost our best credit: Reasonable good harvest weather:

. . .

However 300000 pounds being carried over to our Armys, made
mony still more and more scarcy in England, so as one could hardly
borrow 100 pounds upon the publique security under 13 or 14 per
cent, nor on the Chequer for 30:

. . .

Clerical Influence

29 I went to Lambeth, dined with the A Bishop: there had that
morning ben a Court upon the Complaint against Dr. Watson the
Bishop of Bristol suspended for Simonie; The AB: told me how
unsatisfied he was with the Cannon Law, and how exceedingly
unreasonable all their pleadings appeared to him: After dinner I
mooved him for Dr. Bohune for a preferment promised me for
him; and told him how much I had ben solicited to Bespeake his
suffrage for the Deane of Carlisle, to succeede the Bishop of that
Diocesse, now very old: As also concerning Okewood Chapell etc:

. . .

Gloomy Prospects

[1697. January] 31 The weather continuing so exceeding fierce,
so as since that tirrible winter 12 years since, the like had not ben
known, much corne not coming up, much rotted by the extraordinary wett before the frost, and the ground so hard, as in many places
now pl ... threatning a Dirth: Mony yet so scarce etc: the
Parliament are in greate distresse to furnish another Summers
Campagne: besides people Mechanics begin to rise, as at the
beginning of the greate Rebellion: peace much talked of, but
nothing don; unheard of storms and losse at sea, Newfound Land
surprized by the French: Confusion in Poland about a King; The K
of Spaine not recovered: Conspirasies continualy against K
William, for which this last week Sir J. Fenwick, was beheaded on
Tower Hill: The Lord in mercy prevent further Calamities to this
Church and nation.

Feb: 7 So severely greate has ben this still continuing frost, and
snow, that divers sentinels doing their duty in the Armies and

Townes kept by Garizons, that in Flanders many of them were frozen to death, within an houre or two before they were relieved tho so often: The Duke of Savoy now returning over the Mountain[s], had many of his Guard and troops, Mules and Equipage lost in the Snow, the Duke himselfe hardly escaping:

. . .

Disastrous Fire at Whitehall

[1698. January 2] White-hall utterly burnt to the ground, nothing but the walls and ruines left:

The Zar of Muscovy landed and came to Lond:

. . .

The Tsar of Muscovy at Sayes Court

[February 6] The Czar Emp: of Moscovy, having a mind to see the Building of Ships, hired my House at Says Court, and made it his Court and palace, lying and remaining in it, new furnish'd for him by the King:

27: Our Curat on 8. Zach: 17: A very frosty and hard season, snow and cold:

. . .

[April] 21 The Czar of Mosco[vy] went from my house towards Russia, etc:

. . .

Music with Pepys

[May] 30 I dined at Mr. Pepyss, where I heard that rare Voice, Mr. Pate, who was lately come from Italy, reputed the most excellent singer, ever England had: he sang indeede many rare Italian Recitatives, etc: and severall compositions of the last Mr. Pursal, esteemed the best composer of any Englishman hitherto:

. . .

In the Wake of the Tsar

[June] 9 I went to Deptford to view how miserably the Tzar of Moscovy had left my house after 3 moneths making it his Court, having gotten Sir Cr: Wren his Majesties Surveyor and Mr. London his Gardener to go down and make an estimat of the repairs, for which they allowed 150 pounds in their Report to the L:

of the Treasury:* Then I went to see the foundations of the Hall and Chapell, wharfe and other parts of the Greenwich Hospital: and so returned.

. . .

Captain Dampier 'Buccaneere'

August 6. I din'd at Mr. Pepys, where was Cap: Dampier, who had ben a famous Buccaneere, brought hither the painted Prince Jolo, printed a Relation of his very strange adventures, which was very extraordinary, and his observations very profitable: Was now going abroad againe, by the Kings Incouragement, who furnished a ship of 290 Tunn: he seemed a more modest man, than one would imagine, by the relation of the Crue he had sorted with: He brought a map, of his observations of the Course of the winds in the South-Sea, and assured us that the Maps hithertoo extant, were all false as to the Pacific-sea, which he makes on the S[o]uth of the line, that on the North, and running by the Coasts of Perù, being extremely tempestious:

. . .

Young Jack to Balliol

[1699. February] 17 My Grandson went to Oxford with Dr. Mander, the Master of Bal: Coll: where he was entered a fellow-Commoner:

. . .

Death of Young John

[March] 24 Friday To my exceeding griefe and affliction: after a tedious languishing sicknesse contracted in Ireland, and increased here, died my onely remaining son John: [who had] now ben 6 years one of the Kings Commissioners of the Revenue of that Kingdom, and performed his Employment both with greate ability and reputation, aged 44 years and about 3 moneths: Leaving me one Grandson, now at Oxon, whom I beseech A. God to preserve, and be the remaining support of the Wotton family: Upon this Interruption I could not appeare at Church the following Sonday:

. . .

A Model Undergraduate

[April 16] My Grandson sent me a latin Epist[le] from Oxon, giving me account of the progresse of his studys there, and of his preparation for the receiving of the H. Eucharist, the first time, on Easter Sonday: I beseech God to blesse him, that he may proceede as he has hithertoo:

...

The Duchess of Mazarine

[June 15] Now also died, the famous Dutchesse of Mazarine, in her time the richest Lady in Europ, Niepce to the greate Cardinal Mazarine, and married to the Richest subject in Europ, as is said: she was born at Rome, Educated in France, an extraordinary Beauty and Witt, but dissolute, and impatient of Matrimonial restraint, so as to be abandoned by her husband, came into England for shelter, liv'd on a pension given her here, and is reported to have hastned her death, by intemperan[t]ly drinking strong spirits etc: She has written her owne Story and Adventures and so has her other Extravagant sister, wife to the noble family Colona.

A Bad Example

There died this weeke also Conyers Seymor son of Sir Ed: Seymor, kild in a Duel caused by a slight affront given him in St. Ja: Parke, by one that [was] envious at his Gallantry, for he was a new set-up vaine young fopp: who made a greate Eclat about the Town by his splendid Equipage, not setting any bounds to his pompous living; an Estate of 7000 pounds a yeare falling to him, not two years before, all of which he left at about 2[2] or 23 years of age, to another Brother at Oxford: The general dissolution and Corruption and Atheisme of this period was now in as greate height in this nation among both sexes, as anywhere in Christendome.

...

A Dismal Eclipse

[September 13] There was on Wednesday this weeke great expectations of the Effects of a very dismal Eclipse of the Sun, people expected by predictions of the Astrologer[s] that it would be exceedingly darke: But tho' the morning were very Mirky, yet was the obscurity no other than on other clowdy days: But this I well remember, the whole Nation was affrited by Lilly the Almanack [writer], who foretold what a dreadfull Eclipse that which was called Black monday it would be, insomuch as divers persons were grievously in dread, and durst not peepe out of their house: Yet was that a very bright morning, and the darknesse much like this: It is now above 50 years since, it was indeede succeeded with many revolutions, cruell wars, twixt us and Holland, but this, was preceded by the Death of the K. of Denmark and Q. of Portugal: But thus superstitious people, not considering the natural Course of those Luminarys, looke on what ever haps of Extraordinary as their Effects, who ought to looke up to God the Author of Nature.

. . .

Death of George Evelyn

[October] 4 Wednesday night departed this life my worthy and dear Bro: Geo: Evelyn at his house at Wotton in Surrey in the 83d yeare of his Age, and of such Infirmitys as are usualy incident to so greate an Age, but in perfect memory and understanding: A most worthy, Gentleman, Religious, Sober and Temperate, and of so hospitable a nature as no family in the whole County maintained that antient Custome of keeping (as it were) open house the whole yeare, did the like, or gave nobler and freer Entertainement to the whole County upon all occasions: so as his house was never free, there being sometime 20 persons more than his family, and some that stayed there all the summer to his no small expense, which created him the universal love of the Country: To this add, his being one of the Deputy Lieutenants of the County; and living to be the most antient Member of Parliament living: He was Born at Wotton, Went to Oxford, Trinity Coll: from the Free Schole at Guilford, Thence to the Midle Temple, as gent: of the best quality did, tho' with no intention to study the Law as a Profession: He married the Daughter of Colwall, of a worthy and antient family in Leicester-[s]hire, by whome he had One son; she dying in 1643, left George her son an Infant, who being educated liberaly, after Traveling abroad, returning home, married one Mrs. Goare; by whom he had severall Children but left onely 3 daughters: He was a Young man of a good understanding, but over Indulging to his Ease and pleasure, grew so very Corpulent, contrary to the constitution of the rest of his fathers relations, that he died: after my Bro: his

Father had married a most noble and honourable Lady, relict of Sir Jo Cotton, she being an Offley, a worthy and antient Staffordshire family by whom he had severall Children of both sexes: This lady dying left onely 2 daughters and a son: the younger daughter dyed, before Mariage: The other lived long as a Virgin, and was afterward married to Sir Cyrill Wych, a noble learned Gent: sonne to Sir Wych: he had ben Ambassador at Constantinople: Sir Cyrill was afterwards Made one of the Lords Justices of Ireland: Before this Mariage her onely Bro: John Maried the daughter of Aresfeild of Sussex of an honorable family, whom he left a Widow, without any Child living: He dying about Anno 1691 and his wife not many yeares after, without any heire: My Bro: resettled the whole Estate on me: His sister who maried S[ir] C. Wych having had a portion of 6000 pounds to which what was added was worth above 300 pounds more: The 3 other Grandaughters, with what I added to theirs about 5000 pounds each: [This] my Bro: having seene performed, died this 5t of Octob: in a good old Age, and greate Reputation: and making his beloved Daughter my Lady Wych sole executrix (leaving me onely his Library and some Pictures of my Father, Mother etc:) She indeede buried him with extraordinary solemnity, rather as a Noble man, Than a privat Gent: There were I computed above 2000 people at the funerall, all the Gent of the County doing him the last honour: This performed 20th I returned to Lond, where I came the day before, leaving my Concernes at Wotton, 'til my Lady should dispose of her selfe and family: and sending onely a servant thither to looke after my Concerns:

. . .

A Thames Fog

[November 8?] There happned this Weeke so thick a Mist and fog; that people lost their way in the streetes, it being so exceedingly intense, as no light of Candle, Torches or Lanterns, yeilded any or very little direction: I was my selfe in it, and in extraordinary danger, robberys were committed betwene the very lights which were fixt between Lond: and K[e]nsington on both sides, and whilst Coaches and passengers were travelling: and what was strange, it beginning about 4 in the afternoone was quite gon by 8, without any wind to dissipate it. At the Thames they beate drumms, to direct the Watermen to make the shore, no lights being bright enough to penetrat the fogg:

. . .

Public Security

[November 24] The Parliament met and adjourned for a Weeke.

Horrible roberys, high-way men, and murders committed such as never was known in this Nation since Christian reformed: Atheism, Dissensions, prophanesse, Blasphemy among all sorts: portending some signal judgement, if not amended: upon which a Society set on foote, who obliged themselves to endeavour the reforming of it, both in London and other places, which began to punish offenders, and put the laws in more strict Execution: which God Almighty prosper.

Never was so gentle, Calme, dry, yet seasonable and temperate weather thro all the seasons of the yeare, as this has ben:

. . .

Public Corruption

[December 10] Continuance of warm spring weather: The Parliament reverse the prodigious donations of the Irish forfeitur, intended to be set a part for dischargeing the vast national debt: And calling some great persons in highest office in question for setting the greate seale to an arch pyrates being pardon'd, and Comissioned to take and bring other pyrats infesting Commerce, had turned pyrate again, and brought prizes into the W: Indies, suspected to be connived at, upon [shares] of the prey: by which some greate men were brought into suspicion: but the prevaling part in the house, called Courtiers, out voted the Complaints, or Country part, as for most part they do; not for being more in number, but more vigilantly attending the house, thro neglect of their duty:

. . .

Return to Wotton

[1700. January] 25 I went to Wotton, the first time, after my deare Brothers funerall, to settle my Interest and Concernes there, and furnish the house with necessarys, thro my Lady Wyche and

Nephew [Glanvill] being Executors, having sold and disposed of what goods were left of my Brothers.

...

'Exorbitant Numbers of Attourneys'

[February 4] The Parliament Incorporate the old E. India Company. Voted against the Scots invading or settling in the Darien as prejudicial to our trade with Spaine: Voted that the Exorbitant Numbers of Attourneys (now indeede swarming and evidently causing suits and disturbance, by eating out the Estate of people, provoking them to go to law etc) be lessened; Voted that it should not be in the power of Popish parents, to disinherit their Protestant Children:

...

Moral Reform

[March] The nation being now grown to so unsufferable a passe, and height of Atheisme and profanesse: some Religious persons both in the Citty and Country, entred into a kind of fraternity to attempt a reformation, by a more than ordinary discountenancing immorality and irreligion, upon all occasions; Into this Society entred divers persons of quality, and for that end, some Lectures, were set up, as in particular in the Citty of Lond: Bow-church or St. Paules, where preached the most Eminent of the Cleargy, after the reading of a declaration set forth by the King, to suppresse this universal and growing wickednesse, which already began to take some effect, as to the Common Swearing and [oaths] in the mouths of people of all ranks: and 25 this day preached Dr. Burnet Bishop of Salisbery, befor the Lord Mayor and a very greate Congregation: on 27: Pro: 5. and 6 verse, Open Rebuke is better than seacret love: applyed to the present designe of proceeding in their Indeavor of Reforming the publique dissolution.

...

Commissioners for Ireland

[27] The Parliament did now nominate 14. Persons to go Commissioners into Ireland, in order to dispose of the Confiscated Estates in Ireland, towards payment of the Debts of this Nation contracted in the late Warr; but which the King had in greate

measure given to some of his greate favorits of both sexes, Dutch and other of little merite, and very unseasonably [as] appeared: That this might be don, without suspition of Interest in the Parliament, but for the publique, It was determined that no Member of the House, should be of the Commission, and was therefore to be supplyed by severall Country Gent: and persons of quality, and reputed Integrity:

...

Christ's Hospital and Greenwich

[April 1] The Lord Major, Sherifs, Aldermen etc went with a procession of the Children etc, brought-up in Christs Hospital: among which the 40 Blew-Coate Boys instructed in Mathematics and designed for the sea, with their mathematical Instruments in their hands, going to St. Brides according to custome:

3. I went, with Sir Chr: Wren, Surveyor of his Majesties Workes and Buildings, to Kensington, to present the King with the Model and several drafts ingraved, of the Hospital now erecting at Greenewich for Sea-Men, The A: Bish: of Cant: introducing us; His Majestie receiving us with greate satisfaction, and incouraging the prosecution of the Work:

...

Lords Versus Commons

10 The greate Contest betweene the Lords and Commons concerning the Lords power of amendments and rejection of certaine bills, tack't to the money bill, carried onely for the Commons for them against the Lords, was this days Event, which went so high, as every body almost believed would have either provoked the K to Adjourn, or dissolve them: But by Gods mercy and providence it is prevented: However this Tacking of Bills is a novell practise, suffered by Charles II. who being continualy in want of mony, let any thing passe rather than not have to feede his extravagant favorits etc:

Mr. Nagg our late lectur[er] preached on 5: Hosea 15:

The greate contest betweene the Lords and Commons about passing the Bill for monys, to which they had tack't so many other considerable demands, (and which indeede was but a later practice caused by the continual want of mony to which Charles the 2d had brought himselfe by his profusion and favorits) was at last assented to, with greate difficulty, Voices being equal on both sides, and accidentaly carryed by one Voice; all the Bishops following the Court: going out save one: So as neere 60 Bills passt, to the greate triumph of the Commons, and Country part, but high regret of the Court, and those to whom the King had given large estates in Ireland, of lands, more necessary to discharge the prodigious arrears and debts of the publique, t[h]o it must be confessed, that this successe of theirs, must needes lessen the King, and the interest of the Court, which I foresee will be hard to recover; so apprehensive the Nation are of yeilding any advantage they have gotten, as being now the onely people in Europe who have preserved their libertys, and unwilling to come under a despotic power, as those in Fr: Denmark, Sweden and our neighbours grone under: And pity it is, that things should be brought to such extremitys; The government of this Nation being so equaly poised betweene King and Subject: But we are satisfied with nothing; and whilst there is no perfection on this side heaven, mi thinks both might be contented, without straining things too farr:

. . .

A Profane Age

[May] There never had ben, in any mans memory, so glorious a Spring, such hope of aboundance of fruits of all kinds, and [so] propitious a yeare, and yet never a more profane, and atheistical age: most of the youth and others Atheist[s], Theists, Arians and Sectaries, which God of his mercy reforme:

. . .

Suicide at All Souls

[June 16] Mr. Creech fellow of All-Soules in Oxon: an Excellent Poet and Philosopher who published Lucretius with notes in Latine, and an English translation, with many other pieces, and [seemed] to be of a grave and sollid temper, was found hanged, none knowing upon what occasion or apparent discontent or Cause, his Circumstances being so very easy, for besides one of the best fello[w]ships in the University, he had a living, I am told worth 200 pounds per ann: This disaster much astonished me, who knew him . . .

. . .

The Royal Succession

[July 7] The death of the Duke of Gloucester, dying of the smallpox, is very astonishing, a hopefull child of 12 or 13 years old, and the onely Child of the Princesse Ann by the Prince of Denmarke, she having had and ben with child of many sonns and daughters, but commonly none living, and often misscarying: So as now there is none to succeede to this Crowne, according as lately settled by Parliament on the late Revolution, but [on] some Protestant Prince, the next I think being the Prince of Hanover* Grandson, to the Q: of Bohemia, sister to K. Charles the first: otherwise, I think, descending (if the P: of Wales be utterly excluded) on the Dutchesse of Savoy, daughter to the princes Henrietta, Sister to Charles the first: Wher the Crowne will now Settle, should the Princesse of Denmark breed no more to live, is matter of high speculation to the Politic:

. . .

An Exotic Estate

September 13 A Considerable Estate in land, faire house, richly furnished, Plate, Mony etc being fallen to my Son in Law, Draper, at Adscome neere Croydon: I went with my Wife thither and stayed there til the 26, when I returned back to Wotton:

During the time of my being with my son and daughter: I went to see divers seats of the Gentry neere it, 16 as [Marden], a barren Warren, bought by Sir Ro: Clayton, who building there a pretty House, made such alteration by planting not onely with infinite store of the best fruit; but by so changing the natural situation of the hill, valleys and solitary mountains about it, that it represented rather some forrain Country, producing as it were spontaneously pines, fir, Cypresse, Yew, holly, Juniper intermingled with walks, mazes, precipices, and other so as one would easily fancy himself in some forrain Country, naturaly solitudinary, and exceedingly and pleasantly Exottique, the trees being come to their perfect growth and all preserved with uttmost Care, so as I, who had some years before seene it in its natural and baren condition was in admiration of it: The lande was purchased of Sir J. Evelyn of God-Stone, and by the Industry, and vast charge of this opulent Citizen, thus improved for pleasure and retirement: He and his Lady, entertained us with greate civility:

. . .

And a Ruined One

20: I went to see Bedington, the antient seate of the Carews formerly and in my remembrance, a noble old structure, capacious, and in forme of the buildings of the Age in Hen: 8. and Q. Eliz: [time] and proper for the old English hospitality, but now decaying with the house it selfe, heretofore adorned with ample Gardens, and the first Orange trees that ever were seene in England, planted in the open ground, and secured in Winter onely by a Tabernacle of boards, and stoves, removable in summer; thus standing 120 yeares large and goodly Trees and laden with fruite, but now in decay as well as the Grotts and other curiositys, Cabinets and fountaines in the house and abroade, thro the debauchery and negligence of the Heires, it being now fallen to a Child under age, and onely kept by a servant or two from utter delapidation. The Estate and Parke about it also in decay: the negligence of a few years, ruining the Elegances of many:

. . .

Pepys in Clover

23: I went visite Mr. Pepys at Clapham, who has there a very noble, and wonderfully well furnished house, especialy with all the Indys and Chineze Curiositys, almost any where to be mett with, the Offices and Gardens exceedingly well accomodated [for pleasure] and retirement:

. . .

Smallpox at Balliol: a Brave Master

[November] 5 Came the newes of my deare Grandsons (the onely male of my family remaining) being fall'n ill of the Small-pox at Oxford, which after the dire effects it had, taking a way two of my Children (Women grown) exceedingly Afflicted me: But so it pleased my most mercyfull God, that, being let-blood, at his first complaint of uneasinesse; and the extraordinary Care of Dr. Mander, head of the Coll: and now Vice-chancelor, (who caused him to be brought out of his owne Chamber, and lodg'd in his owne Appartment, Bed and Bed-Chamber) with the advise of his Physitian, and care of his Tutor: That as they came out kindly, separatly, and but few: and no evil symtom accompanying: There was all faire hopes of his doing well, to our infinite Comfort, and refreshment; as [appeared from] the account, which was se[n]t us by letter every day since their appearance, by letters either from the V: Chan: himselfe, or his Tutor: for which Almighty-God be forever praised and depended on:

. . .

A Crisis in Spain

There was no other discourse at this time, amongst the Polit[it]ians and speculatists, save this great and stupendious Revolution of Spaine, given to the Fr: King[s] Grandson by the will of that King: and it was looked on as a coup d'Adresse in the French, amusing our K. William and the rest, about a partition, without which the Spanish Counsels had never made this alteration; for they dreaded nothing so much as the dismembring of those Dominions, and this 'tis believed, induced them to make the King settle it by Will:

. . .

Battle of Narva

[December] The Ctzar of Moscovy (who came with a greate Army to beseige Narva, and reduct that important place to greate straites) is defeated by the Swedes, the Seige raised, and a greate Batell fought, where in the losse on the Ctzars side were slayne 10000, The Artillery and Baggage Taken, The King in person, with a far unequal number, obtaining the Victory, to the joy of all those potentates, who dreaded the Ctzars having any thing to do in the Baltick, which was the aime of the barbarous Prince:

. . .

The Spanish Succession

[1701. February] The Parliament met on the 6t: To whom the K. recommends their care about a Successor, the Pri: of Denmark not likely to have any child live: The shipping, and Harbours, The supplying the defects of the funds to pay of the greate debt of the Nation, the burden of the poore Tax, the security of the Prot: Religion etc.

To which the[y] returned Answer that they would besides all this endeavour the peace of Europ against all, its molesters etc:

But these Resolutions were so late and untimely, that the Fr:

King, who had out witted all Europ by Contriving the K of Spaines will, that before they could do any thing Considerable by concerting matters of this exceeding greate Moment: with the Emperor, Hollanders and Northern princes, The French had seized on all Flanders, and the state of Millan, and pour'd into them greate Armies; so as the Dutch were forc't to owne the New King Philip: and all this may be imputed to our sole neglect of breaking-up the late Parliament and not meeting of this til too late by a fatal stupidity . . .

. . .

Wotton Again

[April] 23d. I returned from Wotton by Greenwich, where my deare Wife being gon, thinking to have the benefit of the aire on the heath, for the recreation of her breath and lungs exceedingly still afflicted of the Cough, fell into a Feaver and Pleurisy, of which she was hardly relieved to my greate sorrow; but leaving her better the next day, businesse hastened me to Lond:

. . .

[May 11] It was now so greate a drouth, no raine considerable having fallen in some moneths, that a famine is feared, to all those other Judgements Impending on us, but which God avert:

My daughter Draper was delivered of a Daughter safely, for which God be praised; and my Wife gathering strength apace.

. . .

The Hanoverian Succession

[June 11] The parliament had now settled the Succession on the house of Hanover, of which there was an antient Lady of the Electoral palitine famely living, and the duke her son: with other usefull Accts that now passed: All the world being now big with expectation of action, the Emp: Army approaching Italy, and by this actualy gotten into it, against all mens expectation considering how the French had guarded the Avvenues: Nor were the Hollanders lesse industrious to keepe the French from Insulting on them, which the French every day threatened by the hostile preparations he made in Flanders: etc:

. . .

A Coaching Breakdown

[20] My Wife going into Surry, The Ax[l]etree of the Coach firing on Bansted downe, they endeavored to quench it, with the fat of the meate was caried with them and a bottle of sack, to refresh them on the way, no water neere them til they came to Letherhead.

...

Summer at Wotton

[July] The heate of the Season, exceedingly disposes me to drowsinesse, to which 'til of late I was never subject: But this I must impute to my age etc.

8 I went with my Family for the rest of the summer to Wotton, dined at my son Drapers at Adscomb.

I made a New Coach and Charriot this yeare:

...

The Season was very dry:

19 A poore old Labourer falling off from the Hay Cart, not any considerable height, but pitching on his head, breaking his Collar-bone, and doubtlesse disordering his braine, tho neither quite speechlesse, and let blood but without effect, died, to my exceeding sorrow and trouble, it being in my Haying:

...

Old Age

[October] 31 I was this day 81 years old Compleate in tollerable health considering my Great Age: God also delivered my Grandson sick at Oxford of the smalpox, for which and many other preservations, continuing my familys health, I rendred (as most bounden) my sincere Accknowledgements:

The weather grew suddainly Cold, hard frosts and snow.

...

The King returned from Holland: The frost relenting with seasonable weather: I planted the Elme walke in the back of the Meadow:

...

Death of William III

[1702. March 8] The King having had a fall from his horse as he was hunting, which broke his coller bone, and being himselfe much

Indisposed before and Aguish, with his former long Cough and other weaknesse, put into a Feaver, died at Kensington this Sunday morning about 8 a clock, to the extraordinary disturbance of the whole Citty, and I feare, to the Interests of the whole nation, in this dangerous Conjuncture, without Gods Infinite mercy: Matters both abroad, and at home being in so loose a posture, and all Europe ready to breake out into the most dangerous Warr that it ever suffered, and this Nation especially being so unprovided of persons of the Experience, Conduct and Courage, just as we were concluding this Confederacy so long concerted with the Emp: and other Princes, to resist the deluge of the French: How this may concerne the measures hitherto taking: God onely knows: The Parliament sate all this day and, I think all last night, and Queene Ann Proclaym'ed at the usual places, and Ceremonys: These two days have ben warm and bright as Summer, all people else, especialy the Souldiers holding downe their heads: God has some greate thing to do, grant it may be to our good, and his Glory etc.

The Reign of Anne
1702–(1706)

Queen Anne Proclaimed and Crowned

[March 11] There was orders published in print, after what manner the publique Mourning for the King was expected to be, as to the Clothes of persons of quality: In the meanetime, there seemed to be no sort of alteration, or Concerne in the people, upon the Kings death but all things pass't without any notice, as if he had still ben alive: Onely the Shopkeepers, who had provided store of Silke and other modish things, complained of the deadnesse of Trade they feared would insue: The Queene was proclaymed with the usual Ceremonies, the greate men, Lord Mayor and Aldermen etc: crouding to Kisse the Q: hands and felicitate her Accession to the Crown: The Wind not favoring, tho the weather like summer, no Intelligence from abroad.

. . .

[April] 23 Was Queene Ann Crowned with all possible magnificence and Pomp, the AB of York preaching on
It was a bright day, and every body much pleased and satisfied.

. . .

Repairs at Wotton

[26] My Wife going to Wotton for a few days, to se what the Workemen had don in repairing the house not yet finish'd: and my steward came up with his Accompt I adjusted all the particulars, finding them very faire: and his Trust honestly m[anaged], amounting to 1900 pounds.

. . .

An Eloquent Preacher

[May] My Lord Godolphin was made Lord High Treasurer of England:
6 I went to Congratulate him.

8 My Wife returned from Wotton:

10 A stranger preached at our Chapell on 63. Psal. 1.
Concerning the necessity Of Early piety, and giving our youth and
first youth to Religion; the greate danger of deferring it to old Age:
A Better Discourse could not be made on the subject, which he did
with great Earnestnesse, and without looking into any Notes,
which was now very rare, most preachers of this Age, constantly
reading their Sermons, which tooke much away from their
operation:

Afternoone another stranger on 6 Luke 37: The Weather very
dry and hot, I was exceedingly surprized with drowsinesse.

. . .

Propagating the Gospel

[June] 19 Being elected a Member of the Society lately
Incorporated for the Propagation of the Gospel in foreine parts, I
subscribed 10 pounds per Annum towards the Carying it on: The
A: Bishop of Cant: being absent, The L. Bishop of Lond. was [vice]
President: when we agreed that every Missioner should besides the
20 pounds to set the person forth, should have out of the stock of
the Corporation 50 pounds per Annum: til his Settlement there
was worth 100 pounds per Annum: and at this meeting we sent a
Young Divine to go to New Yorke.

. . .

27 I went to Wotton with my Family for the rest of the Summer,
whether came my Son-in law Draper with his family to stay with us,
his house at Adscome being New building, so as my family was now
above 30.

. . .

'Retaining my Intellectuals'

[October] 31. Arived now to the 82d yeare of my Age, Having
read over all that past since this day twelve-month in these notes
with my Soule rendring my most solemne Thanks to the Lord,
Humbly Imploring the pardon of my past life, sinns, and
particularly of the Incursions, and frailtys etc not yet fully subdued;
but that by the Assistance of his Grace I may yet be more than
conqueror, making new Resolutions, and imploring that he will
continue his blessed Assistance, and prepare me for my B: Saviours

Comming, that I may obtaine a Comfortable Departure, after so long a terme as has ben hitherto indulged me: Finding by many Infirmitys this yeare (especialy nephritic pains) that I much decline: And yet of his infinite mercy retaining my Intellectuals, and senses in greate measure above most of my Greate Age: I have this yeare, much repaired the mansion house, and severall Tennants, payed some parte of my debts and Ingagements: My Wife Children and Family in Health, for all which I most earnestly beseech Almighty God to accept of these my Accknowledgements, and that if it be his holy will to Continue me yet longer, that it may be to the praise of his infinite Grace, and Salvation of my Soule Amen:

. . .

A Prospering War

[November 1] There was now a full account of the particulars of the Successe of both our Land forces with the Confederates, our taking of so many fortifyed Townes and Territorys which the French had usurpt in Flanders and neerest parts of Germany, with the hapy escape of my L: Marborow our Generall, surprized by a party, as he was returning to Holland after this Winter Campagne: But of the Duke of Ormond (coming from Cales) taking sinking and destroying a greate part of the Spanish Plate-Fleete at Vigo, by a very bold and gallant attacking them in that Harbour to the number of 38 or 40 Ships, Gallions, Men of Warr and all their Equipage and of neer 1000 Cannon, plate and rich Lading etc, for which a day of publique Thanksgiving is appointed thro the whole nation: So as this summers Actions by these and the vast number of prizes (with little losse) and unwonted agreements of the Parliament, now met and sitting, such a concurence of Blessings and hope of Gods future favour, has not ben known in 100 yeares.

The forces also in Italy and on the Rhine prosperous beyond Expectation. Add to these the rich and numerous Returne of our Ships from the E. Indys and all other places.

. . .

There was greate rejoicing for the wonderfull prosperity of our forces by Sea and Land: Lord Marlborow return'd, Sir G: Rooke made a privy Counsellor, of all which the Bishop of Excester has handsomly mentioned in a very honest sermon preached at Paules, before the Queene and both houses; who were wonderfully Huzzas in their passage and most splendidly entertained in the Citty: and all this in so prosperous a Condition, that there has not ben so greate an Union in Parliament, Court, and people in memory of men of this nation, which God in mercy make us thankfull for and Continue—

....

Marlborough a Duke

[December 30] After: [th]e excesse of honors conferred by the Queene on the E. of Marborow, to make him a knight of the Garter, and Duke for the successe of but one Campagne, [that] he should desire 5000 pounds a yeare out of the Post-office to be settled on him was by the parliament thought a bold and unadvised request, who had besides his owne considerable Estate, above 30000 pounds per Ann in places and Employments, with 50000 pounds at Interest: His Wife also (whose originall and his every body knew, and by what merit become such favorite, for his sister was a Miss to K. James the 2d when Duke of York, his Father but a cleark of the Green-Cloth, ingrossing all that stirred and was profitable at Court: But thus they married their daughter 1 to the Sonn of my L. Tress: Godolphin, another to the E. of Sunderland, 3. to the E. of Bridge-Water:) Thus suddainly rising was taken notice of and displeased those who had him til now in greate esteeme: He is indeed a very handsom proper well spoken, and affable person, and supplys his want of acquired knowledge by keeping good Company: In the meane time Ambition and love of riches has no End:

...

Bravery of Benbow

[1703. January 3] Newes of V: Ad: Benbos conflict with a squadron of the French in the West-Indies, in which he was wounded, yet did gallantly behave himselfe, and was sure of an extraordinary successe and prize, had not 4 of his Men of War, stood Spectators without comming to his assistance: for which 2 of their Commanders were tryed and executed by a Councell of Warr, a 3d condemned to perpetual Imprisonment, losse of pay and [Incapacity], the 4th died:

...

Marlborough's Bereavement

[February 28] The duke of Marborow after all his prosperity riches and glory; lost his onely son, who died at Cambridge of the small pox, to the unexpressable sorrow of that family:

. . .

The Earle of Marborow bur[y]ing his son in King's Coll: Chapell in Camb: where he died; tooke shiping a few days after for the Low Countrys to Command as generall:

. . .

The Death of Pepys

[May] 26 This [day] dyed Mr. Sam: Pepys, a very worthy, Industrious and curious person, none in England exceeding him in the Knowledge of the Navy, in which he had passed thro all the most Considerable Offices, Clerk of the Acts, and Secretary to the Admiralty, all which he performed with greate Integrity: when K: James the 2d went out of England he layed down his Office, and would serve no more: But withdrawing himselfe from all publique Affairs, lived at Clapham with his partner (formerly his Cleark) Mr. Hewer, in a very noble House and sweete place, where he injoyed the fruit of his labours in g[r]eate prosperity, was universaly beloved, Hospitable, Generous, Learned in many things, skill'd in Musick, a very greate Cherisher of Learned men, of whom he had the Conversation. His Library and other Collections of Curiositys was one of the most Considerable; The models of Ships especialy etc. Beside what he boldly published of an Account of the Navy, as he found and left it, He had for divers years under his hand the History of the Navy, or, *Navalia* (as he call'd it) but how far advanced and what will follow of his, is left I suppose to his sisters son Mr. Jackson, a young Gent: whom his Unkle had educated in all sorts of usefull learning, Travell abroad, returning with extraordinary Accomplishments, and worth to be his Heire: Mr. Pepys had ben for neere 40 years, so my particular Friend, that he now sent me Compleat Mourning: desiring me to be one to hold up the Pall, at his magnificent Obsequies; but my present Indisposition, hindred me from doing him this last Office:

. . .

A Tactless Sermon

[July] 18 My late severe Conflict, lasting me on Saturday the [10]th past, that I could not go to Church the next day: When the Doctor preached on 27 Pro. 23 Concerning the pride and Luxury of Apparell, which could be applyed to none save my Wife and Daughter, there being none in all the Parish else, but meane people, who had no more than sufficient to cloth them meanely enough etc upon which I told the Doctor that I conceived the sermon had ben more proper to St. James's or some other of the Theatrical Churches in Lond, where the Ladys and Women were so richly and wantonly dressed and full of Jewells: But this reproofe was taken so very ill of the Doctor, that falling into a very furious passion, he hardly spake to me of some days, but preach'd the very same Sermon this day: which was indeed very learned, and fit for a Gallant Congregation; but by no meanes with our poore Country people: Both my Wife and Children having no sort of habits [but] what was Universaly worne by the ordinary persons of their Condition; besides the sobriety and regularity of my owne domestick[s]: He now began to make a shuffling apology for his vehement discourse, that he meant it as one of the national sinns, [we] were to aske God pardon for and reforme, predicting greate Judgements otherwise to succeede it: But all this while sayed not a Word of the pride of the Clergy, their long powdered Perruks, silke Casso[c]ks, Covetousnesse, suppression of those passions they themselves preach against . . .

. . .

Hurricane

[November] 26 The dismall Effects of the Hurecan and Tempest of Wind, raine and lightning thro all the nation, especial[y] London, many houses demolished, many people killed: 27 and as to my owne losse, the subversion of Woods and Timber both left for Ornament, and Valuable materiall thro my whole Estate, and about my house, the Woods crowning the Garden Mount, and growing along the Park meadow; the damage to my owne dwelling, and Tennants farmes and Outhouses, is most Tragicall: not to be paralleled with any thing hapning in our Age [or] in any history almost, I am not able to describe, but submitt to the Almight[y] pleasure of God, with accknowledgement of his

Justice for our National sinns, and my owne, who yet have not suffered as I deserved to: Every moment like Jobs Messengers, bring[s] the sad Tidings of this universal Judgement . . .

. . .

[December] 7 I remov'd with my family to Dover streete, saw the lamentable destruction of Houses and Trees thro all the Journey: and observd it had least injured those trees etc which grew in plaine exposed and perflatil grounds and places; but did most execution where it was pent in by the Villages and among the bottoms of hills:

. . .

Employment for Young Jack

[1704. January 16] My Lord Tressurer gave my Gr: Son, the office of Treasurer of the Revenue of the stampt parchment and paper: Sallary 300 pounds per annum.

. . .

A Serious Alarm

[June 18] Dr. Bathhurst Pres: of Trinity in Ox: (I think the oldest acquaintance now left me in all the wor[l]d), at 86 years age, both start blind, deafe, and memory lost, tho a person of admirable parts and learning no[w] dying, was a serious alarm to me; God of his mercy grant that I may profit by it: He builded a very handsom Chapell to that College and his owne Tomb. Gave a legacy of mony, and the 3d part of his library to Dr. Bohune, his nephew who now went hence to his funerall.

. . .

Battles of Schellenberg and Blenheim

[July 23] Nothing extraordinary from abroad but the Complement of the Emperor to the Queen, and his offer to Create the Duke of Marborow a Prince of the E[m]pire for his Vallor and Conduct and Victory at the Batell of [Schellenberg] against the D. of Bavaria.

. . .

[August 13] This weeke brought over hapy newes of the French and Bavarian Armys defeate by the Confederats, Especialy, by the vallour and Conduct of P: Eugene, and the Duke of Marborow, who vanquished, it, and tooke Marshall Talard their Generall prisoner: This was immediatly brought to the Queene, during the yet pursuite of the Enemys, written and sent by my Co: Parcke (an officer and Ayde de Camp) by the D: of Marlboro in such extreme hast, as he could not particularly describe the rest of the Circumstances and Event, which we hourely expect: But this has so exceedingly over Joyed us, that there is no thing but triumphs and demonstrations of Joy in the Citty and every where:

The weather a little variable, yet seasonable: God Almighty promote and improve this greate newes, to him be glory:

...

The Account of our Victory against the D: of Bavaria confirm'd but the particulars not yet come: The season excessive hot: The taking of Gibraltar [and Ce]uta confirmed:

...

A Stunning Victory

[27] Still greater Confirmaions of the Confederats Victory, the D. of Bavaria quite beaten out of his Country, who now sent their deputys to the Emp, to crave his protection and rescue their Country from utter Spoile: The D. of Marbrow marches over the Rhyne, Beseges Ulm and Landau: The Prisoners and spoile divided into 3 parts, to the Emp, English and Dutch: tis estimated the Fr: lost 40000 men kild and Taken, such a defeate as never was given in Europ these 1000 years:

The pope summons the Card primate of Poland to Rome, for crowning Vladislau their new King etc: this Victory breaks all the Fr: measures and designes, most providentialy for Europ:

...

Celebrating Victory

[September] 7. This day was celebrated the Thanksgiving for the late great Victory with the uttmost pomp and splendor by the Queene, Court, greate officers, Lord Major, Sheriffs, Companys etc the streets scaffolded from Temple-barr (where the L. M[a]yor presented her Majestie with the Sword, which she returned), every Company ranged under their Banners, and Citty Militia with out the rails, which were all hung with Cloth suitable to the Colour of the Banner, the L. Major, sherifs and Aldermen in their Scarlet roobs on their Caparisoned Horses: The knight Martiall and pensioners on horse, the Footguard: The Queene in a rich Coach with 8 Horse, none with her but the Dutchesse of Marlbrow, in a very plaine garment, The Q: full of Jewells, Musique and Trumpet[s], at every Citty Company: The greate officers of the Crown and nobility and Bishops all in Coach of 6. Horses, besides innumerable Spectators in this order went to S. Paules where the Deane preached etc after which the Queene went back in the same order to St. James: The Citty and Companys, feasting all the Nobility and Bonfires and Illuminations at night: Note that there was Musick composed by the best Masters of that art, to accompany the Church musique and Anthems etc to all which (after a[n] exceeding wet and stormy day) succeeded one of the most serene and Calmest bright-day[s], as had ben all the yeare:

. . .

[October 22] The Queene on one side Lords and Comm: with extraordinary expressions of grace and kindnesse, congratulating their meeting, after the late Successes, and intimations of need of supplys to finish the humbling the French etc: and the Lords and Commons satisfaction of her government, and the like Congratulations of successe in Germany, gave hopes of a perfect and unanimous agrement of this Sessions just now begun:

. . .

31. Being my Birth-day, and 84th yeare of my life, After particular Reflection on my Concernes and passages of the yeare; I set some considerable time of this day a part, to recollect, and examine my State and Condition with giving God thanks, and acknowledging his infinite Mercys to me and mine, beging his blessing for the past, and imploring his protection etc for the yeare following:

. . .

Marlborough's Return

[December] 9 my L. Clarendon presented me with the 3. Voll. of his Fathers History of the Rebellion: The D of Marbrough arived in Eng: bringing the Count de Talard and many Prisoner[s]: Tra[r]bach surrendered, and the Houses of Parliament complement him and his Victorys. 17 My Indisposition yet hindred me from going to church this day:

[1705.] Feb. 4 . . . In the afternoone a Scotchman; 1 John 4. 16: drowsinesse againe surprized me: as often of late in the afternoone.

9 I went to waite on my L. Tressurer where was the Victorious Duke of Marlborow, who came to me and tooke me by the hand with extraordinary familiarity and Civility, as formerly he was used to doe without any alteration of his good nature. He had a most rich George in a Sardonix set with Diamond of an inestimable Value: for the rest very plaine: I had not seene him in 2 yeares and believed he had forgotten me:

. . .

Newton's Burning-Glass

[June 17?] I went to the R: Society, where were Tryals with Sir E Newtons Burning-glasse: which did strange things as to mealting whatever was held to it in a moment: one of the most difficult was common Slate, which lasted longer than Iron, Gold, brasse, Silver, flint, brick etc which it immediatly mealted, calcined and Vitrified: The Glasse was composed of 7 round burning glasses of about a foote diameter, so placed in a frame, as to cause all their Sun-beams to meete in one focus onely:

. . .

A Marriage Proposal and Promotion for Jack

I went to Greenewich with my Wife, daughter, Gr Son, Mrs. Boscawen, and her daughter, then proposed as a Wife for him etc: To see the Hospital, which now began to take in wounded and emerited Sea-men, who were exceeding well provided for, the Buildings now going on very magnificent; dined at my servant, J. Strickland, and Returning visited Mr. Cresset my Tennant at Says Court: This by water:

24 St. J. Baptist—a Stranger at our Chapell on 1. Tim: 6. 6:

[After]noone Dr. Lancaster: 6. Micha 8: The season was so hot, that I was exceeding drowsy, which I pray God to pardon.

[So]me refreshing showrs, a greate fleete of Merchants from Lisbon came home, nothing else of [m]oment:—I had a sore fall out of my bed accidentaly—without much harme God be praised.

. . .

July My L Treasurer made my Gr—son one of the Commission-ers of the prizes, the sallary 500 pounds per Annum: Greate drowth—

[8] My Gr: son went this morning with Sir Sim: Harcourt the Solicitor Gen to Windsor to waite [on] my L. Treasurer, to whom I wrote to excuse my not being able to waite on him my selfe [etc:]

There having for some time ben a proposal of Marying my Gr—Son to a daughter of Mrs. Bosca[wen] Sister of my Lord Treasurer now far advanced:

. . .

His Marriage Settlement

[August] 23 Mr. Solicitor being returned from the Judges Circuit: was finished my Gr:sons marriage settlement, and given to be Ingrossed, giving him my Intire Estate, reserving onely the possession of it during my life, and the absolute disposure of the personal Estate, to be disposed of by my Will: etc: The lease of the House, and intire furniture of my house at London I give absolutely to my deare Wife:

. . .

I was now very severely afflicted with the stone, and severall other Afflictions and Infirmitys of my greate Age:

. . .

And Marriage

[September] 18 Tuesday my Gr: Son was Married by the Arch-Bishop of Cant: in Lambeth Chapell: to Ann, Daughter to Mrs. Boscawen, sister to the L. Godolphin, L. High Treasurer:— And, with aboundance of Relations on both sides, most magnificently Entertained with supper that night, by her Mother:

Most of the rest of this Weeke spent in receiving Visites of greate persons.

. . .

26. We invited as many of the Re[l]ations of Mrs. Boscawen and of my L. Treasurer as were in Towne etc., to the number of 18 to Dinner, which was as greate as the solem[n]ity of Marriage of my Grandson etc required:

. . .

A Great Age

[October] 31. I am this day arived to the 85 yeare of Age, Lord teach me so to number the days to come that I may apply them to wisedom better than hitherto I have done, for J C sake.

. . .

The Approaching End

[1706. January] 27 The Raine and a Thaw upon a deepe Snow, hindred me from going to Church.

. . .

His infirmities increasing, John Evelyn died at his house in Dover Street on 27 February and was buried at Wotton on 4 March. His epitaph follows on the next page.

Epitaph

Here lies the Body
of JOHN EVELYN Esq.
of this place second son
of RICHARD EVELYN Esq.
who having serv'd y^e Publick
in several employments, of which that
of Com'issioner of y^e Privy Seal in y^e
Reign of K. James y^e 2^d was most
Honourable: & perpetuated his fame
by far more lasting Monuments than
those of Stone, or Brass; his Learned
& usefull works fell asleep y^e 27th day
of February $170^5/6$ being y^e 86th Year
of his age in a full hope of a glorious
resurrection thro' faith in Jesus Christ.
Living in an age of extraordinary
events, & revolutions he learn't
(as himself asserted) this truth
which pursuant to his intention
is here declared
That all is vanity wch is not honest,
& that there's no solid Wisdom
but in real Piety.
Of five Sons, & three Daughters
borne to him from his most
vertuous, & excellent Wife
MARY sole daughter, and heiress
of S^r $RICH^d$ BROWNE of Sayes
Court near Deptford in Kent
onely one daughter SUSANNA
married to WILL^m DRAPER
Esq. of Adscomb in this County
survived him, y^e two others
dying in y^e flower of their
age & all y^e Sons very young
except one nam'd JOHN, who
deceasd y^e 24th of March $169^8/9$
in y^e 45th year of his age,
leaving one son JOHN, & one
daughter ELIZABETH.

Further Reading

Virginia Woolf, 'Rambling Round Evelyn' in *The Common Reader*, London, 1925, pp. 110–20, written in 1920 for the tercentenary of Evelyn's birth.

Lord Ponsonby of Shulbrede, *John Evelyn*. London 1933.

W. G. Hiscock, *John Evelyn and his Family Circle*. London, 1955.

John Bowle, *John Evelyn and his World, a Biography*. London, 1981.

W. Upcott, Evelyn's *Miscellaneous Works* (London, 1825) remains a convenient collection of his writings other than the *Diaries*.

Notes

Page viii. This account is based on evidence cited by E. S. de Beer, *The Diary of John Evelyn*, (Clarendon Press, 1955) Vol. I, Introduction pp. 55–4.

Page 9. *Evelyn at Oxford*: In 1637 Thomas Lawrence had been appointed Master of Balliol, a conservative scholar afterwards a chaplain to Charles I. In 1648 a more radical Master, Bradshaw, would oust him. Balliol was then one of the poorest of the Colleges and had not attained its later eminence.

Page 17. *A Glimpse of the Wars*: Since 1621 the Dutch had renewed their war with Spain, and were doing well out of it, blockading Antwerp and capturing trading posts in the Far East and the Americas. Since 1635 they had gained the alliance of the French.

Page 23. *Ports*: gates.

Page 27. *Collin*: Cologne.

Page 28. *The Spanish Netherlands*: Since 1598 they had been ruled by Habsburg 'archdukes': Albrecht, brother of the emperor Rudolf II, and his wife the Infanta Isabella, daughter of Philip II of Spain, who after 1621 had ruled alone until succeeded in 1633 by the Cardinal-Infante Don Fernando of Spain.

Page 33. *cancell'd*: enclosed with lattice-work.

Page 34. *Lord Arundel*: Thomas Howard, second Earl of Arundel (1585–1646), grew up under the shadow of his Catholic father's (the fourth Duke of Norfolk's) imprisonment and death in the Tower for alleged treason against Elizabeth I. 'Restored in blood' by James I and by a rich wife, he bought back substantial estates and became Earl Marshal of England, but in 1642 avoided the Civil War and settled in relative poverty at Padua. He had, however, already accumulated a great art collection and library, which were inherited, after the Dukedom had been restored in 1660, by his descendant, Henry, sixth Duke of Norfolk (d. 1684). The sixth duke – who had little interest in the collections and after his wife's death married his mistress, the daughter of the Keeper of the Wine Cellar to Charles II – was persuaded by Evelyn to present the Arundelian Library to the Royal Society and the Arundelian Marbles to the University of Oxford.

Page 38. Braineford: Brentford.

Page 43. Achate: agate.

Page 52. Chartres: Chastres, now Arpajon.

Page 71. the Duke: Ferdinando de Medici (reigned 1627–70). He managed to keep out of the Thirty Years War, despite pressure from France and Spain, and was a notable patron of science and the arts. Though he had failed to defend Galileo, he had allowed him to reside in his territory after he had been condemned.

Page 75. Est: It is here.

Page 78. Cavalcado of Innocent X: Gian Battista Pamphili (1574–1655) came of a Roman family, but had made his career as papal legate in Spain. He was hostile to French and Portuguese interests, and is the subject of a well-known portrait by Velasquez.

Page 96. (1) But he enjoyes another World: there follow four lines deleted by Evelyn.

(2) *Neapoli* 1644: Evelyn may have broken off the *Kalendarium*, begun between 1660 and 1664, at this point. He started it retrospectively again in 1682.

Page 105. Mezzo Carne, Mezzo Legno: half flesh, half wood.

Page 127. Evelyn here refers to the Gregorian or New Style Calendar initiated by Gregory XIII in 1582, and adopted in France and most of Catholic Europe. The English would adhere to the Julian or Old Style Calendar until 1751, by then eleven days in advance of the other. Both Calendars would have been equally familiar to educated Englishmen in Evelyn's time.

Page 141. Tallie douces: engravings.

Page 179. μετ᾽ [πολλῆς] φαντασιας : with great pomp.

Page 180. General Monck Acts: George Monck, Duke of Albemarle (1608–1670) came of Devon gentry near Torrington and fought for Charles I until in 1644 he was taken prisoner at Nantwich and imprisoned in the Tower, where the King sent him £100. But by 1646 he served in Ireland for the Parliament, became military governor of Ulster and got a large estate. He then did decisive service for Cromwell in 1650 at Dunbar and became C.-in-C. in Scotland. Appointed a 'General at sea' in 1653 he defeated the Dutch off Portland and in a greater battle in which van Tromp was killed off the Dutch coast. Reverting to his command in Scotland, he subdued a Royalist rising and quelled radical discontent in his own army, and on the Protector's death supported Richard Cromwell until, as Monck put it, he 'forsook himself'. In command of the best disciplined and best paid army in Great Britain in 1659, when the other generals dispersed the Rump Parliament, Monck occupied Edinburgh and the border fortresses, declared against 'arbitrary power', and outfaced General Lambert. He then forced the restored Rump Parliament to admit the members 'secluded' during the Interregnum and to issue writs for a free election, thus, in effect, declaring for a Restoration of the King. Monck was a stout, short, energetic man determined to make a 'prudent' settlement, an able politician as well as a first-rate soldier popular with his men. At the Restoration his younger brother, Nicholas, became briefly Provost of Eton and Bishop of Hereford.

Page 185. *to breake*: to divulge.

Page 190. *A Westminster School Election*: Dr Busby's long and 'awful' reign was still in progress, and he took great pains to prepare his scholars for the Elections.

Page 192. *Fumifugium*: the full title was *Fumifugium: or the inconveniencie of the aer and smoak of London dissipated.*

Page 194. *The Portuguese Queen*: Catherine of Braganza 1638–1706, was the daughter of King João IV of Portugal (1640–56), whose resistance to Spain had been enhanced by the long-standing alliance, commercial and naval, with the English. The Portuguese, long anxious to consolidate the alliance, offered Tangier, Bombay, and a huge dowry; and the French, still hostile to Spain, favoured a marriage likely also to thwart Dutch trade. Catherine, after a cloistered and pious upbringing, found it difficult to adapt to the Restoration Court, and in 1666 miscarried of an heir to the British throne – her most decisive non-contribution to history; but she learned to put up with the infidelities of her husband and even to hold her own. In 1692 she retired to Portugal, and in 1704, the year after the Anglo-Portuguese Methuen Treaty had begun to make port fashionable in England, she became a popular Regent of Portugal for her brother, Pedro. She had popularized tea-drinking in England, and died very rich, by no means the nonentity she is often depicted.

Page 212. *the invective I* . . . *dedicated to his Majestie and publish'd*: Evelyn is referring to his *Fumifugium* (see p.xxx).

Page 231. (1) *Madamoiselle Quirreval*: Louise Renée de Kéroualle (Quirreval) (1649–1734), the daughter of a Breton gentleman with a manor near Brest, came to England in 1670 with Henrietta, Duchesse of Orléans, Charles II's sister, after whose death she returned to be maid of honour to the Queen. By 1672 she had borne the King a son, Charles Lennox, afterwards Duke of Richmond, and in 1673 she was created Duchess of Portsmouth and by Louis XIV Duchesse d'Aubigny. In spite of her unpopularity as a Catholic, she proved the most politically active and influential as well as the most expensive of the King's mistresses, and retained her position until his death. She then retired to her estate in France, pensioned by the French Government.

(2) *Gibson*: Grinling Gibbons, born in Rotterdam, came of Anglo-Dutch descent, his father a Yorkshire carpenter. He was the greatest genius in English wood carving and a good sculptor; his first major work was in rebuilt St Paul's, and in many City churches. He also worked at Trinity College, Cambridge, at Chatsworth and Petworth and many other great houses. He was Master Carver in Wood to the Crown from the reign of Charles II to that of George I.

Page 233. (1) *Mrs. Nellie*: Nell Gwyn (1650–87) born either in Drury Lane or Hereford, became an orange vendor, then an actress. Small, merry and vivacious, by 1667 she had captivated Charles II, and was popular as against the French mistress, Louise de Kéroualle ('Madame Carwell'), particularly after she had remarked 'Pray, good people, be civil; I am the Protestant Whore.' Charles Beauclerk, her eldest son by the King, he created Duke of St Albans, and James II, mindful of his brother's wish that she 'should not starve', settled an estate on her with remainder to St Albans, in Nottinghamshire. She never learned to write, but one of her descendants became Bishop of Hereford.

(2) *Dutches of Cleaveland*: Barbara Villiers, Countess of Castlemaine and Duchess of Cleveland (1641–1709), a descendant of a half-brother of George Villiers, Duke of Buckingham, was daughter of Viscount Grandison, a Royalist killed in the Civil War, and wife of Roger Palmer, afterwards Earl of Castlemaine. She probably became the mistress of Charles II on the night of his return to London in May 1660 and bore him three sons: Charles FitzRoy, Duke of Southampton and Cleveland; Henry, Duke of Grafton; and George, Duke of Northumberland. In 1670 the King created her Duchess of Cleveland, as 'the ornament and prize of virtue'. But she was displaced as *maitresse en titre* by Louise de Kéroualle, Duchess of Portsmouth, and took a series of lovers, including the young John Churchill, afterwards Duke of Marlborough. She was the most spirited of the Monarch's mistresses, though Portsmouth was considered even more rapacious.

Page 238. *Lady* ——: Louise Renée de Kéroualle, (see note to p.231).

Page 252. *Sir William Petty*: For another and entertaining version of his life, see John Aubrey, *Brief Lives* (ed. Lawson Dick, London, 1950), pp. 237–41.

Page 255. *This day was my deare friend Mrs Blagg maried … the Duke*: this fact, retrospectively recorded here, was not known to Evelyn until 26 April 1676. (See also note to p.894 on Sidney Godolphin.)

Page 258. *My Lord Berkeley*: John Berkeley, first Lord Berkeley of Stratton, had been Charles I's Ambassador to Queen Christina of Sweden and MP for Heytesbury, Wilts. In 1643 he had helped to win the Royalist victory at Stratton in Cornwall and to capture Exeter, which he held until 1645. In 1647 he attended the flight of Charles I to Lymington which ended disastrously at Carisbrook. He had then fought for the French against the Spaniards, and in 1658 was created baron Berkeley of Stratton. In 1670 he was appointed Lord-Lieutenant of Ireland.

Page 260. *Din'd with* ✡: this was Evelyn's shorthand for Margaret Godolphin *née* Blagge.

Page 282. *Monsieur Jardine*: Chardin, later Sir John Chardin.

Page 285. *Sir Stephen Fox*: (1627–1716) born at Farley, Wilts, he became a chorister at Salisbury Cathedral and trained in book-keeping. He helped Charles II to escape after Worcester and in Paris took charge of the King's and Clarendon's households. After the Restoration he became First Clerk of the Green Cloth and Paymaster-General, MP for Salisbury, then for Westminster, and was knighted. Appointed a Lord Commissioner of the Treasury, he resigned as Paymaster-General in 1680, having made a vast fortune, part of which he devoted to Chelsea Hospital and to 'pewing the body of the Cathedral Church' at Salisbury. He served James II, but came to terms with William III and died at Farley very rich, the grandfather of Charles James Fox the politician.

Page 364. *My L. Godolphin*: Sidney Godolphin, first Earl of Godolphin (1645–1712), third son of Sir Francis Godolphin of Godolphin, Breage, Cornwall, and brought up in the household of Charles II, had been MP for Helston and St Mawes, and in 1679 a Lord of the Treasury. Loyal to James II, he had, with Halifax, negotiated with William of Orange at Hungerford, and remained, despite Jacobite sympathies, a Commissioner for the Treasury under William III. Under Anne he and Marlborough for eight crucial years dominated government, but, in face of Whig hostility, in 1710 the Queen dismissed him. He was an able financier and a patron of the turf, and by his marriage to Evelyn's friend, Margaret Blagge, had a son, Francis, who succeeded him. His patronage was decisive for both Evelyn and his grandson 'Jack', who married his niece.

Page 386. *Sir Robert Ashwood*: Evelyn's error for Sir Henry Ashurst.

Page 404. Evelyn's bailiff reported that the Tsar's entourage were 'right nasty': they were found to have broken windows, smashed furniture, and 'damnified' the garden, presumably in festive Muscovite mood.

Page 412. *the Prince of Hanover*: George Louis, the future King George I.

Index

Note: The abbreviation E is used in this index for John Evelyn (1620–1706).

Petre, William Petre, 4th Baron (c. 1626–84), imprisoned in Tower, 274

Pett, Peter (1593–1652), 378

Petty, Lady (Elizabeth), 253, 254

Petty, Sir William (1623–87), 252–5, 436

Peyton, Sir Thomas (c. 1613–84), 136, 151

Phelips, Robert (1619–1707), 357

Philip V, King of Spain (1640–1701), succeeds to Crown, 414; Spanish Netherlands acknowledge as King, 415

Philips, Coll:, see Phelips

Phillips (Philips), Edward (1630–96?), 265

Philosophic Society, see Royal Society

Pierce, Edward, senior (fl. 1640–66), 159

Pierce, Thomas (1622–91), 267, 274, 279

Pierson, see Pearson

Pietro, Signor, see Reggio

pirates, Prettyman robbed by, 131; packet boat chased by, 131–2; E's books safe from, 141; E's journey delayed for fear of, 144; corruption suspected over pardon of, 408

Pisa, 67–8

Pius II, Pope (r. 1458–64), 73

Plaat, De (the Plaet), 29

plague (pestilence), of 1625, 4; of 1636, 8; Ireton dies of, 146; great plague of 1665, 204–5; keeps E from church, 215

plantations, English, French Protestant refugees in, 330; all Negroes to be baptized, 340

plate, of York Minster, 161

Plautii, tomb of the, 100

Pliny the elder (AD 23–79), his interest in Vesuvius, 91

Plot, Robert (1640–96), 256

plots: see Assassination Plot, Gunpowder Plot, Popish Plot, Rye House Plot

Plume, Thomas (1630–1704), 205

Plymouth, declares for William of Orange, 364; merchantmen in Bay, 380

Po, river, 102, 112

poison, discussions and experiments at Royal Society, 191; spiders, 192

Poix (Pois), 138

Poland, siege of Vienna raised, 307; internal troubles, 402; the Pope reprimands the Cardinal, 425

Pollexfen (Pollixfen), Sir Henry, 359

Pontius Pilate, 58

Popes, see Alexander VII (1655–67) and Clement XI (1700–21)

Popham, Alexander (1605–69), house of, 154

Popish Plot (1678), 272, 274, 302

Porta, Giacomo della (1537–1602), 100

portents, 292

Portman, Sir William (c. 1644–90), 331, 332

portraits, Kneller's of E, 375; Verrio's of Charles II, 382

Portsmouth, 201; fortifications, 10; siege of, 38; E and Pepys to, 337–8; James II at, 341; Town Hall, 341; Mary of Modena to, 363; Prince of Wales to, 364; ships at, 399

Portsmouth, Louise Renée de Kéroualle, Duchess of (1649–1734), 435, 436; comes to England, 231; and Charles II, 238, 321; created Duchess, 255; splendour of her apartments at Whitehall, 258, 307–8; entertains Moroccan ambassador, 295; E attends her in her dressing room, 307; her son, 311; the dying Charles II's concern for, 318

Portugal, 435

Portugal, Maria Sophia, Queen of (1666–99), 406

Poule, see Powle

Powell, Sir John, 359

Powle, Henry (1630–92), 288, 289

Pratt (Prat), Sir Roger (1620–84), 209

prayer, E's, 419–20

preaching, none on Christmas Day, 151; a 'phanatical' preacher, 152; the new curate at Deptford, 293; E drowsy during sermons, 293, 419, 427; E hears sermon at Lee, 299; Bishop Andrewes' style out of fashion, 305; Dr Ken to Trinity Company, 312; on Christian vigilancy, 334; on necessity of early piety, 419

Presbyterians, Presbyterianism, in Amsterdam, 21; in Geneva, 123; the minister 'Presbyterianly affected', 170; displeased, 372

presents, Russian ambassador to Charles II, 198; Moroccan ambassador to Charles II, 295

Preston Beckhelvyn, 129

Preston, Sir Richard Graham, Viscount (1648–95), dines with Sir Stephen Fox, 361

Prettyman (Pretyman), Sir John (1612–76), 151

Prettyman (Pretyman), William (d. 1688), has charge of Sayes Court, 128; goes to France, 129; robbed by pirates, 131; E receives a letter from, 155; godfather to E's son, 166; E and, 168

Primaticcio, Francesco (1504–70), work at Fontainebleau, 48

THE WORLD'S CLASSICS

A Select List